Jane Austen and her Readers, 1786–1945

Jane Austen and her Readers, 1786–1945

Katie Halsey

ANTHEM PRESS
LONDON · NEW YORK · DELHI

Anthem Press
An imprint of Wimbledon Publishing Company
www.anthempress.com

This edition first published in UK and USA 2013
by ANTHEM PRESS
75–76 Blackfriars Road, London SE1 8HA, UK
or PO Box 9779, London SW19 7ZG, UK
and
244 Madison Ave. #116, New York, NY 10016, USA

First published in hardback by Anthem Press in 2012

Copyright © Katie Halsey 2013

The author asserts the moral right to be identified as the author of this work.

All rights reserved. Without limiting the rights under copyright reserved above,
no part of this publication may be reproduced, stored or introduced into
a retrieval system, or transmitted, in any form or by any means
(electronic, mechanical, photocopying, recording or otherwise),
without the prior written permission of both the copyright
owner and the above publisher of this book.

British Library Cataloguing-in-Publication Data
A catalogue record for this book is available from the British Library.

Library of Congress Cataloging-in-Publication Data
The Library of Congress has cataloged the hardcover edition as follows:
Halsey, Katie.
Jane Austen and her readers, 1786–1945 / Katie Halsey.
p. cm.
Includes bibliographical references and index.
ISBN 978-0-85728-352-8 (hardback : alk. paper)
1. Austen, Jane, 1775–1817–Criticism and interpretation–History.
2. Austen, Jane, 1775–1817–Appreciation.
3. Austen, Jane, 1775–1817–Influence. 4. Austen, Jane, 1775–1817–Knowledge–Literature.
5. Austen, Jane, 1775–1817–Books and reading. 6. Books and reading–Great Britain–History.
7. Reader-response criticism–Great Britain. 8. Authors and readers–Great Britain–
History. I. Title.
PR4038.B6H35 2012
823'.7–dc23
2012000479

ISBN-13: 978 1 78308 050 2 (Pbk)
ISBN-10: 1 78308 050 7 (Pbk)

This title is also available as an ebook.

CONTENTS

Acknowledgements   vii

Part One

Introduction   3

1. Jane Austen's Reading in Context   17
2. Jane Austen's Negotiations with Reading   37
3. Jane Austen's Games of Ingenuity   57

Part Two

Introduction   89

4. Austen's Readers: Contexts I   101
5. Austen's Readers: Contexts II   117
6. Austen's Readers I: Affection and Appropriation   135
7. Austen's Readers II: Opposition and Resistance   153
8. Austen's Readers III: Friendship and Criticism   171
9. Austen's Readers IV: Sociability and Devotion   189

Conclusion   209

Notes   215
Bibliography   257
Index   279

ACKNOWLEDGEMENTS

In a work dedicated to exploring questions of reading and readers, my first debts of thanks must go to those who have been my own readers at various stages of the production of this book. I am grateful to Caroline Gonda, Anne Henry, Alison Hennegan, Cora Kaplan, Bharat Tandon, Daniel Neill, Robert Douglas-Fairhurst, Mary Jacobus, Michèle Cohen, Larry Klein, Corinna Russell, Kate Griffiths, Louise Joy, Luke Houghton, Daisy Hay, Simon Eliot, Mark Towsey, Dale Townshend, and Anthem's anonymous readers, all of whom have shaped this work in different ways. I have benefited in more ways than I can hope to mention from conversations about Jane Austen with friends and colleagues over many years. I cannot name them all here, but I hope they know who they are.

I am indebted to many people who gave me access to the documentary and manuscript material I used in this book, including the wonderful staff of the Chawton House Library, Senate House Library, the National Art Library, the National Library of Scotland, the London Women's Library, Cambridge University Library, the Bodleian Library, Glasgow University Library, the British Library, Innerpeffray Library and the Houghton Library, Harvard. I am particularly grateful to William St Clair, John Spiers and Petronella Haldane for generously allowing me to use their private collections. For their help in tracking down or pointing me towards sometimes obscure material, I must thank Jenny McAuley, Sarah Johnson, Sandra Cummings, Jennie Batchelor, Gillian Dow, Wim van Mierlo, Karen Attar, Rosalind Crone, Bob Owens, Shafquat Towheed, Kate Macdonald, Hilary Adams and Tom and Elizabeth Heydeman. Thanks, too, to Janka Romero and Tej Sood for their patience.

An earlier version of Chapter 3 section ii first appeared as 'The Blush of Modesty or the Blush of Shame', *Forum for Modern Language Studies*, 42.3 (July 2006). Part of Chapter 3 section iii appeared as 'Spectral Texts in *Mansfield Park*', in Cora Kaplan and Jennie Batchelor (eds), *British Women's Writing in the Long Eighteenth Century: Authorship, Politics and History* (Palgrave Macmillan, 2005), and a small part of the section on Margaret Oliphant in Chapter 8 first appeared in '"Critics as a Race are Donkeys": Margaret Oliphant, Critic or Common Reader?', *Journal of the Edinburgh Bibliographical Society*, 2 (2007). I offer my thanks to the publishers for permission to reuse this material.

I would like to acknowledge the financial support provided by the Arts and Humanities Research Council, the University of Stirling, the University of London, Emmanuel College, Cambridge, the Charles Oldham Fund, the Jane Austen Society, the late Dr Herchel Smith and the trustees of the Chawton House Library.

Part One

INTRODUCTION

I am very strongly haunted by the idea that to those Readers who have preferred P&P. it [Emma] will appear inferior in Wit, & to those who have preferred MP. very inferior in good Sense.[1]

Her exquisite story of 'Persuasion' absolutely haunted me.[2]

This book is about the complex and unequal relationships between texts and readers. These take place in the realm of the imagination, although they have a partial manifestation in the material, in the form of writing. The first part of the book focuses on Jane Austen's negotiations with her reading, her reinterpretations of her period's strictures about reading women and women's reading, and her representations of readers in the novels, letters, juvenilia and fragments. It also discusses aspects of her style that have far-reaching ramifications in the responses of her readers. Part Two considers the textual and historical contexts of her works, and the kinds of relationships that historical readers have had with Austen and her novels. By examining Austen's British readers' views about reading generally, and specifically about reading Austen, as represented in their letters, journals, memoirs, critical writing and autobiographies, we come to a better understanding both of the qualities of Jane Austen's works, and of the practice of reading in Britain in different historical periods.[3] My aim throughout this work is to maintain a dual focus on Jane Austen and her readers, conceiving of the relationship between them as a kind of conversation: a dynamic two-way process wherein readers respond to the novels, but the novels and characters are also brought to life, re-imagined, re-created and re-invented in and through the reading experience in its totality. Unlike Claire Harman's popular biography, *Jane's Fame* (2009), which explores Austen's reception over two centuries, and explicitly sets out to explain 'how Jane Austen conquered the world', thus focussing on the phases and growth of Austen's reputation,[4] my aim is to show not only how the responses of Austen's readers can help to explicate Austen's works, but also how their reactions to Austen's works can illuminate her readers and their social, cultural and literary preoccupations for us.

Discussion of the reception of Austen's works is certainly not new. As early as 1957, Lionel Trilling suggested that 'it is possible to say of Jane Austen, as perhaps we can say of no other writer, that the opinions which are held of her work are almost as interesting, and almost as important to think about, as the work itself'.[5] Brian Southam's two invaluable *Critical Heritage* volumes made many of these 'opinions' more widely available to scholars and researchers from 1968 onwards. The 1990s, with their spate of Austen films and adaptations, and the period of Austen-mania that followed Colin Firth's appearance in the BBC's 1995 adaptation of *Pride and Prejudice*, brought Austen's readers and viewers once again to the notice of Austen critics, and initiated a renewed focus on the 'ordinary' reader (i.e. the reader who is not a professional literary critic). Claudia Johnson's ground-breaking article, 'The Divine Miss Jane: Jane Austen, Janeites, and the Discipline of Novel Studies' (1996) made the argument that 'Austen's reception and readership merits substantial consideration' through an analysis of the role played by Austen's readers and critics in the foundation of the discipline of novel studies.[6] Johnson focussed on the figure of the 'Janeite' – someone who celebrates Jane Austen with 'a militantly dotty enthusiasm' and for whom reading Austen is 'the ecstasy of the elect'[7] – and analysed responses to Austen's 'queerness' with particular reference to the Janeite and anti-Janeite controversies of the early twentieth century, arguing that Austen critics had much to gain 'by bringing non-normalizing Austenian readings back into view'.[8] Johnson's chapter on 'Austen cults and cultures' in *The Cambridge Companion to Jane Austen* (1997) drew on much of the same material to make the claim that the recuperation of ordinary readers' responses to Austen's works 'may help us all'.[9] Deidre Lynch's edited collection, *Janeites: Austen's Disciples and Devotees* (2000), in which Johnson's 'The Divine Miss Jane' was reprinted, emphasized the historical importance of readings of Austen, arguing that 'inquiry into readerships and their readings' is 'productive and politically pertinent'.[10] The collection brought together case studies that ranged from discussions of Austen's earliest readers to analysis of Edward Said's reading of Austen. In the wake of these works, in *Jane Austen and the Morality of Conversation* (2003), Bharat Tandon argued that 'a history of readings can […] yield a series of responses to something that the original text might be argued to have been doing'.[11] Annika Bautz's *The Reception of Jane Austen and Walter Scott* (2007) to some extent provided 'a history of readings' of Austen's works, though with some important omissions, while Claire Harman's *Jane's Fame* and Emily Auerbach's *Searching for Jane Austen* (2004) popularized the field. In the early years of the twenty-first century, a number of critics, led by John Wiltshire's insightful *Recreating Jane Austen* (2001), considered films and adaptations as creative 'readings' of Austen's works.

In this book I do not discuss films, television adaptations, prequels, sequels, spin-offs or other manifestations of creative responses to Austen's works. Nor do I discuss her influence on the literary output of her successors, although I hope that my account of the relationship between Austen's indirect and confidential style, and the questions debated by her female literary successors, will help to expand our notions of the extent of Austen's literary legacy. Johnson's valuable focus on 'non-normalizing' readings of Austen led her to concentrate on the particular qualities of Janeite readings, and to prioritize the readings of early twentieth-century readers; I aim to provide a more extensive historical coverage of Austen's readers from 1786 to 1945, and to consider the contexts of the reading experiences discussed in greater detail. While the material discussed in this book inevitably partially overlaps with that considered in the critical works above (there is, sadly, only a finite number of traceable recorded responses to Austen's writing), I also consider some previously unused (and little used) print sources as well as archival and manuscript material that has never before appeared in the public domain.[12]

Trilling perceptively identifies the dangers as well as the benefits of engaging with opinions of Jane Austen's work, pointing out the 'intensely personal and social' nature of the partisanship of Austen's readers, as well as warning against the kind of extravagant admiration of the works that 'seems to stimulate self-congratulation in those that give it, and to carry a reproof of the deficient sensitivity, reasonableness, and even courtesy, of those who withhold their praise.'[13] Critics are, as Trilling rightly points out, like all readers, prone to such 'extravagantly personal' responses to Jane Austen.[14] Trilling describes a body of opinion which holds that 'it is not Jane Austen herself who is to be held responsible for the faults that are attributed to her by her detractors, but rather the people who admire her for the wrong reasons and in the wrong language and thus create a false image of her'.[15] It has been my intention throughout this book to consider the responses of Austen's readers – including her 'detractors' – on their own terms, rather than as 'right' or 'wrong', 'true' or 'false', but no doubt my own prejudices will be apparent to my readers.

*****

Jane Austen's novels bear the allusive traces of her own reading (which I discuss in Chapters 2 and 3), while her reputation is affected by the appropriations of generations of readers. Her name, like that of many authors, is imbued with an extraordinary resonance. Indeed, it has become a critical truism to note that 'Jane Austen' has, over the last two centuries, come to stand for a number of different, sometimes conflicting positions. Claimed by feminist literary history, by the canonical Great Tradition, and by the mass media,

'Jane Austen' is at once the transgressive 'mother of the novel', a serious moral writer, and the epitome of demurely mob-capped nineteenth-century ladylike domesticity. She is figured simultaneously as both a serious professional writer and an untutored genius. Austen belongs both to a tradition of female writers and to the very different patriarchal canon, and she is appropriated for a number of different movements, literary or otherwise. She is used to represent health and wholesomeness in comparison to the sensation fiction of the 1860s, to epitomize Englishness in the 1920s, to define perfection of style, to typify (however anachronistically) a Victorian ideal of domesticity, to take only a very few examples of how Austen has been and is deployed. She is a writer who enjoys critical acclaim and wide popularity, claimed by high, low and middlebrow culture alike, her novels adapted for television, Hollywood and Bollywood, topping the polls as Britain's favourite writer, and yet still admired within the literary academy. Her six novels have been subjected to every school of analytical or critical discourse, and her juvenile and manuscript works have received substantial attention in recent years. Austen's name therefore has considerable cultural significance.

Jacques Derrida suggests that the proper name in fact represents something quite other from the person who bears that name:

> The naïve rendering or common illusion is that you have given your name to X, thus all that returns to X, in a direct or indirect way, in a straight or oblique line, *returns* to you, as a profit for your narcissism. But as you *are* not your name, nor your title, and given that, as the name or the title, X does very well without you or your life, that is, without the place toward which something could *return* – just as that is the definition and the very possibility of every trace, and of all names and all titles, so your narcissism is frustrated *a priori* by that from which it profits or hopes to profit [...] That which bears, has borne, will bear your name seems sufficiently free, powerful, creative and autonomous to live alone and radically to do without you and your name.[16]

Following this line of argument, in 'Spectres of Engels', Willy Maley persuasively suggests that the work of Engels has become subsumed by Marx: '"Marx," the proper name of Marx, has attached itself to, and has absorbed, other names and texts apparently independent of Marx "himself"'.[17] Jane Austen's proper name functions in a similar way: the name 'Jane Austen' is, one might say, haunted by the ghosts of readings past. The peculiar level of investment in claiming Austen for one's own, and some of the results of doing so, are explored in Chapters 6 and 9. For now, it is sufficient to remark the valence of her name, and to suggest that one of the consequences of the nature of Austen's reputation is, as my quotation from Derrida's work suggests, to complicate the relationship between Austen and her historical readers: images of 'Jane Austen' frequent the thoughts and writings of Jane Austen's readers in complex and conflicting ways.[18] Mary Russell Mitford (in my second epigraph) describes Austen's *Persuasion* haunting her visit to Bath; as we see in Chapters 6 to 9, Mitford was not alone among later generations of readers and writers in feeling Austen's spectral presence both during the actual experience of reading one of her novels and beyond it.

Austen's writing is famously elliptical and spare. I argue in Chapters 2 and 3 that the endings of Austen's novels are undercut and subverted, leaving readers with a potentially uncomfortable or potentially fruitful sense of some kind of omission or lack. As Virginia Woolf noticed, her style 'stimulates us to supply what is not there', because the 'trifle' Austen provides 'expands in the mind' of the reader.[19] In Lacanian terminology, the sparseness of her style forces the reader to make good a 'refusal of satisfaction',[20] as the enigmas of Austen's writing 'expand in the mind' of Austen's readers. Jocelyn Harris argues that Austen herself enjoyed her imaginative engagements with her own reading matter, and I agree (as can be seen in Chapters 2 and 3) with Harris's assessment of Austen's 'confident, even cheerful intertextuality with other authors', and her account of Austen's 'deliberate, powerful and [...] mainly conscious choice to revisit and remake these earlier authors, out of respect, companionship, and even love', a process in which resistant mockery and parody, wild exaggeration and deliberate misapplication of tone and register play a central role.[21] Virginia Woolf acutely identified an essential aspect of Austen's writing – its stubborn and continual refusal to take life and itself entirely seriously – when she wrote (of the Juvenilia) about the 'note [...] which sounds distinctly and penetratingly all through the volume', the 'sound of laughter', suggesting that 'the girl of fifteen is laughing, in her corner, at the world'.[22] If we forget the 'light & bright & sparkling'[23] aspects of Austen's work, or, in other words, we fail to notice how very funny she really is, we do the writing itself a very serious disservice.

Austen's niece Marianne Knight remembered 'how Aunt Jane would sit quietly working beside the fire in the library, saying nothing for a good while, and then would suddenly burst out laughing, jump up and run across the room to a table where pens and paper were lying, write something down and then come back to the fire and go on quietly working as before'.[24] She also remembered the 'peals of laughter' from behind her Aunt Jane's closed door as Jane, Cassandra and Marianne's older sister Fanny read the novels aloud. Marianne thought it 'very hard that we should be shut out from what was so delightful'.[25] I firmly believe that acknowledging laughter as one of Austen's creative impulses is essential to an understanding of her rich and complex relationship with her literary predecessors, and recognizing the 'peals of laughter' and the 'delight' generated by reading Austen helps to explicate some of the responses of her readers. In Chapters 6, 7, 8 and 9 I discuss both the energies generated by resistance and the pleasures of appropriation. My focus on the joy of the intertextual obviously owes much to the theoretical paradigms of Roland Barthes, and my interest in the resistant and oppositional is both narratological (for which the dominant models are to be found in the work of M. M. Bakhtin) and feminist. In acknowledging these theoretical debts I take this opportunity to point out my own acts of readerly appropriation, and acknowledge the ways in which I, like any reader, may be influenced by my own reading.

Throughout this book, I work with two paradigms of readers. The first is the hypothetical reader, derived from the reader-response theory of Mikhail Bakhtin, Hans Robert Jauss, Wolfgang Iser, Stanley Fish, Michel de Certeau and Roland Barthes, and the feminist renegotiations of such theory by Judith Fetterley, Shoshana Felman, Jocelyn Harris, Kathy Mezei, Lynne Pearce, Sara Mills, Elizabeth Flynn and Patrocinio Schweickart among others. The second is the historical reader, represented here through the published and private writings of readers from 1786 (when Austen first started to show her juvenile writings to her family, and hence responses to the works began) to 1945 (when the end of the Second World War ushered in an era of new media, such as radio and television, and print began to lose currency as the primary means of mass communication). The responses of Austen's readers from 1945 to the present day are outside the scope of the current volume.[26] The model for analysis of the historical reader is to be found in the work of book-historical scholars, such as Robert Darnton, Roger Chartier, Jonathan Rose, David Vincent, Simon Eliot, Anthony Grafton, Mary Hammond, Andrew Murphy and Kate Flint. That there is a tension inherent in using these two models concurrently is immediately apparent: actual historical readers rarely (if ever) react in the ways that hypothetical readers can be made to do, so reader-response and historicist criticism seldom work comfortably together. It is my belief that the conflict generated by my choice to use both paradigms is not only interesting in itself on a meta-critical level, but more crucially that such tension points to a battle that occurs in the very process of reading Austen's texts. This is the clash between the ideal reader presupposed in her writing – a reader who is a function of the text – and the actual reader who may or may not be prepared to meet the demands made of the ideal reader, and whose responses are outside textual control. An actual reader may, of course, choose complicity with the narrative voice, becoming to some extent an ideal reader, or may choose to be, to borrow Judith Fetterley's phrase, a 'resisting reader', whose resistance is to the coercion of narrative or stylistic structures and who maintains a difference and distance from the ideal reader.[27] Examples of both compliant and resisting readers are discussed in Chapters 6 to 9.

Readers do not, however, resist or obey only the structures within texts. Nobody reads in a cultural vacuum, and reading can never be innocent of the influences of social, political and economic structures, both those of the moment and the past, as I discuss in the second part of the book. I have designated readers who resist the external pressures of their social and cultural *milieux* as 'oppositional' readers, to differentiate them from the 'resisting' readers described above. Chapters 4 and 5 provide some specific textual and critical background to the responses of Austen's readers, and in Chapters 6, 7, 8 and 9, I endeavour to place the reactions of Austen's readers in some of their historical and cultural contexts, explicating the particular kinds of responses enabled by certain contexts and cultures. This book does not aim to cover all possible contexts for the reading experience, concentrating instead on the material qualities of the text and nineteenth-century theories about the nature and purpose of reading. My primary focus is on gender, and so I do not discuss in any detail, for example, geographical, political, religious or financial contexts, and there is little strictly economic or class-based analysis, though it is probable that all these approaches would illuminate the material considered here in important and different ways. This material has been selected from a wide survey of all known extant responses to Austen's work,[28] and has been chosen because it represents both the most common and the most suggestive and interesting kinds of response, but it must be acknowledged that any history of reading or response is, almost by definition, partial. It is impossible for any researcher in the field of the history of reading to ignore the fact that the act of reading is very rarely recorded (for many, reading was, and is, too ordinary an action to merit writing about), and even if recorded, the evidence may not survive (written and printed materials are vulnerable, destroyed not only by accidents such as fire and flood, but also sometimes by deliberate choice). Scholars are dependent on the survival of records of reading that are skewed in terms of gender (more records written by men than women exist), social class (the belongings of the rich, including manuscripts of their letters and diaries, tend to survive better than those of the poor, while autobiographies and biographies tend to be written by and about extraordinary, rather than ordinary people), and historical period (material of a more recent date is more plentiful, simply because of the destructive effects of time). In addition, the acts of reading that are recorded tend to be those that arouse intense emotion or one kind or another, while the vast majority of reading experiences must in fact be quite the opposite. Rarely does a reader (unless under compulsion) bother to record what may be the most common response of all to a text: boredom. But however partial the history, however self-selecting the responses of her readers, they nonetheless have a story to tell about the nature of Austen's appeal and the enduring value of her works.

*****

Jane Austen herself was a resisting reader. In her criticism of the internal structures of Mary Brunton's *Self Control* (1810), for example, she wrote in a letter to Cassandra, 'I am looking over Self Control again, & my opinion is confirmed of its' [*sic*] being an excellently-meant, elegantly-written Work, without anything of Nature or Probability in it. I declare I do not know whether Laura's passage down the American River, is not the most natural, possible, every-day thing she ever does. –'[29] Although she approves of its morality, recognizing it to be an 'excellently-meant' work, she resists the improbability of its plotting. Her resistance is thus seen to be to the structures of the text itself, rather than to external factors surrounding it. We should also note that Austen comments again on the absurdity of Laura's adventures in a letter to her niece Anna Lefroy, in which she teasingly suggests that she will write 'a close Imitation of "Self-control" as soon as I can; – I will improve upon it; – my Heroine shall not merely be wafted down an American river in a boat by herself, she shall cross the Atlantic in the same way, & never stop till she reaches Gravesent [*sic*]. –',[30] and again in her parodic 'Plan of a Novel according to hints from various quarters', which bears a strong resemblance to these comments to Anna.[31] Austen thus turns the improbability of Brunton's plotting to ironic purposes of her own.

Austen was also an appropriative reader, as when she takes on Samuel Richardson. 'Dear me!' she exclaims. 'What is to become of me! Such a long letter! – Two & forty lines in the 2ᵈ page. – Like Harriot Byron I ask, what am I to do with my Gratitude? –'.[32] Here, she bathetically borrows Harriet's phrase in order to subvert it, turning the seriousness of Harriet's 'Gratitude' to Sir Charles Grandison into her exaggerated thanks for Cassandra's letter. In so doing, she unerringly points out that there is something exaggerated, or excessive, about the 'Gratitude' of the original text, although she simultaneously enacts the tenderness inherent in both Harriet's feelings for Sir Charles and her own for Cassandra. Such intertextual teasing is common between the sisters, and, like Austen's criticism of *Self Control*, shows Austen's amused ability to resist and appropriate for her own purposes what she perceived as ridiculous or unnatural in the writing of others. As we see in Chapters 2 and 3, such acts of resistance and appropriation are characteristic of Austen's reading and writing practices.

In her reading and writing, though not in her life, Austen frequently resisted or opposed social and literary conventions too, mocking the prevailing conventions that suggested reading novels was either dangerous or intellectually unacceptable, and commenting wryly on the 'pretension' and 'self-consequence' of those who were ashamed of reading them:

> I have received a very civil note from Mrs Martin requesting my name as a Subscriber to her Library [...] As an inducement to subscribe Mrs Martin tells us that her Collection is not to consist only of Novels, but of every kind of Literature &tc &tc – She might have spared this pretension to *our* family, who are great Novel-readers & not ashamed of being so; – but it was necessary I suppose to the self-consequence of half her Subscribers.[33]

She defines her position as a reader in opposition to one of the cultural stereotypes discussed in Chapter 5: that of the reader described in Walter Scott's review of *Emma* for the *Quarterly Review*, for whom 'a novel is frequently "bread eaten in secret"',[34] who is ashamed of her secret and depraved taste. Both resistance and opposition are for Austen not painful, but amusing. Defiance, it seems, is pleasurable. In *Sense and Sensibility*, Elinor Dashwood, faced with Robert Ferrars' inanities and nonsense, 'agreed to it all, for she did not think he deserved the compliment of rational opposition'.[35] 'Rational opposition' truly is a 'compliment' in Austen's novels and letters, a compliment that extends to her attitude towards her literary predecessors. Many of Austen's readers pay her a similar courtesy. Rational opposition to Austen's novels is often more interesting than wholehearted devotion; Chapters 6 to 9 explore the complicated ways in which the qualities of resistance, opposition and appropriation I have identified as characteristic of Austen's reading and writing are translated into others' comments about her.

At the heart of all of Austen's novels is the question of what it means to be an intelligent woman in a patriarchal world, which is also importantly at stake in the women readers' responses to Austen discussed in Chapters 6, 7 and 8. Tellingly, one of Jane Austen's earliest readers, Miss Isabella Herries, disliked *Emma* on the grounds that she 'objected to my exposing the sex in the character of the Heroine.'[36] All Jane Austen's heroines face situations in which their own intellectual and/or sexual energies come into direct conflict with the power structures that limit their life choices. Energy is thus thwarted, and forced to take a different course – either sublimation or the formation of potentially disabling somatic symptoms. Chapter 2 discusses the situation of Fanny Price in detail, but other examples would include the diversion of Emma Woodhouse's intelligence and energy into the fantasy world of the 'imaginist'[37] and matchmaker, the low-level depression of Anne Elliot, who, is constantly struggling against 'a great tendency to lowness,'[38] and Marianne Dashwood's dramatic illness when her desires are thwarted. It is no coincidence that Marianne's desire for Willoughby is represented as both literary and sexual, beginning with a shared taste for Shakespeare and compounded by Willoughby's physical attractiveness. It could be argued too that, although Elizabeth Bennet's behaviour frequently pushes the bounds of propriety to their limits, her flyting flirtation with Darcy provides a (just) legitimate use of the quality of intelligence within the marriage market, and thus allows Elizabeth the unusual freedom of directing her intellectual energies into a course congenial to her. We should note, however, that Elizabeth's 'pert' and 'vulgar' behaviour did not win her favour with many early readers, revealing the extent to which her behaviour courts risk. Lady Jane Davy, for example, remarked on the 'unrelieved' depiction of 'vulgar minds and manners' in *Pride and Prejudice*,[39] and even Mary Russell Mitford, one of Austen's greatest apologists, deplored 'the entire want of taste which could produce so pert, so worldly a heroine as the beloved of such a man as Darcy'.[40]

John Wiltshire has beautifully demonstrated the way in which repression of desires manifests itself in somatic symptoms in Austen's novels.[41] Marianne Dashwood's is a case in point, as is that of *Sanditon*'s Parker sisters, whose thwarted energies are diverted into Diana's 'activity run mad' and Susan's absurd invalidism.[42] Austen makes her point explicitly in *Sanditon*, contrasting the legitimacy of masculine energy with the limited possibilities available to women. She writes of the Parker siblings:

> It was impossible for Charlotte not to suspect a good deal of fancy in such an extraordinary state of health. Disorders and recoveries so very much out of the common way, seemed more like the amusement of eager minds in want of employment than of actual afflictions and releif [*sic*]. The Parkers, were no doubt a family of imagination and quick feelings – and while the eldest brother found vent for his superfluity of sensation as a projector, the sisters were perhaps driven to dissipate theirs in the invention of odd complaints. The *whole* of their mental vivacity was evidently not so employed; part was laid out in a zeal for being useful.[43]

In this account, 'quick feelings' and 'mental vivacity' are useful to a male property speculator, but are diverted into hypochondria and overly officious altruism in the ladies of his family. All of Austen's heroines and many of her lesser female characters possess, to a greater or lesser degree, 'eager minds in want of employment', and the plots of the novels frequently turn on the consequences. Suppressed or sublimated energies pervade the plots of the novels, and maintaining propriety of demeanour in company when inwardly struggling with mental anguish is incumbent, at one time or another, on all of her heroines.

The displacement of energy that functions on the level of plot is also felt in Austen's style. Although Virginia Woolf thought that 'the chief miracle' of Austen's writing was that she (Woolf) 'could not find any signs that her circumstances had harmed her work in the slightest',[44] a number of critics, from Margaret Oliphant in 1870,[45] Mary Poovey in 1984,[46] to D. A. Miller in 2003[47] and Janet Todd in 2006,[48] have identified the conflicting energies that pulse beneath the surface of Austen's seemingly smooth and unruffled prose style. In his influential essay of 1940, D. W. Harding coined the phrase 'regulated hatred' to describe the presence of unruly energy in Austen's prose style,[49] and critical work making use of Bakhtin's models of dialogism and heteroglossia continues to focus on disruptive energies in the text.[50] In Chapter 3 I discuss some of the ways in which Austen's style contains the presence of potentially destructive but eventually liberating energies, making use of Poovey's formulation of the conflict of the 'proper lady'. In *Persuasion*, Austen describes Anne's 'smiles reined in and spirits dancing in private rapture' as she finally manages a *tête-à-tête* with Wentworth after receiving his letter.[51] Both 'reining in' and 'private rapture' are, I argue, essential to Austen's prose style.

In suggesting that Austen's style bears the hallmarks of a concern to be, in Poovey's phrase, a 'proper lady' in spite of being a professional woman writer, it is not my intention to ignore or devalue the recent important critical work that has re-examined the early nineteenth-century literary marketplace, and shown that the range of opportunities for women in that marketplace was far greater than previously supposed.[52] It is evident both from such scholarship and from primary sources such as letters and diaries that late eighteenth-century and early nineteenth-century women confidently wrote and published substantial quantities of poetry, drama and both fictional and non-fictional prose, and that a large and often sympathetic readership (of which Austen was herself a part) for their productions existed. Nor do I want to perpetuate the surprisingly long-lived and influential (although inaccurate) myth, begun by Henry Austen in his 'Biographical Notice', that Jane Austen 'became an authoress entirely from taste and inclination. Neither the hope of fame nor profit mixed with her early motives'[53] – in other words that she was not serious about her literary endeavours. Q. D. Leavis forcefully made the point that Jane Austen was not an inspired amateur as early as 1942,[54] and the most cursory reading of Austen's letters reveals the interest she took in the reception of her books, and her desire for both literary acclaim and money. She writes to Cassandra that she is 'never too busy to think of S&S. I can no more forget it, than a mother can forget her sucking child'.[55] She longs for the public to like her Elizabeth Bennet: 'I must confess that *I* think her as delightful a creature as ever appeared in print, & how I shall be able to tolerate those who do not like *her* at least, I do not know'.[56] She is concerned that Emma Woodhouse is a heroine 'whom no one but myself will much like'.[57] She cheerfully declares herself 'too vain to wish to convince you that you have praised them [her novels] beyond their Merit',[58] but is 'very strongly haunted by the idea that to those Readers who have preferred P&P. it [*Emma*] will appear inferior in Wit, & to those who have preferred MP. very inferior in good Sense'.[59] She writes of the second edition of *Sense and Sensibility*: 'I cannot help hoping that *many* will feel themselves obliged to buy it. I shall not mind imagining it a disagreable [*sic*] Duty to them, so as they do it',[60] and complains to Fanny Knight that 'people are more ready to borrow & praise [*Mansfield Park*], than to buy – which I cannot wonder at; – but tho' I like praise as well as anybody, I like what Edward calls *Pewter* too'.[61] It is clear that Austen wanted both 'praise' and 'pewter'. Nonetheless, it seems to me true that the plots of Austen's novels, although subverted, do strongly adhere to codes of ladylike propriety, while the stylistic features of her writing enact the pleasures of resistance to these very codes. This is most in evidence in my discussion of Austen's directed indirections of style in Chapter 3.

If there are sublimated energies in Austen's writing, it is also manifestly true that such energies resurface in writing about Austen, although her readers do not always recognize the relationships between them. I have chosen in Chapters 6 to 9 to focus most intensely on the private and critical writing of Austen's readers, because I believe that by doing so we may expand our notion of literary influence to include some important (and hitherto often ignored) ways in which readers interact with texts. The correspondence between Mary Russell Mitford and Elizabeth Barrett Browning (analysed in Chapter 7), for example, clearly demonstrates the negotiations with Austen's name and reputation that allow both writers to come to a stronger sense of their own beliefs and priorities as readers and writers. The comments of Mark Twain and Ralph Waldo Emerson (discussed in Chapter 8) reflect the ways in which reading can relate to questions of national identity and gender. The responses of the Macaulay, Darwin and Kipling families all point to the role played by shared reading in the construction of familial ties and relationships. It is also important to note that many of the implicit or explicit debates, discussions and problems that remain unresolved in Austen's novels – the challenges that Austen lays down to her readers and the questions she invites them to answer – are taken up by those who read her.

This book thus considers the contributions of Jane Austen's novels to important late-eighteenth- and nineteenth-century debates about the nature, purpose and value of women's reading, examining the use Austen made of her own reading, her discussions of reading women within the novels, and aspects of her stylistic practice that have important implications for a hypothetical reader. Austen's novels are discussed within the context of nineteenth-century anxieties about reading women and women's reading, with particular reference to the influence of the conservative conduct literature of the mid- to late-eighteenth century. Austen's style, which itself enacts the dictates of propriety, actually encourages a type of reading – 'hard reading'[62] – that questions the conservative ideologies that conduct books endeavour to perpetuate, and that the marriage plots of Austen's novels appear to support. Austen's readers respond to the hidden energies of the texts with energies of their own, invoking in their own conversations with and about Austen, a number of important arguments. Among these are debates about the role of the critic, the moral value of fiction, the development of the novel, the future of the professional woman writer, the importance of familial or domestic affection, the status of manners and the heart, and questions about what it means to read well. Like ghosts, these issues, even when they are not directly being addressed, hover in the background of my chosen readers' discussions of Austen. *Revenants* indeed, they return unexpectedly, inflecting conversations and discourses with their presence.

Chapter 1

JANE AUSTEN'S READING IN CONTEXT

Jane Austen's Reading

As a child and young woman, living with her family in Steventon Rectory, Jane Austen had access to her father's library of some five hundred volumes, many of which she read, along with books borrowed from friends, neighbours and wider family members. After the family's move to Bath, when her father's library was sold, and the family's second move to Southampton after the death of the Reverend George Austen, Jane Austen borrowed books from the circulating libraries of Bath and Southampton, and enjoyed borrowing and reading books from the private libraries of friends and relations during her sometimes lengthy visits to them. In particular, Austen seems to have relished her brother Edward Knight's library at Godmersham Park, and to have taken full advantage of his collection.[1] While they were in Bath and Southampton, Henry Austen sent his mother and sisters works from London, and they also sometimes received newspapers and periodicals from the same source, and, rather like the Dashwood family in *Sense and Sensibility*, from friends and neighbours. When Jane, Cassandra, Mrs Austen and Martha Lloyd made their home in Chawton, in 1809, the Austens formed part of the Chawton Book Society,[2] and Jane continued to borrow books from both public and private libraries. In the last three years of her life, once she belonged to the prestigious John Murray stable of authors, she received the latest publications as loans from her publisher. Over the course of her life, therefore, Austen had different kinds of access to books and other printed matter, but, in common with her mother, sister and most other Georgian women on a limited income, she very rarely bought books, and when she did, they tended to be as gifts for other people. Those bought or given to her during her youth were sold with her father's books before the move to Bath in 1801, and the frequent purchase of books was simply too expensive for the Austen women during their years in Bath, Southampton and Chawton.[3]

Reconstructing Austen's reading is therefore both difficult and inevitably patchy, since the most obvious source available to the historian of reading – an individual's library – does not exist in Austen's case. We cannot therefore depend on marginal notes or annotations to her books to tell us what she thought, nor even look for evidence of heavy use, such as dog-eared pages and dirty marks, or, conversely, marks of disuse, such as uncut pages. The Austens, in fact, extremely rarely wrote in their books – the outstanding exceptions are James Austen's copy of Oliver Goldsmith's *History of England* in four volumes (1771), in which Jane Austen wrote more than a hundred marginal notes that document her championship of the Stuart dynasty, and, to a much lesser extent, Jane Austen's copies of Vicesimus Knox's *Elegant Extracts*, in which both she and her niece Anna wrote marginalia, and Burney's *Camilla*, in which Austen commented on the ending. The marginalia in both the *History of England* and the *Elegant Extracts* primarily demonstrate Jane Austen's disagreements with received versions of history, reminiscent of Catherine Morland's view of history in *Northanger Abbey* as 'the quarrels of popes and kings, with wars or pestilences, in every page; the men all so good for nothing, and hardly any women at all'.[4] Austen seems, in particular, to have objected to the depiction of the characters of Mary, Queen of Scots, and Elizabeth I in Goldsmith's *History* and the extracts from Hume's and Robertson's *Histories* in the *Elegant Extracts*. Beyond these exceptions, however, in general the surviving copies of Austen family books in the Knight Collection at Chawton House Library tell us little about their readers.[5] Austen did not leave a diary or journal, and unlike many women of her period and class, she does not seem to have kept a commonplace book or album of quotations. We are therefore dependent on the limited marginalia, Austen's surviving letters (a very incomplete record), the quotations, allusions or parodies of literary works found in her novels, juvenilia and unfinished works, and the recorded memories of Austen's nieces and nephews for evidence about what she read, and, sometimes, how she read it.

It is possible to conclude from the existing evidence that Jane Austen read both intensively and extensively, knowing some books almost by heart through repeated re-readings, but also reading a wide and eclectic variety of texts. From the Goldsmith annotations, which show Austen frequently disagreeing with Goldsmith's view of history, and revealing her own sympathies with the Stuart dynasty, we can see that she engaged intensely and sometimes fiercely with authors and arguments that she disliked. Like most readers, she read different books at different times in her life, but returned to old favourites regularly, and responded in various ways to what she read. She read for different reasons, and with varying levels of attention, although, as Isobel Grundy rightly points out, she read like a potential author from a very early age, looking for what she could use, 'not by quietly absorbing and reflecting it, but by actively engaging, rewriting, often mocking it'.[6] As a child and young woman, Jane Austen's access to books was restricted by financial and geographical constraints, but she was also unusually free to choose her own reading matter. George Austen's library was small, but all of his books were available to his children, and, uncommonly in the period, their choice of reading does not seem to have been censored. From childhood, therefore, Jane Austen was used to making her own judgements and decisions about what (and how) she read, albeit within a limited compass.

When her elder brothers went up to university, they returned for the holidays with new books and ideas, many of which they shared with the family members still at home. Family tradition records, for example, that Austen's elder brother James 'had a large share in directing Jane's reading and forming her taste.'[7] At Steventon, books were read both alone and together, aloud and silently. As Paula Byrne demonstrates, the family participated in amateur theatricals, gaining a deep and shared familiarity with certain plays and poetical prologues, including those written by James Austen. Jane Austen, Byrne argues, was 'actively engaged' in the amateur theatricals, not only at Steventon, but also in Kent, Southampton and Winchester.[8] All of the members of the Austen family, like Mrs Morland in *Northanger Abbey*, re-read their favourite books very frequently. Growing up in a family where books were read together and shared around, Jane Austen was used to sharing her thoughts about books with her parents, sister and brothers, and also, crucially, to assuming a shared knowledge and understanding of literary works. This early experience of reading in a small and close-knit community, in which literary allusions were common currency, almost guaranteed to be recognized and understood, and in which certain books were known by heart, was to affect both Austen's later reading practices and her writing style, in profound and important ways. Throughout her life, Austen habitually read with her sister, mother, and any other guests to their various households. Austen's niece Caroline, for example, remembered that Jane Austen 'was considered to read aloud remarkably well' and recalled her reading of Burney's *Evelina* (1778): 'once I knew her to take up a volume of Evelina and read a few pages of Mr. Smith and the Brangtons and I thought it was like a play.'[9] Patricia Howell Michaelson notes that Austen 'almost certainly wrote her novels anticipating that they would be read aloud', and analyses the ways in which such elocutionary effects as emphases, pauses, tone of voice and gestures are represented in Austen's writing.[10] Austen certainly did read her own works aloud to a small and sympathetic audience at various stages of their composition, including after their publication. In addition to Marianne Knight's account of hearing the novels read aloud behind closed doors, scattered references in the letters alert us to the practice of reading Jane's novels aloud in the family circle. As soon as *Pride and Prejudice* was published, for example, the Austens read it with their guest, Miss Benn: 'Miss Benn dined with us on the very day of the Books coming, & in the eveng we set fairly at it & read half the 1st vol. to her – prefacing that having intelligence from Henry that such a work wd soon appear we had desired him to send it whenever it came out.– She was amused, poor soul! *that* she cd not help, you know, with two such people to lead the way'.[11]

The Austens, as a family, were all also used to reading each other's work in manuscript. More information has survived about Jane's manuscripts than those of any other family member, but she was not the only writer in the family. James Austen wrote plays, poetry and *belles lettres*, Mrs Austen wrote light verse, George, Henry and James Austen all wrote sermons, Cassandra Austen wrote charades and verses, and a later generation of nephews and nieces wrote novels. We know that Jane read (and admired) Cassandra's charades,[12] and Henry's sermons.[13] We can surmise that she read the essays James, Henry and their cousin Edward Cooper wrote for James's periodical *The Loiterer* from the fact that she contributed a letter, signed 'Sophia Sentiment' to the periodical in answer to a previous paper.[14] We know that every member of the family who chose to participate in the Austen amateur theatricals read the plays that James wrote for performance at Steventon. We can assume that even if they did not *read* their father's sermons, the members of the Austen family certainly heard them in Steventon Church. And we know that later in their lives, Jane, Cassandra and Mrs Austen read the embryonic novels of Caroline, Anna and James Edward Austen in manuscript form, and that Jane probably helped Anna by writing out the latter's playlet of 'Sir Charles Grandison'.[15] Jane Austen's family and friends also read *her* novels at all points of their composition, from first drafts to published novels, as recorded in her letters and the opinions she collected of *Emma* and *Mansfield Park*. Martha Lloyd, we should remember, had read 'First Impressions' so often that Jane Austen joked in 1799 that 'one more perusal' would enable her to 'publish it from Memory'.[16] There is, therefore, sufficient evidence to say that the Austens, as a reading community, were both producers and consumers, and that part of what bound them together was the shared experience of reading, enjoying, and criticizing each other's works. Reading and writing were communal activities within a close-knit family, and criticism of literary works took place against a common set of shared reading experiences.

Jane Austen's manuscript notebooks, written between 1787 (when she was 12) and 1792 (when she was seventeen), show her assumptions about the kind of reading community who would read her works – one which would share her concerns and point of view – and occasionally they also show the ways in which that reading community actually responded to the works. The three manuscript notebooks are titled *Volume the First*, *Volume the*

Second and *Volume the Third*, and they adhere closely to the conventions of presentation of the fiction and plays that Austen knew – with dedications, chapter headings, where appropriate, *dramatis personae* at the beginning of plays, and so on. They copy, as far as is possible, the typographical conventions of published works. The juvenile effusions in the volumes are all, without exception, parodies of particular works, authors or genres that we know to have been read by the young Austens together. These individual works include the aforementioned Goldsmith's *History of England*, Charlotte Lennox's *Female Quixote* (1752), Richardson's *Sir Charles Grandison* (1753–4), and Berquin's *L'Ami de l'Enfance* (1782–3); genres include the novel of sentiment, the conduct book, the dramatic comedy, the epistolary novel and the history.

By its nature, parody assumes prior knowledge of the work being parodied, and to some extent, it creates a readership which shares the author's sentiments about the works, authors or genres being parodied. That is, after all, the aim of parody – it points out the weaknesses, absurdities and follies of the original, and implicitly asks the reader to align him or herself with the parodist's stance. The internal evidence, in the shape of the dedications to the works, suggests that all of the members of the Austen family, including more distant relatives such as Jane Cooper and Eliza de Feuillide, and their close friends, such as Martha and Mary Lloyd, were expected to read the notebooks. We know that at least two members of Austen's family recognized the parodic nature of the works, as they responded in creative kind. Henry Austen added a very brief parody of another kind of genre – the banker's draft – after one of her dedications. The dedication reads:

To Henry Thomas Austen Esqre –
Sir
I am now availing myself of the Liberty you have frequently honoured me with of dedicating one of my Novels to you. That it is unfinished, I greive [*sic*]; yet fear that from me, it will always remain so; that as far as it is carried, it Should be so trifling and unworthy of you, is
Another concern to your obliged humble.
                        Servant
                                                The Author[17]

Henry Austen – a future banker – wrote in response:

Messrs Demand and Co – please to pay Jane Austen Spinster the sum of one hundred guineas on account of your Humbl. Servant.
                                                      H. T. Austen
£105.0.0.[18]

In these *jeux d'esprit* of a loving brother and sister, we can see the Austen siblings simultaneously acting out and parodying the productions of their future professions, whilst using their shared expertise in parody, learned through resistant and oppositional reading, to amuse one another. Cassandra Austen, the sibling to whom Jane was always closest, also recognized and participated in the spirit of parody of Jane's notebooks. The second item in *Volume the Second* is *The History of England*, written 'by a partial, prejudiced, and ignorant Historian' and dedicated to 'Miss Austen, daughter of the Revd George Austen'.[19] Cassandra is, however, not only the dedicatee of the work; she produced thirteen illustrations which strongly underline the satirical tone of the text, and reflect its political bias (Mary, Queen of Scots is depicted as soft, round and smiling, while Elizabeth I has a gaunt, hook-nosed and unsmiling visage), thus suggesting that she, like Henry, was a reader with attitudes and interests in common with the author. Austen's first assumption about her reading community, at least as evidenced by the notebooks, is that her readers would immediately recognize her works as parodies of particular originals, and that they would share her satirical perceptions of those originals.

The second assumption that Jane Austen appears to have made was that her readers would recognize the relevance of characters and situations to their own lives. All but a small number of her short pieces are dedicated to a friend or family member, and her mock-grandiloquent dedications are carefully designed, not only to ape the more florid specimens that she and her family knew from published works, but also to reflect the character of the work to follow, and the character and situation of the dedicatee. To her young niece, Fanny, she dedicated 'The female philosopher – A Letter', with a mock-serious dedication that sets it up as a parody of the conduct book in letters, made popular in the 1770s and 80s by writers such as Hester Chapone and John Bennett:

> My dear Neice [*sic*]
> As I am prevented by the great distance between Rowling and Steventon from superintending Your Education Myself, the care of which will probably devolve on your Father and Mother, I think it is my particular Duty to prevent your feeling as much as possible the want of my personal instructions, by addressing to You on paper my Opinions and Admonitions on the conduct of Young Women, which you will find expressed in the following pages. I am my dear Neice,
>   Your affectionate Aunt
>   The Author

The 'Ode to Pity', a brief poem at the very end of *Volume the First*, bears the following dedication to Cassandra:

> To Miss Austen, the following Ode to Pity is dedicated, from a thorough knowledge of her pitiful Nature, by her obedt humle Servt.
>
> The Author[20]

In these dedications, she is encouraging her readers, who are, of course, not only the dedicatees of the works, but also the other members of her reading community, to recognize the allusions to situation and character, and to delight with her in her teasing of family members. Edward Copeland points out the pointed humour of the dedication of 'The Three Sisters', a tale in which three sisters vie for the attention of a single man, to her brother, Edward, who became engaged in 1791 to a woman whose two sisters became engaged in the same year.[21] She dedicated one of her plays to the playwright of the family, her brother James, writing in the dedication that it was not as good as his own (perhaps this is an expression of sibling rivalry, or perhaps a genuine tribute to James's abilities). It is impossible to know quite how pointed the satire is in these dedications – is the dedication of *Love and Freindship* to Eliza de Feuillide, with the epigraph, 'Deceived in Friendship and Betrayed in Love', a deliberate reproach to the flirtatious Eliza, who, as Deirdre Le Faye suggests, had been playing off the Austen brothers Henry and James against each other during her visit in 1795?[22] There is little to show how the individual Austens received their dedications, but their existence is enough to suggest that theirs was a reading community that revelled in shared jokes. Jane Austen's later letters, which abound in jokes about books and people, carried on with different family members, confirm the Austen liking for this kind of intimate and allusive humour. The most famous of these was her running joke about wishing to become Mrs Crabbe, but she also clearly had recurring jokes with Cassandra about Harriet Byron's Gratitude and Hester Lynch Piozzi's style, as well as her own relationship with her 'dear Dr Johnson', among many others now lost to a modern readership.[23]

As her letters demonstrate, shared allusions to literary works remained a kind of helpful family shorthand to describe situations or characters throughout the lives of the Austen siblings, as when Jane describes a young man she has just met at a tea party. She depicts the unfortunate Mr Gould thus, in a letter to Cassandra: 'he is a very Young Man, just entered of Oxford, wears Spectacles, & has heard that Evelina was written by Dr Johnson. – '.[24] She need say no more. We are irresistibly reminded of the unfortunate John Thorpe's inability to distinguish between authors – in his case, Ann Radcliffe and Frances Burney – in *Northanger Abbey*.

Similarly, in a letter of 19 June, 1799, Austen neatly characterizes an acquaintance through reference to Swift's *Gulliver's Travels*: 'He [Edward] made an important purchase Yesterday; no less so than a pair of Coach Horses; his friend Mr Evelyn found them out & recommended them, & if the judgement of a Yahoo can ever be depended on, I suppose it may now, for I believe Mr Evelyn has all his life thought more of Horses than of anything else'.[25] More than ten years later, the sisters were still playing the same game. Jane writes to Cassandra in January of 1813 of the activities of the Chawton Book Society: 'Upon Mrs Digweed's mentioning that she had sent the Rejected Addresses to Mr Hinton, I began talking to her a little about them, & expressed my hope of their having amused her […] The Papillons have now got the Book & like it very much; their neice [*sic*] Eleanor has recommended it most warmly to them. – *She* looks like a rejected Addresser'.[26] Like her letters and the juvenilia, all of Austen's published works are, to a greater or lesser degree, written for an audience who would immediately recognize both parodic and serious allusions.

Which then, were the works with which Austen could assume the sort of deep and comfortable familiarity that allows elliptical, joking and glancing allusions? The earliest description of Jane Austen's reading is Henry Austen's account in the 'Biographical Notice of the Author'.[27] Henry remembered his sister's favourite authors as Samuel Johnson, William Cowper, George Crabbe and Samuel Richardson, making particular reference to the latter's *Sir Charles Grandison*. He tells of her early infatuation with 'Gilpin on the Picturesque',[28] writing also that 'her reading was very extensive in history and belles letters', and that she was 'intimately acquainted with the merits and defects of the best essays and novels in the English language'.[29] It perhaps went without saying for Henry that she was also familiar with Shakespeare, the Bible and the Book of Common Prayer, as he does not mention these, although their cadences ring out throughout his sister's writing. When James Edward Austen-Leigh wrote his *Memoir of Jane Austen* (1870), he drew heavily on Henry's account for information about Austen's reading, adding little additional information, although he does suggest that what Henry had called 'extensive' reading in history was actually 'the old guides – Goldsmith, Hume and Robertson'.[30] Although the fact that she read Goldsmith, Hume and Robertson was presumably deduced from her marginal annotations on these authors, neither Henry nor James Edward remark on Jane's strong disagreements with received versions of history, preferring instead to ignore or conceal her independence of mind. James Edward briefly alludes to his aunt's admiration of Sir Walter Scott's poetry and his novel *Waverley* (1814),[31] and quotes her joking determination to read no novels but Maria Edgeworth's, her relatives' and her own. James Edward then turns from Austen's reading to deal with other topics: 'It was not, however, what she knew, but what she was, that distinguished her from others'.[32]

Neither the 'Biographical Notice' nor the *Memoir* gives any indication of the real breadth and catholicism of Jane Austen's reading, but they do give some sense of the books and authors that were most familiar to her in her early and adolescent years. These were the ones that she read within a family circle, and which were the focus of shared familial attention – Johnson, Crabbe, Cowper, Richardson, Shakespeare, Goldsmith, Hume, Robertson, Scott and Edgeworth. It is important that both Henry and James Edward are sensitive to what a person's choice of reading says about him or her, and that their representation of Austen's reading reads as if it could come straight from an eighteenth-century conduct-book reading list.[33] Henry also insists on Austen's preference for Richardson over Fielding on account of Fielding's 'grossness'. This is a tactical manoeuvre – to the early nineteenth-century readership to whom his notice is addressed, this instinctive recoil from Fielding exemplifies the natural elegance of mind that he ascribes to his sister. Similarly, her liking for Johnson and Cowper as moral writers puts her own morality beyond reproach. The slight defensiveness with which James Edward treats his aunt's reading matter – 'it was not, however, what she *knew*, but what she *was*' – and the speed with which he moves away from it suggests some discomfort with this particular topic. It is impossible to know whether James Edward believed his aunt knew too much – that she had read books that were unsuitable for the proper lady to read – or that she knew too little for an educated woman of her time. The impression given by the *Memoir*, however, is that James Edward wanted his readers to perceive his aunt as someone whose natural genius did not need external stimuli, and whose astonishingly brilliant novels owed nothing to previous literary tradition. Austen's knowledge of political and economic works, her reading of the popular but undervalued female-authored novel, and her strongly resistant and oppositional modes of reading therefore go unmentioned by both Henry and James Edward, who, from their different historical periods, and for reasons both personal and politic, are constructing idealized portraits of their famous relation, portraits to appeal to the taste of their publics. In so doing, they choose to mention, of the extensive array of literature Jane Austen read, the books that function as evidence for the person they say she was.

It is not surprising that they should do so – after all, Austen's own novels frequently display a similar awareness of the part books play in denoting character. Time and again, characters reveal themselves through their responses to literature. We think, for example, of shallow Caroline Bingley, who uses books only as props, taking up the second volume of Mr Darcy's book in a contemptible attempt to gain his attention in *Pride and Prejudice*, and compare her to *Mansfield Park*'s Fanny Price, for whom books are the friends and guides that help her to moral growth. *Northanger Abbey* sets John Thorpe's callow and unthinking rejection of all novels except M. G. Lewis's Gothic shocker *The Monk* (1795) and Henry Fielding's somewhat risqué *Tom Jones* (1749) against Henry and Eleanor Tilney's rational liking for all sorts of literature, including novels and history. The cultural resonance of books allows Austen to use them as convenient shorthand to help her readers swiftly understand her characters. Moralists and commentators of Austen's period and onward frequently suggested that 'we are what we read'. In Austen's novels, it might be truer to say that how we use what we read defines us; it is possible, like Mary Bennet in *Pride and Prejudice*, to reduce reading to an arid collection of clichés, or like Sir Edward Denham in *Sanditon*, to 'derive only false principles from lessons of morality'.[34] It is also possible, however, for Austen's heroines to turn reading to good account; Anne Elliot's thoughts of poetic treatments of autumn comfort her as she watches Captain Wentworth flirting with Louisa Musgrove, for example, and a 'fondness for reading' is, for Fanny Price, as it was for Austen herself, 'an education in itself'.[35]

Caroline Austen documented Austen's appreciation of the importance of reading, recalling her aunt's advice to 'cease writing till I was 16', and her statement 'that she had herself often wished she had *read* more, and written *less* in the corresponding years of her own life'.[36] Despite Austen's desire to have '*read* more' in her youth, close study of her letters and novels clearly establishes the wide range and depth of her reading, and it is important to give some idea of the scope of Austen's reading here. In addition to those authors named by her brother and her nephew, we know from scattered references in the letters and novels that Austen knew the authors of the Augustan tradition – Swift, Defoe, Pope, Gay and Addison, for example. She read both male novelists – Fielding, Sterne and Richardson – and contemporary female novelists, such as Maria Edgeworth, Frances Burney, Ann Radcliffe, Elizabeth Inchbald, Charlotte Lennox, Sydney Owenson, Regina Maria Roche, Mary Brunton, Rachel Hunter, Henrietta Sykes, Elizabeth Hamilton, Laetitia Matilda Hawkins and Sarah Harriet Burney. She knew poetry by Milton, George Crabbe, Robert Burns, Thomas Campbell, Wordsworth and Byron, and the sermons of Hugh Blair, Thomas Sherlock and Edward Cooper. She mentions conduct literature by Thomas Gisborne, James Fordyce, Jane West and Hannah More, and plays by Shakespeare, Richard Brinsley Sheridan, John Home, Richard Cumberland, George Colman, Hannah Cowley, Susanna Centlivre and Elizabeth Inchbald. She read political history by Thomas Clarkson, historian of the slave trade and Charles Pasley, historian of the British Empire, travelogues by Joseph Baretti and Lord Macartney, and the correspondence of Hester Lynch Piozzi and Dr Johnson. Although Margaret

Anne Doody points out that 'no foreign poets feature in Austen's letters or her works', and suggests that Austen had 'no interest' in such works,[37] Austen did read novels and educational literature by the French authors Madame de Genlis, Arnaud Berquin and Germaine de Staël, and novels by the German, Johann von Goethe, and at least one play by August von Kotzebue. She read the efforts of relations and acquaintances such as Cassandra Cooke and Egerton Brydges, and the nascent novels of her nieces and nephew.[38] These are only a sample of those directly mentioned in either her novels or letters; critics have also variously argued that Austen also knew authors as diverse as Chaucer, Locke, Rousseau, Johnson, Spenser, Wollstonecraft, Godwin and Choderlos de Laclos well enough for their works to form an important influence on her own.[39] Research in the Knight Collection tells us that she had access, at least for various periods of her life, to a typical eighteenth-century gentleman's library, boasting a wide and miscellaneous range of literature in a number of different languages, including Latin, Greek, French, Italian and Spanish, as well as works on animal husbandry, horticulture and farriery, and the latest law reports, periodicals and sporting journals.

Knowing what Austen read means little, though, unless we also know how she used her reading. Grundy outlines the multitude of ways that Austen interacted with her reading: her pleasure in deliberately mismatching quotation to the occasion; her debunking of literary traditions; her refusal to place the novels within generic boundaries; her 'necessarily tenuous and deliberately oblique relation to [intellectual] debates'; her dislike of pedantry; her comic self-identification with heroines such as Harriet Byron and Camilla Tyrold; her comfortable relationship with her Augustan predecessors and her consistently Johnsonian world view; her judgements of contemporary literature, complicated by multi-layered elements of irony; her 'outrageous teasing' and her merciless treatment of the lack of originality and use of stereotype.[40] Margaret Anne Doody agrees that Austen's use of parody is 'creative, not dismissive'.[41] In *Jane Austen's Art of Memory* (1989), Jocelyn Harris teases out Austen's complex treatment of what she calls Austen's own great tradition: Locke, Richardson, Milton, Shakespeare and Chaucer, and suggests that Austen's memory for books 'energised her art in a manner far more coherent even than "intertextuality"'.[42] Olivia Murphy's work, however, suggests that Austen's relationship with Johnson was less comfortable than Grundy suggests, and that Austen's negotiations with his writing (and that of Richardson) constitute an attempt to 'lay the compulsory didacticism of the eighteenth century to rest'.[43] Harris' most recent book, *A Revolution almost beyond Expression: Jane Austen's* Persuasion (2007) identifies intertextual references to 'Job, Ecclesiastes, the Book of Common Prayer, Chaucer, Shakespeare, Bunyan, the satiric, sentimental, and political writers of the eighteenth century, and the most recent publications of the Romantics, including Wordsworth, Coleridge, Byron, and Scott', and suggests that it is impossible to read the novel without acknowledging the impact of a host of other political, social, cultural and historical referents and contexts on the work.[44] Mary Waldron explores Austen's confrontation with the popular novels of her own time, focusing on her resistance to and mockery of literary stereotypes: stock situations, stock characters and glib morality, and arguing that Austen 'set about a challenge to contemporary assumptions, attempting to free fiction from elements which she thought hampered its readers'.[45] Grundy, Harris, Doody, Waldron and Murphy all see Austen's re-writings of other authors as pleasurably resistant, and laughter, rather than the anxiety presupposed by a Bloomian model of influence, as one of Austen's most important artistic impulses.[46] Waldron identifies the 'hilarious fun' of Austen's writing process, and her 'merciless disrespect' for the structures of the fiction she knew,[47] and, unlike Sandra Gilbert and Susan Gubar, who find in Austen a gendered 'anxiety of authorship',[48] Harris 'detect[s] no trace of anxiety in her'.[49] Harris and Grundy are correct in their claims that Austen 'recognizes no canonical status, acknowledges no literary authority', and 'assumes the sufficiency of her own taste as guide to literary value'.[50] But it is somewhat overstating the case to suggest that there is 'no trace of anxiety' about Austen's use of her reading in the novels, however complicated or displaced.

Jane Austen grew up when the composite figure of the reading public was under close scrutiny. This scrutiny was directed particularly towards reading women, as Jacqueline Pearson argues in *Women's Reading in Britain, 1750–1835: A Dangerous Recreation* (1999). Both what and how a woman read were matters of public interest to eighteenth-century commentators, and Austen's novels were written in a climate that emphasized the personal and political importance of women's reading. Debates about women's reading were often embedded in discussions about what constituted a proper female education, carried out in newspapers, periodicals, conduct books and didactic poetry, and fictionalized and dramatized in novels and plays. Even if Austen had not been familiar with these debates from conversations with friends, acquaintances and neighbours (as she surely was), she encountered them in her reading of conduct books such as Gisborne's *An Enquiry into the Duties of the Female Sex* (1798), novels such as Elizabeth Inchbald's *A Simple Story* (1791) and Hannah More's *Cœlebs in Search of a Wife* (1809), and plays like Inchbald's adaptation of August von Kotzebue's *Lovers' Vows* (1798) and Sheridan's *The Rivals* (1775).

Austen's novels and letters show her to have been profoundly aware of her contemporaries' attitudes towards women's reading, and to have had a clear understanding of the kinds of cultural value assigned to the reading of different literary forms. What follows is a brief survey of the kinds of anxieties articulated by Austen's contemporaries regarding women's reading, in particular their reading of the novel, in order to provide the necessary background to Austen's treatment of the subject, and to locate Austen's own feelings about books and readers in a historical context. This material comes primarily from conduct books for women, written by both conservative and progressive authors, since it is in this material that we find the fears, anxieties and ideological imperatives that surrounded the practice of reading in Georgian and Regency Britain most clearly articulated. It is possible to trace many of Austen's most habitual reading practices in her responses to this literature, which she read both more carefully and less dismissively than has hitherto been suggested.[51]

Conduct Literature for Women: A Brief Overview

There are important and significant differences between conduct books of different kinds. Conduct literature was written by men and women from a variety of social and cultural backgrounds, with very different religious and political affiliations. Austen herself responded in various ways to the differing works of conduct literature that she read. It is, however, the basic similarities, rather than differences, that are relevant here, and on which I shall focus. Conduct literature is situated firmly within New Testament Christianity, and it bases its directives about manners squarely on the assumption that manners are the outward forms of inner principles. Almost without exception, conduct books for both men and women glorify a female ideal of domesticity – a woman who is modest, virtuous, chaste and practical. Erasmus Darwin's ideal female character, for example, 'should possess the mild and retiring virtues, rather than the bold and dazzling ones', and he goes on to warn that 'great eminence in almost anything is sometimes injurious to a young lady'.[52] Women should be intelligent and rational, but they should avoid overt intellectualism and public display – 'Far be it from me to desire to make scholastic ladies or female dialecticians', Hannah More reassures her readers after recommending 'serious study' in the shape of 'dry tough reading' and 'close reasoning'.[53] Affectation and display of any form is frowned upon. It is a constant in conduct literature that a woman's education should derive from Christian principles, and be directed towards encouraging her to live her life in accordance with these principles; only by doing so, the writers claim, will she be both virtuous and happy. It is a woman's duty to improve her mind (within certain necessary constraints) both for her own sake and for her family's (she will be a more agreeable companion for her husband, and better able to educate her children). In line with a number of more politically conservative female writers (More, Hester Chapone, Jane West), Mary Wollstonecraft sums up the end of female education as being 'to prepare a woman to fulfil the important duties of a wife and mother'.[54]

Much of the conduct literature written by men (Gisborne, John Bennett and James Fordyce, for example) is less open about its desire to produce perfect wives and mothers; its rhetoric tends to suggest that self-improvement is a worthwhile goal purely for its own sake. This does not, of course, obscure the subtext that adhering to the advice of conduct literature will improve a girl's chances of a prize in the 'matrimonial lottery',[55] but it does allow the male writers to preserve some coyness about their desire to produce submissive wives for themselves. While Mary Wollstonecraft and the circle around her future husband William Godwin posited a new version of femininity based on the idea that women, like men, are primarily rational creatures, and their physical differences irrelevant in the light of their mental similarities, other writers felt the need to reiterate their more conservative vision of femininity, stressing that men and women are fundamentally different, and thus that the rules that govern the conduct of women should be different to those that apply to men. Whereas men should 'plunge into business', for example, '[d]omestic qualifications' are 'confessedly the highest point of usefulness' in the female sex.[56] Milton's Adam and Eve still form the prototype of gender relations for the conservative writers of the period,[57] and, not coincidentally, a taste for Milton is a marker of good aesthetic and moral taste in the ideal domestic woman.

Conduct literature tends to ignore the complexities of real problems in favour of 'simple' and 'universal' 'truths'. Such books generally share an assumption that the improvement of the individual will lead automatically and inevitably to an improvement of society in general, although individual writers mean different things by the slippery terms 'improvement' and 'society'. Similarly, the debate at the heart of conduct literature for women: 'what constitutes a proper education for a woman?' is the result of the various writers' unanimous assumption that it is possible to educate women into virtue, but what is meant by both 'education' and 'virtue' differs from writer to writer. Because few girls went to school (Jane and Cassandra Austen were relatively unusual in having spent some time away at the Abbey School in Reading), educational writers assumed that young women would get the majority of their education from the books that they read. Most conduct-book writers agree that controlling girls' reading will help to form their moral characters, but how to control their reading, and what they should read are moot questions.

Women's Reading in the Conduct Book

For eighteenth-century commentators, Jacqueline Pearson suggests, the figure of the reading woman is a site of particular cultural anxiety and conflict, because by representing 'both solitary and selfish pleasure and rationality and self-suppression', female reading 'reveals the contradictions in contemporary gender-ideologies'.[58] Reading is figured as both virtuous and potentially dangerous, educative but also seductive. Reading is seductively dangerous because certain books may distract women from domestic duties, they may encourage them to imagine lives for themselves other than those mapped out by convention or duty, and they may provide them with knowledge that propriety demands they should not have. On the other hand, at the same time reading also enlarges and strengthens the mind, thus making the young woman a less vulnerable target for potential seducers or other villains. So reading matter must be carefully selected and controlled – in Hester Chapone's words, for example, a young woman's reading must be 'well-chosen and properly regulated', and she should depend on the advice of an older preceptor when choosing her books.[59]

Literary taste is inextricably linked with moral taste in conduct-book writing. In *Practical Education* (1798), Maria and R. L. Edgeworth explicitly make this connection, writing, 'by early caution, unremitting, scrupulous caution in the choice of the books which are put into the hands of girls, a mother, or a preceptress, may [...] excite in their minds a *taste* for propriety, as well as a taste for literature'.[60] A woman's literary taste can also be used by others to define her propriety or impropriety. The link between 'propriety' and literature is clear, although how to define 'the best poets' and 'improper reading' is less clear. The writers of later conduct books set out to answer this question, either in an explicit reading list or, less explicitly, in the shape of a command not to read novels, plays or certain works of natural history. Such implicit and explicit lists borrow from and feed off one another, with the result that a consensus of approved books begins to emerge. A set of core texts for many authors of conduct literature would include the Marquis of Halifax's *Advice to a Daughter* (1688), Chapone's *Letters on the Improvement of the Mind* (1773), Gregory's *A Father's Legacy to his Daughters* (1774), Madame de Genlis' *Theatre d'Education* (translated 1781), the poetry of Homer, Virgil, Milton, Pope, Dryden, Akenside and Cowper, Shakespeare's plays and poetry, Addison and Steele's essays, Richardson's novels, Hume's, Goldsmith's and Rollin's *Histories*, Blair's *Lectures*, Fordyce's *Sermons*, and, above all, the Bible. Novelists (apart from Richardson, and, in rare cases Frances Burney) are excluded from this list, and novels and romances incur some of conduct literature's most impassioned tirades. Although novels and romances are not technically the same, conduct literature tends to conflate the two, allowing its writers to extend their disapproval of the romance into the newer form of the novel.[61]

The writers of conduct books disapprove strongly of 'those *fictitious stories* that so enchant the mind',[62] presenting themselves in contrast as 'sincere' and 'truthful' despite frequently adopting a fictional persona, addressing a fictional correspondent, or using fictional examples to underscore their points. Bennett criticizes romances because 'the romantick turn, they create indisposes for every thing that is *rational* or substantial. They corrupt all *principle* [...] Such false, over-strained ideas have led many a poor girl to *ruin*'.[63] Fiction is reckoned to be bad for women for a number of reasons: primarily their supposed susceptibility to example, overly developed sensibility, and propensity to idleness and romanticism. Like the Marquis of Caraccioli, who fears that reading romances leads women to a tendency to 'adopt the language of self-importance and affectation, and become [them]selves the heroines of romance',[64] Maria and R. L. Edgeworth are worried that virtuous women will start to act 'in imitation of some Jemima or Almeria, who never existed', and that over-stimulation of the passions by fiction will render women unfit for daily life: 'common food is insipid to the taste which has been vitiated by the high seasonings of art'.[65]

Hannah More believes that 'the indolent repose of light reading' makes women unfit to read serious books, as works of fiction 'soften the mind; they impair its general powers of resistance, and at best feed habits of improper indulgence'. Minds forced in 'the hot-bed of a circulating library' then 'turn out worthless and vapid'.[66] John Bennett sums up the era's dislike of fictional representation when he writes, 'Licentious writings (the produce of so rank an æra), Romances, Novels, Pictures, and the varied *indelicate* representations of the stage will accelerate the last convulsions of virtue and smother the just expiring embers of female reserve'.[67] The sexual language employed by More and Bennett provides a clue to their common resistance to fiction: novels and romances, they believe, are bad in themselves, but more importantly, they weaken the mind, thus making young women unable to resist the encroachments of vice. Becoming addicted to novels is thus the first step on the road to sexual ruin. There are, though, a number of grudgingly approving accounts of novels. Jane West, for example, after a long and impassioned diatribe against the novel, changes tone: 'it would, however, be culpable injustice, to involve all fictitious narrative in this severe censure [...] a well-written novel is the best introduction to the knowledge of life and manners, and may justly claim to be the associate, but not the substitute of graver studies'.[68] Like Bennett, who explicitly recommends *Sir Charles Grandison*, West singles out Richardson's novels as likely to 'transfuse some devout sentiments into the most cold and worldly bosom'. Goldsmith (presumably referring to *The Vicar of Wakefield*) is recommended for his 'simplicity, innocence, and nature'.[69]

Conduct books emphasize not only the control of reading matter, but the manner in which young ladies must read. The Edgeworths and More advocate scrupulous censorship in order to ensure that nothing potentially corrupting should be seen. The works of Buffon, for example, are 'absolutely inadmissible into the library of a young lady'.[70] Reading aloud to a daughter, but skipping 'immoral' passages, insisting that a young woman reads only in company, or demanding a form of self-censorship ('Let whatever she peruses in her most private hours be such as she needs not to be ashamed of reading aloud to those, whose good opinion she is most anxious to observe', advises Gisborne)[71] are other ways in which young women's reading is controlled and restricted. Reading is conceptualized as a sociable activity. Ideally, a young woman will read in the domestic circle (rather than alone in her closet, where what and how she reads cannot be monitored), and she will discuss what she reads with her parents or preceptor, so that any misapprehensions into which she slips can be corrected. To some extent, then, the practices of communal reading in the Austen family answered well to conduct book directives about the necessity for a young woman to read in company, though the often mocking, resistant and oppositional nature of those communal reading practices did not.

Enacting an uneasy recognition of the gap between theory and practice, conduct literature is riddled with contradictions about reading. Young women's reading needs to be chosen and regulated by their parents, older friends or preceptors, and they should be given little choice in what they read because otherwise they will turn naturally to novels, but it is also a young woman's duty to be able to make judgements and to discriminate: to 'improve your discernment',[72] a duty impossible to fulfil if the material over which to exercise discernment is taken out of her hands. Hannah More, despite her view that Buffon should be banished from a young lady's library, suggests that 'to those who exercise a habit of self application a book of profane history may be made an instrument of improvement' and *vice versa*:'[W]ithout this habit the Bible itself may, in this view, be read with little profit'.[73]

Uneasily concurrent with the desire to restrict reading and limit individual desire, exists the wish to teach young women to read closely and carefully, to become autonomous self-regulating readers who will be able to make informed choices about reading for their future children. Mary Wollstonecraft insists that 'till women are more rationally educated, the progress of human virtue and improvement in knowledge must receive continual checks', and that 'to become respectable, the exercise of their understanding is necessary'.[74] Many less politically radical writers were in fact saying much the same thing. When Coleridge writes disdainfully of 'the present much-reading but not very hard-reading age',[75] he is echoing a century of conservative conduct-book writers, who promote 'hard reading'[76] in order to 'harden the mind for more trying conflicts', 'correct' a 'spirit of trifling', and 'abstract her [the reader] from the world and its vanities'.[77] In *An Enquiry into the Duties of the Female Sex*, Gisborne suggests that the young female reader should 'accustom herself regularly to bring the sentiments which she reads, and the conduct which is described in terms, more or less strong, of applause and recommendation, to the test of Christian principles'. She must not only read difficult books; she must engage in a meaningful moral dialogue with the text. 'In proportion as this practice is pursued or neglected, reading will be profitable or the reverse'.[78] Engagement and interaction with the text are thus the necessary preconditions of profitable reading, and the development of critical skills is encouraged on the grounds that literary criticism is moral criticism; literary taste is moral taste.

In a similar vein to Gisborne, Bennett advises his young female correspondent: 'Do not read much, at a time. Meditation is the stomach, which digests this food; you should *reflect* many hours, for reading *one*'.[79] Unlike novels and romances, which are 'devoured', serious reading demands reflection and digestion. The metaphor of reading as feeding is a common one – Gisborne describes the desire to read novels as 'an appetite [...] too keen to be denied',[80] while Hannah More advises young ladies (after a proper course of preparation) 'to swallow and digest such strong meat, as Watt's or Duncan's little book of Logic'.[81] And the metaphor is telling – the control of reading is one way of controlling unruly appetites and curbing indulgence. Just as a young woman should not be greedy for food, she should not have an 'insatiable appetite' for novels, as both imply a lack of self-control that could eventually affect the structures of social control. What the more conservative authors of conduct literature fail to account for is the possibility that, once a girl has learned to read 'improving books' carefully and critically, to 'meditate' and 'digest', there is nothing to stop her transferring her reading skills and reading habits to other kinds of literature, including novels. She may even begin to read conduct books critically, and start to question the modes of taste and behaviour that they set up and privilege. A woman's challenge to conservative conduct literature can appear either directly (like Wollstonecraft's *Vindication of the Rights of Woman*), or more obliquely, through irony, parody or satire, as Austen's does.

In *Desire and Domestic Fiction* (1987), Nancy Armstrong argues that the conduct literature of the eighteenth century made possible the conditions under which Jane Austen was to write her novels. By the time Austen wrote her books, she suggests, the 'domestic ideology', promoted and perpetuated in conduct books, had 'acquired power akin to that of natural law', with the result that 'the rules governing sexual relations laid out in the conduct books could be taken for granted'.[82] Unlike Richardson, who had to 'new-Model [the] Affections' of the reader in defiance of earlier notions of sexual relations,[83] Armstrong suggests that 'Austen knew perfectly well her readers had identified those rules not only with common sense, if not always with nature, but also with the form of the novel itself'.[84] However, Austen's novels are not simple dramatizations of virtue rewarded, unlike, for example, Hannah More's conduct-book-as-novel, *Cœlebs in Search of a Wife*. Austen's novels unswervingly depict the complexity of life, and in the process, they reveal and expose the contradictions in the 'domestic ideology' expounded by such writers as Hannah More.[85]

Austen responds with both amusement and sincerity to conduct literature, and the ideas it articulates, gleefully exposing affectation and absurdity, calmly appropriating tone and register, undercutting and subverting both diction and directives. However, she also engages seriously with the flaws in its ideological demands. Austen's novels belong in a tradition that believed in the importance of educating women to read more selectively, more carefully and, crucially, more intelligently. Notwithstanding her reservations about conduct literature itself, Austen trusted in the value of that tradition, and she develops a style of writing that both demands and teaches 'hard reading'.

Ilona Dobosiewicz, indeed, reads Jane Austen's novels as constituting a sustained critique of the 'patriarchal canard' perpetuated by eighteenth-century conduct literature.[86] She suggests that Austen systematically rejected the ideology of the conduct book in order to posit a new form of domesticity, based on female-only relationships: mothers and daughters, sisters and female friends. In fact, Austen's relationship with the various writers of conduct literature is much more complicated, involving commitment to many similar moral ideals, but simultaneous dedication to the demands of her own chosen genre: the novel. In the following chapter, Austen's responses to her reading of different conduct books and authors are discussed, both to clarify her position in her period's debates about women's reading, and to serve as an example of how Austen read and used other types of reading matter.

Chapter 2

JANE AUSTEN'S NEGOTIATIONS WITH READING

Jane Austen was far from opposed to the central tenets of conduct literature, with its strong emphasis on New Testament Christianity, propriety and good manners, prudence, economy, modesty and good sense. Her early anti-heroine, Camilla Stanley, of *Catharine; or, The Bower*, for example, is described in terms that are strongly reminiscent of the conservative conduct-book writers of the late eighteenth century:

> Those years which ought to have been spent in the attainment of useful knowledge and mental improvement, had been all bestowed in learning drawing, Italian and music, more especially the latter, and she now united to these accomplishments, an understanding unimproved by reading and a mind totally devoid either of taste or judgement.[1]

Similarly, when Austen writes of Harriet Smith's riddle-book that 'the only literary pursuit which engaged Harriet at present, the only mental provision she was making for the evening of life, was the collecting and transcribing all the riddles of every sort that she could meet with, into a thin quarto of hot-pressed paper, made up by her friend, and ornamented with ciphers and trophies',[2] she is both mocking Harriet's vapidity, and making a serious point about her intellectual deprivation. She does so in terms that reflect Hannah More's concerns that women are educated 'exclusively, for the transient period of youth, when it is to maturer life we ought to advert'.[3] Mr Darcy's claim that a truly accomplished woman 'must yet add something more substantial, in the improvement of her mind by extensive reading'[4] is both good sense and a compliment to Elizabeth at Miss Bingley's expense; it is also reminiscent of Thomas Gisborne's recommendation that 'every woman' should acquire 'the habit of regularly allotting to improving books a portion of each day'.[5] Anne Elliot's recommendation that Benwick's 'daily study' should include 'such works of our best moralists, such collections of the finest letters, such memoirs of characters of worth and suffering, as occurred to her at the moment as calculated to rouse and fortify the mind by the highest precepts, and the strongest examples of moral and religious endurance'[6] shows similar influences.

Jane Austen shares a standpoint with many of the writers of conduct books, but she is not a writer for whom agreement (or even admiration) precludes mockery. Her favourite novel, Richardson's *Sir Charles Grandison*, was ruthlessly digested into a brief humorous skit for the entertainment of her young niece, and Sir Charles himself appears, both diminished and comically exaggerated, in the person of Charles Adams, in the early *Jack and Alice*. The sentimental novel is satirized in *Love and Freindship* [sic], and the conventions of the epistolary novel exploited to the extent of ridicule in *Lesley Castle*. When Austen was herself dying, she wrote the marvellous mockery of invalids and invalidism that is *Sanditon*. 'I hope I never ridicule what is wise or good. Follies and nonsense, whims and inconsistencies *do* divert me, I own, and I laugh at them whenever I can', says Elizabeth Bennet in *Pride and Prejudice*.[7] Austen's impulse to ridicule, to make jokes (even about inappropriate subjects such as still-born babies) is most evident in the juvenilia and her letters, but was never entirely curbed even in her most mature fiction. Laughter was both a habitual cast of mind for Jane Austen and a powerful artistic impulse, as she recognized herself: 'I could not sit seriously down to write a serious Romance under any other motive than to save my Life, & if it were indispensable for me to keep it up & never relax into laughing at myself or other people, I am sure I should be hung before I had finished the first Chapter'.[8] It is for this reason that conduct literature provides her with useful material for intertextual parody. By exploiting the potential of shared reading, Austen could be assured of shared jokes, jokes at the expense of a genre that combines the wise and good with the foolish and inconsistent.

Austen's Appropriations and Subversions

> I do not rhyme to that dull elf
> Who cannot image to himself.[9]

> I do not write for such dull Elves
> As have not a great deal of Ingenuity themselves.[10]

When Jane Austen misquotes Walter Scott's *Marmion* to Cassandra, it is a paradigmatic act of appropriation. In a letter of 1808, she had asked Cassandra, 'Ought I to be very much pleased with Marmion? – as yet I am not'.[11] Austen's question tells us about the pressures of Scott's reputation on potential readers (she knows that there are those who think she ought to be pleased with *Marmion*) and about her own independence of judgement (she is not). Five years later, Austen cheerfully requisitions the quotation for her own purposes, turning Scott's phrase, intended to rouse the reader into imagining the stirring scenes of Wilton's heroism at the Battle of Flodden, into a discussion of the prosaic question of typography in the first edition of *Pride and Prejudice*: 'There are a few Typical errors – & a "said he" or a "said she" would sometimes make the Dialogue more immediately clear – but "I do not write for such dull Elves / As have not a great deal of Ingenuity themselves"'.[12] Austen thus diminishes the grandeur of Scott's rhetoric by changing its context, while she simultaneously makes an implicit claim for the larger impact of her own writing. Where Scott claims only to address the readers of poetry ('I do not rhyme'), Austen's claim relates to the readers of every kind of writing ('I do not write').[13] Where Scott imagines only a single reader ('that dull elf'), Austen envisages a plurality ('such dull Elves'). Scott's elfin readership is all-male ('himself'); Austen's embraces both sexes ('themselves'). Austen thus light-heartedly claims a larger readership than the most popular writer of the day, and, in the process, changes the terms of what it can mean to be a reader. To read her work, she suggests, readers need 'Ingenuity', not only the ability to 'image'. Reading therefore needs skill as well as imagination. Austen's appropriation of Scott is, of course, a double joke – both a gentle jibe at Scott's inflated rhetoric, and a teasing invitation to an ingenious reader (her sister) to recognize the allusion. Cassandra, Austen assumes, is not one of those 'dull elves' who do not have the 'Ingenuity' to recognize what she is doing with Scott. Like so many jokes, this one has its serious side: reading Austen really does demand 'Ingenuity'.

In her appropriation of Scott, Austen demands that her reader (in this case, Cassandra) should bring her knowledge of Scott, and the connotations of his name, to bear on an individual text, in the process making explicit the 'ingenious' habit of reading she requires. We will now return to her use of conduct literature as a particularly apposite example of how this process works. In a letter to Martha Lloyd, Austen demonstrates just how closely she has read Hester Chapone and Hannah More, jokingly laying out the pattern for their evenings together on her imminent visit:

> I come to you to be talked to, not to read or hear reading. I can do *that* at home; & indeed I am now laying in a stock of intelligence to pour out on you as *my* share of Conversation. – I am reading Henry's History of England, which I will repeat to you in any manner you may prefer, either in a loose, disultary [*sic*], unconnected strain, or dividing my recital as the Historian divides it himself, into seven parts, The Civil & Military – Religion – Constitution – Learning & Learned Men – Arts & Sciences – Commerce Coins & Shipping – & Manners; – so that for every evening of the week there will be a different subject.[14]

Margaret Anne Doody suggests that this may be a parody of 'the Scottish historian's pride in his seven divisions, as elaborated in his "General Preface"'.[15] But it is also the case that, as Austen describes it here, her reading conforms exactly to that recommended by Chapone's *Letters on the Improvement of the Mind* and More's *Strictures on the Modern System of Female Education*, which both recommend the disciplined and regulated study of history as an important portion of a girl's reading. Austen describes herself as not only reading history, but reading it in the manner prescribed by Chapone – not to give herself pleasure, but in order to be able to discuss her reading in the domestic circle, to provide herself with material for intelligent 'Conversation'. Austen offers Martha the choice of a 'loose, disultary, unconnected strain' (this reads like a sly reference to her own joyfully parodic *History of England*, 'by a partial, prejudiced & ignorant historian',[16] a work which Martha might well have read, since she was a dedicatee of one of Austen's other juvenile works, and hence can be assumed to be part of the reading community for the juvenilia) or the authorized division that 'the Historian' himself has made, arranging the history into portions for each evening of the week. Her apparent willingness to divide her narration 'so that for each evening of the week there will be a different subject' is reminiscent of the numerous conduct books that present themselves as series of evening conversations (Priscilla Wakefield's *Mental Improvement* (1794–7) or Carracioli's *Advice From a Lady of Quality* (1779), for example), and suggests that Austen is thinking of such texts as she writes. Austen first ironically presents herself as the sort of reader that Chapone approves, but then ends flippantly, 'with such a provision on my part, if you will do your's by repeating the French Grammar, & Mrs Stent will now & then ejaculate some wonder about the Cocks & Hens, what can we want?'[17] The bathetic introduction of Mrs Stent's 'wonder about the Cocks & Hens' serves as a timely reminder that the entirely improving conversations imagined in the preceding sentences are self-consciously fictitious, and not to be taken seriously. Such joking can only take place among friends for whom an evening evoked in such terms was a cliché familiar from their shared reading, and among whom the intertextual references can be taken for granted.

Pride and Prejudice, destined for a wider readership, contains a similarly intertextual joke at the expense of James Fordyce's *Sermons for Young Women* (1765), a joke that depends for its effect on the idea that we can know a person by their reactions to their reading. Mr Collins, invited to read aloud to the ladies after dinner, readily assents. A book is produced:

> But on beholding it (for everything announced it to be from a circulating library) he started back, and begging pardon, protested that he never read novels. Kitty stared at him, and Lydia exclaimed. – Other books were produced, and after

some deliberation he chose Fordyce's Sermons. Lydia gaped as he opened the volume, and, before he had, with very monotonous solemnity, read three pages, she interrupted him.[18]

Mr Collins, 'much offended', at this interruption, observes: "'I have often observed how little young ladies are interested by books of a serious stamp, though written solely for their benefit. It amazes me, I confess; – for, certainly, there can be nothing so advantageous to them as instruction'".[19] On one level, we need only understand that Mr Collins has chosen a dull and pompous text which represents his own pomposity, while Lydia and Kitty are unused to reading anything but frivolous novels, and so are unable to attend to 'books of a serious stamp'. This would simply be another example of Austen's use of reading to denote character. However, Austen's joke is multi-layered, and deeply embedded in contemporary prejudices and preconceptions about books and reading. Mr Collins' choice of Fordyce's *Sermons* suggests he is familiar with conduct-book directives about what a young woman should and should not read, while his reaction to the sight of a circulating library book is perfectly judged to make him appear as a convention-bound fool, familiar with the reputation of circulating libraries, but not what they were really like.

Recent scholarship, building on Paul Kaufman's classic study of circulating library catalogues, has established without doubt that circulating libraries, far from stocking only vapid and worthless romances, in fact contained a variety of different texts.[20] Although, in most circulating libraries, fiction did constitute the largest part of their collections, from many circulating libraries it would also have been possible to borrow works on agriculture, domestic economy, travel, medicine, history, geography, politics and mathematics, as well as conduct books, sermons, poetry, biographies and children's books, not to mention newspapers and periodicals. Some circulating libraries also stocked sheet music, and, in remoter areas, necessities such as firewood, in addition to trinkets and ornaments like those that tempt Charlotte Heywood in *Sanditon*. Mr Collins assumes, like Hannah More, that a circulating library is a 'hot-bed' of impropriety, whereas actually such institutions provided serious intellectual fodder in addition to their holdings of more frivolous items. In a novel where realizing the unreliability of first impressions is vital to self-knowledge and growth, Mr Collins thus gives the most literal possible demonstration of judging a book by its cover, and demonstrates simultaneously his over-strict adherence to codes of propriety and his refusal to form opinions of his own. Austen's first readers, her own family members, 'great Novel-readers & not ashamed of being so',[21] and habitual borrowers from circulating libraries, would, we must assume, have seen the joke straight away.

Northanger Abbey contains Austen's most explicit defence of the novel, in defiance of public opinion, although a brief early indication of Austen's commitment to the genre appears in *Catharine; or, The Bower*, where novels are described as 'books universally read and admired'.[22] Henry Tilney, too, suggests in *Northanger Abbey* that novels are more 'universally read and admired' than Catherine Morland believes, telling her that young men 'read nearly as many as women', and that 'I, myself, have read hundreds and hundreds'.[23] Austen's defence of the novel in *Northanger Abbey* should be set clearly in its context as a response not only to 'the Reviewers'[24], but also to a particular passage in Mr Collins's favoured Fordyce's *Sermons*. It seems clear from the textual evidence that Austen had Fordyce's *Sermons* either to hand or very clearly in her memory as she wrote the passage in *Northanger Abbey*. Fordyce writes:

> I say nothing now of Novels and Romances, having had occasion to speak of them so largely in a former discourse. But I must not omit to recommend those admirable productions of the present century, which turn principally on the two great hinges of sentiment and character; joining description to precept, and presenting in particular the most animated sketches of modern manners, where the likeness is caught warm from life; while the powers of fancy, wit, and judgment, combine to expose vice and folly, to enforce reformation, and in short but spirited essays to convey the rules of domestic wisdom and daily conduct. I need not here name the Spectator [...] How much are both sexes indebted to their elegant pens, for a species of instruction better fitted perhaps than most others of human device, to delight and improve at the same moment; such is its extent, its diversity, its familiarity, its ease, its playful manner, its immediate reference to scenes and circumstances with which we are every day conversant![25]

Austen answers Fordyce:

> 'And what are you reading, Miss – ?' 'Oh! it is only a novel!' replies the young lady; while she lays down her book with affected indifference, or momentary shame. – 'It is only Cecilia, or Camilla, or Belinda;' or, in short, only some work in which the greatest powers of the mind are displayed, in which the most thorough knowledge of human nature, the happiest delineation of its varieties, the liveliest effusions of wit and humour are conveyed to the world in the best chosen language. Now, had the same young lady been engaged with a volume of the Spectator, instead of such a work, how proudly would she have produced the book, and told its name; though the chances must be against her being occupied by any part of that voluminous publication, of which either the matter or manner would not disgust a young person of taste; the substance of its papers so often consisting in the statement of improbable circumstances, unnatural characters,

and topics of conversation, which no longer concern any one living; and their language, too, frequently so coarse as to give no very favourable idea of the age that could endure it.[26]

Austen rejects Fordyce's too-easy dismissal of the novel by appropriating his approval of the characteristics of the periodical essay for the novel itself: 'animated sketches of modern manners' in Fordyce becomes 'thorough knowledge of human nature' in Austen; 'the powers of fancy, wit, and judgment' becomes 'the greatest powers of the mind' and 'the liveliest effusions of wit and humour'. She then turns to Fordyce's complimentary remarks about the *Spectator*, retorting that, rather than representing 'scenes and circumstances with which we are every day conversant', actually 'the substance of its papers so often consist[s] in the statement of improbable circumstances, unnatural characters, and topics of conversation, which no longer concern any one living'. Rather than 'elegant pens', the *Spectator*'s writers use 'coarse' language, and it cannot 'delight and improve' because 'either the matter or manner will disgust a young person of taste.' The young person's taste has already been formed to disapprove of the *Spectator*, Austen implies, so the *Spectator* can have no part to play in either delight or instruction. Both Austen and Fordyce are implicitly referring to the Horatian principle that works of literature should both delight and instruct, a principle that underpinned much eighteenth-century writing about fiction, and was espoused by the editors of the *Spectator* themselves, Addison and Steele. In Austen's reconfiguration of Fordyce, the very nature of the *Spectator* is under threat; if it is no longer either *dulce* (sweet) or *utile* (useful), it can have no purpose.[27] When we look at *Northanger Abbey*'s defence of the novel in this context, it becomes evident that Austen is redefining the novel in relation to the periodical essay as a more realistic as well as a more instructive representation of 'modern manners'. Austen's engagement with Fordyce makes clear her position in her period's debates about suitable reading for young women: they are better off reading novels than the books recommended to them by an outdated morality. It is no coincidence that Austen returns to Fordyce in *Pride and Prejudice*'s multi-layered joke outlined above; her real and serious objections to his treatment of the novel find comic resolution in her decision to expose his views through the idiotic Mr Collins.

Northanger Abbey also contains Austen's most sustained exploration of the trope of the young woman led astray by her reading. As conduct books would predict, Catherine Morland does confuse her reading with reality, interpreting real life through the lens of the Gothic novel. But *Northanger Abbey*, the most parodic of Austen's finished novels, proclaims both its debt and its resistance to conduct literature from the moment Catherine, at the age of fifteen, rejects 'books of information' for those which 'were all story and no reflection'.[28]

A heroine who prefers Gothic novels to 'real, solemn history'[29] should (like one who is excessively sentimental), in conduct-book terms, end in ruin. Austen does not, however, allow this to be the case, for Catherine's fate is no worse than an ignominious return home as 'a heroine in a hack post-chaise'.[30] Austen also insists that Catherine's judgement has not been ruined by her reading. Although she is bitterly humbled by Henry's discovery of her suspicions about his father, and recognizes her mistakes as an 'infatuation', which 'might be traced to the influence of that sort of reading which she had there indulged',[31] Catherine also, 'upon serious consideration', still believes General Tilney 'to be not perfectly amiable'.[32] His behaviour in turning her out of the house is, as Eleanor Tilney recognizes, 'intolerable', and insulting, 'of the greatest consequence to comfort, appearance, propriety, to your family, to the world'.[33] Catherine's ability to read General Tilney's character is perfectly sound; she just mistranslates it into a particular idiom – the Radcliffean Gothic – in which neither she nor the General belongs. Catherine's reading, then, leads her into errors about situation, but does not seriously affect her judgement or understanding of character.

In *Sanditon*, Austen further subverts the trope that women will be led astray by their reading of novels by re-gendering it. She portrays, in Charlotte Heywood, a young lady who is 'sufficiently well-read in novels to supply her imagination with amusement, but not at all unreasonably influenced by them',[34] and sets her beside Sir Edward Denham, who, in contrast, 'derive[s] only false principles from lessons of morality, and incentives to vice from the history of it's [*sic*] overthrow'.[35] Charlotte, unlike Sir Edward, learns valuable lessons from her reading of novels. Picking up a volume of Burney's *Camilla* reminds her of Camilla's disastrous ventures into debt: 'She took up a book; it happened to be a volume of *Camilla*. She had not *Camilla*'s youth, and had no intention of having her distress – so, she turned from the drawers of rings and broches [*sic*], repressed farther solicitation and paid for what she bought'.[36] She is able to separate fiction from reality, enjoying 'fancying the persecutions which *ought* to be the lot of the interesting Clara, especially in the form of the most barbarous conduct on Lady Denham's side', but finding 'no reluctance to admit from subsequent observation, that they appeared to be on very comfortable terms'.[37] Sir Edward, on the other hand, 'had read more sentimental novels than agreed with him'.[38] Just like the foolish women described by the Edgeworths, 'who have been much addicted to common novel-reading', and who are thus 'always acting in imitation of some Jemima, or Almeria, who never existed',[39] Sir Edward identifies with Richardson's Lovelace, feeling 'that he was formed to be a dangerous man – quite in the line of the Lovelaces'.[40] The reading of 'such authors as have since appeared to tread in Richardson's steps, so far as man's determined pursuit of woman in defiance of every opposition of feeling and convenience is concerned', had 'occupied the greater part of his literary hours, and formed his character', with the result that 'Sir Edward's great object in life was to be seductive'.[41]

Sir Edward, in fact, is a model of many of the deficiencies more usually ascribed to the female reader. Not only does he have a propensity to identify with literary characters, he also scatters his quotations about with no real understanding of their context or meaning. This is a fault that Hannah More attributes particularly to women: 'it is not difficult to trace back to their shallow sources the hackney'd quotations of certain *accomplished* young ladies, who will be frequently found not to have come legitimately by any thing they know'.[42] In order to make an unfounded claim to taste and intelligence, Sir Edward, like Mr Collins, or one of the 'reviewers' satirized in *Northanger Abbey*, spouts clichés about 'the mere trash of the common circulating library', and claims to be 'no indiscriminate novel-reader'. Sir Edward's dislike of novels made up of 'vapid tissues of ordinary occurrences'[43] is possibly a tongue-in-cheek reference to Austen's own novels, or, perhaps, to her favourite *Sir Charles Grandison*, and his rejection of such works as failing to inspire 'useful deductions' suggests his own inability to 'deduce' correctly. Austen thus encourages her readers to see, in defiance of conventional wisdom, that a 'sober-minded' young lady may be a better reader than a 'downright silly' man with neither a 'clear brain' nor a 'strong head'.[44] Anne Elliot's recommendation of 'a larger allowance of prose' to Captain Benwick in *Persuasion* is a similar moment; Anne 'feel[s] in herself the right of seniority of mind' and so reverses the hierarchy of instruction in which Benwick would have, by virtue of his sex, the right to educate her.[45]

In *Catharine; or, The Bower*, Austen light-heartedly mocks conduct literature's self-importance, directly parodying More's *Strictures on Female Education* in the person of Mrs Percival, the heroine's affectionate, but ridiculous and old-fashioned aunt, who significantly gives her niece Hannah More's *Cœlebs in Search of a Wife* to read.[46] In the *Strictures*, More argues that the future of the nation depends on the behaviour of its individual women:

> What an accession would it bring to the public strength, could we prevail on beauty, and rank, and talents, and virtue, confederating their several powers, to come forward with a patriotism at once firm and feminine for the general good [...] I am persuaded, if many a one, who is now disseminating unintended mischief, under the dangerous notion that there is no harm in any thing short of positive vice [...] could be brought to see in its collected force the annual aggregate of the random evil she is daily doing, [...] she would start from her self complacent dream.[47]

More's rhetoric, with its martial vocabulary, is a call for action. Her desire for 'a patriotism at once firm and feminine' represents a real belief that the women of England have a part to play in reconstructing the manners and morals of the people of England. Austen turns this martial rhetoric into the weak justification of a fussy and old-fashioned woman: when Kitty displeases her aunt by sitting alone in her bower with a young man, Mrs Percival is convinced 'that every thing is going to sixes and sevens and all order will soon be at an end throughout the kingdom'. Her reasoning is, like More's, that 'the welfare of every nation depends upon the virtue of it's [*sic*] individuals, and any one who offends in so gross a manner against decorum and propriety is certainly hastening it's [*sic*] ruin'.[48] Hannah More's argument is similar, in that the behaviour of individuals *does* matter, but Mrs Percival has transformed More's argument that women can cause social change into one that forces them to resist it. Catharine, on the other hand, opposes such an interpretation of her behaviour, saying teasingly to her aunt, 'upon my honour I have done nothing this evening that can contribute to overthrow the establishment of the kingdom'.[49] Mrs Percival responds that she has been giving 'a bad example to the world, and the world is but too well disposed to receive such', but Catharine exposes her aunt's lack of logic, replying, 'I *can* have given an example only to *you*, for you alone have seen the offence'.[50] Mrs Percival loses the battle of logic, and Kitty has the last word in the argument, as Mrs Percival's concern for her niece's moral well-being immediately gives way to exaggerated concern for her own health, which trivializes and undermines her opinions of young women and the state of the nation. Austen's representation of Mrs Percival's misreading of Hannah More neatly exposes both the self-important tone of More's text, and the foolishness of those who misread it. In order to do this, Austen depends on her readers' recognition of these echoes of More's rhetoric, the verbal clues that let her readers share the joke.

The question of misreading conduct books recurs in the priggishly tedious character of *Pride and Prejudice*'s Mary Bennet. In *An Enquiry into the Duties of the Female Sex*, Gisborne writes:

> To every woman, whether single or married, the habit of regularly allotting to improving books a portion of each day [...] cannot be too strongly recommended. I use the term *improving* in a large sense; as comprehending whatever writings may contribute to her virtue, her usefulness, and her innocent satisfaction, to her happiness in this world and the next.[51]

There is little to cavil at here, and in fact Austen does not disagree with Gisborne – in *Mansfield Park*, Edmund Bertram swiftly recognizes that Fanny's abilities will be best served by her 'fondness for reading, which, properly directed, must be an education in itself'[52] – but the danger of relying on 'improving books' at the expense of using one's own intellectual faculties is demonstrated by Mary Bennet, whose determined culling of extracts and 'observations of thread-bare morality' makes her neither lovable nor intelligent.[53] When Lydia elopes, Mary's attempt to console her sisters with a paraphrase of Mr Villars' advice to Evelina in Fanny Burney's eponymous novel fails completely, because her reading has destroyed her ability to sympathise with her sisters' emotions, or to understand the reality of Lydia's plight.[54] To Mary, Lydia is merely another example, no longer a sister, but, as she puts it, a 'useful lesson'.[55] It is no wonder that Elizabeth lifts up her eyes in amazement at Mary's words. Readerly identification of Mary's ineptitude is deepened by the recognition that the ideas she spouts as consolation are not her own. Like Mr Collins, her feelings are inauthentic and dictated by convention rather than sympathy. Austen assumes a readership sophisticated and experienced enough to appreciate this.

'Books of a Serious Stamp': Austen Questions the 'Domestic Ideology'

The most serious aspect of Austen's negotiations with conduct literature is her rejection of the easy answers to moral and social dilemmas provided by such books. Nancy Armstrong suggests that the conduct book had provided a 'grammar of female subjectivity', which 'awaited the substance that the novel and its readers, as well as the countless individuals educated according to the model of the new woman, would eventually provide'.[56] The novel, she suggests, was to become the means by which the maxims of conduct literature were to be fleshed out. In the process, as we shall see, those maxims were challenged and proved wanting. There are a number of places in Austen's works where she demonstrates how impossible it is to live one's life by conduct-book aphorisms. These include the complications inherent in Elinor Dashwood's promise of silence to Lucy Steele, the painful insight into Fanny Price's mind as she struggles to behave as she believes she should, Emma Woodhouse's inability to stick to the excellent reading lists she draws up, and Anne Elliot's constant struggle against her tendency to depression, to take only a small number of examples. Conduct literature's internal contradictions and attendant frustrations are dramatized in Austen's novels, where the realities of a situation do not allow straightforward responses.

When the demands of characterization mean the exposure of the hollowness of some area of conservative morality, Austen ruthlessly exposes it, as we will see in her treatment of Fanny Price. If subverting a convention provides a more believable plot, Austen insists on doing it. She even points out that she has done so, as when the narrative voice speaks directly to the reader in *Northanger Abbey*:

> I must confess that his affection originated in nothing better than gratitude, or, in other words, that a persuasion of her partiality for him had been the only cause of giving her a serious thought. It is a new circumstance in romance, I acknowledge, and dreadfully derogatory of an heroine's dignity; but if it be as new in common life, the credit of a wild imagination will at least be all my own.[57]

The convention that a woman should not show her love for a man until he has declared himself is a commonplace in both conduct books and eighteenth-century novels (and this is the second joking mention of it in *Northanger Abbey*). Austen's readers are clearly invited to recognize the gap between 'romance' and 'common life', and to laugh with Austen's narrator at the idea that one would need a 'wild imagination' to accept that a man could fall in love with a woman simply because she is in love with him. In the process of laughing at the convention, we are encouraged to believe that Austen's version of the process of falling in love is truer than that depicted elsewhere. This brief moment in *Northanger Abbey* also includes a characteristically Austenian subversion of Richardson. In *Sir Charles Grandison*, it is perfectly acceptable for Harriet Byron's love for Sir Charles to 'originate in nothing better than gratitude' – indeed, Harriet makes it her justification for falling in love with him before he has declared himself. In *Northanger Abbey*, Austen ironically ('I must confess') re-genders the 'gratitude' masculine, attributing it to Henry Tilney. In so doing, she exposes the social and literary conventions that see gratitude as a respectable motivation for love in a woman, but cannot conceive of it ('it is a new circumstance in romance') as the motivation for a man.

In *Persuasion*, Austen explicitly separates conventional 'morality' from 'truth', writing:

> Who can be in doubt of what followed? When any two young people take it into their heads to marry, they are pretty sure by perseverance to carry their point, be they ever so poor, or ever so imprudent, or ever so little likely to be necessary to each other's ultimate comfort. This may be bad morality to conclude with, but I believe it to be truth.[58]

Austen's narrator's loyalty, this passage suggests, is to truth, rather than to morality, and again, the common sense argument employed by the narrator encourages Austen's readers to trust her version as truth. Exposing the conventions of others, fictional or otherwise, allows the narrator to enlist the reader in a confederacy of 'hard readers': those who see what others cannot.

When Catherine Morland returns home, heartsick and mortified, from her trip to Northanger Abbey, her mother's remedy for Catherine's unhappiness is to suggest to her 'a very clever Essay in one of the books upstairs [...] about young girls that have been spoilt for home by great acquaintance', a cure entirely (and absurdly) in keeping with the spirit of the conduct literature from which Mrs Morland takes her loosely applied system for her ten children's education.[59] For Mrs Morland, faced with Catherine's 'silence and sadness'[60] – a problem she does not understand – the obvious solution is to turn to a greater authority than her own: that of 'improving books'.[61] In so doing, she obeys the dictates of conduct literature, which invariably recommends both submission to authority and respect for 'those books from which you can learn true wisdom'.[62] Catherine's mother thus acts with propriety. Mrs Morland's conduct-book cure would, of course, have as little effect on Catherine's lassitude as the remembrance of her great-aunt's lecture on dress has on her vanity earlier in the novel;[63] fortunately it is never put to the test as Henry Tilney appears at Fullerton and banishes Catherine's sadness for good. In *Northanger Abbey*'s final subverted 'moral', which 'leave[s] it to be settled by whomsoever it may concern, whether the tendency of this work be altogether to recommend parental tyranny or reward filial disobedience',[64] Austen undercuts the seriousness with which conduct literature recommends filial obedience as a religious duty. She also alludes again to Richardson, who brought the doctrine of filial obedience into the public eye in *Clarissa* (1747–48).

In *Mansfield Park*, however, Austen creates a novel in which questions of 'parental tyranny' and 'filial disobedience' cannot be dismissed so lightly. Fanny Price is, in many ways, a perfect conduct-book heroine, whose principles and manners cannot be faulted. She is gentle, modest, innocent, helpful and unaffected; she reads 'the best books' and learns from them; she is never forward or witty; she is prudent and does not allow others to read her feelings. The thought of filial (or near-filial) disobedience revolts her – with Edmund, she censures Mary Crawford for making a flippant remark about her uncle, the Admiral, as 'very wrong', and 'very indecorous', and her own contribution to the conversation is to describe her as 'very ungrateful'[65] – and she sheds tears when her own uncle leaves for Bermuda because she cannot love him as much as she believes to be right. Yet Fanny is very rarely happy, a fact that immediately demonstrates the fallacy of Gisborne's claim that 'those principles of conduct [...] will lead probably to a considerable share of happiness in the present life'.[66] Indeed, Austen's depiction of Fanny Price's agonies of mind is one of the novel's great strengths, as the narrative explores the mind of a young girl desperate to do what is right but imposed on by a flawed authority. This flawed authority is not only the older generation in *Mansfield Park*, represented most strongly in Fanny's mind by Mrs Norris, and later by Sir Thomas Bertram, but a social order in which modesty, gentleness, self-denial and respect for authority could still be forced on young women as moral duties.

From the first paragraph of the novel, in which the details of the history of the three Ward sisters are given, and Miss Maria Ward is described as 'three thousand pounds short of any equitable claim' to her marriage, Austen lays out the part played by social expectations in the lives of young women.[67] In *Mansfield Park*, matrimony really is the 'manoeuvring business' that Mary Crawford thinks it.[68] Maria Bertram's confused thinking about marriage, in which she cannot distinguish between 'duty' and desire, 'moral obligation' and financial gain,[69] is the result of the different pressures under which she has grown up – Mrs Norris' continual flattery and hints, the expectations of the neighbourhood, 'who had, for many weeks past, felt the expediency of Mr. Rushworth's marrying Miss Bertram', her father's anxious desire that she should be good, and the necessity of repressing her real feelings when he is nearby.[70] Brought up in a society where marriage is a matter of expediency, and where expediency triumphs over love, Maria's eventual elopement and ruin are hardly surprising.

Though the results of psychological pressure and repression can be seen in the career of Maria Bertram, the most sustained critique of such pressures in *Mansfield Park* is Austen's treatment of Fanny's painful resistance to her relatives' advice that she should marry Henry Crawford. The dilemma facing Fanny is a familiar one: the predicament of the heroine advised by her family to marry against her inclination, and torn between her sense of duty and her own wishes, is explored most famously in Richardson's *Clarissa*, but Fanny's position as a dependent in her uncle's house, who has, since the moment of her arrival, been impressed with the imperative that she should feel 'an extraordinary degree of gratitude', is one that renders the struggle particularly acute.[71] At the ball at Mansfield Park, Sir Thomas' power over his niece is made explicit – his counsel that she should go to bed is 'the advice of absolute power' – while his desire that she should open the ball with Mr Crawford does not allow her 'to hazard another word'.[72] Fanny can hardly bear to tell her uncle her opinion, let alone contradict his. She feels that 'urging her opinion against Sir Thomas's, was a proof of the extremity of the case'.[73] In addition, Fanny suffers from a lack of confidence in her own judgement allied to a strong desire to please others. Austen's exploration of Fanny's resistance to coercion is an important criticism of the doctrine of unwavering obedience to authority, and her depiction of Sir Thomas's attempts to manipulate his niece is, as Claudia Johnson suggests, a powerful analysis of the problems that arise when that authority is flawed.[74]

When Sir Thomas and Fanny first discuss Henry Crawford's proposal, it is in the old schoolroom, where 'the terror of his former occasional visits to that room seemed all renewed'.⁷⁵ Fanny's habitual awe of her uncle leaves her at a disadvantage when he tells her of his conversation with Crawford, and his casual assumption that his discourse must be giving her pleasure leaves her little opportunity for speech. Fanny has to break through all her habits of respect for her uncle's opinions and her gratitude for his kindness (his concern about the fire at the beginning of the chapter is beautifully placed to remind the reader of Fanny's strong sense of obligation and her past of neglect and hardship) before she can even speak. She is 'forced by the anxiety of the moment even to tell her uncle that he was wrong'– the 'even' a marker of just how daring a move this seems to Fanny – but her uncle does not listen properly.⁷⁶

Instead, he uses a number of arguments to bring her to a state of mind which is 'all disorder', and to make her believe 'she was miserable for ever'.⁷⁷ Sir Thomas' rising anger is reflected not only in the rising scale of offences of which he accuses Fanny, but also in the tone of his voice, from 'calm displeasure', to 'a voice of authority', to 'a good deal of cold sternness', until he relents somewhat, and speaks 'in a tone of becoming gravity, but of less anger'.⁷⁸ Sir Thomas is, in fact, no mean orator. He tells Fanny 'there is nothing more to be said', putting her off her guard, and then says a great deal more, hoping to catch her out and trick her into betraying a prior attachment.⁷⁹ He uses a number of rhetorical tricks to subdue his niece, including meaningful pauses, repetition and Ciceronian triads, and manipulates her feelings by accusations 'so heavy, so multiplied, so rising in dreadful gradation!'⁸⁰ In his diatribe against Fanny's 'ingratitude', Sir Thomas's accusations are particularly effective, because they strike at the heart of Fanny's image of herself.⁸¹ His notions of goodness, like hers, are those of Gisborne, Chapone and More, and his accusations are couched in terms his niece understands only too well. He tells Fanny:

> I had thought you peculiarly free from wilfulness of temper, self-conceit, and every tendency to that independence of spirit, which prevails so much in modern days, even in young women, and which in young women is offensive and disgusting beyond all common offence.⁸²

Her offence is not so much in refusing Crawford, as in revealing that she has a mind of her own. Sir Thomas complains: 'You can be wilful and perverse, [...] you can and will decide for yourself, without any consideration or deference for those who have surely some right to guide you – without even asking their advice'.⁸³ He considers her, as Fanny recognizes, 'self-willed, obstinate, selfish and ungrateful',⁸⁴ and such a description of her character negates everything that Fanny has striven for all her life. It is no wonder 'her heart was almost broke by such a picture of what she appeared to him',[85] for to Fanny, her refusal of Crawford is not the result of 'independence of spirit', but of her inability to give her heart to him and a deeply felt aversion to his principles, as revealed to Fanny by his simultaneous flirtations with Maria and Julia. It is particularly poignant that she cannot mention the latter objection to her uncle – an objection that would at least give Sir Thomas food for thought – because it would reflect badly on her cousins.

Fanny's hope 'that to a man like her uncle, so discerning, so honourable, so good, the simple acknowledgment of settled *dislike* on her side, would have been sufficient' is, although it proves in the event to be misplaced, not unreasonable; what she has failed to realize, however, is that her uncle, though honourable and good, is not discerning.[86] Unlike her, he sees Henry Crawford not as an unprincipled philanderer but as 'a young man of sense, of character, of temper, of manners and of fortune'.[87] Fanny is more intelligent and more discriminating than her uncle, a situation that the writers of conduct books do not envisage, and the result is that Fanny is accused of vices that she does not have. Like Elizabeth Bennet (more intelligent and less vulgar than her mother), Emma Woodhouse (cleverer than her father) or Elinor Dashwood (more prudent and clear-sighted than her parent), Fanny is forced into the position of owing respect, duty and obedience to someone whose understanding is inferior to her own. Such a situation leads Fanny inevitably into unhappiness and confusion.

From the time Fanny makes her feelings clear to her uncle, he adopts a different strategy: still bent on marrying her to Crawford, he recognizes that on one of Fanny's temper and disposition, 'kindness might be the best way of working'.[88] He heartily commends Henry Crawford's actions as well as his choice, and in an astonishing piece of self-deception, reproaches his niece: 'You cannot suppose me capable of trying to persuade you to marry against your inclinations'.[89] Sir Thomas may truly believe, as he tells Fanny, that 'your happiness and advantage are all that I have in view',[90] but this does not stop him from trying by covert means to persuade her to accept Crawford, as when he meditates his 'medicinal project upon his niece's understanding' to 'teach her the value of a good income' by sending her home to Portsmouth.[91]

Lady Bertram, too, plays her part on working on Fanny's sense of duty, raising herself from her usual state of near-catatonic indolence to offer 'almost the only rule of conduct, the only piece of advice, which Fanny had ever received from her aunt in the course of eight years and a half', which is 'that it is every young woman's duty to accept such a very unexceptionable offer as this'.[92] Even Edmund, for all his kindness and sympathy for Fanny, forwards Crawford's attempts to win her by drawing him out on subjects he knows will appeal to Fanny, and by leaving them *tête-a-tête* while he buries himself in the paper.[93] He even tries to persuade her that she *ought* to love Crawford, telling her, in syntactical constructions designed to do away with *her* thoughts and feelings: 'I cannot suppose that you have not the *wish* to love him – the natural wish of gratitude. You must have some feeling of that sort'.[94] Edmund will not listen to Fanny's anxieties and reservations, 'scarcely hearing her to the end', and sweeping them all away under the strength of his own certainties.[95] Fanny is not convinced by her cousin, recognizing that his desire to vindicate Crawford comes not from a hope for her happiness, but from the wish to promote his own. Fanny's understanding cannot be imposed on, but her sense of duty and gratitude can. Edmund has more than the power of a kind friend; he has 'the kind authority of a privileged guardian', and it takes all Fanny's resolve (and her secret love for him) to resist the arguments he puts to her.[96]

The fact that Fanny's friends and relations consider her potential match with Henry Crawford a great stroke of luck for her, and believe themselves to be working to promote her happiness, does not obscure the fact that they are trying to persuade Fanny to do what she knows would be wrong, and that the struggle Fanny feels is the conflict between her long-ingrained habits of obedience and duty and her desire to do right. The struggle is so difficult because she has been brought up to believe that they are one and the same thing; that duty to her uncle and aunt will inevitably lead her to behave in the same way as that directed by her principles and understanding. When she finds that this is not the case, Fanny suffers greatly from uncertainty. Life, she finds, is more complicated than it appears in improving books, and duty is not always self-evident.

A simple interpretation of *Mansfield Park* would see Fanny Price as a perfect conduct-book heroine, whose struggle to be good is naturally and conventionally rewarded eventually by marriage to the man she loves. *Mansfield Park*, however, is not so undemanding a novel. Austen intimates that such an ending is not entirely 'natural' by insisting on an alternative possibility:

> Would he [Henry Crawford] have deserved more, there can be no doubt that more would have been obtained; especially when that marriage had taken place, which would have given him the assistance of her conscience in subduing her first inclination, and brought them very often together. Would he have persevered, and uprightly, Fanny must have been his reward – and a reward very voluntarily bestowed – within a reasonable period from Edmund's marrying Mary.[97]

Fanny's sense of duty not only could, but 'must', Austen shows us, have led her into marriage with a man whose principles she had good reason to mistrust. The certainty ('there can be no doubt') with which Austen puts this alternative demonstrates the real danger that Crawford poses to Fanny. In the end, of course, she marries Edmund, not Henry Crawford, and her duty and inclinations are fortunately combined since Sir Thomas (conveniently) has wearied of 'ambitious and mercenary connections', and has begun to prize 'more and more the sterling good of principle and temper', and so is able to give his 'joyful consent' to Fanny's marriage to Edmund.[98] The path down which Fanny could have been led by her sense of duty and obligation is, however, firmly marked out, and it suggests Austen's resistance to the belief that virtue is always rewarded.

'Let other pens dwell on guilt and misery. I quit such odious subjects as soon as I can, impatient to restore every body, not greatly in fault themselves, to tolerable comfort, and to have done with all the rest'.[99] So begins the last chapter of *Mansfield Park*, which speedily assigns to the characters of the novel their various fates, and, in passing, undercuts the didactic convention that the good should be rewarded and the bad should be punished. For three volumes, Jane Austen's pen has dwelt on both guilt and misery in her depiction of the fine shades of Fanny's mind. Fanny frequently feels guilty that she does not live up to her own internal standard of conduct, and *Mansfield Park* is both an exploration of the misery and constraint that such a standard of conduct entails, and a clear-sighted look at the pressures created by social expectations. Some of Austen's first readers may have seen *Mansfield Park* as a straightforwardly conservative moral tale, but in fact much of the novel's power lies in the way it undermines and questions the very 'truths' that conduct books so confidently assert.

Henry James patronisingly suggests that it could be 'argued against' Jane Austen 'that where her testimony complacently ends the pressure of appetite within us presumes exactly to begin'.[100] We need not 'argue against' Austen to believe that the pressure of appetite does result (at least partly) from a complacent ending in *Mansfield Park*. It is also possible to believe that the reader's appetite is deliberately, not unconsciously, stimulated by the narrative voice. When Austen's narrator insists on the 'natural' transfer of Edmund's love from Mary Crawford to Fanny at the end of *Mansfield Park*, it raises far more questions than it answers:

> I purposely abstain from dates on this occasion, that every one may be at liberty to fix their own, aware that the cure of unconquerable passions, and the transfer of unchanging attachments, must vary much as to time in different people –. I only entreat everybody to believe that exactly at the time when it was quite natural that it should be so, and not a week earlier, Edmund did cease to care about Miss Crawford, and became as anxious to marry Fanny, as Fanny herself could desire.[101]

The narrator goes on in the next paragraph: 'With such a regard for her, indeed, as his had long been, a regard founded on the most endearing claims of innocence and helplessness, and completed by every recommendation of growing worth, what could be more natural than the change?' The offer to the reader of free choice in deciding the duration of the process deliberately obscures the fact that we are being asked to make a far greater leap of faith in believing that Edmund could change his affections at all. The over-insistence on the 'natural', and particularly the question 'what could be more natural?' point to alternative possibilities: Edmund might have remained in love with Mary Crawford, or the 'endearing claims of innocence, helplessness and growing worth' might have held no charms for him. We question, in other words, how 'natural' the change really is. The tensions and ironies that cluster around the word 'natural' in this novel are extremely revealing.

As when Austen emphasizes the alternative ending to *Mansfield Park* – the Fanny–Henry and Edmund–Mary marriages – the reader is here simultaneously complicit with the 'rightness' of the outcome as drawn by Austen, and made aware of the chasm between fiction and reality. *Mansfield Park*'s subverted ending thus deliberately emphasizes the difference between what is 'natural' and what only claims to be so. The narrative voice hence asks the reader to question the assumption underlying a marriage plot – that the heroine and hero will marry – just as, earlier, the narrator dismisses the assumption that virtue is rewarded and vice punished. The narrative voice thus problematizes both the generic and the moral conventions that dictate the ending of *Mansfield Park*. The 'complacency' that James attributes to Austen is in fact purposely and consciously undercut. And many of Austen's readers throughout the two hundred years since the book's publication have recognized the problematic nature of Austen's 'natural' ending, suggesting that, in fact, the alternative ending was either more probable or more satisfying. Many of the early opinions of *Mansfield Park* collected by Jane Austen deal with the ending's controversial nature, and suggest that it promoted lively debate in Austen family circles. The frequent occurrence of the word 'natural' in this collection of opinions is particularly worthy of note. While Mrs James Austen 'thought Henry Crawford's going off with Mrs Rushworth, very natural', both her son Edward Austen and her nephew Edward Knight thought the opposite. Edward Austen 'objected to Mrs. Rushworth's Elopement as unnatural', and 'Henry C.'s going off with Mrs. R – at such a time, when so much in love with Fanny, [was] thought unnatural by Edward [Knight]'. Other members of Austen's family similarly found the ending not to be 'natural' at all. Austen's niece, Fanny Knight, for example, was 'not satisfied with the end – wanting more Love between her & Edmund – & could not think it natural that Edm^d. sh^d .be so much attached to a woman without Principle like Mary C. – or promote Fanny's marrying Henry'. Miss Clewes, the governess to Austen's Knight nieces and nephews, agreed with Fanny, while both Austen's brother Henry and her acquaintance John Pemberton Plumptre could not decide which man would marry Fanny: 'I had not an idea till the end which of the two w^d .would marry Fanny, H. C. or Edm^{d}'.[102] In 1958, Donald Windham would have similarly preferred the alternative ending, though E. M. Forster was horrified to discover this:

> How *could* you have thought – even with Sandy's persuasive reading – that she was going to let Fanny marry Henry Crawford? Your main argument seems to be that if Edmund and Fanny invite you to Mansfield Park you will not want to go. As if they would ever invite you! Edmund – now a clergyman – will have other and flatter fish to fry.[103]

Such reactions (as well as the persistent critical belief that *Mansfield Park* is somehow a 'problem novel')[104] suggest that readers did (and do) respond to the subversive energies of *Mansfield Park*, finding the novel's ending both troubling and uncomfortable. What could be more natural?

Jane Austen, as we have seen, was familiar with the debates over women's reading that took place in the pages of the conduct books of the eighteenth and early nineteenth centuries, and her own novels contain both vignettes in which these debates are briefly enacted, and more prolonged studies of their effects. There is much of the 'wise and good' in conduct books, and Austen recognizes it. However, she parodies conduct literature's inflated rhetoric and scare-mongering about women's reading, exposing the falsity of the trope of the young woman led astray by her reading in Catherine Morland, and then re-gendering it in Sir Edward Denham. She mocks those who take such rhetoric too seriously in Mr Collins and Mary Bennet, and turns denunciations of novels and romances into a defence of the novel in *Northanger Abbey*. She delights in intertextual joking at the expense of different conduct books, and enlists the reader as complicit in her exposure of conventions. Austen also takes seriously the effects of the pressures imposed on women by their reading, creating a sustained critique of the 'domestic ideology' in *Mansfield Park* by her representation of the agonies of Fanny Price's mind and the narratological device of the gap between the demands of the structure of the plot and the comments of the narrative voice. Austen's novels demand from a reader what Coleridge called 'hard reading', and Austen herself characterized as 'Ingenuity'. The following chapter discusses the relationship of Austen's prose style to the questions of gender, reading and ideology explored in this chapter.

Chapter 3

JANE AUSTEN'S GAMES OF INGENUITY

In *The Proper Lady and the Woman Writer*, Mary Poovey argues that Jane Austen 'assumed that a novel could simultaneously gratify the cravings of the imagination and provide moral instruction', and that 'she thus manages to satisfy both the individual reader's desire for emotional gratification and the program of education prescribed by traditional moral aestheticians'.[1] Chapter 1 outlines the 'program of education prescribed by traditional moral aestheticians', with particular reference to its directives about female reading and their relationship to the status of the novel. Poovey's central assumption that Austen's novels find a way to combine pleasure and instruction is certainly correct (although I do not believe they do so entirely to the service of the 'domestic ideology', as Poovey suggests), as is her belief that 'at their most sophisticated, Austen's rhetorical strategies harness the imaginative energy of her readers to a moral design'.[2] However, in the light of the material considered in Chapters 1 and 2, Poovey's suggestion that Austen could 'assume' that a novel could provide moral instruction is surprising, particularly when set in the context of the reputation of the female-authored novel in Austen's period.

The evidence suggests that Austen's society 'assumed' rather the opposite from the position outlined by Poovey: that whatever potential for good the novel might have, in practice it was more likely to cause harm. Hannah More claims in the *Strictures* that, rather than being written to provide moral instruction, 'such is the frightful facility of this species of composition that every raw girl while she reads, is tempted to fancy that she can also write [...] Capacity and cultivation are so little taken into the account, that writing a book seems to be now considered as the only sure resource which the idle and illiterate have always in their power'.[3] Conversely, of course, we have also seen Jane West's 1806 defence of Richardson on the grounds that his works transfuse piety into the minds of his readers. However, even by 1816, when Austen had already published four novels, the anonymous reviewer of the *Gentleman's Magazine* did not take the genre seriously, writing only that 'a good Novel is now and then an agreeable relaxation from severer studies'.[4] Richard Whately, in his influential review of *Northanger Abbey* and *Persuasion* in the

Quarterly Review of 1821, writes, 'the times seem to be past when an apology was requisite from reviewers for condescending to notice a novel' and that 'the delights of fiction, if not more keenly or more generally relished, are at least more readily acknowledged by men of sense and taste'.[5] In fact, though, the status of the novel as a genre remained under consideration until at least the end of the nineteenth century.

When Austen published her first novel in 1811, she, like her contemporaries, understood that the very act of writing and publishing a novel signalled the author's willingness to engage in a long-running debate about the value and validity of the genre. Frances Burney writes in the Preface to *Evelina*: 'In the republic of letters, there is no member of such inferior rank, or who is so much disdained by his brethren of the quill, as the humble Novelist: nor is his fate less hard in the world at large, since, among the whole class of writers, perhaps not one can be named of which the votaries are more numerous but less respectable'.[6] Edgeworth presented *Belinda* as 'a Moral Tale – the author not wishing to acknowledge a Novel' because 'so much folly, errour [*sic*], and vice are disseminated in books classed under this denomination, that it is hoped the wish to assume another title will be attributed to feelings that are laudable, and not fastidious'.[7]

The narrator of *Northanger Abbey* attempts to rehabilitate the reputation of the female-authored novel, commending *Cecilia*, *Camilla* and *Belinda*, and calling for team spirit: 'Let us not desert one another; we are an injured body', even as she rebukes the writers of novels who disown their own creations.[8] Austen clearly recognizes the body of opinion against the novel: 'no species of composition has been so much decried. From pride, ignorance, or fashion, our foes are almost as many as our readers', but insists that 'our productions have afforded more extensive and unaffected pleasure than those of any other literary corporation in the world'.[9] We saw in Chapter 2 that Austen reacted to her contemporaries' diatribes against reading the novel in a variety of ways: by attributing a fear of the novel to the idiotic Mr Collins, she neatly exposes the idiocy of the fear; by claiming for the novel the qualities attributed to the irreproachable periodical essay, she legitimizes it; by exposing and re-gendering stereotypes such as the girl led astray by romances, she indicates the absurdity of the stereotype, and by parodying the sententious style of writers such as Chapone or Gisborne, she reveals the emptiness of the *sententiae*. Her own sane and rational novels, with their emphasis on the domestic and the everyday and their small cast of characters and limited social milieu, form a corrective not only to the more absurd and melodramatic sentimental and Gothic novels of her era, but also to the commentary that tars all novels with the same brush.

Austen's prose style enacts a similar corrective to notions of the novel's frivolity, demanding the kind of strenuous reading previously more usually associated with non-fictional prose. Mary Poovey argues that Austen, like Mary Shelley and Mary Wollstonecraft, was driven by the dictates of propriety, as manifested in the domestic ideology, to use strategies of 'indirection and accommodation', which appear at the level of content and form, 'as resolutions blocked at one level of a narrative and then displaced by other subjects that are more amenable to symbolic transformation'.[10] Austen does employ strategies of indirection that are grounded in conduct-book notions of propriety. However, although Poovey and Gilbert and Gubar see such strategies as limiting and defensive, they can also be seen as pleasurable and defiant, forming part of the game of 'Ingenuity' that Austen plays with her readers. Where Poovey argues that Austen 'attempts to convert the pleasure generated by imaginative engagement into a didactic tool' in the service of conservative morality,[11] it could be argued that, on the level of style, Austen's strategic indirections – which include her characteristic free indirect discourse, her use of allusion and her parodic narrative voice – stem from and create a resistance to the ideology that her novels' plots appear to endorse. Austen's style, Mary Lascelles suggests, creates a special bond between author and reader, a bond that makes readers complicit in the demands of the narrative voice and excludes those who do not understand that particular relationship: Austen's writing is 'as elliptical and indirect as talk among friends, where intuitive understanding can be counted on'.[12] This style results at least partly from Austen's early reading and writing experiences within a close and intellectually compatible reading community.

However, the narrative voice also plays tricks on the reader, leading us into false conclusions, and exposing the ways in which conventions of different kinds dictate our responses to both literature and life. The questions raised by Austen's style are thus epistemological and moral: her novels demand that her readers question not only what they know, but how they know it. They require 'hard reading', not just of the novels themselves, but of the conventions and assumptions the novels satirize. 'Hard reading' is both playful and strenuous: to take part in the games of the narrative voice a reader has to learn to read extremely carefully, in the ways that the writers of conduct books recommend. In this chapter, three ways in which Austen plays with and manipulates her readers' expectations are explored: free indirect discourse, her use of the feminine blush, and her deployment of literary allusion.

Games of Ingenuity I: Austen's Free Indirect Discourse

Throughout her novels and juvenilia, Austen uses varieties of what M. M. Bakhtin calls 'double-voiced discourse'.[13] In his exposition of 'double-voiced discourse', Bakhtin describes the intensification of others' intonations in a certain discourse or a certain section of a work as a 'game' that allows two consciousnesses to co-exist, either harmoniously or antagonistically, in a single utterance. He identifies three types.[14] In both the first and second types, 'the other person's discourse is a completely passive tool in the hands of the author wielding it. He takes, so to speak, someone else's meek and defenseless discourse and installs his own interpretation in it, forcing it to serve his own new purposes'.[15] In the third type of double-voiced discourse, on the other hand, 'the other's words actively influence the author's speech, forcing it to alter itself accordingly under their influence and variety', thus subverting or complicating the writer's authority.[16]

This chapter is concerned with the second and third types of double-voiced discourse, and more specifically with Austen's use of parodic narration (defined as 'introducing into the narration or into the principles of construction a conventionalized discourse, stylized or parodic')[17], parodically represented characters, hidden dialogue and 'discourse with a sideways glance at someone else's work',[18] that is, literary allusion. In Chapter 2, we saw a number of examples of Bakhtinian parodic narration, where Austen's narrative voice dismisses or subverts narrative conventions in *Mansfield Park*, *Northanger Abbey* and *Persuasion* ('Let other pens dwell on guilt and misery', 'I purposely refrain from dates on this occasion', 'What could be more natural?';[19] 'I will not adopt that ungenerous and impolitic custom so common with novel writers', 'it is a new circumstance in romance, I acknowledge';[20] and 'Who can be in doubt of what followed?'[21] for example). Austen's use of parodic narration is not limited to these three works. A parodic narrative voice appears, to a greater or lesser degree, in all of her works. It is evident in *Pride and Prejudice*'s spoof-aphoristic first line: 'It is a truth universally acknowledged, that a single man in possession of a good fortune, must be in want of a wife'.[22] It appears, too, in the exposure of the fictionality of the omniscient narrator in *Emma*'s narrator's sly insertion of the 'truth' about Jane Fairfax's letter that 'there might be some truths not told',[23] and the device of *Lady Susan*'s abrupt ending: 'Whether Lady Susan was, or was not happy in her second choice – I do not see how it can ever be ascertained – for who would take her assurance of it, on either side of the question?'[24] In *Sense and Sensibility*, we hear of Marianne Dashwood's 'extraordinary fate' in being 'born to discover the falsehood of her own opinions, and to counteract, by her conduct, her most favourite maxims'.[25] In this description, Austen parodies both Marianne's views on second attachments, and the melodramatic novels in which heroines really are 'born to an extraordinary fate', much as she mocks the same convention in Catherine Morland's lack of heroic qualities in the first line of *Northanger Abbey*: 'No one [...] would have supposed her born to be an heroine'.[26] In *Sanditon*, too, the narrative voice parodies exemplary heroines: 'I make no apologies for my heroine's vanity. If there are young ladies in the world at her time of life, more dull of fancy and more careless of pleasing, I know them not, and never wish to know them'.[27] Parodic narration, Bakhtin's model suggests, enlists the reader on the side of the narrator against the thing being parodied. It thus strengthens the bond between narrator and reader, making a reader believe that he or she has privileged knowledge of the writer's intentions.

Characters represented parodically may also strengthen the narrator-reader bond. In *Sanditon*, Austen clearly tells the reader that Mr Parker reveals himself through his conversation: 'where he might be himself in the dark, his conversation was still giving information, to such of the Heywoods as could observe'.[28] Austen's characteristic free indirect discourse, in which Mr Parker's conversation is presented, not explicitly, but through a supposedly neutral narrative voice, is a challenge to readers to 'observe' the 'information' about Mr Parker that it provides:

> The sea air and sea bathing together were nearly infallible, one or the other of them being a match for every disorder, of the stomach, the lungs or the blood. They were anti-spasmodic, anti-pulmonary, anti-sceptic, anti-bilious and anti-rheumatic. Nobody could catch cold by the sea; nobody wanted appetite by the sea; nobody wanted spirits; nobody wanted strength. They were healing, softing [*sic*], relaxing – fortifying and bracing – seemingly just as was wanted – sometimes one, sometimes the other.[29]

It does not take 'a great deal of Ingenuity' to recognize that we are hearing Mr Parker's enthusiastic voice through the narrator's here, and our response is directed by one word: the neat 'seemingly' that deflates Mr Parker's eloquence and exposes its hyperbole. The ingenious or observant reader swiftly realizes, like Charlotte Heywood, that Mr Parker is 'an enthusiast': his enthusiasm for *Sanditon* carries him beyond good sense.[30]

In *Emma*, we hear Harriet Smith in a narrative voice that comes to us through Emma's recognisable tones:

> Could she but have given Harriet her feelings about it all! She had talked her into love; but alas! She was not so easily to be talked out of it. The charm of an object to occupy the many vacancies of Harriet's mind was not to be talked away. He might be superseded by another; he certainly would indeed; nothing could be clearer; even a Robert Martin would have been sufficient; but nothing else, she feared, would cure her. Harriet was one of those, who, having once begun, would be always in love. And now, poor girl! she was considerably worse from this re-appearance of Mr Elton. She was always having a glimpse of him somewhere

or other. Emma saw him only once; but two or three times every day Harriet was sure *just* to meet with him, or *just* to miss him, *just* to hear his voice, or see his shoulder, *just* to have something occur to preserve him in her fancy, in all the favouring warmth of surprize [*sic*] and conjecture.[31]

We are clearly in Emma's mind at the beginning of this extract – the 'alas!' and 'poor girl!' are markers of Emma's sympathies, and the colloquialism of 'he might be superseded by another; he certainly would indeed; nothing could be clearer' shows the speed of Emma's thoughts. Emma's inveterate snobbery appears in the phrase 'even a Robert Martin would have been sufficient', and her impatience with Harriet seeps through in a representation of Harriet's breathless reporting: '*just* to [...] *just* to [...] *just* to [...] *just* to'. The absurdity (as well as the pathos) of Harriet's situation is neatly encapsulated in '*just* to hear his voice or see his shoulder', as we imagine Harriet cataloguing glimpses of every disassociated body part. The sense of the absurd is strengthened at the end of the paragraph, when 'his air as he walked by the house – the very sitting of his hat', are cited, still within the narrative voice, 'all in proof of how much he was in love!'. The exclamation mark reiterates Emma's impatience and Harriet's silliness. Harriet is judged in Emma's terms, Harriet's voice distorted by Emma's parody, all still within a purportedly neutral narrative voice. However, Emma, too, in her arrogance, her snobbery, and her belief that the emotional world of others is within her control, is being censured. As readers, we can laugh with Emma at Harriet, but we are also aware of Emma's own faults and absurdities. The purpose (in this case to present Emma as in need of humility) is strengthened by the parody inside the narrative voice.

When Anne Elliot joins her father and sister in Bath, their voices echo through Austen's narrative:

> They had the pleasure of assuring her that Bath more than answered their expectations in every respect. Their house was undoubtedly the best in Camden-place; their drawing-rooms had many decided advantages over all the others which they had either seen or heard of; and the superiority was not less in the style of the fitting-up, or the taste of the furniture. Their acquaintance was exceedingly sought after. Every body was wanting to visit them. They had drawn back from many introductions, and still were perpetually having cards left by people of whom they knew nothing.[32]

The phrasing as well as the content ('exceedingly sought after', 'every body was wanting to visit them', 'perpetually having cards left') makes it evident that the views expounded in this passage are those of Sir Walter and Elizabeth, not a neutral narrator. Their egotism and vanity is parodied by letting their voices ring through the narrative. We next begin to hear William Elliot in the narrative voice, relayed through Sir Walter/Elizabeth:

> They had not a fault to find in him. He had explained away all the appearance of neglect on his own side. It had originated in misapprehension entirely. He had never had an idea of throwing himself off; he had feared that he was thrown off, but knew not why; and delicacy had kept him silent. Upon the hint of having spoken disrespectfully or carelessly of the family, and the family honours, he was quite indignant. He, who had ever boasted of being an Elliot, and whose feelings, as to connection, were only too strict to suit the unfeudal tone of the present day! He was astonished, indeed! But his character and general conduct must refute it. He could refer Sir Walter to all who knew him; and, certainly, the pains he had been taking on this, the first opportunity of reconciliation, to be restored to the footing of a relation and heir-presumptive, was a strong proof of his opinions on the subject.[33]

Sir Walter/Elizabeth's voice ('it had originated in misapprehension entirely') shades into Mr Elliot's ('ever boasted of being an Elliot', 'too strict to suit the unfeudal tone of the present day!' 'astonished, indeed!'). The exclamation marks clearly indicate Elliot's feigned indignation. The narrative then (after the semi-colon) returns to the consciousness either of the listening and judging Anne or to Sir Walter/Elizabeth ('certainly', 'a strong proof of his opinions on the subject'). The reader has no way of telling whether we are in the mind of a trustworthy or untrustworthy character, or listening to the voice of an ironic narrator at this moment. The views and opinions contained within the narrative voice are not explicitly identified as belonging to one or another of the characters; nor does any one of them carry greater formal weight than another.

Although the context and the plot clearly indicate the direction a reader's sympathies should take, on the level of style, the narrative voice occludes the differences between sympathetic and unsympathetic characters, allowing both fools and villains to have their voices heard in the same space as heroes and heroines. A reader could thus (theoretically) choose to take the narrative voice at face value: to believe that popular and charming Sir Walter and Elizabeth live in the best house in town, and that Mr Elliot's feelings on the subject of family honour are genuine. At this point, a reader can already make a shrewd guess about the truth of Sir Walter/Elizabeth's claims, but cannot yet know whether Mr Elliot is sincere. The voices within the narrative thus destabilize the reader, simultaneously asking us to judge and to suspend judgement.

Austen's narrative voice is notoriously hard to pin down, not least in the ways outlined above. It also contains the 'active type' of double-voiced discourse, in which different voices, both parodic and serious, conflict with one another. The following passage from *Mansfield Park*, for example, is again in the narrative voice. The prevailing consciousness is Edmund's, although this is not made explicit. Within Edmund's tones, however, we also hear Maria's and Julia's, filtered through and parodied by Edmund's disapproval.

> His sisters, to whom he had an opportunity of speaking the next morning, were quite as impatient of his advice, quite as unyielding to his representation, quite as determined in the cause of pleasure, as Tom. – Their mother had no objection to the plan, and they were not in the least afraid of their father's disapprobation. – There could be no harm in what had been done in so many respectable families, and by so many women of the first consideration; and it must be scrupulousness run mad, that could see any thing to censure in a plan like their's, comprehending only brothers and sisters, and intimate friends, and which would never be heard of beyond themselves. Julia *did* seem inclined to admit that Maria's situation might require particular caution and delicacy – but that could not extend to *her* – *she* was at liberty; and Maria evidently considered her engagement as only raising her so much more above restraint, and leaving her less occasion than Julia, to consult either father or mother.[34]

Edmund's presence in the narrative voice makes itself felt in the repetition of the disapproving 'quite as [...] quite as [...] quite as', and in the phrases employed: 'impatient of his advice', 'unyielding to his representation', and 'determined in the cause of pleasure', all of which ring with Edmund's moral righteousness and disappointment at his failure to convince his sisters. Maria and Julia's speech patterns and characteristic turns of phrase are then represented: 'not in the least afraid', 'so many women of the first consideration', 'scrupulousness run mad'. The punctuation of free indirect discourse is interesting at this point; it is almost represented as direct speech, using a dash to introduce each speaker (a perfectly acceptable convention in the eighteenth-century novel, though becoming obsolete by Austen's time) but it keeps the syntax of indirect speech ('their mother had', 'there could be no harm').[35] Their voices are thus simultaneously separated from and subsumed into Edmund's, allowing a reader to hear their justifications but only framed by Edmund's commentary on them ('Julia did seem inclined', 'Maria evidently considered'). Edmund's voice is conflated with the narrator's, which should suggest that the narrator shares his position, but the fact that Maria and Julia's voices are not formally identified as theirs, either, complicates the narrative position. A dialogue between two opposed positions, neither of which has greater stylistic authority, is thus played out within the narrative voice, and neither Edmund's disapproval of the theatricals nor the ladies' justifications get the final say: Edmund is 'still urging the subject' when Henry Crawford enters and interrupts them. Fanny, of course, provides a commentary on her cousins' justifications of the play, but the destabilizing influence of Maria's and Julia's common-sense arguments in the narrative voice undermines the certainty of Fanny's moral position. Most of the time, in Austen's novels, a reader attuned to the shifts in the narrative voice finds no difficulty in recognizing the moral, ethical or literary allegiances towards which we are nudged, but occasionally we are confronted with moments when the narrative voice is deliberately baffling and we are faced with the limits and limitations of our ability to interpret. To elucidate these moments, we will now turn to Austen's use of a near-ubiquitous device in eighteenth-century fiction: the female blush, which teaches readers the importance of reading not only texts, but social situations, more carefully.

Games of Ingenuity II: 'Eloquent Blood' – Austen's Use of the Blush[36]

'It might with truth be said that "her eloquent blood spoke through her modest cheeks"', writes Henry Austen of his sister.[37] This part of Henry's idealized portrait adapts John Donne's lines on Elizabeth Drury: 'We understood / Her by her sight: her pure and eloquent blood / Spoke in her cheeks, and so distinctly wrought, / That one might almost say, her body thought'.[38] It is worth noticing, as Ruth Bernard Yeazell does, that the word 'modest' is Henry's addition, reflecting an unconscious assumption that 'eloquent blood' can 'speak' only in the cheeks of a 'modest' woman.[39] This assumption is not surprising, given the frequency with which the trope of the modestly blushing female appears in eighteenth- and early nineteenth-century writing – from conduct books and journals to poetry and novels – and the extent to which the innate ambiguity of the blush tends to be ignored or suppressed. Blushes, both real and figurative are ever-present. From Richardson's Pamela Andrews (1740) and Fielding's Sophia Western (1749) to Burney's Evelina Anville (1778) and More's Lucilla Stanley (1808), the ingenuous heroine's blushes mirror both the modesty and superiority of her mind. The *Female Reader* makes this clear when it assures young women that 'It is not necessary to speak to display mental charms, the eye will quickly inform us if an active soul resides within; and a blush is far more eloquent than the best turned period'.[40] The eighteenth-century moral writers who concern themselves with female education and behaviour tend to assert that the ability to blush inevitably represents innocence and modesty – although, as Ruth Bernard Yeazell points out in her *Fictions of Modesty* (1991), 'no doubt a more or less equivocally the blood could speak lay behind so much insistence on a blush both modest and innocent'.[41] A text without a conservative moral agenda, such as John Cleland's *Fanny Hill* (1748–49) can afford to explore the blush's equivocal nature, as when the eponymous heroine makes the transition from innocence to sexual experience. During her first sexual encounter, Fanny Hill, aroused by the caresses of the prostitute Phoebe, comments that 'even my glowing blushes expressed more desire than modesty';[42] the conventional symbol of her modesty is thus transformed into the signal of her sexuality. By contrast, Gregory's best-selling and influential *A Father's Legacy to His Daughters* refuses to recognize that the blush may hint at more than modesty:

> Pedants, who think themselves philosophers, ask why a woman should blush when she is conscious of no crime? It is sufficient answer, that nature has made you blush when you are guilty of no fault, and has forced us to love you because you do so. – Blushing is so far from being necessarily an attendant on guilt, that it is the usual companion of innocence.[43]

He chooses to ignore the possibility that a blush of guilt (at least on the faces of women like his daughters) could exist. Similarly, the *New Lady's Magazine* tells its readers, 'shamefacedness carries the very colour of virtue, and that blush which spreads itself over her face, is a mark of her abhorrence of vice'.[44] In such accounts, shamefacedness, paradoxically, is proof that a woman has done nothing shameful; only the innocent can still blush. In Burney's *Evelina*, for example, the heroic Lord Orville rejects the idea that a virtuous young lady could blush for any impure reason: when the foppish Mr Lovel claims that he has 'known so many different causes of a lady's colour, such as flushing, – anger, – *mauvaise honte*, – and so forth, that I never dare decide to which it may be owing', he is swiftly put in his place by the assembled company, and Lord Orville comes to Evelina's defence, taking the true motive of her blush (embarrassment) for granted.[45] This brief exchange demonstrates the way that the blush can provide the reader with privileged knowledge that characters within the novel may not have: Mr Lovel may read Evelina's complexion wrongly, but, as readers, we cannot do so because we have access to her inner thoughts, rather than only to the surface of her skin.

In *Tristram Shandy* (1759–66), Laurence Sterne exposes and undercuts the convention of the novelistic blush, laying bare the strategy that allows the reader to interpret blushes correctly:

> – You shall see the very place, Madam; said my uncle Toby. Mrs. Wadman blush'd
> – look'd towards the door – turn'd pale – blush'd sli

natural colour – blush'd worse than ever; which for the sake of the unlearned reader, I translate thus –

'L – d! I cannot look at it –
What would the world say if I look'd at it?
I should drop down, if I look'd at it –
I wish I could look at it –
There can be no sin in looking at it.
I will look at it'.[46]

Deliberately 'translating' the blush for the 'unlearned reader', Sterne plays with the convention that allows readers to imagine that they translate blushes for themselves, pointing out the author's place in manipulating our interpretations. Tristram's 'translation' also points to the *knowingness* of the Widow Wadman's blush; she blushes, not because her thoughts are pure (as Evelina would), but because they are not – the 'it' that she so desires to see is the wound in Uncle Toby's groin. Far from being 'a mark of her abhorrence of vice', as the *New Lady's Magazine* would have it, her blush is the complicated mark of her curiosity, shame and knowledge.

Like *Tristram Shandy*, Jonathan Swift's 'Cadenus and Vanessa' (1713) makes an explicit link between women's blushing and sexual knowledge: 'They blush because they understand',[47] a line quoted in Richardson's *Pamela* as a comment on the ladies' abilities to understand a sexual innuendo:

'…Who, that sees her fingers, believes not, that they were made to touch any key?' He laughed out, and, 'O, parson!' added he, ''tis well you are by, or I would have provoked a blush from the ladies'. 'I hope not, Sir Simon', said Mrs Jones; a man of your politeness would not say any thing that would make ladies blush'. 'No, not for the world', replied he; 'but if I had, it would have been, as the poet says,

They blush, because they understand'.[48]

Pamela herself comments that 'one of the chief beauties of the sex seems banished from the faces of [aristocratic] ladies', because 'they not only don't know how to blush themselves, but they laugh at any innocent young creature that does, as rustic and half-bred; and (as I have more than once heard them) toss their jest about, and their *double meanings*, as they own them, as freely as the gentlemen'.[49] In Pamela's mind, the ladies are so brazen that even their knowingness does not shame them into a blush; by contrast she represents herself as 'covered in blushes' when the ladies make suggestive comments about her own beauty.[50]

Fictional eighteenth-century young (and not so young) women – even modest heroines – do blush from shame, although rarely from sexual shame, and novels repeatedly demonstrate that the innocent blush is often more complicated, never quite as innocent of knowledge, as it seems. Young women in fiction blush for a number of different reasons: from embarrassment at praise; from shyness or timidity when entering a public place; from consciousness of being admired or consciousness of inferiority; from indignation or anger; from a fear of doing wrong; from shame at having done wrong, or seeming to have done wrong; from mortification, and from an inability to dissemble. This last is most important to eighteenth-century moral writers; the blush is assumed to be a guarantee of authentic emotion, a safeguard against feminine deceit. Blushing speaks the language of the heart, a language that the lips may be denied from uttering. The natural rose of a country girl's cheeks is frequently contrasted to the artificial rouge used in the inauthentic world of the fashionable or the depraved (a marker of Sir Walter Elliot's inability to value the authentic is his wish that Lady Russell 'would only wear rouge' in *Persuasion*).[51] While using rouge can consistently counterfeit colour in an elderly or sallow face, only emotion can make the colour come and go, as it does in the face of the modest heroine, whose blushes cannot be faked. In *Evelina*, Lord Orville compliments Evelina's natural complexion, by contrasting it to that created by rouge:

> The difference of natural and artificial colour, seems to me very easily discerned; that of Nature, is mottled, and varying; that of art, *set*, and *too* smooth; it wants that animation, that glow, that *indescribable something* which, even now that I see it, [in Evelina's face] wholly surpasses all my powers of expression.[52]

Lord Orville rightly reads Evelina's sincerity in her blushes, even though he is not privy to the emotions that prompt her colour.

The blush informs a spectator, then, that the young woman is capable of authentic emotion, but it does not always reveal what that emotion might be. In *Northanger Abbey*, Catherine Morland is unable to read her friend Isabella's blush: after telling Isabella that she does not want to marry her brother, Catherine says, 'you know, we shall still be sisters', referring to Isabella's engagement to James Morland. Austen presents Isabella's reply: '"Yes, yes" (with a blush), "there are more ways than one of our being sisters. – But where am I wandering to?"'[53] Catherine, in her innocence, does not recognize that Isabella's blush denotes the possibility that the two could 'be sisters' if Catherine were to marry Henry Tilney and Isabella his brother, Captain Tilney. The reader, on the other hand, sees exactly where Isabella is 'wandering to'. In *Mansfield Park*, too, Sir Thomas cannot read his niece Fanny's blushes. At the pivotal moment when

Sir Thomas tries to ascertain Fanny's motive for rejecting Henry Crawford, he suggests to her that her affections may already be engaged. After this:

> He paused and eyed her fixedly. He saw her lips formed into a *no*, though the sound was inarticulate, but her face was like scarlet. That, however, in so modest a girl might be very compatible with innocence; and chusing at least to appear satisfied, he quickly added, 'No, no, I know *that* is quite out of the question – quite impossible.'[54]

Sir Thomas concludes that Fanny is not already in love, but the reader knows that her affections are indeed engaged; her blush is not of innocence, but of guilt. While Fanny's blush truly tells the language of her heart, her uncle does not speak its language, and so cannot interpret it correctly.

Unlike Sir Thomas, a reader, to whom Fanny's thoughts are usually open, has a better chance of understanding Fanny's blushes. Although the emotions prompting her blushes are not always explicit, we are generally close enough to what Fanny has been feeling or thinking to interpret her colour better than the rest of the characters around her. And often, Austen chooses to explain a blush, to do away with the necessity for interpreting it ourselves. This device is a staple of eighteenth-century fiction –Evelina, for example, writes of herself that she is 'blushing for her unworthiness',[55] while Mary Hays' Emma Courtney writes to Augustus Harley, 'I blush, when I reflect what a weak, wavering, inconsistent, being, I must lately have appeared to you'.[56] The blush is straightforward; we know that it is a feeling of unworthiness that brings the colour to Evelina's cheeks, and a sense of shame to Emma's. The convenience of the blush as a signal that allows the narrator and the reader to share privileged knowledge about the emotions that have caused the blush helps explain its popularity as a novelistic device, and thus its ubiquity in the eighteenth-century novel.

Austen is not averse to using the blush in this way. Mr Knightley, for example, on hearing of Harriet's refusal of Robert Martin, 'actually looked red with surprize [*sic*] and displeasure'.[57] In the early *Catharine; or, The Bower*, the eponymous heroine enters a ball, with 'a glow of mingled Chearfulness [*sic*] and Confusion on her Cheeks', while her aunt is described as 'colouring with anger and Astonishment'.[58] Later, Catharine, too, finds herself 'blushing with anger at her own folly'.[59] The emotions – surprise, displeasure, cheerfulness and confusion, anger and astonishment – are all clearly laid out for the reader to see. In *Mansfield Park*, Fanny Price's 'soft skin, […] so frequently tinged with a blush' does not always need readerly interpretation, for we are often told why she blushes.[60] We hear of her 'colouring at such praise' and colouring with anger when Mary Crawford speaks mockingly of religious services.[61]

On being pressed to take the part of Cottager's Wife, Fanny grows 'more and more red from excessive agitation', and, having reprimanded Henry Crawford later in the novel, she 'trembled and blushed at her own daring'.[62] Talking to William, her cheeks are 'in a glow of indignation' when she hears that the Gregory girls will not speak to him.[63] Other characters – Sir Thomas, Henry, Mary, even Edmund – misinterpret Fanny's blushes, but even when we do not have an explicit guide to Fanny's emotions, we learn not to misread her because of their mistakes. Unlike Mary Crawford (who imagines Fanny's colour denotes a liking for Mary's brother, and thus attributes her blushes to a knowingness Fanny certainly does not possess), we begin to understand what a modest girl's blushes really mean from our proximity to a truly modest heroine. We are thus taught through our own superior degree of knowledge over the other characters, what proper responses should be, and how misreading and misunderstanding can come about. Mary Crawford reads Fanny's skin wrongly; she also consistently responds wrongly to moral dilemmas. Because of our special bond with the narrator, we are able to recognize and learn to condemn her responses to both skin and situations.

In *Persuasion*, however, Austen undercuts her own use of the blush-as-narrative-bond. Anne, having listened to talk of the connection between the Crofts and Mr Wentworth, the curate of Monkford, walks out 'to seek the comfort of cool air for her flushed cheeks', saying to herself, 'a few months more, and *he*, perhaps may be walking here'.[64] The chapter ends immediately, and straight after the chapter break, the narrative voice briskly explains, '*He* was not Mr. Wentworth, the former curate of Monkford, however suspicious appearances may be, but a captain Frederick Wentworth, his brother'.[65] The narrator firmly points out that we should not assume that we can read Anne's blush or her secret thoughts. If we do, we will draw the wrong conclusions.

In *Emma*, Austen more consistently exploits and subverts the special relationship with the narrator as seen through the device of the blush. Emma Woodhouse, the 'imaginist' who enjoys creating the narratives of other people's lives, repeatedly misinterprets the blushes of Jane Fairfax and, to a lesser degree, those of Harriet Smith. Harriet's blushes are initially fairly transparent (correctly, and conventionally, the *ingénue* smiles and blushes each time Emma speaks to her of Mr Elton's supposed regard, she blushes as she sits for her picture, her cheeks glow as she reads Robert Martin's declaration of love, and she blushes with shame as she destroys her treasured mementoes of Mr Elton). However, as her experience of love and friendship increases, her complexion becomes harder for Emma to read. When others talk of Frank Churchill, and Harriet's countenance remains unmoved, Emma attributes this to Harriet's improved strength of mind. Harriet, who habitually blushes when she has even the smallest thing to hide, does *not* blush, which ought to inform Emma of her indifference to Frank, but Emma refuses to attend to the signs. Even when Harriet colours in astonishment at the idea that she might care for Mr Churchill, crying, 'You do not think I care about Mr Frank Churchill', Emma interprets Harriet's blushes as mortification and her sincerity as fortitude.[66] Emma does not remain long in error, for she and Harriet soon understand one another. Her self-deception over the history she creates for Jane Fairfax is, however, much more long-standing.

Watching Jane after she has received the anonymous gift of the pianoforte (which is supposed by most of Highbury to have come from Miss Fairfax's guardian, Colonel Campbell, but which Emma suspects to be a love-offering from Mr Dixon), Emma interprets Miss Fairfax's 'blush of consciousness with which congratulations were received' as 'a blush of guilt which accompanied the name of "my excellent friend Col. Campbell"'.[67] Emma is right to discern both a blush of consciousness (Jane later acknowledges how much she has hated having to tell lies) and a blush of guilt (for she knows the piano has come from Frank Churchill, and allowing others to believe it is from Colonel Campbell is a sin of omission if not of commission), but the narrative she creates from these blushes is entirely inaccurate.

The next day, Emma sees Jane Fairfax blush again, a 'deep blush of consciousness', when Frank Churchill tells her that a piece of music he picks up was danced at Weymouth.[68] Emma immediately fits this blush into the imaginary love affair she has created between Miss Fairfax and Mr Dixon, reflecting that the 'smile of secret delight' that accompanies the blush of consciousness is the result of her 'very reprehensible feelings' towards her friend's husband.[69] Frank Churchill, a master of deceit, recognizes and exploits the ways in which a blush can be misinterpreted – not only does he encourage Emma in her self-deception over the two blushes above, he also suggests to Emma that he will impudently admire the 'Irish fashion' of Jane's curls, 'and [Emma] shall see how she takes it; whether she colours'.[70] Although Emma does not see whether or not Jane colours, Frank has provided a screen for himself. If Jane blushes at something he says to her, or if her face reveals her feelings by a blush, he has provided them both with an excuse for it. Frank knows that the eloquent blood in a girl's cheeks can be made to tell lies. Later, during the dinner at Hartfield, Jane Fairfax blushes as she explains her desire to walk to the post office, and again when Mr John Knightley hopes that she will soon be surrounded by her dearest connections. Those around her imagine she innocently thinks of her friends the Campbells and Dixons; it later transpires that she must have been thinking of Frank. Emma, though, ascribes Jane's 'glow both of complexion and spirits' to the receipt of an imaginary love-letter from

Ireland, correctly reading both discomfort and pleasure in her blushes, but misreading the circumstances behind them.[71]

Mr Knightley, on the other hand, reads Jane's blushes more perceptively than Emma, recognizing, in the children's game of letters, that the 'blush on Jane's cheek' gives the word *blunder* 'a meaning not otherwise ostensible'.[72] Almost immediately afterwards, Frank pushes the word *Dixon* towards Jane, who is 'evidently displeased', and 'blushed more deeply than he [Mr Knightley] had ever perceived her'.[73] Mr Knightley, a better reader of complexions than Emma, does not leap to the conclusion that Jane is in love with Mr Dixon. Instead, he continues to suspect Frank of 'some inclination to trifle with Jane Fairfax', and tries to warn Emma of the 'symptoms of attachment between them'.[74] Once the whole story of the engagement has come out, Mrs Weston, too, can understand Jane's blushes, telling Emma, 'she then began to speak of you, and of the great kindness you had shown her during her illness; and with a blush which showed me how it was all connected, desired me, whenever I had an opportunity, to thank you – I could not thank you too much – for every wish and every endeavour to do her good'.[75] Mrs Weston correctly interprets the 'blush that showed how it was all connected' as an acknowledgement of Jane's jealousy of Emma. Blushes may well show how things are connected; as Emma (and with her, a reader) finds out, they may also lead one to make connections that are not there. With Emma, as readers, we are swept along in the narrative that she has created, and, with Emma, we learn that the blush can be deceptive. What we do not realize, of course, on a first reading of *Emma*, is how much of the narrative of Jane Fairfax's blushes is in Emma's imagination; a story created, not by the narrator, but by Emma. Because we see the action of the novel so consistently from Emma's viewpoint, and because her tones are so frequently embedded within the narrative voice, we do not know at first when Emma is wrong. We cannot know on a first reading, that the privileged knowledge we assume we have is faulty.

It is not surprising that we should assume that we can read and interpret blushes correctly in *Emma*, because our interpretation of Emma's own blushes is guided so that we do understand them. We witness Emma stopping 'to blush and laugh at her own relapse' when she momentarily lapses back into matchmaking.[76] We are able to interpret her 'little start, and a little blush' at the news of Mr Elton's engagement as the result of surprise and embarrassment at the memory of his ill-fated proposal to her.[77] We understand (better, perhaps, than Emma does) the 'faint blush' with which Emma notices the 'warmth' of Mr Knightley's interest in Jane Fairfax as that of consciousness of Mrs Weston's belief in his *tendresse* for her, and unconscious dislike of the idea that anyone else could be of romantic interest to Mr Knightley.[78] At the ball at the Crown, when Mr Elton refuses to dance with Harriet, Emma's 'heart was in a glow, and she feared her face might be as hot', and a reader recognizes Emma's anger as the emotion prompting the heat of her face.[79] With her; we feel that she deserves the mortification of being 'under a continual blush all the rest of [her] life' over the 'senseless tricks' she plays to bring Harriet and Mr Elton together, and we both recognize and feel with Emma when she 'recollected, blushed, was sorry' at Mr Knightley's reproach to her after the Box Hill incident.[80] Similarly, we understand her feelings as her colour is heightened in front of Mr Knightley by the unjust praise her father bestows upon her attentiveness to the Bateses.[81] Once Emma knows the secret of Frank and Jane Fairfax's engagement, she 'could not speak the name of Dixon without a little blush', a blush that demonstrates her shame at the tissue of nonsense she created, and later, she is obliged, when talking to Frank, to blush and forbid the name being pronounced in her hearing.[82] Her 'glowing cheeks' as Mr Knightley tells her that he already knows of the engagement suggest to Mr Knightley that she may be suffering from love for Frank, but we are explicitly told that 'it occurred to her that he might have called at Mrs Goddard's in his way' – the glow, we gather, comes from a fear on her part that he may have seen Harriet.[83] Later, Emma has a 'blush of sensibility on Harriet's account', for which 'she could not give any sincere explanation [to Mr Knightley]', but the reader knows that Emma's blush conceals Harriet's liking for Mr Knightley as well as Emma's guilt at being the one preferred.[84] Having trusted the narrator's accounts of Emma's blushes, we think we are in a position to trust her account of others' blushes.

Yet Jane Fairfax's blushes show that the complexion can be misread, not only by characters within the novel, but by a reader. Like the Widow Wadman's blush, and Anne Elliot's glowing cheeks, the history of Jane Fairfax exposes the way the blush is used as a fictional device, and challenges the assumptions that we make about our ability to interpret novelistic codes. It teaches us, in other words, about the ways we read, the assumptions we make as we are amassing knowledge. When Mr Darcy and George Wickham first come face to face in *Pride and Prejudice*, both change colour: 'one looked white, the other red'. Elizabeth, 'all astonishment at the effect of the meeting', yearns to know the meaning of it. 'It was impossible to imagine; it was impossible not to long to know'.[85] Like Emma, Elizabeth wants to interpret complexions, and it is significant that her desire is couched in terms of longing for knowledge. Like Emma, Elizabeth is swiftly drawn in to believe what is not true when she hears Wickham's tale; her search for knowledge has gone awry. It is not only Elizabeth, Mary Ann O'Farrell suggests, who may misread what the complexions mean: 'correct assignment of colors to characters (correct reading of somatic signs) has sometimes proven difficult for readers of this passage, especially, perhaps, for first-time readers; [...] one need not know at this point in the novel that Darcy's is the righteous, angry blanching, Wickham's the embarrassed blush'.[86] One certainly need not know that it is Darcy who turns white and Wickham red; indeed, an equally plausible explanation is that Darcy's is the red of anger, and Wickham's the white of fear. Or, as Elizabeth might think, Darcy is white from unjustified resentment, and Wickham red from justified anger. Neither Elizabeth nor the reader, in other words, should find a somatic sign in either men or women entirely trustworthy; knowledge of character is a tricky business, and making and acknowledging mistakes is an essential part of acquiring knowledge. It is particularly difficult for a reader to make the necessary judgements, especially when the narrator deliberately refuses to explain the reason for a blush, as Austen does here. She uses the same trick, teasingly, when she describes Mr Knightley blushing after being accused by Emma and Mrs Weston of a liking for Jane Fairfax. The blush is deliberately left ambiguous: 'Mr Knightley was hard at work upon the lower buttons of his thick leather gaiters, and either the exertion of getting them together, or some other cause, brought the colour into his face'.[87] The device is used again in *Persuasion*, when Anne realizes she has been misattributing Lady Russell's fixed regard on the window curtains to the sight of Captain Wentworth: 'Anne sighed and blushed and smiled, in pity and disdain, either at her friend or herself'.[88] The reader cannot know (though we may guess) whether Mr Knightley's colour results from his exertion or his secret thoughts, and we are not allowed to know whether Anne blushes for herself or for Lady Russell. We are thus faced with the necessity for interpretation, and with the limits of our understanding.

The blush, then, like the narrative voice, can be both a transparent indicator of a character's feelings, and an agent of misdirection. The characters in *Pride and Prejudice*, *Persuasion*, *Mansfield Park* and *Emma* tend to think that a blush can always be read without difficulty, failing to realize that, when eloquent blood speaks in a person's cheeks, it is worth listening very carefully to understand what it is really saying. Provided with greater evidence of what is happening below the surface of the skin, a reader initially learns to think that his or her degree of knowledge is superior to that of the characters in the novel; she feels a bond with the narrative voice from which these characters are excluded. However, as we see in *Emma*, a reader must then learn that the very existence of such a bond between narrator and reader is not straightforward. Katherine Mansfield identifies the appeal of Austen's novels as lying in the fact that 'every admirer of the novels cherishes the happy thought that he alone – reading between the lines – has become the secret friend of their author'.[89] Austen's use of blushes in *Emma* teaches us that becoming the 'secret friend' of the author brings us face to face with our interpretative limitations. As Emma learns to read social experiences and character more carefully, more discriminatingly and more humbly, so we learn to read texts with greater care and humility, becoming in the process more 'ingenious' in our reading habits.

Games of Ingenuity III: 'The True Learning for a Lady' – Austen's Use of Literary Allusion

In Hannah More's *Strictures*, she suggests that a woman should 'read the best books, not so much to enable her to talk of them, as to bring the improvement she derives from them to the rectification of her principles',[90] and claims that 'well-informed persons will easily be discovered to have read the best books, though they are not always detailing lists of authors'.[91] Both comments suggest that, if a young lady talks of books, she will be accused of showing off her accomplishments. More's later work, *Cælebs in Search of a Wife* (1808), presents an exemplary heroine, Lucilla Stanley, who demonstrates both her impeccable taste and her knowledge of literature through a speaking silence in the presence of her father and prospective suitor. The hero, looking for a wife, claims that 'the true learning for a lady' is 'a knowledge that is rather detected than displayed',[92] and is delighted to find that Lucilla does not overtly display her learning. Charles (the *cælebs* of the title) finds instead that 'it was easy to trace her knowledge of the best authors, though she quoted none'.[93] Lucilla is, in fact, extremely modest about her intellectual abilities, blushing deeply and going so far as to leave the room to avoid the necessity of revealing her knowledge of Latin.

When Jane Austen, writing to the Prince Regent's librarian, 'boast[ed]' that she was 'the most unlearned, & uninformed Female who ever dared to be an Authoress' she was undoubtedly mocking both herself and the convention that demanded young ladies should be modest about their learning.[94] Although the tone of the letter is playful, the issue of female pedantry was a serious one for an 'Authoress' like Austen. Unlike Fielding's 'sagacious readers', who are explicitly gendered male, and so can legitimately revel and delight in his classical allusions, Austen's implied reader has to find a quieter pleasure in more deeply embedded references.[95] One of the ways in which Austen turns the dictates of propriety to her own uses is through her deployment of literary allusion, and in particular through what are here termed 'spectral texts' – literary works that hover in the margins of her novels, not always directly acknowledged, but always reflecting or refracting some of the novels' central concerns about ethics and morality.[96] These texts are often not directly acknowledged (showing off what one has read is, after all, unladylike), or alluded to so briefly as to seem unimportant, but they are nonetheless a part of the fabric of the novels, and enrich and complicate the relationship between narrative voice, heroine, and reader. Austen's use of spectral texts is explored here through a reading of *Mansfield Park*.[97]

Most critical discussions of intertextuality in *Mansfield Park* have focused on Elizabeth Inchbald's *Lovers' Vows* (1798) to the exclusion of all other texts.[98] Critics from Lionel Trilling to Claudia Johnson divide over the function of Inchbald's adaptation of August von Kotzebue's controversial radical, sentimental German Jacobin play in the structural centre of *Mansfield Park*, arguing for its purpose in the novel as political, moral, structural or thematic, and enlisting it as evidence of Austen's conservatism, radicalism or feminism, her Platonic, Evangelical or Anglican beliefs, her approval or disapproval of the theatre, even her coded homoerotic desires.[99] The extent of critical attention to *Lovers' Vows* pays tribute to its unsettling presence in the moral and political framework of *Mansfield Park*, the nature and consequences of which are examined at the end of this section. But such critical discourses also tend to ignore the importance of alternative intertexts in the novel, most notably William Cowper's *The Task* (1785) and Crabbe's *Tales* (1812), which bear the weight of the discussion here.[100] A close interrogation of the presence of these more politically conservative texts exposes the subtle ways in which Austen's readers are manipulated, and reveals the artistic strategy behind some of the more problematic moments in *Mansfield Park*. The presence of Cowper and Crabbe both simultaneously references a conservative morality, and undercuts it with ironic distance. By recognizing and identifying the kind of intertextual conversation that is occurring in the pages of *Mansfield Park*, we should come to a clearer understanding of what is at stake, morally and intellectually, in the action of the novel.

It is evident from Austen's letters to different members of her family that literary references were an habitual way of expressing emotions and describing events and people; a means of sharing thoughts in a fashion that other family members could immediately and effortlessly understand. This tendency, as we have seen, is carried over into Austen's novels, in which books, poems and plays are evoked with the tacit assumption that the reader will understand the implications of the references. Sometimes, of course, the assumption is mistaken. *Lovers' Vows*, for example, no longer resonates with the *louche* allure that made it so appealing to Mr Yates, and Home's *Douglas* (quoted by Tom Bertram as evidence that his father had no objection to acting), no longer means very much to a modern reader, despite its enormous popularity in the latter half of the eighteenth century.[101]

In *Mansfield Park*, as in all her works, Austen uses literary references both to make her characters understand each other, and as broad hints to help her readers understand the characters better. When Maria Bertram, coquetting with Henry Crawford at Sotherton, quotes the starling in Sterne's *A Sentimental Journey* (1768), for example, she suggests that she feels trapped in a cage, and thus allows him to offer himself as a liberator. Furthermore, she demonstrates her knowledge of a text that wholeheartedly endorses the passion of love and frequently excuses lapses of decorum on the grounds that feeling is more important than propriety. Maria's reading thus reveals her as a woman with whom Henry can flirt with impunity, and hints to a reader that her passions are stronger than her sense of propriety. When Mary Crawford wittily parodies Hawkins Browne's 'Address to Tobacco' in imitation of Pope, she reveals herself as the imitator of an imitator, and thus as insincere and shallow.[102] Her reading, like Maria's, betrays and exposes her. These literary references resonate with more information than the characters that quote them can hear or understand, thus creating a complicated bond: a link between narrator and reader based on the assumption of shared attitudes to the texts quoted. As in the use of the blush as a narrative device, once such a link has been established, it may be exploited either by confirming or refuting the reader's assumptions.

According to her brother Henry, Jane Austen's favourite moral writers were 'Johnson in prose, and Cowper in verse'.[103] Austen refers to or quotes Cowper in *Sense and Sensibility*, *Northanger Abbey* and *Emma*, and a number of times in her letters. It is surely no coincidence that Fanny Price quotes Cowper twice (*The Task* and 'Tirocinium') and paraphrases Johnson (*Rasselas*) in *Mansfield Park*. Books are Fanny's primary way of understanding the world and, for Fanny, as for her creator, quotations and allusions are a habit of mind, a way of expressing how she feels. Indeed, on occasion they are the only way in which she can speak the language of the heart. Fanny habitually retreats from the pains and uncertainties of her life at Mansfield to the East room and her books and comforts. Her choice of reading is important, as reading forms her mind. It is clear from the selection that Edmund casually picks up when he visits her in her own domain – Lord Macartney's *Journal* of his embassy to China, Johnson's *Idler* and Crabbe's *Tales* – that the books that Fanny reads are an accurate reflection of her character, consistent with the various aspects of her personality. Macartney's *Journal*, with its careful descriptions of Chinese customs and the author's sympathetic and sensitive curiosity about the habits of the citizens of other nations, is paralleled by Fanny's desire to know more about her uncle's affairs in the West Indies. Johnson's *Idler* reflects and represents her moral code, while Crabbe's *Tales* show Fanny's poetic sensibilities, demonstrated elsewhere by her sensitivity to nature and beauty and her love of Cowper. Her choice of Crabbe also shows her thoroughly unexceptionable literary taste. Crabbe's status as a poet whom everyone could admire is well-illustrated by Mary Russell Mitford's comment on the subject to her correspondent Mrs Hofland in 1819: 'Do you like Crabbe? But that is a silly question. Everybody likes Mr. Crabbe to a certain point. He is the only poet going of whom everybody thinks alike'.[104] A similar point is made in *The Champion*'s review of *Emma* of 1816: 'Our authoress, though no great dabbler in poetry or quotations, quotes Cooper [*sic*] – It would perhaps not be difficult to account for the fact of every lady's admiring Cooper'.[105] These comments suggest that there is certainly nothing eccentric about liking Crabbe and Cowper; their work demands general approval from ladies who are *au courant* with literary criticism.

Austen herself knew and loved Crabbe's poetry. Crabbe's *Parish Register* provided the name of *Mansfield Park's* heroine, and his *Tales* supplied subject matter with which Austen could work. Austen-Leigh suggests that his aunt enjoyed Crabbe, 'perhaps on account of a certain resemblance to herself in minute and highly finished detail', and relates her long-running jest on the subject: 'if she ever married at all, she could fancy being Mrs Crabbe'.[106] Austen's letters bear out Austen-Leigh's anecdote. She writes, 'I am in agonies. – I have not yet seen Mr. Crabbe', and was 'particularly disappointed at seeing nothing of Mr Crabbe' at the theatre.[107] She tells Cassandra, on hearing of the death of Mrs Crabbe, that she will 'comfort *him* as well as [she] can'.[108] Isobel Grundy reminds us that Austen more than once uses the pose of husband-hunting to signal her specifically literary admiration of a man.[109] Crabbe is the signifier of a private joke in Austen's letters, and it may be that he plays a similar role in *Mansfield Park*.

In the preface to his *Tales*, Crabbe writes of his intention that 'nothing will be found that militates against the rules of propriety and good manners, nothing that offends against the more important precepts of morality and religion'.[110] This description immediately marks the work as suitable reading for a young lady, particularly one like Fanny who finds the characters in *Lovers' Vows* 'so totally improper for home representation'.[111] Crabbe's poetry is, though, also characterized by a robustly cynical world-view. This kind of full-bodied cynicism had no place in the female-authored novel, but the shadowy intertextual presence of Crabbe in *Mansfield Park* helps Austen to imbue conservative moral views with the scepticism natural to her.[112]

The tale of most relevance to *Mansfield Park*, and to Fanny's situation in particular, is 'The Confidant' (Tale XVI). In this tale, the lovely Anna is a dependent relation, who has the 'painful office' of attending 'on a lady, as an humble friend'. Her 'station', like Fanny's, 'frequent terrors wrought', and the description of her duties is strongly reminiscent of Fanny's attendance on Lady Bertram:

> Her duties here were of the usual kind –
> And some the body harass'd, some the mind:
> Billets she wrote, and tender stories read […]

We witness Fanny's 'body harrass'd' as she rests on the sofa with a head-ache after cutting roses in the hot sun, and the trials to her 'mind' from Mrs Norris's importunities; we see her getting through the difficulties of Lady Bertram's needlework for her, and reading to her (although Fanny reads Shakespeare, rather than 'tender stories'). When Anna is described as playing music 'At a request that no request convey'd', we are reminded of Sir Thomas' 'advice of absolute power' at the end of the Mansfield Ball.[113] Anna 'veil'd her troubles in a mask of ease / And showed her pleasure was a power to please'.[114] For Fanny too, veiling her troubles is second nature, and 'pleasure' is the 'power to please'. Failing to please makes her miserable, and her happiest moments are when she earns her relatives' praise. Although Anna's story differs from Fanny's in that the main part of the tale takes place after she has been removed from her dependent situation by marriage, before her marriage, she is 'shamed and frighten'd' by proposals from men who gaze on her face 'with careless freedom', and who '[speak] their purpose with an easy air',[115] just as Fanny is frightened by Crawford. There is enough of Anna in Fanny to make Fanny's reading of Crabbe's *Tales* suggestive. Crabbe's tone when discussing Anna is gently satirical, and, although he is broadly sympathetic to his heroine, he nonetheless remains at a distance from her. This is reflected in Austen's narrative voice. Though the majority of the action *is* represented by Fanny's perceptions of it, the narrator maintains a space between them. There are places in *Mansfield Park* where the reader is encouraged to see through Fanny, as when, for example, waiting for Edmund and Miss Crawford to finish riding, she translates her own jealousy and feelings of exclusion into concern for Edmund and the horse, and displaces her irritation with Edmund onto Mr Crawford:

> She must not wonder at all this; what could be more natural than that Edmund should be making himself useful, and proving his good-nature by any one? She could not but think indeed that Mr. Crawford might as well have saved him the trouble; that it would have been particularly proper and becoming in a brother to have done it himself; but Mr. Crawford, with all his boasted good-nature, and all his coachmanship, probably knew nothing of the matter, and had not active kindness in comparison of Edmund. She began to think it rather hard upon the mare to have such double duty; if she were forgotten the poor mare should be remembered.[116]

The syntax gives Fanny away. In 'she must not wonder', Austen represents Fanny wrenching her thoughts away from the fact that she does wonder why Edmund should be so involved in teaching Mary Crawford. The rhetorical question, 'what could be more natural?' is once again a clue to the alert reader, gesturing to the fact that Fanny does *not* think it 'natural' that Edmund should help anyone but her. The phrase 'she could not but think' is a beautiful example of Fanny's capacity for self-delusion, since the previous sentence has demonstrated precisely that Fanny *can* stop herself from thinking certain things. Her willingness to blame Mr Crawford rather than Edmund is thus revealed as the displacement strategy it really is. Similarly, when she begins to think about the mare, the phrase 'if she were forgotten' undercuts her sympathy for the mare; the 'she' does not even need to be italicized for a reader to hear its self-pitying tone. A reader may see through Fanny's eyes, but the same reader also perceives her self-delusions. Crabbe's robust scepticism thus makes an appearance in *Mansfield Park*, toned down and translated into a quieter sort of ironic distance.

Cowper's poem *The Task*, too, is always in the background of *Mansfield Park*, present in Fanny's thoughts. Because Fanny's consciousness is the filter through which a reader sees and understands the majority of the action of *Mansfield Park*, Cowper is therefore frequently present in the narrative too, as a contrapuntal accompaniment to the narrative voice. In *Mansfield Park*, as in *The Task*, the reader feels clearly that 'God made the country, and man made the town'.[117] Although the suggestion that country life is preferable to the dissipations of a town is in no way confined to Austen and Cowper, the singular congruence between the attitudes expressed in *The Task* and *Mansfield Park* seems significant. *The Task*'s approbation of a retired domestic life and its disapproval of the joys of the town are reflected in the contrast between Fanny's quiet steadiness and longing for peace, and the noise and bustle of the rest of the characters. Cowper writes:

> Possess ye therefore, ye who borne about
> In chariots and sedans, know no fatigue
> But that of idleness, and taste no scenes
> But such as art contrives, possess ye still,
> Your element; there only, ye can shine
> There only minds like yours can do no harm.[118]

Mary Crawford, whom 'nothing ever fatigues [...], but doing what I do not like', and who, looking at Nature's beauty in the Parsonage shrubbery, can 'see no wonder in this shrubbery equal to seeing myself in it', is clearly one of these.[119] 'In cities foul example on most minds / Begets its likeness',[120] says Cowper, in lines that explain Edmund and Fanny's conversation about the influence of example on Mary's 'tainted' mind.[121] In London, among her own set, a mind like hers can do no harm; at Mansfield, out of her artificial element, Mary Crawford's mind can and does cause harm. The town is an evident evil in *Mansfield Park* – Maria's longing for a town house tempts her into her disastrous marriage with Rushworth, while Mary's delight in the gaieties of London reveals her as an unsuitable mate for Edmund. Henry's choice of

London over Everingham causes his elopement with Maria, and Tom's town dissipations lead him to the brink of death. Put crudely, the narrative voice and deserving characters in *Mansfield Park* seem to share Cowper's taste for the country, while the less deserving do not.

Cowper's description of 'the sedentary [who] stretch their lazy length / When custom bids, but no refreshment find / For none they need', finds its embodiment in Lady Bertram, snoozing on the sofa.[122] His disapproval of those who indulge too much in 'the repose the SOFA yields' is reflected in the fact that Fanny, as Julia does her the justice to point out, is 'as little upon the sofa as any body in the house'.[123] Lady Bertram playing cards is the quintessence of Cowper's lines about those card players who cannot play, as, with Henry Crawford at her elbow, she 'sits / Spectatress both and spectacle, a sad / And silent cipher, while her proxy plays'.[124] The choice of the noun 'cipher' is telling – earlier in the novel Mrs Grant describes Lady Bertram as 'more of a cipher now than when he [Sir Thomas] is at home'.[125] Crawford's and Rushworth's enthusiasm for improvement confirms Cowper's view that 'improvement [...] the idol of the age, / Is fed with many a victim'.[126] As Alistair Duckworth has shown, Henry's indifference to his estate, Everingham, bears out Cowper's disappointment that 'estates are landscapes, gazed upon awhile, / Then advertised, and auctioneer'd away'.[127]

Sir Thomas's view that Maria should not be allowed to return to Mansfield because she 'had destroyed her own character, and he would not by a vain attempt to restore what never could be restored, be affording his sanction to vice, or in seeking to lessen its disgrace, be anywise accessory to introducing such misery in another man's family, as he had known himself',[128] is exactly paralleled by Cowper's wistful evocation of 'old time', when 'she that had renounced / Her sex's honour, was renounced herself / By all that priz'd it; not for prud'ry's sake, / But dignity's, resentful of the wrong'.[129] Sir Thomas, we might remember, is the embodiment of 'dignity' in *Mansfield Park*.[130] Cowper's description of the proper behaviour of a clergyman (*Task* ii, 395–544) is exactly congruent with Edmund's conception of his own role and behaviour, and his account of the same to Mary Crawford.[131] Cowper contrasts the sincere preacher, '[i]n doctrine incorrupt; in language plain; / And plain in manner' with the theatrical one, who 'seek[s] to dazzle me with tropes / [...] and play his brilliant parts before my eyes'.[132] In *Mansfield Park*, Edmund, who cannot say a *bon-mot*, and is 'a very matter of fact, plain spoken being', is contrasted to Henry Crawford who claims that he would enjoy the performative aspect of being a clergyman, imagining himself before a sophisticated London audience who could appreciate his rhetorical powers.[133]

Fanny Price's thoughts frequently run along the same lines as Cowper's, a fact emphasized by the similarities between Cowper's description of himself as a 'stricken deer' outside the herd of mankind and Fanny's position as a lonely and wounded outsider at Mansfield.[134] When Fanny, hearing of Rushworth's plans for Sotherton, thinks of Cowper's avenues: 'Does not it make you think of Cowper? "Ye fallen avenues, once more I mourn your fate unmerited"', it is the most obvious of the places where Cowper is directing her thoughts on nature, but far from the only one.[135] Sitting in the shrubbery with Miss Crawford, she rhapsodizes over the evergreen:

> '…How beautiful, how welcome, how wonderful the evergreen!– When one thinks of it, how astonishing a variety of nature! – In some countries we know the tree that sheds its leaf is the variety, but that does not make it less amazing, that the same soil and the same sun should nurture plants differing in the first rule and law of their existence.'[136]

Cowper, too, muses on the many varieties of trees and differences of their properties, while looking out over trees in *Task*, i, 300–320. Earlier in the novel, in the drawing room, gazing out into the starry night, Fanny again speaks like Cowper: 'Fanny spoke her feelings. "Here's harmony!", said she, "Here's repose! Here's what may leave all painting and all music behind, and what poetry only can attempt to describe. Here's what may tranquillize every care, and lift the heart to rapture!"'[137] Cowper's poetry, in which 'my descriptions are all from nature: not one of them second-handed', and whose 'delineations of the heart are from my own experience',[138] does 'attempt to describe' the starlit harmony and repose of a night in the country:

> Come evening once again, season of peace,
> Return sweet evening, and continue long!
> Methinks I see thee in the streaky west,
> […]
> Not sumptuously adorn'd, nor needing aid
> […]
> A star or two just twinkling on thy brow.[139]

Fanny's 'rapture' comes from 'harmony', 'repose' and tranquillity; Cowper finds 'composure' in the 'gentle hours' of the 'Winter Evening'.[140] Speaking from the heart, then, Fanny's most sincere feelings are conflated with the ideals of the poet.

Mansfield Park is thus saturated with Cowper's poem, but because many of the allusions outlined above are extremely subtle, while reading *Mansfield Park*, we become acquainted with Cowper, as Henry Crawford says of Shakespeare, 'without knowing how'. 'It is part of an Englishman's constitution', continues

Crawford, 'His thoughts and beauties are so spread abroad that one touches them every where, one is intimate with him by instinct'.[141] Cowper is one of the few writers consistently recommended by the authors of late-eighteenth-century conduct literature for women, and Hannah More quotes Cowper's address to domestic happiness as the epigraph to her *Strictures*.[142] According to such writers as More and Jane West, Cowper ought to be part of an Englishwoman's constitution; his style and subject matter are particularly suited to the ideal of female domesticity that they advocate. Fanny Price's love of Cowper is in keeping with her modesty, her timidity, her self-abnegation, her struggles with envy and with independence of spirit. The books that Fanny loves have created her mindset and ideals, and so reinforce them for the reader. It is also entirely appropriate that Cowper's presence in the text is very rarely directly mentioned, and largely no more than indirectly felt; as an undercurrent both to Austen's prose and to Fanny's thoughts, it is proper that he should be perceived only as a subtle echo of ladylike reading. Like the ingenuous heroine's blushes, Austen's literary allusions might be seen as the external evidence of the morality and taste beneath the surface of the skin or the text. Like the blush, they are also more equivocal than they seem.

Austen's use of spectral texts is not limited to texts as comforting as Cowper's, and *Mansfield Park* is not a novel that offers unqualified approval of the values Fanny acquires from her reading, as we saw in the previous chapter. The presence of Kotzebue/Inchbald's *Lovers' Vows* also complicates any suggestion that Austen's literary allusions simply reinforce a conservative moral ideology. The play is more intrusive than other spectral texts because it is less ideologically congenial to the dominant narrative consciousness (Fanny's). Where Cowper, Johnson, Macartney, Shakespeare and Crabbe positively reinforce Fanny's ideals, *Lovers' Vows* presents her with an entirely different version of her pupil-mentor bond with Edmund in the shape of the relationship between Amelia and Anhalt, and with shocking alternative modes of thinking about love. *Lovers' Vows* thus creates dissonance rather than resonance in *Mansfield Park*, and in a novel where the narrative voice and the heroine's consciousness are so often one, *Lovers' Vows* creates an uncomfortable distance between Austen's artistic achievement and Fanny's disapproving conscience. This partly explains the weight of critical reference to the play, and the multiple attempts to explicate the relationship between the two texts.[143]

E. M. Butler claimed in 1933 that *Lovers' Vows* plays a crucial structural part in *Mansfield Park*, analysing the similarities in plotting and character development in the two works and contending that *Mansfield Park* translates *Lovers' Vows* into the life of an English country family and reasserts the moral standards subverted by Kotzebue/Inchbald.[144] Dvora Zelicovici extends Butler's argument to suggest that 'Austen chose *Lovers' Vows* for her actors precisely because the play shares the same moral premises and poses the same moral problems as her book'.[145] According to Zelicovici, the failure of the Bertrams is that, unlike the characters in *Lovers' Vows*, they do not learn the right moral lessons. In contrast to E. M. Butler, Zelicovici thus sees *Lovers' Vows* as epitomizing the values that Mansfield Park should teach its occupants, and *Mansfield Park* its readers. Her view that the intertextual structure of the novel is instructive is extremely suggestive. If it is the case that *Lovers' Vows* poses moral questions and demands the learning of moral lessons, then it is equally true that *The Task* requires similar attention. The lessons to be drawn from each text are, however, politically and morally opposed, leaving the reader to make his or her own choice of what to believe.

Brian Wilkie suggests that *Mansfield Park*'s status as a 'problem novel' is rooted in its structure, claiming that the action of the novel takes place in two structural realms: a probing of morality and a sustained examination of Fanny's personal growth.[146] We could, however, conceptualize *Mansfield Park*'s structure as an intertextual conversation between two systems of morality, represented by Kotzebue on the one hand, and Cowper on the other. The 'problem' of the novel could thus be explained by the dissonance created by such a dialogue. We could also interpret the 'problem' of the novel as its disturbing strength: the jostling presence of alternative systems of morality within the same novel forestalls a reader's desire to come to simplistic political or moral conclusions. It is for this reason that critical accounts of *Mansfield Park* that read the novel only in relation either to *Lovers' Vows* or to conservative morality fall short; *Mansfield Park* is a not a showcase for an ideology, but a battleground of value systems, and the battle is over the complex and messy question of how an individual should live.

Mansfield Park is a novel in which readers are usually kept close to Fanny Price's thoughts and feelings, and her ethical judgements influence our way of seeing. In this way, the moral guides that Fanny reads become in a sense moral guides that we have read, comfortable and comforting guides to future conduct. However, the writers she rejects – Kotzebue, Inchbald, Sterne – also haunt *Mansfield Park*'s readers, reminding us of a code of values quite other than Fanny's. Austen's use of Cowper and Crabbe is thus not just a way of demonstrating her reading or knowledge in a ladylike manner, and her use of *Lovers' Vows* cannot be purely understood as a matter of thematic or structural convenience. Although the artistic strategy of spectral texts is grounded in conservative notions of feminine propriety, in *Mansfield Park*, their interplay subversively undermines the very notions of propriety that the novel ostensibly approves. Spectral texts covertly interact with the plot of the novel, allowing alternative modes of thinking into the enclosed world of Mansfield Park, providing a sometimes harmonious, sometimes discordant counterpoint to the main moral melody, and resisting the too-easy conclusion of the last chapters of the novel. Like an objectionable point made by a clever barrister, struck from the record but lodged in the minds of the jurors, the messages of *Mansfield Park*'s spectral texts remain with Austen's readers: ghostly and unsettling voices in our memories.

Games of Ingenuity: The Rules

The directed indirections of Austen's prose style, in which Austen first creates and then subverts a bond of understanding between narrative voice and reader, involve her readers in some complicated interpretative games, all of which demand the recognition of alternative codes of morality or behaviour from those apparently endorsed by the plots of the novels. These games encourage the reader to resist both the consolations of ideology and the comforts of fictional form, by exposing the extent to which narrative authority can be used to deceive as well as to enlighten. In Austen's novels, questions of authority are rarely entirely separate from questions of gender. In *Persuasion*, Anne Elliot tells Captain Harville that she 'will not allow books to prove any thing' because they document the point of view of men, rather than women: 'Men have had every advantage of us in telling their own story'.[147] Similarly, Catherine Morland objects to 'real serious history' because it contains 'nothing that does not vex or weary me [...] the men all so good for nothing, and hardly any women at all'.[148] Narrative authority, we are neatly reminded, historically belongs to men: 'the pen has been in their hands'.[149] In Austen's hands, the pen exposes the ways in which readers, in particular female readers like Catherine Morland, can be 'vexed and wearied' by both ideology and fictional convention, and presents opportunities for resistance through the games in which readers can join with the narrative voice.

Part Two

INTRODUCTION

In the previous chapters, I suggested that Austen's novels provide models of resistance and change for a hypothetical reader, through what William Galperin calls the 'counter-hegemonic practices of reading' she makes available.[1] I also proposed the argument that these practices were grounded in gender-related strategies of indirection. In my argument, the hypothetical reader recognizes the tension between, for example, *Pride and Prejudice*'s realistic social criticism and its final 'aesthetic gratification',[2] or *Mansfield Park*'s apparent conservative moral ideology and its complicated intertextual structure, resisting collusion with the norms of taste that the novels set up. Reading in this way, I have argued, is both strenuous and ludic. For the hypothetical reader, reading, as Johanna M. Smith puts it, is 'not passive consumption' but instead a form of production.[3]

But did Austen's actual historical readers take up the teasing challenges of her prose style? Discussing Richardson's *Clarissa*, Ruth Perry argues that '*Clarissa* got under the skin of women of Richardson's generation because, as with Lady Mary Wortley Montagu, their lives provided the raw materials for his imagination'.[4] *Clarissa*, in other words, represented women readers to themselves. Austen's novels, drawing on and rewriting Richardson, also 'got under the skin' of their readers (and still do). Both troubling and consoling, they, like Richardson's, reflect the experience of intelligent, articulate women in cultural situations unsympathetic to their intelligence and eloquence. Unlike *Clarissa*, Austen's novels provide happy endings for such women, thus holding out the possibility that society can accommodate, even reward, women like Elizabeth Bennet, witty, impertinent and eloquent. Where Clarissa Harlowe's fate is deliberately made 'extraordinary' and 'unusual',[5] that of Austen's heroines is (however ironically) contrived to seem as 'natural' as possible. Unlike Clarissa's, their characters are presented not as extraordinary but as recognisably ordinary, and a number of Austen's first readers and reviewers noticed this immediately. Austen's collection of opinions of *Mansfield Park*, for example, contains Anne Sharpe's view of her characters as 'drawn to the Life – so *very*, *very* natural & just', Fanny Cage's opinion that the characters were 'natural & well supported', Mrs Bramstone's comment that the character of Fanny was 'so very natural', and Lady Gordon's opinion:

> In Miss A–'s works, & especially in M. P. you actually *live* with them [the characters], you fancy yourself one of the family; & the scenes are so exactly descriptive, so perfectly natural, that there is scarcely an Incident or conversation, or a person that you are not inclined to imagine you have at one time or other in your Life been witness to, born a part in, & been acquainted with.[6]

It seems probable that the sense of 'living with' the characters identified by Lady Gordon results from Austen's choice to keep her readers within, or close to, the consciousness of her heroine, thus seeing 'the family' of Mansfield Park primarily through Fanny's eyes. It is also, though, the result of Austen's use of free indirect discourse. Not only do we see and hear Sir Thomas, Lady Bertram, Maria, Julia, Tom, Edmund and Mrs Norris through Fanny's eyes and ears, we also hear their voices through the narrative voice. The omniscient narrator does, of course, sometimes move out of Fanny's consciousness, and speaks in a different voice to comment on the characters and the action, but as we saw in the previous chapter, this voice frequently remains inflected with the characteristic tones and inflections of the Bertram family's own voices. It is no wonder that Lady Gordon felt that she could fancy herself one of the family, and that she had 'been witness to' the scenes depicted in the novel, since Austen's style creates precisely this impression.

It was not only *Mansfield Park* that prompted comments on the realistic mode of Austen's writing. Austen's acquaintance Mrs Guiton thought *Emma* 'too natural to be interesting',[7] and William Gifford, editor of the *Quarterly*, similarly approved of *Pride and Prejudice*'s ordinariness, particularly its avoidance of the more absurd and unrealistic features of the fashionable Gothic romance: 'no dark passages, no secret chambers; […] no drops of blood upon a rusty dagger – things that should now be left to ladies' maids and sentimental washerwomen'.[8] T. H. Lister made the point in 1830 that Austen's characters 'act and talk so exactly like the people whom they [her readers] saw around them every day'.[9]

Many of Richardson's readers strongly resisted Clarissa's fate, begging her creator to let her live. Lady Bradshaigh even wrote an alternative ending, in which Clarissa remains alive to serve as 'Example & Benefit to her fellow creatures'.[10] Austen's heroines, embedded in happy marriage plots, to some extent gave readers of Bradshaigh's persuasion what they had wanted from Richardson: her virtuous heroines do not die, but live on, as 'Example & Benefit' to others. Some of the readers under discussion in the next chapters find in Austen's novels reflections of their own lives, and take comfort in

Austen's 'civilizing social accommodations';[11] but there are also those who resist, refusing to see any relevance to themselves in Austen's novels. Some respond, not to the happy endings of the marriage plots, but to the anarchic energies contained within and hidden by her shapely sentences, and to the problems and difficulties subsumed into, but not resolved by, the novels' ostensibly happy endings. Some readers did (and do) respond to Austen's teasing invitation to exercise 'ingenuity' in their readings of the novels, while others refuse or ignore that invitation. And it is important to stress that many readers either dislike or are completely indifferent to Austen's novels and the majority do not record their responses to them at all. It is salutary, when thinking of such readers, to remember what Lady Anne Romilly had to say about *Emma*: 'I have read both *Emma* and [illegible]. In the first there is so little to remember, and in the last so much one wishes to forget, that I am not inclined to write about them'.[12] Romilly's friend, Maria Edgeworth, did 'write about' *Emma*, in a letter to her half-brother, but hers is a response that reminds us of another kind of reading experience: one in which the reader is simply baffled by the book in hand.

> There was no story in it, except that Miss Emma found that the man whom she designed for Harriet's lover was an admirer of her own—& he was affronted at being refused by Emma & Harriet wore the willow – and smooth, thin water-gruel is according to Emma's father's opinion a very good thing & it is very difficult to make a cook understand what you mean by smooth, thin water-gruel!!'[13]

The focus throughout the chapters that follow is on real readers and the material conditions of their reading experiences. This is therefore not a conventional reception history, as it does not dwell only on critical accounts such as reviews, essays and articles. Instead, these chapters present a history of the ways in which individual readers encounter texts and literary figures. Neither are these chapters a conventional study of literary 'influence', which would trace quotations, allusions or situations from the published writing of one author into the publications of another.[14] The 'posthumous life' of a writer involves different kinds of influence, many of which are not purely literary.[15] Authorial reputation, for example, can affect a reader simultaneously with the content of that author's novels. Cultural stereotypes and societal expectations can exert pressure on readers, as can the physical conditions of the reading experience. It is on these too-often ignored factors that the following chapters concentrate.

Critical accounts of reading Austen have tended to suppose, either implicitly or explicitly, that the novels are written for posterity in some form – a hypothetical reader, an ideal reader, a Bakhtinian *super addressee*, whose perfect understanding of the texts can be taken for granted. The previous chapters make use of a similar kind of theoretical framework, suggesting ways in which Austen's texts encourage a plurality of meanings, and assuming that a reader may be able to read in such a way as to keep all of these meanings concurrently active. The following chapters consider actual, rather than hypothetical, readers, and emphasize the complexities of the actual practice of reading, taking it to be incontestable that any act of reading takes place within particular social, historical and cultural contexts.[16]

It is obviously impossible to trace all of Austen's readers' interactions with her novels, or even to attempt to recreate a truly representative sample (as argued on pages 9–10), and so these chapters present a selection of readers whose responses to Austen's novels are particularly deeply engaged and thus repay careful study. As discussed previously, it could, of course, be argued that this material is self-selecting, as many (indeed most) readers leave no trace of their reading, no record of their engagement (or otherwise) with a text, and those who do are those on whom the text has made an impression, not the many readers like Anne Romilly, for whom what they read does not seem worth recording, or those who do not have the time or leisure to comment on their reading. As Simon Eliot writes, one of the most important caveats to any discussion of records of reading experiences is that 'any reading recorded in an historically recoverable way is, almost by definition, an exceptional recording of an uncharacteristic event by an untypical person'.[17] Those readers who were indifferent to Austen's work, or who did not record their reactions to her writing therefore do not (indeed, cannot) feature in this book, but they should nonetheless be kept in mind as a counterbalance to the powerful reactions that are discussed in Chapters 6 to 9.

Interpreting accounts of reading is problematic, for a number of reasons to do with the nature of reading itself. Readers read different books for different purposes, we read critically or uncritically, we concentrate, or we skim-read. We read because we think we should or because we want to (and often the two are not distinguishable in our minds). We read alone, or with others, with and against the grain, and factors completely unrelated to the texts themselves affect how we feel about what we are reading. Modern readership research reminds us of the multitude of ways people both read and perceive their reading. Researchers are extremely careful to distinguish between ways of reading – 'glanced at', 'looked at', 'flicked through', 'read', 'read carefully' are all categories which demand different types of analysis – and between situations in which readers read: at the hairdresser, on the train, in a bookshop or at a news-stand, at home, in a library and so on.[18] Even with sophisticated interview techniques designed to eliminate the factual errors, or the errors of memory that people make about their own reading, readership research rarely returns hard and fast answers, and the question of how to establish the quality of reading in any given instance is one that remains contested.[19]

Accounts of reading, in other words, may not be reliable: the 'I' of a journal or letter is in many ways no less fictional, no less created, no more 'real' than the 'I' of a poem, or the first-person narrator of a novel. A letter-writer, for example, may communicate different feelings to different correspondents, write deliberately to deceive, or may express him- or herself ambiguously. Letters (particularly between close friends or family members) may, like Austen's, contain in-jokes, interpretation of which depends largely on recognition of tone and context. Journals are vulnerable to being read by unfriendly eyes, and may therefore withhold or doctor the truth, however confessional they might appear.[20] Memoirs and autobiographies, written some years on from the original act of reading, describe the remembrance of that act, not the act itself. Moreover, as Daniel Allington and others point out, the act of writing about reading is regulated by generic conventions which are, though often unrecognized or not analysed, as important as those that govern literary genres.[21]

Difficulties of interpretation are compounded when we deal with accounts from a historical period at a distance from our own. In *The Making of English Reading Audiences, 1790–1832* (1987), Jon Klancher warns of the difficulties of trying to reclaim the answers to the questions 'how did readers understand the texts they read? And how were those texts used?' on the grounds that 'historical evidence offers few and scattered answers'.[22] The answers it does yield are notoriously difficult to interpret. Accounts of reading that resurface from a historical period do not necessarily tell us what the individual reader really thought or felt about certain books or about the practice of reading (although they may); instead they might tell us much about prevailing prescriptions on books, and ideas about reading. Klancher counsels that we should 'resist the ambition to reclaim [...] lost understandings in some consummate act of historical recovery. A certain blank space in cultural memory must not be filled, the space of an otherness that marks an unbridgeable difference between their reading and ours'.[23] William St Clair agrees: 'even if we are willing to regard the written records of individual responses as reliable, as we probably normally should, they too are written texts which were produced by their authors, within the generic conventions of a specific historical time, with implied readers and intended rhetorical effects in mind'.[24] Anecdotal evidence, such as written accounts of individuals' responses to their reading, therefore demands careful handling, but it does have a value of its own. Unlike more strictly empirical data, such as publishing figures, lending library records, and booksellers' receipts, the accounts of reading that form the basis of the following chapters tell us not only what their writers read, but, more interestingly, what they claimed to think about it. Klancher's emphasis on the 'otherness' of historical readings is right, and yet the desire for a better understanding of the readers of the past is not necessarily an attempt to bridge an 'unbridgeable difference' between their reading and ours, nor need it be an attempt to dehistoricize the practice of reading. Rather, an attempt to analyse the reading of previous eras should and does *demand* the recognition of that difference, and should and does shed light on the conditions that created those readings. Research into the ways that readers responded to Jane Austen tells us not only more about the novels themselves, but also about the social and cultural conditions in which her novels were received, and the cultural debates and preoccupations with which they and their readers engaged.

Individual accounts of reading, while they may tell us little about general patterns of behaviour, do tell us at least as much about ways of thinking, or 'mentalities', to use St Clair's term, as statistical evidence. Anecdotal evidence can tell us, for example, as sales and publication records cannot, about books that readers have not necessarily read, but with which they were familiar through the lengthy extracts quoted in the reviews of the nineteenth-century periodical press, or because the work had been repeatedly read aloud to them. Individual accounts of reading can tell us how readers responded to texts, revealing important truths about the emotional or affective aspects of reading. They reveal, as statistics cannot, the multi-faceted nature of the reading experience. And, as Eliot writes, despite all the obstacles involved in the interpretation of anecdotal evidence of this kind, 'however difficult it is to face, it will be the development in the history of reading which will make sense of all the other aspects of the history of the book – or not, if we don't manage to crack it.'[25] It is, of course, dangerous to generalize from the particular. The aim of the following chapters is therefore to concentrate on the individual, to describe and analyse individual reading interactions within their various contexts without endeavouring to construct a singular narrative about reading over the *longue durée*.

By focusing on Austen's historical rather than hypothetical readers, we return to a subject that preoccupied Austen herself. W. H. Auden writes, in 'Letter to Lord Byron' (1937):

> But tell Jane Austen, that is, if you dare,
> How much her novels are beloved down here.
> She wrote them for posterity, she said;
> 'Twas rash, but by posterity she's read.[26]

Auden's suggestion that Austen said she wrote 'for posterity' is slightly misleading, although it is certainly true that 'by posterity she's read'. There is no direct evidence that Austen ever claimed to be writing for posterity; unlike her male Romantic contemporaries – Keats, Shelley and Byron in particular – Austen never explicitly wrote about her desire for a posthumous life of fame.[27] Indeed, Cassandra Austen, her closest confidante, was astonished to find that her sister's novels survived so long into the nineteenth century: 'Is it not remarkable that those Books have risen so much in celebrity after so many years? I think it may be proof that they possess intrinsic merit', she wrote to her niece Anna Lefroy in 1844.[28] There is, of course, both a gendered and a generic implication here. Where male poets such as Byron could make grandiose claims about their own future poetic fame – 'My epitaph shall be, my name alone', wrote Byron in 1809, for example – because they knew that they were participating in a high-culture tradition, the female novelist could not take the future of the genre for granted, and she was also hindered by the conventions that demanded female modesty.[29] Austen certainly wrote for publication – her continuing resolve in the face of the refusal of 'First Impressions' and Crosby's dilatoriness over *Susan* is proof enough of her determination to have her books published and read – but publication does not guarantee readerships in posterity. In fact, as we have seen, Austen first wrote for her family and her intimate friends, in the form of the juvenilia. The six novels, including those written once Austen was a published author, also bear the traces of having been written for a small and close circle of friends. Lisa Lewis correctly suggests that Austen's jokes are 'like a secret smile between sisters or old friends',[30] and I would argue that Austen's novels have the quality of 'confidential' writing, to use Donald Reiman's helpful terminology.[31]

Austen may indeed privately have hoped that her novels would survive the test of time, but what we can say for certain is that she was extremely interested in the novels' effects on the readership of her own time. On 22 November 1814, she enjoined her niece Anna to 'make everybody at Hendon admire Mansfield Park';[32] she collected as many of her readers' opinions as she could, and she frequently reported comments about her novels back to Cassandra. Austen, as she wrote to James Stanier Clarke in December of 1815, was 'very strongly haunted' by the idea that her readers would dislike her works.[33] Even when dismissing the 'dull elves' for whom she did *not* write, her readers were on Austen's mind.

The opinions of *Mansfield Park* and *Emma* collected by Jane Austen are the first recorded responses to her novels, and they usefully document not only what her earliest readers made of Jane Austen's works, but also the priorities and preconceptions about literature in the reading community of which Jane Austen was herself a part. It is possible to perceive in these early readers' responses many of the themes that were to emerge in critical writing about the novels over the course of the nineteenth century. We have already seen, for example, the emphasis placed on the question of whether or not the events and characters in the novels were 'natural', or 'unnatural' – a focus which suggests that these early readers recognized both the importance and the novelty of Austen's insistence on verisimilitude in fiction. As we see in the next chapters, Austen's fidelity to detail and rejection of excess would also be noted, commented on and discussed in successive readers' responses to her work, and the extent to which verisimilitude alone could qualify an author as a high artist was a question that exercised both her critics and her ordinary readers, from the time of the first publication of the novels onwards. *The Champion*'s 1816 review of *Emma* provides a good example of the terms in which this sort of debate began to be formulated in the early years of the nineteenth century:

> The imitative arts – and novel-writing is the art of imitating in a narrative the scenes of life – are productive of two distinct gratifications: – one, arising from the intrinsic beauty of grandeur of the objects represented, and the other, from the skill of the artist, shown in representing objects of an ordinary, and at the same time so familiar a nature, as to invite an easy comparison between the prototype and the imitation, and to draw the intellectual faculties into a pleasing criticism on the merits of his imitative efforts. The latter, rather than the former, is the principal attraction which we hold out to our readers in recommending to them the volumes before us [...] She presents nature and society in very unornamented hues; and yet, so strong is the force of nature, that we will venture to say, few can take up her work without finding a rational pleasure in the recognitions which cannot fail to flash upon them of the modes of thinking and feeling which experience every day presents in real life.[34]

Austen's ability to 'give fiction the perfect appearance of reality', as Richard Whately put it in 1821, would become the cornerstone of discussions and defences of her art in the nineteenth century and beyond,[35] and we will see the fullest elaboration of this debate in the epistolary conversation between Mary Russell Mitford and Elizabeth Barrett Browning, discussed in Chapter 7.

Austen's earliest readers also seem to have been preoccupied with deciding which of Austen's works or characters they thought superior to the others. Austen frequently recorded such opinions as Mrs Lefroy's, on *Emma*: 'Mrs. Lefroy – preferred it to M P – but liked M P. the least of all'.[36] Mrs Dickson, who 'bought *Mansfield Park*' (though history does not relate whether she was one of those encouraged to do so by Anna at Hendon), thought it 'not equal to P & P',[37] and hers appears to have been a relatively common response. Mrs Dickson also 'did not much like' *Emma*, thinking it '*very* inferior to P. & P.'[38] Mrs Lutley Sclater liked *Emma* 'very much', thinking it 'better than M P',[39] while Miss Murden thought *Emma* 'certainly inferior to all the others'.[40]

This comparative mode of criticism exemplified here was also popular in (and possibly learned from) critical writing, which frequently attempted to rank or place writers and works within the emerging canon of British literature.

Austen's family and friends were alive, it seems, to their role as critics of the linguistic and literary quality of the novels, and commented on the technical features of novel-writing, such as characterization, expression, narrative structure, dialogue, and the moral or educational value of the works. The effectiveness of Austen's characterization was particularly commended by these readers, as seen in the discussion of how 'natural' the characters are, as well as in such comments on *Mansfield Park* and *Emma* as 'excellent delineation of character' (Lady Robert Kerr, on *Mansfield Park*), 'characters like all the others admirably well drawn & supported' (Anna Lefroy, on *Emma*), 'the Characters are natural & well supported' (Frank Austen, on *Mansfield Park*) and 'the best-drawn character in the book' (Henry Sanford, on *Emma*'s Mrs Elton),[41] and also by the critics. Of *Sense and Sensiblity*, the *British Critic*'s reviewer remarked that 'the characters are happily delineated and admirably sustained'[42] and that the characters of *Pride and Prejudice* were 'remarkably well drawn and supported'.[43] The phrases 'well drawn' and 'well supported' (sometimes in combination) appear no fewer than seven times in the collection of opinions, suggesting that these were qualities that Austen's readers knew that they should be looking for. Readers also remarked on the quality of Jane Austen's style and expression. Fanny Cage and Lady Robert Kerr commented on the language of *Mansfield Park*, recording diametrically opposed opinions: 'language poor' (Fanny Cage), 'Elegant Language' (Lady Kerr).[44] Mr and Mrs James Austen found *Emma*'s 'language different from the others; not so easily read', though Miss Bigg thought the opposite: 'Language superior to the others'.[45] There is clearly a class element to Mrs Pole's commentary on Austen's language: 'everything is told [...] in a manner which clearly evinces the Writer to *belong* to the Society whose Manners she so ably delineates'.[46] Such comments suggest that Austen's readers had a keen ear for language and dialogue, and that they thought it important to get it right. Anna Lefroy, herself a fledgling novelist, took note of the role of dialogue in *Emma*, commenting that she 'thought one or two of the conversations too long'.[47] Frank Austen too noticed dialogue, writing of *Mansfield Park* that 'many of the Dialogues' were 'excellent'.[48] These members of Austen's family were in good company; in his review of *Emma*, Walter Scott noted that in his view, the 'merit' of the author lay in 'a narrative conducted with much neatness and point, and a quiet yet comic dialogue, in which the characters of the speakers evolve themselves with dramatic effect'.[49]

Narrative structure was also noticed, not only by Austen's publisher, Egerton, whose job it was to evaluate the quality of novels, and who thought *Mansfield Park* praiseworthy for being 'so equal a Composition',[50] but by other, less professional, readers. Mr J. Plumptre, for example remarked of *Mansfield Park*'s plot that 'the plot is so well contrived'. Jane Austen's brother Charles, on the other hand, 'thought it wanted Incident'.[51] The plot-related criticism of lack of incident was repeated by Benjamin Lefroy in relation to *Emma*.[52] Austen's early readers, it seems, were not only literary, but cultural critics. Taking seriously her role as a moral and cultural arbiter, Lady Kerr commented on *Mansfield Park*'s 'pure morality' and 'sound sense', calling *Mansfield Park* 'a most desirable as well as useful work'.[53] Miss Sharpe thought the same: 'of its good sense & moral Tendency there can be no doubt'.[54] Mrs Cage echoed these comments, writing of *Emma* that 'no one writes such good sense & so very comfortable'.[55] In their focus on the good sense and morality of the works, they echoed the tone and content of the reviewing culture of their era – the first review of an Austen novel, the *Critical Review*'s review of *Sense and Sensibility*, for example, commented on the 'excellent lesson which it holds up to view', as well as the 'useful moral which may be derived from its perusal', calling these 'essential requisites' of a work of literature.[56] Successive critics would follow this line of argument, and readers would respond both positively and negatively to their perceptions of Austen as a moral writer, as we see in the following chapters.

Early readers did not, however, only see the serious 'beauties' and 'morality' of Austen's novels. Many remarked on the comedy of the writing. Anna Lefroy was 'delighted' with 'all the humourous [sic] parts' of *Mansfield Park*.[57] Mary Cooke 'enjoyed Mr Rushworth's folly', and Mr Plumptre found that 'Mrs Norris amused me particularly'.[58] 'The family at Upton Gray' were 'all very much amused' with *Emma*, and Mrs Cage 'was nearly killed with those precious treasures!' (Harriet Smith's relics of Mr Elton), thinking them 'Unique, & really more fun than I can express'.[59] Early critics, too, noted the 'great spirit' of *Pride and Prejudice*,[60] 'the strain of genuine natural humour' and 'amusing' qualities of *Emma*,[61] and the 'delicate humour' of *Northanger Abbey* and *Persuasion*.[62]

In addition to what we might call technical critiques, there is also a more personal element to Austen's friends' and family members' comments, particularly to those on character. Many readers were keen to pick their favourite characters. Miss Bates appears to have been surprisingly popular, while Fanny Price divided readers, just as she does now. Miss Bates was preferred by Jane Austen's niece, Anna (her other favourites were Mr Knightley and Mrs Elton).[63] Mrs Cage also liked Miss Bates, calling her 'incomparable',[64] Henry Sanford was 'delighted with Miss Bates,' while 'Miss Bates [was] a great favourite with Mrs. Beaufoy', of Upton Gray.[65] More lukewarm praise was bestowed by Miss Bigg, who 'liked Miss Bates much better than at first' on a second reading of *Emma*, and Anna's husband, Benjamin Lefroy, who found 'Miss Bates excellent, but rather too much of her'.[66] Turning to Fanny Price,

Austen's brother Frank thought her 'a delightful Character', and her niece, Fanny Knight, was 'delighted with Fanny'.[67] Jane Austen's other adult niece, Anna, on the other hand, 'could not bear Fanny', and Jane Austen's own mother 'thought Fanny insipid'.[68] Critical writing of this period also focuses heavily on character, perhaps because, as the reviewer for the *New Review* of 1813 suggests, it was thought necessary to understand the characters 'for the better comprehension of the story',[69] but also because the reviewers (like Austen's acquaintances Lady Gordon and Mrs Pole), wished to comment on how recognizably true-to-life these characters appeared:

> The singular merit of her writing is, that we could conceive, without the slightest strain of imagination, any one of her fictions to be realized in any town or village in England, (for it is only English manners that she paints,) that we think we are reading the history of people whom we have seen thousands of times, and that with all this perfect commonness, both of incident and character, perhaps not one of her characters is to be found in any other book.[70]

Perhaps because they felt they were indeed 'reading the history of people whom we have seen thousands of times', many early readers emphasized their empathetic involvement with the characters, often in the form of 'liking' or 'disliking' a particular character, as when Fanny Knight remarked that she 'should like J[ane] F[airfax] – if she knew more of her'.[71] Miss Bigg similarly 'expressed herself as liking all the people of Highbury in general, except Harriet Smith – but cd. not help thinking *her* too silly in her loves'.[72] Mr Knightley, according to Austen's nephew James Edward, was 'liked by everybody'.[73] Many of these readers also write about the characters as if they were real people, as when Mary Cooke thought that Fanny Price 'ought to have been more determined on overcoming her own feelings, when she saw Edmund's attachment to Miss Crawford.'[74] Mr and Mrs Leigh Perrot, Jane Austen's uncle and aunt, 'pitied Jane Fairfax and thought Frank Churchill better treated than he deserved.'[75] Fanny Knight recorded a less sympathetic emotional response: she 'could not bear Emma herself', while Miss Sharp on the other hand was 'pleased with the Heroine' but 'dissatisfied with Jane Fairfax'.[76] Miss Lloyd was 'delighted with Fanny', but 'hated Mrs Norris'.[77] Personal responses to characters also sometimes took the form of recognizing either oneself or acquaintances in the characters. Miss Isabella Herries, for example, was 'convinced that I [Austen] had meant Mrs. & Miss Bates for some acquaintance of theirs – People whom I never heard of before.'[78] Mrs Dickson 'liked [*Emma*] the less, from their being a Mr. and Mrs. Dixon in it.'[79] And, with what we hope is impressive self-knowledge, though it might perhaps be its very opposite, Mrs Bramstone 'thought Lady Bertram like herself'.⁸⁰ Such responses to the works remind us of the many ways in which readers may respond to texts simultaneously, mixing seemingly more 'objective' criticism of style, language or execution with intensely personal reactions to characters and works.

The rhetoric of friendship and affection, liking and disliking, which permeates so many of the responses to Austen's characters and novels in these early responses, is discussed in detail in the following chapters of this volume. In Mary Ann O'Farrell's 'Jane Austen's Friendship' (2000), O' Farell attempts to think through 'what is involved in construing authorship and readership as friendly activities'.⁸¹ She suggests that 'talk of friendship often idealizes or reduces that complex and intense relation'.⁸² While this is no doubt in general true, the accounts of reading figured as friendship explored in the following chapters seem to me on the contrary to provide ample evidence of both the complexity and the intensity of readers' relationships with Jane Austen and her works. In so doing, they help to expand our notions of both reading and authorial 'influence'.

Chapter 4
AUSTEN'S READERS: CONTEXTS I

Before turning to consider individual readers in detail, it is important to sketch out some of the significant contexts within which readers encountered Austen's works. As Anthony Mandal has recently brilliantly demonstrated, placing Austen's novels within the context of the late eighteenth and early nineteenth-century publishing trade allows us to better understand both her novels and their relationship to the popular fiction of her period.[1] Here, we will deal first with the material qualities of the books in which the works were found, since these can play an important part in influencing readers. When Charlotte Brontë first came across *Pride and Prejudice* in late 1847, she wrote to G. H. Lewes of the 'accurate daguerrotyped portrait of a common-place face' that she found in it.[2] Most critics take this to be a metaphorical description, but as Brian Southam points out, '"commonplace" engraved portraits of Elizabeth Bennet face the reader on the title-pages of Bentley's 1833 edition of *Pride and Prejudice*'.[3] Were Brontë's responses to reading Austen coloured by the kinds of illustrations she encountered in the novel? Was she, consciously or unconsciously, influenced by them? Without knowing which edition Brontë was reading, it would be impossible to know the extent to which Charlotte Brontë's impressions of Austen's work – 'an accurate daguerreotyped portrait of a common-place face; a carefully fenced, highly cultivated garden, with neat borders and delicate flowers; but no glance of a bright, vivid physiognomy, no open country, no fresh air, no blue hill, no bonny beck [...] elegant but confined houses' – represent descriptions of actual illustrations, metaphorical descriptions of Austen's writing, or a combination of the two.[4] Given the editions on the market in 1847, it is most likely that Brontë was reading *Pride and Prejudice* in the Bentley's Standard Novels edition, reprinted many times between 1833 and 1869, but there are three other possibilities (H. G. Clarke's two-volume 1844 edition, closely printed in tiny type, one of Thomas Egerton's three original editions of 1813–17, or the American 1838 edition by Carey, Lea and Blanchard of Philadelphia). Only Bentley's edition was illustrated.

If it was Bentley's edition that Brontë read (as seems probable given the relative sizes and prices of the editions on the market),[5] she was not alone in finding the illustrations 'common-place'. Thomas Babington Macaulay was similarly unimpressed by the frontispiece and title page of Bentley's 1833 edition of *Persuasion* and *Northanger Abbey*:

> The publisher of the last volume of poor Miss Austin [*sic*] has succeeded in procuring two pictures decidedly worse than the worst that I ever saw before. Get a sight of the Book next time you go to a circulating library at Liverpool; and tell me whether Henry Tilney be not the most offensive Varmint man that you ever saw. The artist must have read the book carelessly and must have confounded the adorable young parson with John Thorp [*sic*]. As to Miss Anne, sitting under a hedge, her appearance at once vindicates all Captain Wentworth's doubts as to her identity with the pretty girl whom he had known, and renders the final triumph of his constancy so admirable as to be almost incredible.[6]

He also disliked the images in Bentley's *Pride and Prejudice*: 'Pride and Prejudice is out. I bought it yesterday. The pictures are worse than ever.'[7] Macaulay was disappointed to find that the illustrations did not live up to the quality of the writing, but there is also a sense in these letters that the pictures do not represent the way he imagined the characters. Throughout Macaulay's private letters, his intimate knowledge of Austen's novels is plain; he refers knowledgeably and allusively to minor characters, he challenges his correspondents to identify quotations and catchphrases, and he aptly matches Austenian allusions to relevant situations in his own life. Macaulay had read Austen's novels in their un-illustrated form (i.e. in the Egerton and Murray editions) before encountering them in Bentley's edition, and it is thus the disjunction between his own mental pictures of characters and situations and their physical pictorial representation in this edition which prompts his comments. Macaulay's is, of course, not an unusual response. Austen herself found it hard to find a picture of Elizabeth Bennet when she went looking for one in an exhibition of portraits in London, and in our own time, viewers of the film and television adaptations of the novels very often comment on the fact that the actors playing Austen's characters do not look as they should.

Kathryn Sutherland has recently suggested that the experiences of reading Austen by generations of readers are affected by stylistic choices made first by Austen's early publishers (or, possibly, the printers who set her works), and then by generations of editors, who tidied up her punctuation and thus polished her style.[8] Sutherland's work suggests further fruitful avenues of enquiry for the historian of reading, not least because so many different factors affect the reading experience of a novel, or indeed, any other work of writing. Readers respond to the kinds of textual choices about punctuation outlined by Sutherland, but in addition to these, they also respond to the materiality of the book itself, commenting on the quality of the paper, binding, font, type and edition size. They may remark on the capabilities of the translator (if relevant) or editor, the attractiveness, or appropriateness of the illustrations, the financial value of the book, or indeed the value it represents for money. If a new technology of production is in use (linotype, stereotype, print on demand, for example), readers may record their responses to it, or if reading manuscript material, they frequently notice the legibility or appearance of the hand.

Recent work in the history of reading reminds us of the variety of different features that make up the reading experience. Simon Eliot persuasively makes the case for the importance of different kinds of lighting in defining the Victorians' reading experiences, and insists on the relevance of cost.[9] Paul Dobraszczyk, Mike Esbester and Adrian Bingham remind us of the role of layout in influencing particular habits of reading.[10] Ruth Clayton Windscheffel describes the 'rhythms of reading' that dictated Gladstone's reading practices.[11] Mark Towsey points to the pressures and societal expectations that can govern reading communities.[12] Robert Darnton, Andrew Hobbs and Stephen Colclough separately describe the ways in which physical place affects readers' expectations and their experiences of text,[13] and Jan Fergus helpfully foregrounds the place of social class in influencing readers' access to and choices of textual matter.[14] Thomas Wright, in particular, reminds us of material conditions in his account of the insistent physicality of Oscar Wilde's relationship with his books.[15] A survey of recorded accounts of reading experiences between 1450 and 1945 will reveal the extent to which readers do remark on material issues.[16] Given the frequency and extent of historical readers' comments on these things, we must extrapolate from this evidence the assumption that at least some, and very probably most, of Austen's readers were either consciously or unconsciously affected by the material aspects of the books they read, even when they do not explicitly comment on these issues.

In his autobiographical account, *Solo Trumpet: Some memories of Socialist agitation and propaganda* (1953) Thomas Jackson, the son of a master craftsman, remembered reading the 'huge Family Bible' of his childhood in the 1880s. He continues:

> That Bible, with its illustrations by Gustave Doré and Felix Philipotteaux, was a joy and solace for years. Especially the battle-pictures and those of storm and wreck. There was one of Joshua's army storming a hill fortress – with the great iron-studded door crashing down before the onrush of mighty men with huge-headed axes – that never failed to thrill.[17]

Evidently, the Bible's illustrations made a far stronger impression on the young Jackson than its text; nonetheless he also remembered its 'fine fat type' as well as its brass binding. Jackson also noted the physical qualities of other books that he encountered:

> I happened upon some fat volumes of Campbell's "British Poets", the complete works of from four to eight poets in each volume which cost me 6d. apiece. They had shabby worn leather bindings, and the type was on the small side and closely set. But I ploughed through them, doggedly, as if reading for a bet, or an imposed task.[18]

Again, it is the books' physical appearance – their width, their shabby bindings and small, closely set type – along with their price which make a greater impression on their reader than the contents, which he 'ploughed through' with 'little sense, and a dwindling understanding'.[19] Thomas Jackson worked as a reading boy at a printer's workshop, which may partly explain his interest in type and physical appearance, but many readers with no such professional interest also remark on the physical features of the books that they are reading. A woman surveyed by the Mass Observation project in 1942, for example, told the recorder that she chose her books by the length of the book, and the size of its type. She also comments unfavourably on the wartime practice of issuing long books in single volumes:

> As I'm a quick reader, naturally I choose fairly thick books of average size with medium print. Never the large type. I like a substantial book, not one that I can finish quickly. On the other hand I don't like books of the size of *Gone with the Wind* or *Anthony Adverse*, some 900 pages. Either of these books should have been issued in two volumes.[20]

The prolific author V. S. Pritchett, too, noticed type size, and was offended, both by Marie Corelli's political opinions, and by the patronisingly easy words allied to the 'large type' in which her collection of newspaper articles, *Free Opinions*, was set:

> I moved to Marie Corelli and there I found a book of newspaper articles called 'Free Opinions'. The type was large. The words were easy, rather contemptibly so. I read and then stopped in anger. Marie Corelli had insulted me. She was against popular education, against schools, against Public libraries and said that common people like us made the books dirty because we never washed, and that we infected them with disease.[21]

Authors are perhaps particularly sensitive to type. Robert Louis Stevenson described himself as a 'gourmet in type', preferring the *Portfolio* to the *Saturday*

Review on the grounds that 'the P[ortfolio]. is so nicely printed'.[22] Arnold Bennett wrote of the *Adelphi* that 'the type is entirely without distinction'.[23] Vera Brittain noticed the 'closely-typed pages' of St John Ervine's biography of General Booth, *God's Soldier*,[24] while Dorothy Wordsworth described Thomas Clarkson's *Portraiture of Quakerism* as 'a very well-looking Book, with enough of stuff in each page, not too large margins, and a good type'.[25] 'What an admirable and clear type this most readable book is printed in!', enthused George Otto Trevelyan, in a marginal note to his copy of Frances Trollope's *The Ward of Thorpe-Combe*, dated 'June 18, 1928'.[26] Trevelyan was clearly even more interested in the type of his books than most authors. Three years earlier, he had noted the difference between his copy of Herodotus, and the 'fine, clear legible type' of his Thucydides,[27] and in the biography of his uncle, Thomas Babington Macaulay, Trevelyan was at pains to impress upon his readers the physical attributes of Macaulay's copy of Plato, and how these struck a reader. The 'ponderous folio, sixteen inches long by ten broad' was 'published in Frankfurt in 1602', and contained 'nearly fourteen hundred closely-printed pages of antique Greek type [...] The Latin translation by Marsilius Ficinus, arranged in parallel columns by the side of the original text, presents an aspect of positively revolting dullness.'[28] There is no doubt that Trevelyan was correct in his assumptions: poor type and layout certainly can put a reader off the work in hand. Indeed, as Claire Harman points out, Mary Augusta Austen-Leigh accounted for 'the slow growth of Austen's fame in the 1830s, 40s and 50s' by 'blaming the smallness of the print used in [Bentley's] Standard Novels series, "ill-suited to any but young and strong eyes"'.[29]

Variations in the size or colour of lettering can, of course, also affect the reading experience, as the scribes of medieval manuscripts, and the printers of sixteenth-century books of hours, books of days and prayer books knew well. For their often semi-literate readerships, these books provided visual cues to help the user follow along while someone else read aloud.[30] An entry in Ruskin's diary from 13 August 1872 nicely illuminates the way in which such variations can affect the reading experience, even of the competent and fluent reader: 'Took up Renan's "St Paul" as I was dressing, and read a little. A piece of epistle in smaller type caught my eye as I was closing the book: "Graces a Dieu pour son ineffable don"'.[31] Here, the smaller type catches the eye, owing to its difference from the rest of the book.

Bindings, too, often come in for remark, and sometimes even dictate a person's choice of book, as this war-time reader discloses:

> Most of the books I choose from the free library are for the wife. I cast my eye over the books vaguely searching for likely looking binding. If one catches my eye, such as a new looking book, I glance at the title and author. If that looks

promising, I take the book out and scan the synopsis, if there is one, and then scan the first page, before flicking over the pages and reading snatches of the dialogue. If there seems to be plenty of action, I choose the book. I avoid books about the present or last war.[32]

Robert Southey, hunting in Dr Williams's Library (then in Redcross Street) for information about Joan of Arc in 1797 also found that the state of a book's binding could be a clue to its contents:

> A hackney coach horse turned into a field of grass falls not more eagerly to a breakfast which lasts the whole day, than I attacked the old folios so respectably covered with dust. I begin to like dirty rotten binding, & whenever I get among books pass by the gilt coxcombs & yet disturb the spiders.[33]

Readers comment both admiringly and disparagingly on the binding of books that they see. Katherine Mansfield, visiting Mudie's Library in January 1904, 'had some peeps into most lovely books, & the bindings were exquisite'.[34] Vita Sackville West was delighted by the 'lovely leather binding' of the copy of *Orlando* sent to her by Virginia Woolf, in 1928.[35] Ruskin thought Elizabeth Barrett Browning's poems deserved a 'golden binding',[36] while Arnold Bennett thought so highly of the binding of the copy of *Candide*, given to him by Mr Bagguley, a book-binder in Newcastle-under-Lyme, that he wrote to congratulate the craftsman on his 'extraordinary art'.[37] Conversely, Leonard Woolf disliked Bernard Dutton's 'hundreds of books in horrible print & binding', although this did not stop him reading them.[38] And Samuel Pepys deliberately bought his copy of Michel Millot's pornographic *L'Ecole des Filles* 'in plain binding (avoiding the buying of it better bound) because I resolve, as soon as I have read it, to burn it, that it may not stand in the list of books, nor among them, to disgrace them if it should be found'.[39]

Readers are also, frequently, aware of the importance of finding or reading a particular edition or translation. Norman Nicholson, indeed, implies that reading the wrong edition could cause a reader to dislike a writer for the rest of his life: 'We had met Dickens before, but only "The Old Curiosity Shop" and "The Chimes", both of which, in their mean little school editions, were enough to sour a boy against the novels for the rest of his life'.[40] Of course, an elegant or luxurious edition does not necessarily make a work more comprehensible, though it might make the reading experience marginally more enjoyable. Thomas Carter first read Milton's *Paradise Lost* 'in a thick volume with engravings and copious notes, probably a copy of Bishop Newton's edition of that noble poem.' He found it, however, 'little better than "a sealed book". Its versification puzzled me, while the loftiness of its subjects confused my understanding'.[41] On the other hand, Harriet Martineau claimed to have met with the same work at the age of seven in an ugly, 'plain, clumsy, calf-bound volume', but immediately to have thrilled to the poetry, feeling that 'my mental destiny was fixed for the next seven years'.[42] In fact, readers often comment on the disjunction between a book's physical appearance and their response to the text within, as when the labourer Thomas Burt recorded reading Shakespeare for the first time in the 1860s:

> I now read for the first time 'The Tempest', 'Measure for Measure', 'Love's Labour's Lost', and many other of Shakespeare's comedies, besides the supreme tragedies, among [them] the greatest creations of the human intellect, 'Hamlet', 'Macbeth', 'Othello' and 'Lear'. From no 'edition de luxe' did I read. The plays were published by Dick, cost me one penny each, a sum well suited to my means. No matter that the price was small and the paper poor; no matter that there were neither theatre nor stage, neither actors or orchestra. All the more scope was given to fancy and imagination.[43]

It is clear from the surviving historical evidence that readers do respond (and always have responded) to the material features of the books they encounter, as well as the non-material qualities of the texts that they read.[44]

A proper understanding of the experiences of Austen's historical readers as they encountered her works therefore demands a certain degree of knowledge about the physical attributes of the books in which her works appeared. Because it is rare (though not unknown) for readers to name the particular editions of Austen's works that they have read, it is usually necessary to hypothesize, based on the editions available at different times, and any other available evidence. It is, however, often possible to generalize about the *kind* of book being read, if not the precise edition, impression or copy.[45] To this end, what follows is a very brief description of the attributes and availability of the major editions of Austen's works from 1811 to 1945.

Major Editions of Austen's Novels, 1811–1945

Early editions

Austen's first three novels, *Sense and Sensibility*, *Pride and Prejudice* and *Mansfield Park* were all published anonymously by Thomas Egerton, in 1811, 1813 and 1814 respectively. Two editions of *Sense and Sensibility*, three of *Pride and Prejudice* and one of *Mansfield Park* were published by Egerton. All were published in three duodecimo volumes. The type was Caslon Pica roman – a fairly standard choice – and was well spaced, with 23 to 29 lines per page on average, and plenty of spacing around the text. There were no illustrations. The works appear to have been bound in ordinary boards of various colours, although of course those copies sold to collectors and some private libraries were often rebound. These features were absolutely typical of the early nineteenth-century novel. Simon Eliot writes: 'Early nineteenth-century novels were often published in two, three, or more volumes; commonly in duodecimo size – smaller than most modern octavo novels. The type would usually be large with generous spacing between the lines and wide margins [...] most novels would have been issued in temporary bindings of grey cardboard.'[46] Egerton was a moderately successful publisher, whose productions were popular with the proprietors of circulating libraries, and readers encountering any of Austen's novels in Egerton's editions would have seen little to differentiate them from any other novels by an unknown but respectable writer.

The second edition of *Mansfield Park* was published not by Egerton, but by John Murray, in 1816 as '*Mansfield Park*: a Novel in three volumes by the author of "Pride and Prejudice"'. John Murray was a more influential publisher than Egerton, with a stable of authors including the wildly successful Lord Byron and Sir Walter Scott, and John Murray II himself was a considerably more flamboyant character than Egerton. Austen's decision to change publishers was a sign both of her own growing confidence as an author, and of the success of her first three novels. It would also have suggested to her readers that they were reading a more fashionable novelist than those published by Egerton. The second edition of *Mansfield Park* does not, however, differ substantially, visually, from the first. The type is the same, the layout is almost identical, and the binding was again in ordinary boards. The text is, however, different – Austen had revised the first edition and changed a number of technical details as well as making minor changes of spelling and punctuation. Although the second edition of *Mansfield Park* did not sell well, Austen's choice of Murray as a publisher was a shrewd commercial decision, as the success of *Emma* testifies.

Emma was also published by John Murray in December 1815 (though dated 1816), and was the last of Austen's works to be published before her death. It was published as '*Emma*: a Novel in Three Volumes by the Author of "Pride and Prejudice", &c, &c.', and shares the same visual features as the second edition of *Mansfield Park*. Austen's choice of John Murray as her new publisher was vindicated by the fact that Murray asked Sir Walter Scott (another Murray author) to review it in the *Quarterly Review* (a Murray publication, notorious for 'puffing' Murray's authors). Murray suggested a group review of all of Austen's novels, mentioning *Pride and Prejudice* in particular as worthy of note.[47] Given that he also advertised *Pride and Prejudice* (but none of Austen's other novels, which are relegated to an '&c&c'), on the title page of *Emma*, it seems likely that Murray recognized that this was the work that had made Austen popular, and thus would help to sell her other works. Readers who read *Emma* and *Mansfield Park* in the Murray editions were being subtly encouraged to think of the works as being like *Pride and Prejudice*. The frequency with which Austen's early readers directly compare the works to each other may thus be in part attributable to this marketing decision. *Emma* also appeared in a very small American edition by Mathew Carey of Philadelphia in 1816. This was similar to the English edition although its type was different (Long Primer as opposed to Caslon) and the spacing was less generous (an average of 38 or 39 lines per page instead of the average 25 or so of the English edition).

Austen's first four novels were published anonymously, and a certain amount of speculation about their authorship can be found in the early readers' responses to these works. Annabella Milbanke (the future wife of Lord Byron) 'wish[ed] much to know who is the author or *ess* as I am told'.[48] Sarah Harriet Burney speculated that *Pride and Prejudice* was by 'Mrs Dorset' [Catherine Anne Turner Dorset]: 'Do, I entreat, tell me by whom it is written; and tell me, if your health will allow you, *soon*. I die to know. Some say it is by Mrs Dorset...'[49] This rumour was clearly current; Margaret Mackenzie wrote to her brother that 'it is said to be by Mrs. Dorset, the renowned authoress of *The Peacock at Home*'.[50] Lady Boringdon was also 'suspected of having written the two novels: "Pride and Prejudice" and "Sense and Sensibility"'.[51] *Northanger Abbey* and *Persuasion*, however, published in four volumes by John Murray, visually similar to the previous works, and brought out the winter after Austen's death in July of 1817, carried Henry's 'Biographical Notice' of the author, and identified Jane Austen as the author of these and the previous novels, which put an end to the speculation about their authorship. Henry's 'Biographical Notice' also gave readers an image of the author – gentle, modest, family-orientated and amateur – which was to prove extremely durable and influential.[52]

Since those described above were the only editions of Austen's novels in existence between 1811 and 1832, it can be assumed that British readers encountering her works in this period read them in the relatively elegant Egerton and Murray editions, although it is also possible that some readers became familiar with snippets of her novels through extracts in the periodical press, given that reviews and articles of this period tended to quote fairly extensively from the work under review.[53] A very small number of British readers might have encountered the American edition of *Emma*, though this seems relatively unlikely, because of the small size of the edition.[54] Austen's books were advertised for sale at prices ranging from 15*s* (*Sense and Sensibility*) to £1.4*s* (*Northanger Abbey* and *Persuasion*). Given that an average annual wage for an unskilled labourer in 1815 was about £45, that of a teacher approximately £50, and a skilled printer approximately £80,[55] it is clear that the Murray and

Egerton editions would only have been easily affordable by members of the gentry and aristocracy. To put these figures in context, the purchase of *Sense and Sensibility* for an unskilled labourer of this period would have represented roughly a week's wages. Members of the working classes and the 'middling sort' who wished to read Austen's novels did have other means of gaining access to print, but regrettably such readers leave little trace in the historical record. The recorded responses of Austen's early readership thus show a substantial bias towards the gentry and aristocracy, although it is probable that a far wider readership, who encountered the novels in circulating, subscription and association libraries, in the collections of their employers, or as loans from the private libraries of the aristocracy, also read the Egerton and Murray editions.[56]

Bentley's Standard Novels series

In 1832, Richard Bentley bought the copyrights of all Jane Austen's novels, which he issued as five volumes (*Persuasion* and *Northanger Abbey* were published together in one volume) in his 'Standard Novels' series. These were small, closely printed, cloth-bound books, originally available for purchase separately, but, from October 1833, also as a collected edition. The individual volumes cost 6*s*, while the collected edition was priced at 30*s* for the five volumes. These editions were frequently reprinted and reissued until 1869, and were, as Gilson points out, the market leaders between 1833 and 1870.[57] In 1866, the latest reprint of the collected edition still cost 30*s*, later reduced to 21*s*.[58]

The vast majority of Austen's readers during this period were therefore most likely to have encountered her work in Bentley's edition, and to have seen the illustrations commented on by Lord Macaulay and Charlotte Brontë. Prices of books relative to average earnings dropped steadily over the course of the nineteenth century, thus making the novels in Bentley's Standard Novels series available to a wider range of readers by the end of the century than they had been at the beginning. They were certainly affordable to professional men in the mid-century: Charles Dickens bought a complete set in April 1837, making use of an author's discount,[59] and, despite his dislike of the illustrations, Macaulay bought all Austen's novels in Bentley's edition in 1833.[60] Lest we should imagine that Bentley's edition suddenly made Austen available to the working classes, however, Simon Eliot's detailed analysis of book prices in the nineteenth century reveals that book-buying remained the preserve of the aristocracy and the middle classes until the beginning of the twentieth century and even beyond: 'Prices that British book historians tend to regard as cheap – 2*s*, 3*s* 6*d*, 5*s*, and 6*s* – were, in practice, almost certainly middle-class prices.

In other words, a book's price would have to go below 1s, if not way below that price (perhaps down to sixpence or less), to attract a significant working-class buying readership'.[61] Bentley's edition, then, was well beyond the financial reach of working-class readers to buy, although, like the Egerton and Murray editions, Bentley's books reached a deeper and wider readership through both lending and second-hand channels.

Bentley's decision to include Austen's novels in the Standard Novels series was therefore more significant in signalling to readers that Austen was a writer worthy of being included in such a series, than in making her work more available across the social spectrum. His edition did, however, make her work much more affordable for the middle classes. These books were also the first illustrated editions of Austen's work published in England, with steel-engraved frontispieces and second title pages containing engraved scenes from the stories.[62] The illustrations depict Austen's characters in the clothes, accessories and hairstyles of the 1830s, rather than those of the period in which the books were written and first published. As Gilson implies, these illustrations thus subliminally encouraged readers of the 1830s to think of the books as contemporary fiction, and Austen's characters as their own contemporaries.[63] Bentley's edition also included (with *Sense and Sensibility*) a revised and expanded version of Henry Austen's 'Biographical Notice' which continued to influence readers' perceptions of the author.

Other Victorian editions

Between 1833 and 1890, Bentley's edition faced some competition from a number of different published editions of Austen's novels, including (but not limited to) a cheap edition of *Pride and Prejudice* and *Sense and Sensibility* by H. G. Clarke of London (1844), a collected edition by Carey and Hart of Philadelphia (1845), and Tauchnitz editions (designed for readers on the Continent of Europe only) between 1864 and 1877. These were smaller books, closely printed, and much less elegant than the original first editions. Like Bentley's, these editions were aimed at an emergent middle- and lower-middle-class market, and many were destined for the library and second-hand markets.

Routledge's Railway Library series and Munro's Seaside Library

In 1857, Routledge issued *Mansfield Park* and *Northanger Abbey and Persuasion* in the Railway Library series, designed to make literature cheaply available to travellers, and presumably destined for W. H. Smith's new railway bookstalls.[64] Previously (1851), George Routledge had brought out *Sense and Sensibility* and

Pride and Prejudice in one volume with a frontispiece of Elizabeth Bennet in costume appropriate to 1851. Routledge reissued these novels (and *Emma*) in the 1870s, again with frontispieces depicting characters in high Victorian dress, thus continuing the trend set by Bentley's 1830s illustrations of depicting Austen's characters in contemporary dress. In 1880–81, George Munro of New York published all the novels in a very cheap series called 'The Seaside Library'. The culture of the Victorian publisher's series is a phenomenon in its own right, and outside the scope of this monograph,[65] but it is important to note here that in the mid- to late Victorian period, Austen's novels were included in a number of different series, found in the cheap and popular 'yellowback' format as well as in more expensive and elegant editions, such as that of 1875, by Groombridge and Sons, illustrated with lithographs by A. F. Lydon. Alongside a growing body of critical work that commended Austen over the popular Victorian gothic, melodramatic and sensation novelists, her inclusion in a variety of series marketed towards the growing Victorian middle-class family signalled to readers that Austen was a respectable author, acceptable to a wide spectrum of literary tastes. The 1880s also finally made her properly accessible to a book-buying working-class readership – the Seaside Library advertised works at prices between 10 and 20 American cents, though it is difficult to know how many copies actually crossed the Atlantic to be read by British citizens.

J. M. Dent's edition, 1892

The first edition of Austen's work to include editorial commentary was J. M. Dent's ten-volume set of 1892, edited by R. Brimley Johnson. The illustrations in this edition, Gilson notes, depict the characters in Regency dress, setting the trend for illustrations after this edition, and representing an effort to place the novels in their original historical and social context.[66] When Austen's work appeared in an edition that included scholarly editorial apparatus, it was a sign to readers that these were now novels to be taken seriously as literature, rather than as light entertainment. This shift in perception is paralleled both by the rising seriousness with which the study of English literature was treated during the late nineteenth century onwards, and by Austen criticism from the 1870s, in which Austen is described as 'a great name in literature' in Richard Simpson's influential review of James Edward Austen-Leigh's *Memoir*,[67] as a 'classic' by Mary Augusta Ward in her review of Lord Brabourne's edition of the letters,[68] and as a 'genius' by Henry James in 1885.[69] Her 'marvellous literary skill' is so well-established that it could even be explicitly taken for granted by Leslie Stephen in 1876.[70]

George Allan's edition of Pride and Prejudice, *1894*

In 1894, George Allan published *Pride and Prejudice* with a preface by George Saintsbury and illustrations by Hugh Thomson. This edition is significant for two reasons, the first being the coinage, in Saintsbury's preface, of the term 'Janeite' (spelled 'Janite' by Saintsbury), a term that would come to be adopted to describe Austen's ardent fans in the years immediately following, and which marks a particular phase in the growth of Austen's reputation. The second is Hugh Thomson's extremely popular illustrations, which, Claire Harman writes, 'redrew the boundaries between the author's ownership of a text and an interpreter's, abducting *Pride and Prejudice* into the land of kitsch'.[71] The edition was extraordinarily successful, selling 11,603 copies in the first year, with 3,500 sent to America. It was reprinted many times over the next few years, and 25,000 copies had been sold by 1907.[72] Editions of *Sense and Sensibility, Emma, Mansfield Park, Northanger Abbey* and *Persuasion*, all illustrated by Thomson and published by Macmillan followed swiftly, in 1896 and 1897, with the result that Thomson's illustrations saturated the market. Any reader encountering Austen's works for the first time at this period would hence be more likely to see them in an edition decorated with Thomson's somewhat whimsical illustrations than in any other.

Chapman's edition, *1923*

While the Macmillan editions and Thomson's illustrations worked to make Austen better known to the reading public in general, the work of ensuring Austen's place in the literary canon was continued by R. W. Chapman's magisterial scholarly edition of the 1920s. Chapman's edition, in line with principles of editorial best practice, collated all the editions of the novels published in the author's lifetime, and, in the case of the juvenilia and unfinished novels, published as *Minor Works* in 1954, consulted the manuscript sources. This edition, which attempted to render Austen's texts as she had written them, retaining her characteristic spellings and punctuation as well as the original volume divisions, established Austen as an author whose work deserved close textual attention, and whose stylistic choices needed to be taken seriously. It was an important moment in the history of Austen's literary reputation. Concurrently with the more scholarly efforts of Brimley Johnson and Chapman, between 1880 and 1930, expensive luxury editions, such as Bentley's 'Steventon Edition' of 1882 (which cost 63*s* the set) were published, and very cheap editions proliferated from the early years of the twentieth century onwards. This, along with the publication of related Austeniana, such as that described in Chapter 9, prompted Henry James to comment on the 'stiff breeze of the commercial' that had made Austen's works so very popular by 1905.[73]

The appearance of Austen's manuscript works also affected the way in which she was perceived. The earliest of her juvenile works to be published was *The Mystery*, a very brief playlet, probably written in 1788, which was included in the second edition of James Edward Austen-Leigh's *Memoir of Jane Austen* (1871), along with some verses, *Lady Susan*, *The Watsons* and *Sanditon*. Her marginalia in Goldsmith's *History of England* were reproduced in 1920, and her letters (in the Brabourne edition) appeared in 1882, but it was not until 1922 that more of Austen's manuscript works became publicly available, with the publication of the manuscript notebook *Volume the Second*, under the title *Love and Freindship*. The remainder of the juvenile and manuscript works were not published until Chapman's edition of the *Minor Works* in 1954. It is obvious both from the reviews and contemporary readers' responses that readers did not quite know what to make of the messy and anarchic juvenile and other manuscript works in the context of Austen's reputation for effortless elegance and propriety. In 1871, for example, R. H. Hutton called *Lady Susan* 'interesting only as the failures of men and women of genius are interesting', and suggested that 'the subject was too bold'.[74] Virginia Woolf found the manuscript works most interesting because 'the second-rate works of a great writer are worth reading because they offer the best criticism of his masterpieces'.[75] Reading *The Watsons* changed her opinion of Jane Austen; from seeing her as an 'effortless' writer, Woolf began to appreciate the 'preliminary drudgery' involved in Austen's writing process.[76]

The Critical Tradition

The tale of Austen's critical fortunes – modest success in her own time, followed by a lapse into relative obscurity until her rediscovery in the 1840s by such critics as G. H. Lewes and Thomas Babington Macaulay, a gradual rise to greater fame through the latter decades of the nineteenth century into full blown 'Austenolatry' from the 1880s onwards; her canonization into the Great Tradition as a serious moral writer, the re-examination by feminist criticism in the 1970s and other schools of literary theory in the 1980s, followed by the runaway success of the Austen television and film adaptations of the 1990s and 2000s – is well-known, and is covered in extensive detail elsewhere.[77] The extent to which criticism defines or influences readers' responses is less well scrutinized, and is also difficult to measure, but it is nonetheless an important consideration when attempting to establish the context of responses to Austen's novels. In a diary entry for 1 July 1876, Lady Charlotte Schreiber describes the attention she bestowed on Jane Austen's novels in response to

Macaulay's criticism. It is possible that she is referring to Macaulay's review, 'The Diary and Letters of Mme D'Arblay' of 1843, in which he likens Austen to Shakespeare,[78] but, given the amount of time that had elapsed between the publication of the review and Schreiber's diary entry, it is more probable that she had seen one of the many advertisements for Austen's novels which extracted phrases from that review.[79] Schreiber writes:

> I have been studiously reading four of Miss Austen's novels, incited thereto by Macaulay's praise, *Pride and Prejudice, Northanger Abbey, Persuasion, Mansfield Park*. I like the first least of all; I think I like the last the best, but I cannot quite make up my mind whether I am alive to their very great merit. For the epoch at which they appeared, some sixty years ago, they are very remarkable.[80]

Schreiber is hesitant, as shown by her language ('I think I like', 'I cannot quite make up my mind'). Her uncertainty reflects her disappointment that she should need to differ from Macaulay, that her 'studious reading' has not provided her with the comfortable sense that she, like the great man, is 'alive to their very great merit'. As we see in the next chapters, a number of readers recorded responses to Austen's novels that, like Schreiber's, demonstrate an awareness of Austen's critical reputation, both resisting and appropriating the critical discourses surrounding her name.

Chapter 5

AUSTEN'S READERS: CONTEXTS II

Stereotypes of the Reading Public

Moralists and other cultural commentators of the late eighteenth century were, as we have seen, particularly concerned about the reading habits of young female readers. Their worries and concerns were both intensified and developed in the nineteenth century. Born of the explosion of cheap print in the middle of the nineteenth century, and the increase in mass literacy over the course of the century, concerns about the abilities of the reading public more generally frequently surfaced in visual art, fiction, and, in particular, the periodical press, throughout the nineteenth century.[1] During this period, therefore, whichever edition they happened to be reading, and however they responded to the material qualities of the book itself, Austen's readers were faced by particular cultural stereotypes about reading, which affected the ways in which many of them, particularly her female and labouring-class readers, responded to fiction generally, and also to her novels in particular. The material considered here is taken from a wide and deep survey of periodical publications, from highbrow literary reviews such as the *Edinburgh Review*, *Blackwood's Edinburgh Magazine* and the *Quarterly Review*, through general interest periodicals such as *Tinsley's Magazine* and *The Quiver* to more esoteric material, such as *The What-Not*, *The Ladies' Treasury*, *The Cabinet of Fashion and Romance* and *The Englishwoman's Magazine and Christian Mother's Miscellany*. The periodical publications considered have different ostensible aims, they are directed towards different consumer groups, they enjoy different political, moral and intellectual reputations and cultural resonances, and they deal with different subjects and are written in a range of different registers. Within many of the periodicals, there are several different kinds of writing – literary critical, fictional, scientific, geographical or historical, sociological and domestic, for example. The material covers a long historical time-span, from 1800 to 1945. Despite all the apparent and real differences between different types of periodical publications, and different historical time periods, what is most striking about this material is the similarity of image and theme in its depictions of the reading public, and the ways in which these versions of the reading public consistently appear even in writing that is not ostensibly about readers or reading.

In an article on the novel in the *Church of England Quarterly Review* of 1842 the reviewer writes:

> The great bulk of novel readers are females; and to them such impressions (as are conveyed through fiction) are peculiarly mischievous: for, first, they are naturally more sensitive, more impressible, than the other sex; and, secondly, their engagements are of a less engrossing character – they have more time as well as more inclination to indulge in the reveries of fiction.[2]

The gendered fears of the *Church of England Quarterly Review* are familiar to us from the conduct literature of the eighteenth century, and need not be repeated here, but a distrust of fictional forms dates back at least as far as the banishment of the poets from Plato's Republic on the grounds that 'the mimetic poet sets up in each individual soul a vicious constitution', and that 'its power to corrupt [...] even the better sort is surely the chief cause of alarm'.[3] All imitative art, says Socrates in the *Republic*, is antithetical to truth; imitations are at least a third remove from truth.[4] As Austen was growing up and writing her novels, rejections of mimetic art forms, as we have seen, tended to centre on the popular novel, the case for poetry having been largely made and won long before the end of the eighteenth century. A deeper resistance to any form of imitative art can, however, still be detected in such writing as John Bennett's, and, indeed, in many of the reviews of the nineteenth century, including some of those of Austen's novels. As the nineteenth century wore on, the novel did become a more culturally valid form, as successive generations of writers developed and moulded the genre in different ways, and the periodical writing of the period reflects this change to some degree, usually praising certain types of fiction at the expense of others. Nonetheless, the cultural stereotype of the 'habitual reader of fiction' remained a handy straw (wo)man for reviewers and critics to berate throughout the period.[5]

In Sheridan's *The Rivals* (1775), Lydia Languish, thrown into a panic at the sound of her approaching censorious relatives, directs her maid Lucy to hide all the novels that she has recently brought back from Bath's circulating libraries:

> Here, my dear Lucy, hide these books. – Quick, quick. – Fling *Peregrine Pickle* under the toilet – throw *Roderick Random* into the closet – put *the Innocent Adultery* into the *Whole Duty of Man* – thrust *Lord Aimworth* under the sopha – cram *Ovid* behind the bolster – there – put *the Man of Feeling* into your pocket – so, so, now lay *Mrs Chapone* in sight, and leave *Fordyce's Sermons* open on the table.[6]

This scene clearly caught the imagination of its readers. When Walter Scott reviewed *Emma* for the *Quarterly Review* of March 1816, he referred to the scene casually and allusively, assuming his readers would recognize the reference: 'it is not upon Lydia Languish's toilet alone that Tom Jones and Peregrine Pickle are to be found ambushed behind works of a more grave and instructive character', for, he said, a novel is frequently 'bread eaten in secret', and, even 'among the crowds who read little else, it is not common to find an individual of hardihood sufficient to avow his taste for these frivolous studies'.[7] We are reminded of *Northanger Abbey*'s Catherine Morland and Isabella Thorpe, who 'shut themselves up, to read novels together', and of the 'hardihood' of the narrator's avowal of her taste for novels in defiance of 'the Reviewers'.[8] Scott goes on to trace the history and development of the novel, from its early days as 'the legitimate child of the romance', to the 'style of novel [that] has arisen, within the last fifteen or twenty years',[9] which depends not on 'a wild variety of incident' or 'the splendid scenes of an imaginary world', but on 'a correct and striking representation of that which is daily taking place'.[10] Scott recognizes the difference in Austen's novels from those of the sentimental and romantic schools, and makes the point that an Austen novel 'affords to those who frequent it a pleasure nearly allied with the experience of their own social habits; and what is of some importance, the youthful wanderer may return from his promenade to the ordinary business of life, without any chance of having his head turned by the recollection of the scene through which he has been wandering'.[11] Scott conflates the verisimilitude of Austen's novels with their inoffensive tendencies. In so doing, he gives voice to the commonly expressed fear that other novels, though not this one, 'turn the heads' of young people by opening up imaginary vistas to them.

Scott was not, of course, the only reviewer of the Regency period to praise Austen's novels because of their difference from the more outrageous excesses of the sentimental, romantic or gothic novels and romances of the previous century, but reviewers also noticed favourably their difference from the works of their own era: the 'numerous novels which are continually presenting themselves to our notice'.[12] *Pride and Prejudice*, for example, is described as 'very far superior to almost all the publications of the kind which have lately come before us', in January of 1816.[13] In March 1818, the *British Critic*'s reviewer contrasted *Northanger Abbey* and *Persuasion* extremely favourably with the 'dull and exhausting' perusal of the generality of novels.[14] In the 1860s, Austen's novels were recommended as a healthy corrective to the sensation novels of that period.[15]

Although Richard Whately's unsigned review of *Northanger Abbey* and *Persuasion* for the *Quarterly Review* of 1821 claimed that the times were past when reviewers needed to 'plead the necessity of occasionally stooping to humour the taste of their fair readers' for reviewing a novel, in fact, apologies for noticing novels continued to appear with some regularity.[16] The talking 'in threadbare strains of the trash with which the press now groans' of the anti-novel reviewers, which already had a long history by the time Jane Austen complained of it in *Northanger Abbey*,[17] persisted well into the late years of the nineteenth century, although softened from the full-scale tirades of the previous century.[18] A distrust of fiction also became increasingly conflated with the notion of a feminized reading public over the course of the century, as we will see. One thread that runs consistently through the periodical writing of the nineteenth century is the incompetence, vulgarity or lack of discernment of the bulk of the reading public. Against the mass of the vulgar is set a hypothetical reader whose discrimination, aesthetic and moral taste, intelligence, and industry are profound, characterized as a deep- and hard-reader rather than a 'much-reader', and with whom the readers of the periodical, magazine or article are encouraged to identify.[19] Both 'reading public' and the 'hard-reader' are, of course, equally illusory ideological constructions, but they were nonetheless influential models with which historical readers could and did engage.

Louisa Emily Dorrée's article in *The Quiver* of 1884 is typical of advice given, not only to young girls, but to the reading public in general, to pursue 'a regular course of study' instead of enjoying 'light reading':

> How many girls give up their regular reading when they have left the schoolroom! They rejoice in their liberty, and spend much more time than is needed for recreation, which we all require, in light reading. Will they believe me when I tell them that they would enjoy their stories much more if they kept to a regular course of study upon some given subject?[20]

Blackwood's Edinburgh Magazine similarly claims: 'it may be granted that of all reading [,] novel-reading, as usually performed, is the slightest of intellectual exercises – one that may be discontinued with the least perceptible loss to the understanding'.[21] It is, however, also true that this view of novels existed alongside a growing defence of 'light reading', or at least of novels of which the reviewers approved. The anonymous reviewer of 'Recent Novels' in the *Edinburgh Review* of 1853, for example, suggests that 'genius stamps its own signet on every performance, whatever be the kind of work it takes in hand; and nowhere is its impress more deep and unmistakeable than in those volumes which reproduce in fiction the richest and most genial realities of life'.[22] He also writes:

> Hundreds of readers who would sleep over a sermon, or drone over an essay, or yield a cold and barren assent to the deductions of an ethical treatise, will

be startled into reflection, or won to emulation, or roused into effort, by the delineations they meet with in a tale which they opened only for the amusement of an idle hour.[23]

This view (reminiscent of Sidney's claim in the *Defence of Poesie* (1595) that 'Esop's Tales [...] whose prettie Allegories stealing under the formall Tales of beastes, makes many more beastly than beasts: begin to hear the sound of vertue from those dumbe speakers') reinforces the idea that the majority of the reading public, unlike the reviewers, were unable to read in a discerning manner.[24] According to such accounts, the members of the reading public were incapable of the mental effort involved in appreciating sermons, essays or ethical treatises, and 'won to emulation, or roused into effort' almost against their will and certainly without their personal agency. It therefore makes the claim for fiction's value at the expense of fiction's readers.

In 1862, a writer for the *Ladies' Treasury* claimed that 'nine persons out of ten read little else' but novels,[25] and 'T. A.' (Thomas Arnold the younger) of *Macmillan's Magazine* wrote of 'the jaded palate of the habitual reader of fiction in our day'.[26] The 'habitual reader of fiction' was collapsed into the mass of the reading public, characterized as a multitude of mindless, easily led readers of trashy novels, incapable of telling good literature from bad. *The Leisure Hour* of 1852 quotes S. T. Coleridge in order to encourage readers in their attempts to discriminate between literary wheat and chaff:

> Coleridge has said that there are four classes of readers. The first he compares to an hour glass; their reading being as the sand – it runs in and runs out, and leaves not a vestige behind. A second class resembles a sponge, which imbibes every thing, and returns it in nearly the same state, only a little dirtier. A third class he likens to a jelly bag, which allows all that is pure to pass away, and retains all the refuse and the dregs. The fourth class may be compared to the slaves in the diamond mines of Golconda, who, casting aside all that is worthless, preserve only the pure gem.[27]

The ideal reader, it is clear, is the 'slave' who preserves the 'pure gem' of knowledge, while the reading public in general fall into the categories of hourglasses, sponges and jelly-bags. The passage is unsettling; if readers are 'slaves' then reading must be in some way coercive, readerly activity must be dictated by a tyrannical master. *The Leisure Hour*'s reviewer does not seem to find this authoritarian model problematic, and makes little further comment, taking it for granted that his readers will accept without question the premise that reading needs to be difficult to be worthwhile, as well as the idea that there are many readers who are not prepared to put in the hard work it takes to 'preserve the pure gem' from their reading. Implicitly, therefore, the reader is encouraged to be one of the few: a member of the 'fourth class' of readers, a 'hard reader' rather than a 'much reader'.

In a similar strain, in an article entitled 'Books and their Uses' in the first issue of *Macmillan's Magazine* (1859–60), 'Doubleday' (Alfred Ainger) writes:

> There are those who read because some work is in fashion, and it were bad taste not to be able to talk of it. There are those who read, in order to give the public the benefit of their judgment – those mysterious men, the critics. There are those who read indiscriminately with morbid wideness of taste, as the savage devours the earth. Lastly, there are those who read little, but with discernment; whose books are their honoured friends – 'the souls who have made their souls wiser'.[28]

There is a casual sneer at 'fashion', and an evident rejection of 'morbid wideness of taste' in favour of 'discernment' here. The article, like many others, makes it clear that 'the danger in this much written-for age is of reading too much'.[29] Thomas Arnold blames the reading public for the number of 'worthless books' on the market:

> Those who launch upon the book-sea with no better previous training than the greater number of our middle-class schools supply, will be deterred by no amount of bad taste, bad English, and literary crudity, from reading what is suited to the barbarous condition of their intelligence. So the law of supply and demand works; and, to meet the notions of such readers, a plentiful crop of like-minded writers arises; and an unprecedented circulation of worthless books is the inevitable result.[30]

F. T. Palgrave partially agrees, although he suggests that the problem lies in the way people read rather than what they read:

> The root of the wrong appears to be, that people, unless profession or scientific interest influences them, go to books for something almost similar to what they find in social conversation. Reading tends to become only another kind of gossip. Everything is to be read, and everything only once; a book is no more a treasure to be kept and studied and known by heart, as the truly charming phrase has it, if deserving that intimacy.[31]

Palgrave suggests that the reading public of 1760, compared to that of 1860, though smaller, was 'deeper and more earnest' in its approach to books; fewer people read but those who did read better. In 1860, he suggests, the public are 'much-readers', rather than deep readers. Of course, the reviewers and moralists of the 1760s had made almost exactly the same complaints about a perceived move from intensive to extensive reading in *their* reading public. Two decades after Palgrave, Mary Arnold concurred that public taste had deteriorated, declaring, 'taste is laxer, the public easier to please, and book-making more profitable' than it had been one hundred or even fifty years before.[32] Even those writers who defended the habits of the reading public – Mowbray Morris, the writer of 'General Readers; by One of Them' in *Macmillan's Magazine*, for example – agree with the idea that current readers read more widely and less deeply than those of previous times:

> To read the best in literature; to read it always, and to read it only. Wise counsel; but who shall fulfil it? Does not such an education pre-suppose a condition of mind and fortune – one might almost say, too, of body – rare indeed in this much-harassed age, if possible at all?[33]

Instead of denigrating, he celebrates the wide-ranging reading that other reviewers considered a demerit in the reading public: 'So long as our whims be not dangerous, do not lead us to the books which promote "filthiness and foolish talking", we may be content to read, I do think, as the whim seizes us', turning from *Don Quixote* to the *Woman in White*, and from *The Pilgrim's Progress* to *Westward Ho!* with equal pleasure and profit.[34] The tide of feeling was, however, against him.

In *Tinsley's Magazine* of 1867, the pseudonymous Aunt Anastasia exhorts her 'niece' to a different approach to reading. Admitting, 'I am an old maid with the prejudices of my age and condition', she goes on to give some robust advice to her fictional correspondent.[35] The premise of this brief sketch is that, having observed her niece's addiction to the Mudie's Lending Library novel during a recent visit, Anastasia wishes to give her some good advice. She thus condemns both the amount of time given to the reading of novels and the fact that 'you do not read novels on any system of selection', instead relying on 'Mr. Mudie's catalogue, the daily papers, and the *Saturday Review*'. She also deplores the 'feverish rapidity'[36] of her reading. Anastasia considers her niece to be 'half-drunk, in the sense of moral intoxication, and that too on the coarsest and most injurious kind of intoxicating literary liquor', to 'the destruction of the intellectual appetite and digestion'. The niece will not read Anastasia's own books: 'the production of the finest intellects of our own and of past times', because her mind 'cannot swallow or digest wholesome food any longer'. Anastasia encourages her to develop her own critical faculties 'by rejecting absolute belief in newspaper criticism, and, as you must read novels, do a little criticism for yourself'.[37] She next exerts the strongest criticism on a novel left behind by her niece, and censures it on the grounds that 'this book, and also many others which bear a regrettable likeness to it, are written by women, are chiefly read by women, represent to men who read them the feelings, views, and opinions of women concerning life and its desirabilities'.[38] She thus objects to the lack of literary merit in trashy novels, but even more to the image of women created and perpetuated in their pages. She fulminates against the state of 'intellectual imbecility' to which the women who read such books are brought,[39] and against her niece's 'denaturalised state of mind',[40] and ends with the hope that she might learn to prefer 'the good novels over the bad'.[41] Nearly fifty years before, in the *Quarterly Review* of October 1820, William Gifford had made many of the same points about the effects of bad novels on a female readership:

> We have had too frequent reason of late to lament, both in female readers and writers, [...] the infection of that pretended liberality, but real licentiousness of thought, the plague and the fearful sign of the times. Under its influence they lose their relish for what is simple and sober, gentle or dignified, and require the stimulus of excessive or bitter passion, of sedition, of audacious profaneness.[42]

Aunt Anastasia's strictures are of interest here because they recapitulate in tone, imagery and content the arguments of the conduct books of the late-eighteenth century against the novel and the romance. While the old-fashioned aunt is a stock literary figure of fun (as we saw in Austen's portrayal of Mrs Percival in *Catharine; or, The Bower*), the comments Anastasia makes are nonetheless in tune with those of the rest of the periodical writers of the 1860s. Her advice is clearly to be taken seriously, despite the element of caricature implicit in her portrayal. There is, as in the conduct books of the eighteenth century, a backward-looking element in much of the advice meted out to the reading public in the periodicals of the Victorian age; a suggestion that the previous age knew better how to conduct itself, and that the readers as well as the novelists of that time were greater than those of the present day. The reviewer of *The Ladies' Treasury* compares Maria Edgeworth, Walter Scott and Jane Austen favourably to the sensation novelists of the 1850s and 60s, for example, and *Clarissa* is invoked to glorify the tastes of the eighteenth century in comparison to those of the nineteenth:

> What the people for whom *Clarissa* was written thought of the book, everybody knows; and no stronger proof of the inveterate aversion to prolixity in our time could be adduced than the fact that so few have had the courage to make themselves acquainted with a work which was the 'sensation' of its own epoch.[43]

The novelists of the past are, in fact, credited with astonishing powers in an article of 1870 in *Blackwood's Edinburgh Magazine*, where the claim is made that reading just one good novel in girlhood could prevent a short attention span for the rest of a person's life:

> There are many women desultory, restless, incorrigible interrupters, incapable of amusing themselves or of being amused by the same thing for five minutes together, who would have been pleasanter and so far better members of society if once in their girlhood they had read a good novel with rapt attention – one of Walter Scott's or Miss Austen's, or, not invidiously to select among modern great names, if the Fates had thrown it in their way, Sir Charles Grandison – entering into the characters, realising the descriptions, following the dialogue, appreciating the humour, and enchained by the plot.[44]

While this article makes a strong claim for the improving powers of fiction, it also assumes that the 'desultory, restless' woman is a reader of bad novels. Both 'Aunt Anastasia' and the *Blackwood's* reviewer make the assumption that the reading public for bad novels was primarily feminine, and the assumption is made explicit in a *Macmillan's Magazine* article of 1886:

> 'All people, with healthy literary appetites love them', wrote Thackeray, calling novels the sweets of literature, just as all people with healthy physical appetites have a sweet tooth somewhere in their head. A later witness declares that women are the chief patrons of fiction, and of the bulk of current fiction this, I suppose, is true; for, without offence either to our novelists or their patrons, the modern novel can hardly be expected to have much flavour for what is known as a masculine appetite.[45]

The reviewer goes on to make the case that men may enjoy the novels of the 'Old Masters of their craft', namely Fielding, Scott and Dickens, but that 'female taste is too delicate for these strong meats'.[46] The discerning reader (capable of recognizing and appreciating an 'Old Master') is characterized as masculine, while the 'chief patrons of fiction' are female. Given that it is assumed that fiction makes up the bulk of the reading matter read by the public, the reading public is thus feminized. Even where it is not explicit, the feminization of the reading public can be detected. Ainger's sneer at 'those who read because some work is in fashion, and it were bad taste not to be able to talk of it', for example, is directed at the female section of the population, so often derided for their interest in fashion and talk. When F. T. Palgrave describes bad reading practice as 'only another kind of gossip' he consigns it to a traditionally feminine realm, while comparing it to a better type of reading: that influenced by 'profession or scientific interest'. Both profession and scientific interest are the domains of men; women are thus implicitly excluded from the worthwhile practices of the discerning reader. Despite the presence of female authors, critics and editors throughout the nineteenth century, the fictional foolish 'reading public' evoked in periodical writing, from the *Ladies' Magazine* to the *Quarterly Review*, tends to be understood as broadly made up of women, or effeminate men.

Half-hearted defences of 'the girls' can be found throughout the latter half of the century,[47] but a prevailing, if false, notion of a feminized fiction-reading public that conflated femininity with novels, and the reading of novels with a lack of literary or critical discernment, was thus the background against which both male and female readers of fiction experienced Austen's novels during the nineteenth century.

Readers' Responses to Cultural Stereotypes

With such encouragement from the reviewers to differentiate themselves from 'the generality of readers',[48] it is no wonder that intelligent and literate readers of fiction attempted to distance themselves from the stereotypes of the 'mere novel reader',[49] or 'the novel-reading public'.[50] Jane Austen noted that Mrs Lefroy, although she liked *Mansfield Park*, 'thought it a mere Novel', a fine example of faint praise that illuminates the form's lack of cultural capital in the early nineteenth century.[51] As we saw in Chapter 1, in the Austen household, such views had little currency. The defence of the novel in *Northanger Abbey* is a lengthening and elucidation of a long-held position, which dislikes the 'pretension' and 'self-consequence' of those who pretend to disapprove of novels.[52] Among Austen's early readers, Mary Russell Mitford sounds a similar note to the Austens, writing to Sir William Elford in a letter of 1824, of her own *Our Village*: 'as you, in common with all sensible people, like light reading, I say again that you will like it'.[53] Thomas Moore, too, writing to Samuel Rogers in June of 1816, was not afraid to recommend a novel: 'Let me entreat you to read *Emma* – it is the very perfection of novel-writing – and I cannot praise it more highly than by saying it is often extremely like your own method of describing things – so much effect, with so little effort!'.[54] Not everyone, however, as Walter Scott perceptively noted in the review of *Emma* discussed above, was prepared to admit to a liking for 'light reading': Felicia Hemans teasingly anticipates that her correspondent, Matthew Nicholson, will 'assume a very good grave, *mentorial* face, & give me a long lecture, when I tell you I have also *been guilty* of reading a *Romance*' [Jane Porter's *The Scottish Chiefs* (1810)]. Hemans had clearly internalized some of her period's views of the dangers of fiction, going on to claim, 'I am by no means an Advocate for *Historical*

Novels as they bewilder our ideas, by confounding truth with fiction'.[55] Mary Berry, looking back in later life on what she had read by 1781, believed that she had picked up all sorts of misinformation about the world 'from much desultory and often improper reading', by which she meant fiction.[56] In 1800, she engages with what, by then, was a long-running debate on exactly how novels were detrimental to young people:

> The false pictures given of human life in most novels, and which alone (in my opinion) makes them dangerous reading for young people, is, not that the sentiments and conduct of the hero or heroine are exalted above the common level of humanity, for there is no well-conceived novel which is not read by many an ingenuous and noble mind, who can reflect with pleasure that *they* have acted on some occasion with all the high sense of honour, the exalted generosity, the noble disinterestedness described in their author. But what they must not look for in real life, what they would expect in vain, what it is necessary to guard them against, is, supposing that such conduct will make a similar impression on those around them, that the sacrifices they make will be considered, and the principles on which they act understood and valued, as the novel writer, at his good pleasure, makes them.[57]

Novels are judged here, not on their likelihood to lead a girl to ruin, but on their propensity to raise unrealistic expectations of life. It is an interesting passage because, amongst its confusing and seemingly contradictory sub-clauses, it comes to a clear-sighted recognition of the wrong uses to which we may put our reading, moving away from the tone of righteous indignation that characterizes so many discussions of the novel. It suggests that novels are not wrong in their depictions of virtuous heroes and heroines, for many young people are quite as virtuous as their fictional peers. Instead, Berry says, it is real people who disappoint. It is *right*, Berry seems to be suggesting, to identify with 'the sentiments and conduct of the hero or heroine', but wrong to expect acknowledgement of good conduct and motives from others. Her understanding of the dangers of false expectations shifts a burden of blame away from the novel to the moral blindness of those who do *not* identify with the virtuous examples depicted in novels.

Even when Berry voices the conventional view that 'desultory and heterogeneous reading is the great evil of all young women', she continues:

> Though nobody is more aware than myself that this sort of desultory reading during the first years of (mental) life does often much mischief, and is attended always with a great waste of time, yet it has at least this good effect […], that a love of reading thus natural and thus indulged is often a happy preventive in future life, against more serious follies, more pernicious idleness.[58]

This is a common-sense view that undercuts more excessive denunciations of 'desultory reading'. There are worse things, Berry thinks, than to have a 'natural' love of reading, whatever the reading matter may be, and she suggests that reading actually guards against, rather than leading young women into, 'more serious follies, more pernicious idleness'.

Susan Ferrier, on the other hand, although she herself was a novelist, comments disapprovingly on the genre in 1815, claiming that Mary Brunton's *Discipline* (1814) is 'one of the few novels I think fit for family use'.[59] In 1816, she wrote more favourably of Austen's *Emma* on the grounds that it was deliberately different from the excesses of the Gothic: 'I have been reading *Emma*, which is excellent; there is no story whatever, and the heroine is not better than other people; but the characters are all so true to life, and the style so piquant, that it does not require the adventitious aids of mystery and adventure'.[60] In 1823, Mary Shelley wrote dismissively that 'desultory reading adds to, instead of alleviateting [*sic*] my sorrows', although she found 'a balm in serious and deep study'.[61] Mary Russell Mitford, herself a voracious novel reader, who longed for years to write a novel, and who thought that 'all sensible people' enjoyed 'light reading', still wrote to Elizabeth Barrett Browning in 1844 of the poor taste of 'English novel-readers', using the term as one of abuse, and suggesting that Balzac would be 'too good' for them.[62] Mitford evidently does not categorize herself as an 'English novel-reader', despite being both English and a reader of novels.

Dorothy Wordsworth's letters often contain complaints that she has had no time, or not enough time, to read. Intriguingly, she frequently follows such a comment with an account of reading novels or 'light books'. She writes to Catherine Clarkson in August 1811: 'I have read nothing since I wrote to you except bits here and there and the Novel of John Bunkle, but I am going to set to and read – though I still have some sewing to do'.[63] In April of the following year, she writes to her brother, 'we have not yet been sufficiently settled to read any thing but Novels';[64] the next month she writes, 'we have only read light books yet'.[65] For Dorothy Wordsworth, the term 'reading' clearly means serious study; any other sort of reading has to be described separately. Reading 'light books' can take place in spare minutes, while 'reading' takes time and concentration. This differentiation in terminology reflects Dorothy's understanding of the relative cultural merits of different kinds of reading.

Despite the assumptions most often made by cultural commentators of the period, the extensive reading of nineteenth-century women was rarely limited to the novel or romance, and their reading depended on their political or religious backgrounds, their family situations, their geographical locations, and a host of other factors. William Godwin's step-daughter, Claire Clairmont, for example, her early reading influenced by Godwin, the Shelleys and Byron, and later by working as a tutor in households in France, Italy and Russia, read an astonishing array of literature in at least six languages, including politics, theology, philosophy, novels, poetry, plays, educational theory and history. Her reading seems not to have been censored in any way, and her engagement with what she read both intense and critical. As early as 1814, when Clairmont was only 16, she was able to criticize Shakespeare with confidence, writing, 'in most of Shakespeare's Plays there are generally secondary Plots & Characters which are rather tiresome than interesting, but in Lear there is not a line that does not teem with vigour & energy'. She took exception to Rousseau on the grounds that 'it is indeed partial to judge the whole sex by the conduct of one [Sophie] whose very education tended to fit her more for a Seraglio than the friend & equal of Man'.[66] Clairmont's criticism is here no doubt linked to the continued influence of Mary Wollstonecraft in Godwin's home, as her argument is very similar to Wollstonecraft's in the *Vindication of the Rights of Woman*. Claire Clairmont is certainly atypical in terms of the range of languages in which she could and did read, but the variety of subject matter encompassed by her reading does not appear unusual, even when contrasted with that of much less geographically mobile or politically radical women.[67]

Elizabeth Barrett Browning's early diary[68] similarly demonstrates a wide range and depth of reading in more than one language, and includes Greek Tragedy, ancient and modern poetry, philosophy, theology and 'thousands' of 'novels & Romances'.[69] Her diary for 1831–32 records reading, for example, 'Chrysostom's commentary on the Ephesians', 'Aeschylus', 'the Bible & Horne on its critical study', 'Pindar's 4th Olympic before breakfast', 'the mysteries of Udolpho', 'some of Victor Hugo's & Lamartine's poetry – his last song of Childe Harolde', 'the Cyclopaedia', 'Barnes's Euripides, Marcus Antoninus, Callimachus, the Anthologia, Epictetus, Isocrates', 'Destiny', 'The Inheritance', 'the Alcestis', 'La Bruyère & Cowper', 'the 3d. vol: of Mrs. Shelley', '*Cebes*', 'Keats's Lamia, Isabella, Eve of St Agnes & Hyperion', 'the Endymion', 'Theophrastus', 'some passages from Shelley's Revolt of Islam', [Goldoni's] 'Pamela, & Pamela Maritata', 'Self control' [by Mary Brunton], 'Mr Beverley's pamphlets [...] the letter to the Archbishop of York, & the Tombs of the prophets', 'Dr. Clark's Discourse', 'Dr. Card's sermon on the athanasian creed', 'Dr. Channing's treatise "On the importance & means of a national Literature"', 'Iphigenia' [in Aulis], 'Gregory's apologetick', 'the Hippolytus', 'the Supplices of Aeschylus', 'the Choephori', 'the Eumenides', 'Mr. Joseph Clarke's Sacred Literature', 'the whole of Synesius's poems', and 'four odes of Gregory'. She mentions conversations with others about 'Keats & Shelley, & Coleridge's Ancient Mariner', 'Homer [,] Aeschylus & Shakespeare', and 'Corinne & Mathilde'. A diary entry for 3 April 1832 includes her claim to have read 'every play of Euripides'.[70] On 22 December 1831, she asserts that she has 'left off now my *partial* habits of reading',⁷¹ and on 9 April 1832, she writes, 'and yet I really read nothing superficially'.⁷² The critical comments on her reading scattered throughout the diary suggest that both latter statements are true; Barrett Browning's attention to all her reading, from Aeschylus to Mary Shelley, was extraordinarily close and careful.

Although the reading lists of conduct literature for women prescribed a very restricted diet of reading, it is immediately clear from even the most cursory survey of accounts written by historical readers that prescriptive reading lists do not come close to describing what women read, though they remain a useful index of the ways in which the desire to control women's reading was made manifest. It is hardly surprising that such lists are inadequate: they look backward to the publications of the past century, while new works tumbled rapidly from the presses of nineteenth-century printers. Certain books became fashionable, and once fashionable, desirable.⁷³ Prescriptive reading lists had little chance against the abundance of new books, as the *Critical Review* laments, sneering at 'the readers of novels, who are insatiable after *something new*'.⁷⁴ Mary Shelley's diaries and letters chronicle her urgent desire for new publications throughout the 1820s and 30s – she repeatedly writes to various correspondents asking for 'any pretty new book to lend me',⁷⁵ 'your new Edition'⁷⁶ and 'any new books come out *quite* lately'⁷⁷; she also frequently records reading novels, poems, biographies, works of philosophy and memoirs as soon as they have come out. Ten years later, Harriet Martineau, too, fretted about her lack of 'the only indulgence I have not, – a good supply of books', and goes on to complain: 'the Literary Society here buys only one copy of each new book, and it is weeks, or more likely months before we can get any'.⁷⁸ Although Mary Mitford came to prefer 'old books' and 'the older writers', she also records her reading of 'a vast number of respectable new books', discussing them energetically with her correspondents.⁷⁹ A representative week from her diary of 1819 (Monday 4 to Sunday 10 January), records her reading of both old and new books: [Scott's] 'The Antiquary' (1816), 'some of Miss Edgeworth's Popular Tales & Some of Burke' [Maria Edgeworth's *Popular Tales* (1804) and Edmund Burke's *Reflections on the Revolution in France* (1790)], Henry Fearon's *Sketches of America* (1818), which she describes as 'this pretty book', Burke again, Thomas Love Peacock's *Nightmare Abbey* (1818) and 'more of Burke'.⁸⁰

While female readers certainly did not limit themselves to fiction, many male readers did read novels in abundance. Statistical analysis of a survey of approximately 3,500 recorded responses of reading experience between 1800 and 1900 even shows a slight bias towards male fiction-readers during this period.⁸¹ Given Scott's reputation as the pre-eminent novelist of his age throughout the nineteenth century, it is not surprising that many men of all social classes recorded reading Walter Scott's novels with great pleasure. John Wilson Croker, for example, maintained that he had all of Scott 'by heart',[82] while Byron's Ravenna journal contains the claim that Byron had 'read all W. Scott's novels at least fifty times'.[83] Although this is a characteristically Byronic exaggeration, there was some truth in it. Byron did re-read Scott's novels repeatedly, telling William Bankes in 1820 that he was 'more and more delighted' with Scott's novels every time he read them.[84] Further down the social scale, Adam Mackie, a tenant farmer from Aberdeenshire, wrote in January 1827 of 'occupying my spare time reading Scott's novel of the Abbot', and 'during my spare time reading a novel – The Pirate'.[85] Mackie also recorded reading *Redgauntlet* (1824) and *Guy Mannering* (1815) in the same month, and *Tales of My Landlord* (1816–19) in February.[86] The extent to which Scott's novels were acceptable, even required, reading for anyone with any claim to taste is well demonstrated by James Glass Bertram, who wrote in his autobiography of his days as an apprentice in a book warehouse that, 'curiously enough, the reading of the "Waverley novels" was to me a task of difficulty; and I am ashamed to say that I have only read few of them, "Guy Mannering", "The Heart of Midlothian", "The Bride of Lammermoor" and "St Ronan's Well". "Waverley", although attempted more than once, failed to attract.'[87] Bertram's 'shame' at his failure to enjoy the Waverley novels reminds us, like Austen's appropriation of *Marmion*, of the pressures that Scott's reputation placed on his readers.

Many male readers read novels by other male novelists: the writer of imperialist adventure tales, H. Rider Haggard, enjoyed *Robinson Crusoe* (1719) and *The Three Musketeers* (1844), and his two favourite novels were Charles Dickens' *Tale of Two Cities* (1859) and Bulwer Lytton's *The Coming Race* (1871).[88] Dickens' novels were, as is well known, frequently favourites with both men and women from the time of their publication. But many men read novels of lesser, or questionable, reputation also, including novels by women. Leslie Stephen, for example, indulged in the reading of 'French novels' – telling Oliver Wendell Holmes: 'I am much given to that amusement though I never read de Musset'[89] – and enjoyed the female-authored novel very much. John Wilson Croker wrote, in 1854, of his 'novel reading [...] younger days' when he 'used to read them all from Charlotte Smith to Maria Edgeworth'.[90] George Moore, aged eleven, 'took the first opportunity' of reading Mary Elizabeth Braddon's best-selling sensation novel, *Lady Audley's Secret* (1862): 'I read it eagerly, passionately, vehemently.'[91] Joseph Stamper, son of an iron moulder, was strongly moved by Mrs Henry Wood's *East Lynne* (1861), remembering in later life 'the tears I gulped back over the death of Little Willie!'[92] Charles Kingsley read Charlotte M. Yonge's novel, *Heartsease* (1854), a work aggressively marketed towards young female readers, and told its publisher that it was 'the most delightful and wholesome novel I ever read [...] I found myself wiping my eyes a dozen times before I got through it'.[93] On the other hand, the clergyman Mandell Creighton read Mary Augusta [Mrs Humphry] Ward's *Miss Bretherton* (1884) 'with much interest', but felt that 'it is not a novel of my sort'.[94] And many well-known men – among them Warren Hastings, Henry Crabb Robinson, S. T. Coleridge, William Wordsworth, Robert Southey, Sir James Mackintosh, Francis Jeffrey, John Murray, the Prince Regent, Thomas Moore, Sir Walter Scott, Cardinal Newman, Edward Bulwer Lytton, William Charles Macready, Thomas Babington Macaulay, Alfred, Lord Tennyson, Charles Darwin, Henry Wadsworth Longfellow, Mark Twain, E. M. Forster and Edwin Muir – along with a host of now largely forgotten working men, such as the young labourer, Philip Inman, read the novels of Jane Austen.[95]

Indeed, many of Austen's earliest readers, at least according to the collection of opinions of *Mansfield Park* and *Emma* that she gathered, were men. She recorded the opinions of her brothers, her nephews and various other relatives, connections and friends of the family. Many of these male readers (including two of her brothers, James Austen and Edward Knight, her nephew, Edward Austen, and her niece Anna's husband, Benjamin Lefroy) commented on the Portsmouth scenes in *Mansfield Park*, perhaps because, like Admiral Foote – who was 'surprised that I had the power of drawing the Portsmouth-Scenes so well' – they were startled by Austen's ability to represent scenes that so accurately represented the world of a down-at-heel lieutenant of Marines. Benjamin Lefroy was 'highly pleased with Fanny Price –& a warm admirer of the Portsmouth Scene. – Angry with Edmund for not being in love with her, & hating Mrs Norris for Teazing her'.[96] It is worth noting that Lefroy's response is couched in terms of the emotions he felt – as we have seen, an emotional response to fiction was more usually considered to be the preserve of the 'bad' or female reader, but here we see a man's affective response. Concerns about reading fiction can be identified in the responses of the Rev. Samuel Cooke, who called *Mansfield Park* 'the most sensible Novel he had ever read', and John Pemberton Plumptre, who said that he had 'never read a novel which interested me so very much throughout'.[97] Both comments suggest not only a very real admiration of Austen's skill, but, in their deliberate distancing of *Mansfield Park* from other novels, also a vague disapproval of the novel form more generally.

While elite male readers were frequently able to ignore or transcend the cultural stereotypes about fiction and the reading public that they encountered in the press, it is evident that male readers from the working and aspirant lower-middle classes felt more pressure to refrain from reading fiction.

In the mid-century, the working-class Methodist, Christopher Thomson, absenting himself from Chapel to read fiction from the circulating library, was 'called to account for it', by the elders of the Chapel. To defend himself:

> I pleaded my desire for, and indulgence in, reading. This appeared rather to aggravate than serve my cause. It was evidently their opinion, that all books, except such as they deemed religious ones, ought not to be read by young men. I ventured somewhat timidly to hint, that it was possible for a young man to read novels, and other works of fiction, and still keep his mind free from irreligion and vice.[98]

Thomson plainly recognized that 'all' novels were considered to inculcate 'irreligion and vice', but it is also clear that he himself believed otherwise and was prepared to resist such prejudices. Nonetheless, the social pressure exerted on him shows itself in the (albeit ironically presented) 'timidity' with which he could 'hint' at a different point of view.

Thomas Burt, another working man, comments on the rarity of reading fiction in the Burt family circle in the 1850s:

> There is a novel, 'Uncle Tom's Cabin', which I should not omit to mention, since it made a great sensation when it appeared, and it was the only book of its class brought home by my father. "Uncle Tom" was read aloud in our little family circle, and it gave us many hours of happy, thrilling and not unwholesome excitement.[99]

Evidently, novels were not considered to be, in general, suitable reading, since *Uncle Tom's Cabin* (1852) was 'the only book of its class' read in this way by the Burt family. Again, the language provides a clue to the ideological forces exerted on fiction-readers; Burt's stress on the 'not unwholesome excitement', provided by *Uncle Tom's Cabin* suggests that a much more commonly held view of fiction was that it was in fact unwholesome or unhealthy.

Many working-class male readers record the public prejudice against cheap popular fiction, commenting on their own positive responses to it but showing a clear recognition of how such literature was generally perceived.[100] Thomas Okey, a labourer, writing in 1930, recalled the reading habits of his childhood in Spitalfields in the 1860s:

> The favourite literary pabulum of us boys at school [...] was [...] 'penny bloods' and other Weeklies issued in penny sheets, such as "Sweeny Todd the Barber". Romantic stories of highwaymen circulated freely from boy to boy until reduced to rags: Dick Turpin, Spring-heeled Jack, the gallant Claude Duval, gracefully

dancing on the greensward with the ladies he had robbed, Edith the Captive, Edith Heron, with what impatience we awaited the issue of the next number, with what absorbing interest we followed the thrilling adventure![101]

Okey recognized that this kind of reading was neither 'classical' nor 'healthy', but he insisted that 'what it did was to evoke the reading habit, and to one boy at least that was a valuable endowment'.[102] Okey thus acknowledges, and to some extent complies, with the notion that cheap popular fiction was bad for the reading public, but also opposes himself to it, maintaining that in fact the 'bloods' had instilled in him a 'reading habit' which in and of itself was worthwhile. Mary Berry had expressed similar views on the cultivation of a reading habit in the 1800s.

Readers' responses to the texts they read are inflected by their gender, class and community affiliations, professional and social status, and political and religious beliefs. Hans Robert Jauss suggests that scholars interested in assessing a reader's response to a text should first outline that reader's 'horizon of expectations'. In Jauss's theory, the 'horizon of expectations' is largely dictated by the text; it is essential to consider the historical status of the literary conventions that the text abides by or breaks, and the literary strategies that it enacts, in order to ascertain the ways in which that reader could react to it.[103] An attempt to construct the reader's 'horizon of expectations' must also, though, take account of extra-textual influences, such as the cultural value of a particular form or genre, as well as a particular author's reputation, when attempting to analyse how it is received. In the case of Austen's nineteenth-century readers, the models of readers with which they were presented in the periodical press, as well as the changing cultural status of the novel are particularly relevant to how such readers could and did perceive Austen's novels, which themselves raise questions about the status of the novel, and the cultural value associated with different kinds of reading practices and reading matter.

Chapter 6

AUSTEN'S READERS I:
AFFECTION AND APPROPRIATION

Although discussion of Austen's earliest readers, in the shape of her family and immediate circle of friends, has already informed the argument of this book thus far, we will begin our detailed analysis of Austen's individual readers with the first generation of her literary successors, primarily with female authors, as these are the readers for whom the kinds of questions, problems and issues outlined in the previous chapters are most pressing. Austen's female successors frequently needed to establish themselves, as readers and writers, in opposition to the kinds of stereotypes and clichés discussed in Chapters 1 and 5. This chapter and those following discuss the implications of writers' various interactions with Austen's name in establishing their literary identities. As we will see, over the course of the long nineteenth century, Jane Austen became the publicly acceptable face of the woman writer, and, as literary women, writers from Mary Russell Mitford to Katherine Mansfield and Virginia Woolf compared themselves to Austen. They were also aware of the ways in which they were both implicitly and explicitly compared to her. Their reactions to her reveal important truths, not only about the ways in which Austen's novels acted on her successors, but about those successors' fears, insecurities and doubts about their position in the literary marketplace, their duties as professional women writers, and their responsibilities as women. Their negotiations with Austen's name show up their priorities as readers and writers, manifested in discussions over the characteristics of great literature, the proper behaviour for a professional female writer, the importance of a female tradition, the value of emotional responses, and debates about what a novel should be.

As Kathryn Sutherland argues, Austen's effect on her literary successors, both male and female, was heavily influenced by the biographical myths and semi-myths, begun in the 'Biographical Notice' written by her brother, and perpetuated in Austen-Leigh's popular *Memoir* of 1870.[1] Henry Austen writes: 'Short and easy will be the task of the mere biographer. A life of usefulness, literature, and religion, was not by any means a life of event'.[2]

The uneventfulness of Austen's life was to become a staple of criticism about her, as critics marvelled at her knowledge of the world despite the confines of her life. Aware of the social stigma attached to a professional female writer, Henry claims that his sister 'became an authoress entirely from taste and inclination. Neither the hope of fame nor profit mixed with her early motives [...] It was with extreme difficulty that her friends [...] could prevail on her to publish her first work',[3] and maintains that 'in public she turned away from any allusion to the character of an authoress'.[4] The briefest glance at Austen's letters demonstrates the patent falsehood of Henry's representation – but his squeamish denial of Austen's professionalism was nonetheless to be echoed in the responses of her readers. Henry claims for Austen a prim reaction to Fielding that is certainly not demonstrated in her letters (nor, indeed, in Mary Crawford's cheeky *Rears* and *Vices* pun in *Mansfield Park*).[5] Henry writes: 'Without the slightest affectation she recoiled from every thing gross', driving home the point that Austen's taste was truly refined.[6] Nervous of the effects of Austen's sharp and sometimes caustic wit, Henry insists on her 'candour': 'Faultless herself, as nearly as human nature can be, she always sought, in the faults of others, something to excuse, to forgive or forget'.[7] Henry's is an affectionate and idealized picture, but it was adopted as literal truth by many reviewers and common readers, and its repercussions have been long-lived. It is only in the last thirty years, for example, that literary critics have widely recognized and understood the depth of Austen's commitment to her literary endeavours, or the eclecticism and daring of her reading.

It is, of course, impossible to know how many readers read the 'Biographical Notice', or indeed how many took it seriously as an accurate representation of Jane Austen's temperament and character. We do know that at least one of her readers read and was moved to comment on the 'Biographical Notice' itself. The Rev. Alexander Dyce's first editions of Jane Austen's novels, now held in the National Art Library at the Victoria and Albert Museum in London, all contain fairly extensive marginalia in Dyce's hand. His annotations include corrections of misspellings and typographical errors, explanatory notes about literary or historical allusions, and a comment on the 'Biographical Notice' which reads:

> p. xvii. 'My dearest E.' i.e. James Edward Austen, her nephew, who was then at Exeter College, Oxford, where he read to me the very letter now quoted, on the day it reached him. He is now (1844) the Revd James Edward Austen Leigh, having added Leigh to his name since he succeeded to the property of his aunt, Mrs Leigh Perrot. The Lady last mentioned, Mrs Austen's sister, had an invincible propensity to stealing, and was tried at Bath for stealing lace: the printed account of the trial is extant. The family were dreadfully shocked at the

disgrace which she brought upon them. For many years she lived in seclusion at Scarlets (a handsome place where she died. [no closing parenthesis][8]

This case offers clear evidence of the reading of the 'Biographical Notice,' including the snippet of the letter to James Edward that Henry included in it. It was evidently important to Dyce to set down his connection with the writer, and in doing so to corroborate the veracity of the statements made in the text. How the 'Biographical Notice' influenced Dyce's reading of Austen is impossible to judge, but his marginal notes demonstrate a close and careful engagement with the texts themselves, as well as with the 'Biographical Notice', and a pedantic concern with accuracy, on the level of both typography and context. At the very least, we can say that he read the 'Biographical Notice' carefully and was moved to comment on it, perhaps subconsciously extending his sense of Austen's modesty, gleaned from Henry's description, to the rest of the family by noting their 'shocked' response to the 'disgraceful' Mrs Leigh Perrott. More broadly, we should note that nineteenth-century critical commentary on Austen's work relies heavily on Henry's depiction for both biographical fact and interpretation of the facts, and so disseminated Henry's version of his aunt to those readers who read the literary periodicals.[9]

'Jane Austen' as a figure was cheerfully requisitioned by the (largely male) writers of the periodical press to represent female experience, not as it was, but as they thought it could be. This appropriation complicates Austen's relationship to her female literary successors, making her a difficult and contradictory role model for the professional female writer. One of the founding tenets of feminist theory is Virginia Woolf's emphasis on the importance of thinking back through our mothers if we are women because this will provide a common ground of shared female experience through different historical eras.[10] Thinking back through Austen, however, entails thinking back through a figure whose depictions of female experience (in the shape of her novels) are haunted by the ghosts of biographical semi-myths and fictions about their author. Austen's female readers cannot think back through Austen as mother, therefore, without simultaneously thinking back through the fathers – biographers, critics, reviewers – who re-made her in an image distorted by their own desires and needs.

Many of the accounts of reading Austen considered in this chapter gesture beyond the boundaries of the texts to the broader issues surrounding the development of a tradition of women's writing in the long nineteenth century. It is no doubt unnecessary to stress that the material considered in this chapter was written against a backdrop of social change for women, in which the major legislative changes of the Custody Acts of 1839 and 1873, the Divorce Act of 1857, and the Married Women's Property Acts of 1870 and 1882 are the legal markers. The nascence of the Women's Rights Movement in the middle years of the century, the increasingly visible and vocal activities of the female suffragists, and the granting of partial Women's Suffrage in 1918, affected Austen's successors deeply and personally. Many women of the period mention the long battle to repeal the Contagious Diseases Acts of 1864, 1866 and 1869 as peculiarly important because it impelled them to break the taboos which made 'decent' and 'respectable' women remain silent about sexual abuses and inequities affecting girls and women. For such women, conventional modesty (of the kind praised by writers such as Hannah More) was no longer a social duty, but social irresponsibility. The importance of the establishment of institutions for women's higher education, such as Girton and Newnham Colleges, Cambridge (1869 and 1871), and Lady Margaret Hall and Somerville Hall [now College], Oxford (1878 and 1879), is also relevant. In 1869, Margaret Oliphant jokingly told her commissioning editor, Blackwood, that 'even' the establishment of 'Ladies' Colleges' would not iron out the differences in the ways men and women read and write about their reading:

> I am working at Richardson now, and will send you the paper by the end of the week. I suppose I ought to be ashamed to confess that, tedious as he often is, I feel less difficulty in getting through him than in reading Fielding, and that as a matter of taste I actually prefer Lovelace to Tom Jones! I suppose that is one of the differences between men and women which even Ladies' Colleges will not set to rights.[11] Pray don't tell of me; if I betray my sentiments in public they shall be laid upon the heavily burdened shoulders of what Clarissa would call 'my sex', and your contributor shall sneer at them as in duty bound.[12]

But social change of this nature does have an effect on reading practices, not least by making available to women books that they could not previously have seen, by teaching them the skills of critical analysis, whether literary or otherwise, and by opening the doors to legitimate professional activity. Social change does profoundly affect the professional writer's conception of his or her role, and it also changes the ways in which readers obtain, understand and interact with their reading matter.

Mary Russell Mitford (1787–1865)

For a number of reasons, the names of Mary Russell Mitford and Jane Austen were frequently and pervasively linked together in articles and reviews throughout the nineteenth century. This is partly because of a series of convenient similarities and coincidences, including their shared spinsterhood, the geographical proximity of their final homes (Three Mile Cross and Chawton respectively), the similarity of subject matter encompassed by both writers, and the almost-simultaneous publication of Austen-Leigh's *Memoir* of Jane Austen, and A. G. L'Estrange's *Life of Mary Russell Mitford*, which allowed them to be reviewed together in 1870. The coupling of their names, however, also happens because Mitford was a reader who was haunted by Austen, one who appropriated Austen's texts, stylistically and thematically, into her own writing. She is explicit about her desire to write like Austen, confiding to her friend Mrs Hofland, in a letter of 25 May 1825, that the novel she has in mind 'will be common English life in the country, as playful, and as true, as I can make it, in other words, as like Miss Austen'.[13] It is possible to identify the same desire in other women writers of Mitford's generation, such as Catherine Hutton (1756–1846), who wrote in a letter of November 1838: 'I had always wished, not daring to hope, that I might be something like Miss Austen; and, having finished her works, I took to my own, to see if I could find any resemblance.'[14]

Elizabeth Barrett Browning commented that Mary Mitford's affections and associations sometimes clouded her literary judgement: 'when she read a book, provided it wasn't written by a friend, edited by a friend, lent by a friend, or associated with a friend, her judgment could be fine and discriminating on most subjects, especially upon subjects connected with life and society and manners'.[15] Browning laments the lack of critical detachment in Mitford's analyses of literature, but for Mitford, this very lack of detachment constitutes a type of reading that is deliberately opposed to academic or critical demands for 'impersonality': one in which networks of connection and association are as important as arbitrarily or critically decided notions of literary value.[16] Mary Mitford had little respect for the judgements of critics. In her *Recollections of a Literary Life* (1852), she describes one winter when she amused herself 'by looking through the whole series of the "Monthly Review," reading the contemporary [i.e. eighteenth-century] judgements on Hume and Robertson, on Gibbon and Johnson, on Fielding and Smollett, on Goldsmith and Sterne, and comparing the criticism of the day with the abiding verdict of posterity'.[17] She enjoyed seeing the critics proved wrong by posterity, and believed that the common reader could be a better judge of a work's value. Mitford's entry in the *Dictionary of National Biography* confirms this character trait, describing her as 'catholic and unconventional in her literary judgement'.[18] Mitford can thus be described as an oppositional reader.

Mitford's commitment was rather to the importance of personal association in reading. She writes in the *Literary Life* of 'a pleasure quite apart from that excited by the charming book itself' [Bishop Percy's *Reliques of Ancient English Poetry*, 1765], the pleasure that 'springs from a very simple cause.

The association of these ballads with the happiest days of my happy childhood'.[19] In the dedicatory letter to the *Literary Life*, she writes to Henry F. Chorley, 'as I wrote [i.e. transcribed] line after line of our fine old Poets, many a cherished scene and many a happy hour seemed to live again in my memory and my heart'.[20] She dedicates 8 chapters (of 29) to the category of 'Authors Associated with Places'. Importantly, the association with place is with the place where the book was read, not necessarily the place where the author is from, or even indeed, commonly associated with (although sometimes the two combine). Samuel Johnson, for example, is associated with the scenes of Mitford's early life on the 'breezy Hampshire downs' rather than with London or Lichfield.[21] Each of the 29 chapters begins with some of Mitford's reminiscences about reading the author/s in question, and throughout, there is a strong belief in the value of the personal, combined with trenchant and fearless criticism. Rather than clouding her literary judgement, Mitford believes, associations enable it; 'relish' rather than impersonality is, according to her, a legitimate aim.[22] In her correspondence and her literary works, Mitford deploys Austen with a kind of possessive familiarity through which she justifies her own style of writing, her literary taste, her belief in the values of social propriety and modesty, and her commitment to the importance of personal association and pleasure in reading.

In the *Literary Life*, Mitford describes how her reading of Austen's *Persuasion* coloured her experience of Bath:

> Her exquisite story of 'Persuasion' absolutely haunted me. Whenever it rained (and it did rain every day that I staid at Bath, except one), I thought of Anne Elliott [*sic*] meeting Captain Wentworth, when driven by a shower to take refuge in a shoe-shop.[23] Whenever I got out of breath in climbing up-hill (which, considering that one dear friend lived in Lansdown Crescent, and another on Beechen Cliff, happened also pretty often), I thought of that same charming Anne Elliott, and of that ascent from the lower town to the upper, during which all her tribulations ceased. And when at last, I incurred the unromantic calamity of a blister on the heel, even that grievance became classical by the recollection of the similar catastrophe, which, in consequence of her peregrinations with the Admiral, had befallen dear Mrs. Croft.[24]

In this anecdote, Mitford brings Austen's characters to life in her own mind, and then begins to transform the very city of Bath by inscribing its streets and hills with the fictional events of Austen's novels. Mitford was not the only reader to feel Austen's particular claims on the city of Bath – Elizabeth Wordsworth remarks in her diary of 1866, 'I have been sending two ladies in Bath a copy of "Northanger Abbey" and "Persuasion"'. No one ought to live in Bath and not know them'.²⁵ Nor was Mitford the only reader to feel the peculiar power of Austen's fictionalization of real places. Alfred, Lord Tennyson, for whom Austen was a 'prime favourite,' was inspired to travel to Lyme Regis by Austen's description of the place in *Persuasion*.²⁶ Tennyson's son writes:

> On August 23rd [1867] my father left for Bridport. He was led on to Lyme by the description of the place in Miss Austen's *Persuasion*, walking thither the nine miles over the hills from Bridport. On his arrival he called on [F. T.] Palgrave, and, refusing all refreshment, he said at once: 'Now take me to the Cobb, and show me the steps from which Louisa Musgrove fell.'²⁷

The effectiveness of Austen's characterization is such that a fictional character gives importance and symbolic meaning to a real place in this account; Tennyson desires to see the Cobb not because of its undoubted picturesqueness but because it has upon it 'the steps from which Louisa Musgrove fell'. It is no surprise that Tennyson thought that Austen 'pictured human character as truthfully as Shakespeare', nor that her novels represented 'a bright and true' world.²⁸ His emphasis on the 'truth' of Austen's representations is borne out by his response to the Cobb of Lyme Regis.

Mitford identifies the same qualities in Austen's writing. Her anecdote of being haunted by Austen's characters in Bath works on many levels. This is a genuine tribute to the evocative quality of *Persuasion*; it is also suggestively allusive and self-conscious. Mitford's gentle self-mockery disguises the serious claims she is making for fiction's consolatory powers, but it does not entirely hide them. In the preface to *Literary Life*, Mitford describes the book as 'an attempt to make others relish a few favourite writers as heartily as I have relished them myself'.²⁹ The account above, therefore, is no doubt doctored to make an entertaining anecdote, and to help readers to 'relish' Jane Austen, and yet, in its casual allusiveness to the scenes and characters of *Persuasion*, it assumes a readership with significant previous knowledge of Austen's novel.

Reading beyond the direct allusions to *Persuasion*, the whole account also seems like an in-joke, of the kind that Austen herself delighted in. To be 'haunted' by the ghosts of one's reading brings Catherine Morland, *Northanger Abbey*'s devotee of Gothic novels, irresistibly to mind, particularly given Catherine's propensity, like the young Mitford's, to inscribe places with the preconceptions she brings to them from her reading. Just as Catherine peoples Northanger Abbey with characters from Mrs Radcliffe's *Udolpho*, so Mitford (or at least this representation of her younger self) peoples Bath with characters from Miss Austen's *Persuasion*. *Persuasion* and *Northanger Abbey*, linked geographically and thematically by the Bath scenes in both novels, were also linked by their publication history: Mary Mitford first read *Persuasion* in the John Murray edition that included *Northanger Abbey* (as well as Henry Austen's 'Biographical Notice').

As Mitford makes the geography of Bath meaningful to her, the real is superseded by the fictional; the 'dear friends' in Lansdown Crescent and Beechen Cliff become less real to the narrator than Austen's characters, 'charming Anne Elliot' and 'dear Mrs Croft'. Bath itself flickers between the concrete and the imaginary, retaining its geographical shape, but becoming vague in its outlines as the specificity of place names – Lansdown Crescent and Beechen Cliff – makes way for the fictional ascent from 'the lower town to the upper'. The narrator invokes the power of fiction to magic away the trying incidents of daily life – for her, Austen's characters seem to have an enchanted healing power that charms away the unpleasantness of rain, shortness of breath and even a blister on the heel. They come to life not only to guide her through a strange city, but also to enable the narrator to forget her troubles, even to 'relish' them. Like Anne Elliot herself, trudging towards Winthrop, who deals with the emotional pain caused by watching Captain Wentworth and Louisa Musgrove flirting together by musing on literary quotations, Mitford's younger self survives her troubles by thinking about literature. The comic effect of Mitford's anecdote lies partly in the fact that her narrator's troubles, unlike Anne's, are not those of the heart, but those of the body. The bathetic juxtapositions ('unromantic calamity', the 'catastrophe' of a blistered heel, the 'classical' blister) emphasize the difference between the travails of Mitford's younger self and those of Anne Elliot. And yet, the solace provided by the thought of *Persuasion* to Mitford's narrator is genuine, even if the author is self-mocking, just as the solace provided to Anne by her musings on autumnal poetry is real, even while she is gently mocked by her narrator. As we have seen, Austen's novels demonstrate the dangers of reading badly as well as the benefits of reading well; in this passage Mary Mitford comically makes the benefits of reading fiction manifest as the talismanic use of Austen's novel makes bearable (and even enjoyable) small, everyday woes. Explicitly retracing the geographical and emotional steps of one of Austen's heroines, Mitford implicitly refers to the haunting of another, and replicates Austen's complicated allusiveness and mockery in her own writing. W. M. Thackeray records a similar deployment of Austen's works as consolation, writing in October 1859, 'I have been living at Bath for the last ten days in Miss Austen's novels which have helped me to carry through a deal of dreary time'. Unlike Mitford, Thackeray's geographical location is not Bath; his phrase 'living at Bath' is metaphorical but, like Mitford's account, it pays tribute to the intensity of the reading experience, which ameliorates the 'dreary time' spent in an 'out of the way Inn'.[30]

On another occasion in the *Literary Life*, Mitford both paraphrases Austen and makes the sentiment her own, writing:

> It may be reckoned amongst the best and dearest of our English privileges, that we are all more or less educated in Shakespeare; that the words and thoughts of the greatest of poets are, as it were, engrafted into our minds, and must, to a certain extent, enrich and fructify the most barren stock. Shakespeare came to me I cannot tell how. But my first great fit of dramatic reading was, I am ashamed to say, of very questionable origin; a stolen pleasure; and therefore – alas! for our poor sinful human nature! – therefore by very far more dear.[31]

Mitford's reflections on Shakespeare equate directly with the passage in *Mansfield Park*, discussed in Chapter 3, in which Henry Crawford tells Edmund, 'Shakespeare one gets acquainted with without knowing how. It is a part of an Englishman's constitution. His thoughts and beauties are so spread abroad that one touches them everywhere, one is intimate with him by instinct'.[32] The context is that of 'dramatic reading', since the conversation arises out of the fact that Crawford has been reading Shakespeare's *King Henry VIII* aloud to Fanny and Lady Bertram. Mitford personalizes the idea by recounting her own 'first great fit of dramatic reading', thus conflating the Crawford/Edmund conversation in *Mansfield Park* with her own experience. Mitford's reading of Austen is compliant but possessive, consuming and recreating the works in a form close to, but no longer, their own. Throughout her letters and journal entries, Mitford records her strong emotional and aesthetic responses to Austen's novels, conveying to Elizabeth Barrett Browning her willingness to cut off her right hand if she could 'write one page like her's [Austen's] with the other'.[33] (Austen-Leigh presented this in his *Memoir* as something Miss Mitford had said to him; perhaps he misremembered or misrepresented this, or perhaps Mitford expressed herself in this way more than once).[34] Austen's writing has become a part of Mitford's being to the extent that Austen's novels, as spectral texts, and Jane Austen as spectral presence, imbue her writing.

In February 1815, Mary Mitford writes to Sir William Elford of Jane Austen as 'our great favourite, Miss Austen'. Mitford had made the discovery that Austen was 'my countrywoman; that mamma knew all her family very intimately', and goes on to relate some semi-malicious gossip (later refuted in Austen-Leigh's *Memoir*):

> Mamma says that she was then the prettiest, silliest, most affected, husband-hunting butterfly she ever remembers; and a friend of mine, who visits her now, says that she has stiffened into the most perpendicular, precise, taciturn piece of 'single blessedness' that ever existed [...] a poker of whom every one is afraid.[35]

Mitford conscientiously explains, 'I do not know that I can quite vouch for this account, though the friend from whom I received it is truth itself; but her family connections must render her disagreeable to Miss Austen'.[36] Mitford takes the opportunity in this letter to differentiate 'most writers', who 'are good-humoured chatterers – neither very wise nor very witty', from Austen. She, as 'a wit, a delineator of character, who does not talk', is 'terrific indeed!'[37] Here, Mitford presents herself as an admirer who can yet poke fun at the admired object, rather as Austen herself was wont to make fun of Scott, More or Richardson. Mitford and Sir William swiftly fall into the habit of alluding casually to Austen's novels and characters, and he tells her of Jane Austen's death, which she calls 'a terrible loss!', asking, 'are you quite sure that it is our Miss Austen?'[38] The question is poignant – on one level, of course, it is merely meant to verify the information given, but it simultaneously enacts a sort of possessive anxiety about the writer – the 'quite sure' desires a negative answer, while '*our* Miss Austen' rings with familiarity. In 1843, Elizabeth Barrett Browning writes to Mitford more than once of 'your Miss Austen', confirming Mitford's strong possessive feeling about her.[39]

Mitford's need to engage personally with what she reads is evident in the following comment to William Harness in November of 1852:

> Look at the great novelists of the day, Dickens and Thackeray (although it is some injustice to Thackeray to class them together, for he can write good English when he chooses, and produce a striking and consistent character); but look at their books, so thoroughly false and unhealthy in different ways; Thackeray's so world-stained and so cynical, Dickens's so meretricious in sentiment and so full of caricature. Compare them with Scott and Miss Austen, and then say if they can live. Neither of them can produce an intelligent, right-minded, straightforward woman, such as one sees every day, and a love story from Thackeray could hardly fail to be an abomination.[40]

Mitford gestures to a desire for fiction that represents or reflects her own experience: 'an intelligent, right-minded, straightforward woman, such as one sees every day', a figure she found in Austen and Scott. Whately's review of Jane Austen in the *British Critic* commented that 'her heroines are what one knows women must be';[41] Mitford here appears to be looking, in vain, for a similar sort of characterization in Dickens and Thackeray. Mitford's comment signals too to what she herself calls 'that *esprit de corps* which may be translated into "pride of sex"'; a desire that intelligent and right-minded women should once more take their rightful place in literature.[42] Mitford's interactions with Austen suggest that she did see her own experience depicted in Austen's novels; she had for her both passionate admiration and fellow-feeling. In this, she was not alone.

Sarah Harriet Burney (1772–1844)

For Sarah Harriet Burney, the less successful half-sister of Frances Burney, Austen provided a similarly well-loved role model. From the time of first discovering Austen's novels (which she read in Egerton and Murray's editions), Burney was an enthusiastic admirer. Having borrowed the first edition of *Pride and Prejudice* in December of 1813, she wrote to Elizabeth Carrick:

> Yes, I *have* read the book you speak of, "Pride & Prejudice", and I could quite rave about it! How well you define one of its charecteristics [*sic*] when you say of it, that it breaths [*sic*] a spirit of "careless originality". – It is charming. – Nothing was ever better conducted than the fable; nothing can be more *piquant* than its dialogues; more distinct than its characters. I have the three vols now in the house and know not how to part with them. I have only just finished, and could begin them all over again with pleasure.[43]

Emma was enough to lift her out of 'languour and depression' in 1816, when she wrote to Henry Colburn of her gratitude for the book: 'Many thanks for the loan of "Emma", which, even amidst languor and depression, forced from me a smile, & afforded me much amusement.'[44] She was delighted to hear of a friend's shared taste for Austen's work: 'I am *so* glad you like what you have read of "Emma" and the dear old man's "gentle selfishness." – Was there ever a happier expression? – I have read no story book with such glee, since the days of "Waverley" and "Mannering," and, by the same Author as "Emma," my prime favourite of all modern Novels "Pride and Prejudice."'[45] Burney then compares her own writing and cast of mind to Austen's: 'Fanny Raper likes to languish over stories stuffed, as she says herself, as full of love as a rich plum pudding is full of plums. I never insert love but to oblige my readers: if I could give them humour and wit, however, I should make bold to skip the love, and think them well off into the bargain.'[46] It is evident that Burney, like Mitford and Catherine Hutton, would have liked to write 'like Miss Austen', giving her readers 'humour and wit' if she could. In January of 1838, she wrote to her friend Anna Grosvenor of reading the sixth volume of Lockhart's biography of Walter Scott: 'It delighted me to find he (Sir Walter) thought so highly of my prime favourite Miss Austen – he read her "Pride and Prejudice" three times. *I* have read it as bumper toasts are given – *three times three*! –'[47] Throughout her life, Burney expressed similar sentiments. She delighted in *Emma*, she called *Pride and Prejudice* 'my prime favourite of all modern Novels', and, at the end of her life, held firm to her allegiance, insisting to Henry Crabb Robinson that 'I quite, & always did, prefer Miss Austen'.[48]

Arthur Henry Hallam (1811–1833)

Arthur Hallam is best known as the subject of Tennyson's *In Memoriam A.H.H.* (1849), but he was also, like his friend Tennyson, a poet and an admirer of Jane Austen's works. Writing to his fiancée, Emily Tennyson, in January of 1833, Hallam described his pleasure in re-reading *Emma*:

> I have been reading Miss Austen's Emma, which I had entirely forgotten, with the greatest enjoyment. I think it an admirable book, & I dare say you will agree with me. Miss Austen is an inimitable painter of quiet life. It would be difficult to say where the interest of Emma lies, yet it does interest strongly. There is no fine writing; no laboured description; no imaginative or ideal touches; no working on the feelings. Its magic must be its truth. It is exquisitely true. Life is presented to us, not as it may be taken in rare situations, in picturesque emergencies, but as we see it everyday. Common, workday life, with here & there a suit of best for Sundays. Yet there is nothing trivial. It is what Alfred calls in one of his unfinished poems 'most ideal unideal, most uncommon commonplace.' Dignity in the sentiments, dignity in the style. Quite a woman's book – (don't frown, Miss Fytche – I mean it for compliment) – none but a woman & a lady could possess that tact of minute observation, & that delicacy of sarcasm.[49]

These observations are all both acute and intelligent, but of greatest note is his characterization of *Emma* as a 'woman's book', particularly because this is figured as a 'compliment'. Although, as a male reader of the 1830s, Hallam would have been exposed to the criticisms of fiction and the feminized reading public discussed in the last chapter, he is nonetheless willing to commend Austen's novel, not despite, but *because* it is a 'woman's book'. Hallam's characterization of a women's novel as not only tactful, delicate and dignified (which one might expect), but also as true, admirable and stylistically 'inimitable' suggests that he was willing to take Austen's work, and, by extension, the novel genre seriously. There is crucially, he says, 'nothing trivial' in what Austen writes. To an extent, then, Hallam is an oppositional reader, ignoring or dismissing the expectations of gender and class in his reading of this work. Hallam's references to the 'delicacy' of Austen's sarcasm and the 'tact' of her careful observations also suggest that he identifies something of the subversive subtlety of Austen's art. In this, he pre-empts the comments of Margaret Oliphant in 1870 (discussed in Chapter 8).

After reading *Emma*, Hallam bought Bentley's edition of *Sense and Sensibility*, but he was slightly disappointed in it: 'I do not like it so well. It was her first book, & she does not seem to have attained full ease, & self possession. Yet there are many good things in it.'[50] After *Sense and Sensibility*, Hallam read *Mansfield Park*, in March 1833:

> I have just got through another of Miss Austen's novels, Mansfield Park, which many people vote the best. However although I like it much, and find the same delicacy of touch with delighted me in the others, yet is Emma my 1st. love and I intend to be constant. The edge of this constancy will soon be tried, for I am promised the reading of 'Pride and Prejudice'.[51]

Hallam's description of *Emma* as 'my 1st love' suggests a deep attachment to the book and its characters. This use of emotional language is noteworthy, pointing to an affective, as well as intellectual response to the book, rather like those of Austen's first readers, and a willingness to express his reaction in these terms, despite the negative and feminized connotations of emotional responses to literature found in the periodical press of the period. It is clear that Hallam anticipated the reading of *Pride and Prejudice* with great pleasure, but it is sadly impossible to know whether he ever did read it. There is no mention of the book in subsequent letters, and Arthur Hallam died in Vienna five months later, in September 1833. It is a sad irony that Tennyson's memorialization of Arthur Hallam echoes Hallam's own use of Tennyson's play on 'uncommon commonplace' to describe the experience of loss itself:

> One writes, that 'Other friends remain,'
> That 'Loss is common to the race'–
> And common is the commonplace,
> And vacant chaff well meant for grain.
>
> That loss is common would not make
> My own less bitter, rather more:
> Too common! Never morning wore
> To evening, but some heart did break.[52]

Arthur Hallam, sympathetic and sensitive reader of Jane Austen was, like the writer he so admired, neither common nor commonplace.

Thomas Babington Macaulay (1800–1859)

Thomas Babington Macaulay was, as Henry James cattily put it, Austen's 'first slightly ponderous amoroso', an avowed admirer of her novels both in public and in private.⁵³ His critical appraisals of Austen's work were influential in bringing her into the public eye (and lines from these, used as 'puffs' for her books, helped to sell them). In private Macaulay revelled in reading the novels, and knew them almost by heart. Like Mitford, he was also interested in what others thought of them, taking the time to report various opinions of Austen's works in a letter of 1831 to his sister, Hannah:

> On Saturday I dined at Lansdowne House. We had a small and very pleasant party. [Sir James] Mackintosh was there, and there was a good deal of conversation – chiefly about books [...] We chatted about novels. Everybody praised Miss Austen to the skies. Mackintosh said that the test of a true Austenian was Emma. 'Everybody likes Mansfield Park. But only the true believers – the select – appreciate Emma.' Lord and Lady Lansdowne extolled Emma to the skies. I had heard Wilber Pearson call it a vulgar book a few days before.⁵⁴

This snippet is suggestive in many ways, not least in revealing that as early as 1831, there were those who thought of themselves as 'true believers' and 'the select' in relation to their reading of Austen. Here we see a very early version of what would become 'Janeite' cults and culture in the late nineteenth and early twentieth centuries. The anecdote is also interesting in what it says about the perceptions of the relative value of Austen's different works in the period. Mackintosh's claim that 'everybody' liked *Mansfield Park* while *Emma* was the 'test of a true Austenian' reflects Arthur Hallam's comment that 'many people' 'vote [*Mansfield Park*] the best'.⁵⁵ This may be surprising to a modern readership, for whom the relative appeal of these two works is generally reversed, but it probably reflects a general approbation of *Mansfield Park*'s greater moral seriousness by Austen's early readers. Austen's acquaintance Mrs Carrick commented that 'all who think deeply & feel much will give the Preference to Mansfield Park', and many of the other opinions of *Mansfield Park* collected by Jane Austen, including that of its publisher, Thomas Egerton, also commend its 'morality', as we have already seen.⁵⁶ Approving of a 'moral novel' allowed readers to espouse the socially sanctioned Horatian position with regard to fiction; they could enjoy the entertainment as long as they were imbibing some instruction as well. In contrast, *Emma*'s 'morality' is less immediately obvious than *Mansfield Park*'s, and it is easy to see why, on first reading, a number of readers found it to be frivolous. Jane's brother Francis, for example, thought that there was 'an higher morality in *Mansfield Park*', while their friend Miss Bigg 'objected to the sameness of the subject (Match-making) all through' *Emma*. Their acquaintance Mrs Wroughton went further still, implying that *Emma* was not just inferior to *Mansfield Park*, but that it was potentially harmful, providing ammunition to the anti-religious factions of the period.

Austen recorded that Mrs Wroughton '[t]hought the Authoress wrong, in such times as these, to draw such clergymen as Mr. Collins & Mr. Elton'.[57] Mackintosh's comment that *Emma* functioned as the test of a true Austenian might therefore suggest that 'true Austenians' were those who were willing to adopt a more oppositional position as readers, valuing entertainment over instruction in a novel.

Macaulay's nephew and biographer, George Otto Trevelyan, wrote that 'amidst the infinite variety of lighter literature with which he beguiled his leisure, *Pride and Prejudice*, and the five sister novels, remained without a rival in his affections. He never for a moment wavered in his allegiance to Miss Austen.'[58] This was not strictly true; in 1831, Macaulay wrote to his sister, Hannah, that he believed that Madame de Staël was 'the first woman of her age – Miss Edgeworth, I think, the second, and Miss Austen the third', but, by 1851, he had altered his view, writing in his diary that 'there are in the world no compositions which approach nearer to perfection' than Jane Austen's works.[59] Macaulay told his friend, Macvey Napier, as early as 1834, that an article 'on Miss Austen's novels' was 'a subject on which I shall require no assistance from books', presumably because his knowledge of the works was so full and intimate,[60] and a 'short life of that wonderful woman' was one of the projects that remained unwritten on his death.[61] Macaulay had hoped that the profits from this proposed biography could be used 'to put up a monument to her in Winchester Cathedral'[62], and this hope, reported to readers both in his nephew's biography in 1876, and Austen-Leigh's *Memoir* in 1870, did prompt a letter to the *Times* which recommended that Macaulay's idea should be put into practice.[63] The eventual result was the memorial window in Winchester Cathedral, unveiled in 1900.

James Edward Austen-Leigh wrote of his aunt's knowledge of Richardson that 'every circumstance narrated in *Sir Charles Grandison*, all that was said or done in the cedar parlour, was familiar to her; and the wedding days of Lady L. and Lady G. were as well remembered as if they had been living friends.'[64] Macaulay knew Austen's works as intimately, referring to Austen's characters exactly as if they were living friends and mentioning them frequently and familiarly in his letter. To Hannah in 1833, for example, he writes that 'we, like Mrs. Norris, must always have a spare bed-room'.[65] Earlier in the same year, when Hannah was convalescing on a farm in the country, he encouraged her to drink plenty of milk, writing jokingly, 'I dare say that if, like Miss Smith, you are partial to one of their cows they will call it your cow'[66]. Complaining about having his picture taken, he likens himself one of Austen's characters: 'I begin, like Sir Walter Elliot, to rate all my acquaintance according to their beauty', and elsewhere, to another: 'I, like

Mr. Darcy, shall not care how proud I am'.[67] Phrases such as 'as Mrs Bennet would say', and 'as Sir William Lucas says' are common, particularly in the letters of the 1830s, when Macaulay was buying and re-reading Austen's novels in Bentley's new edition.[68]

Macaulay was unusually fortunate in having an excellent memory and extraordinary powers of concentration. 'His standard of excellence was always at the same level, his mind always on the alert, and his sense of enjoyment always keen', wrote his nephew of Macaulay's reading habits.[69] Apt allusions therefore came quickly to his mind, and these allusions were, of course, not limited to Austen's works. It seems, from his letters and copious marginal annotations, that the authors who came first to mind when Macaulay was commenting on, comparing or criticizing works, were the Classical writers (in particular Plato, Cicero, Horace, Virgil and the Greek tragedians) and Shakespeare. The depth and range of Macaulay's allusions is both astonishing and impressive, but it is noteworthy that his deployment of Austen appears to be more affectionate (if not more familiar) than that of his other favourites. Macaulay's engagement with the Classical authors and Shakespeare was perhaps more intense and philosophical than his reading of Austen – his marginalia are very extensive in his editions of Shakespeare's plays and the writings of the Classical authors, whereas his copies of Jane Austen's novels are hardly annotated – but, as we will see in Chapter 9, it was Austen to whom he habitually turned when he was seeking to say something serious in a light-hearted tone.[70] Trevelyan recorded that 'the writer of a book which had lived was always alive for Macaulay', commenting on the 'sense of personal relation' that Macaulay felt with the authors of the past. 'While he had a volume in his hands he never could be without a quaint companion to laugh with or laugh at; an adversary to stimulate his combativeness; a counselor to suggest wise or lofty thoughts, and a friend with whom to share them.' His books were 'companions', 'comrades' and 'society' to him.[71] For Macaulay, as for Mary Mitford, Sarah Harriet Burney, and countless other unnamed and unremembered readers, Jane Austen was a well-known friend, to whom he had pledged his 'allegiance' and who held first place in his 'affections'.[72]

In the affectionate and deeply engaged reactions of Macaulay and Mitford, and to a much lesser extent, those of Hallam and Burney, we see one model of response to Austen: playful, receptive, and sometimes appropriative. These readers are also, perhaps not coincidentally, prepared to oppose themselves to clichés and stereotypes about fiction and fiction's readers. The responses of these readers suggest that they are willing to participate in the 'games of ingenuity' identified in Chapter 3, in particular by making use of Austen's own trick of deliberately resonant and complex use of literary allusion. Austen's novels themselves become the allusions, and we see both Mitford and Macaulay delighting, as Austen did herself, both in apt and relevant quotation and in deliberately mismatching the register of quotation and occasion. Such readers perform what we might call playful acts of literary friendship, and we will see more of such acts in Chapter 9, when we consider familial and domestic readings of Austen's novels. In the next chapter, however, we will be discussing an alternative model of response: resistant and oppositional reading.

Chapter 7

AUSTEN'S READERS II: OPPOSITION AND RESISTANCE

The 'Austen Controversy' (1841–1845)

Between July 1841 and June 1845, Mary Russell Mitford and Elizabeth Barrett Browning engaged in a long-running affectionate epistolary argument about Jane Austen. Mary Mitford read Austen's novels in the Murray and Egerton editions but it is not known which edition/s Barrett Browning used, though it seems probable that she either owned or borrowed Bentley's edition. In the correspondence, both women demonstrate clearly their own allegiances through their manoeuvrings with Austen's name. They are both, more generally, oppositional readers who choose to define themselves against cultural stereotypes of the 'bad' female reader; in this series of letters, they also come to define their literary selves through their opposition to each other. In the course of their discussion we can trace two different visions of what a novel should be: Mitford's, whose model is Jane Austen, and whose belief is that accurate pictures of conventional life may contain within them the truths of the human heart, and Barrett Browning's, for whom 'Conventional Life is not the Inward Life'.[1] The clash is, in broad terms, between the novel of manners and the novel of psychological life, and between a pre-Romantic and post-Romantic literary sensibility. While Mitford passionately admires Austen, and considers her novels models of great literature, Barrett Browning objects to Austen on the grounds of lack of 'poetry', 'inner life' or 'ideal aspiration'.[2] When discussing Jane Austen, Charlotte Brontë poses the question '[can] there be a great artist without poetry?', and finds Austen 'without "sentiment," without *poetry*', concluding that she therefore 'cannot be great'.[3] Both Brontë's and Barrett Browning's rhetoric is strongly reminiscent of P. B. Shelley's *Defence of Poetry*, in which 'to be a poet is to apprehend the true and the beautiful, in a word the good which exists in the relation, subsisting, first between existence and perception, and secondly between perception and expression'.[4] By this account, the lack of 'poetry' in a writer automatically presupposes the inability to 'apprehend the true and the beautiful'. It is worth remarking here that, although Barrett Browning is a poet, and Brontë a novelist, they follow Shelley in recognizing 'the distinction between poets and prose-writers' as 'a vulgar error',[5] and in conceptualizing 'poetry' not in its 'more restricted sense' as 'arrangements of language, and especially metrical language',[6] but in its more idealized and 'general' sense, as 'the expression of the Imagination',[7] the representative of 'the true and the beautiful'.[8]

In the long-running discussion about Austen, we can piece together an argument not only about the qualities of literature, but about the future of the 'literary lady', the professional woman of letters. By Mitford's own admission, she felt that Joanna Baillie was 'the very pattern of what a literary lady should be', being 'quiet, unpretending, generous, kind, admirable in her writings, excellent in her life'.[9] Elizabeth Barrett Browning, on the other hand, admired George Sand and George Eliot, who were prepared to shun convention in their life and writing, embracing instead, 'warmth', 'passion', 'humanity' and experience. Mitford disapproved of Sand, writing to Mrs Ouvry in 1852 that she had been surprised by Elizabeth Barrett Browning's wholehearted support of George Sand, and explaining censoriously that 'Mrs. Browning did make an idol of talent'.[10] This revealing comment demonstrates both Mitford's sense that 'talent' did not excuse or justify departures from conventional morality, and Barrett Browning's belief in the freedom from social constraint owed to genius. Both Mitford and Barrett Browning were, of course, professional female writers, for whom these questions were not academic but deeply personal. Their perceptions of the intellectual space that a female writer could inhabit are defined by personal experience, and it is telling that, despite the success of female writers of all kinds – poets, dramatists, novelists and critics – in the early years of the nineteenth century, neither Elizabeth Barrett Browning nor Mary Russell Mitford felt entirely secure in her professional role.

The two women also embrace different positions as readers of Jane Austen: Elizabeth Barrett Browning is an oppositional reader, prepared to accept Austen on stylistic terms but staunchly opposed to what she believes Jane Austen represents, while Mitford, as we have seen, is a compliant, indeed possessive reader of Austen. Their positions in what they called the 'Austen controversy' thus show up their different priorities.[11] Both women rely on their mutual affection to bridge the gap between their different literary allegiances, and their opposition to one another over Austen allows them to define, clarify and maintain their respective positions, sometimes by responding directly to what the other writes, sometimes by attributing imaginary sentiments to the other in order to strengthen a particular argument. It is a kind of criticism that comes into being because it is carried out in an affectionate correspondence, making use of a rhetoric of friendship. Because the writers know each other well, they are able to attribute ideas to each other with some degree of accuracy, and because the letter is a private form, they are at liberty to express themselves with some freedom. Most of Mitford's side of the correspondence no longer exists, but Barrett Browning's letters frequently quote Mitford back to her, so some sense of Mitford's letters still remains.

Throughout the Barrett Browning-Mitford correspondence, whenever Barrett Browning is trying to evaluate Austen, she compares her, and asks Mitford to compare her, with another female writer – Frederika Bremer, Ann Radcliffe, Mary Howitt, Maria Edgeworth, Elizabeth Inchbald, Felicia Hemans, Ellen Pickering, Geraldine Jewsbury or Mary Mitford herself – rather than with her male contemporaries or predecessors (the only exception being Walter Scott).[12] Although the 1840s saw some male critics – among them Macaulay and G. H. Lewes – endeavouring to consolidate Jane Austen's reputation by placing her in a tradition of male writers, second only to Shakespeare, Barrett Browning situates Austen firmly in a tradition of female writers, and establishes a hierarchy of female writers within which women should be compared to one another. In so doing, she establishes an alternative canon of writers in which gender is a given, forestalling the 'praise / Which men give women when they judge a book / Not as mere work, but as mere woman's work, / Expressing the comparative respect / Which means the absolute scorn'.[13] Virginia Woolf lamented the female writer's lack of a tradition of thinking back through our mothers, and Barrett Browning herself longed to find her literary grandmothers. When she situates Austen among her female counterparts and makes female writers into her comparative standard of quality, Barrett Browning begins the long work of establishing the importance of such a female tradition.

The argument over Austen begins when Elizabeth Barrett Browning recommends to Mitford Mary Howitt's translation of Frederika Bremer's *The Neighbours* (1842), on the grounds that Mrs Howitt has said that it is 'like Miss Austen'. She entreats Mitford to 'read it my dearest friend, & agree with me that it is delightful', thus desiring Mitford's agreement and wanting to share with her the 'delight' of the book. She repeats Howitt's comment, saying, '"Like Miss Austen" being the best introduction to you possible, "I echo her" – altho' in my private & individual opinion & saving your presence, I do consider the book of a higher & sweeter tone than Miss Austen had voice & soul for'.[14] Barrett Browning's engagement with the work in hand is intimate and personal, describing it as she would a friend or acquaintance, who needs an 'introduction' to another friend. Austen herself adopted a similarly intimate vocabulary when writing of her books, making use of the trope of book-as-acquaintance when she answered a letter on the subject of *Emma* as if her novel were a debutante. Her correspondent (the Countess of Morley) sets up the trope by writing of having been 'most anxiously waiting for an introduction to Emma', and of her delight in having 'the pleasure of her acquaintance'.[15]

Austen responds: 'in my present state of doubt as to her reception in the World, it is particularly gratifying to receive so early an assurance of your Ladyship's approbation'.[16] Austen frequently spoke of her characters as if they were alive, writing jokingly to Cassandra of having been 'very well pleased' at an exhibition 'with a small portrait of Mrs Bingley, excessively like her', and carrying on the joke with a description of the supposed Mrs Bingley's dress: 'in a white gown, with green ornaments, which convinces me of what I had always supposed, that green was a favourite colour with her'.[17] Like Macaulay, other readers often respond to Austen herself, and the books, as well as her characters, as if they were 'living friends'.[18] The American critic and novelist, W. D. Howells, in fact, explicitly claimed to do so: 'She has always been a family cult with us [...] We talk of her as if she were our living friend'.[19] To Anne Thackeray Ritchie, Austen's were 'dear books'.[20] To read Austen, according to such accounts, is to perform an act of friendship, and a personal relationship with the text and the author (however the author is figured by the individual reader) is thus essential. Barrett Browning resists becoming Austen's 'secret friend', and she also refuses to call Austen a 'sister' (unlike writers more congenial to her, even if less talented – 'the sister Jewsbury', for example),[21] but she knows that the phrase 'like Miss Austen' can be used to ensure Mitford's attention to another book, rather as a letter of introduction opens the doors of a new acquaintance. She is therefore prepared to use the rhetoric of friendship to open their discussion.

Barrett Browning tells Mitford that she is 'pleased, & touched ... *charmed for the better*, by [Bremer's] book',[22] and she also feels compelled, the compulsion mirrored in the jerky rhythms of her prose and her lack of punctuation, to compare the writer to Austen:

> There is more poetry, more of the inner life, more of the ideal aspiration more of a Godward tendency in the book than we need seek for or than even you my beloved friend, can, I think, imagine in any book or books of Miss Austen considered in a moment of your most enthusiastic estimation.[23]

Although she apologizes to Mitford ('saving your presence'), for her contrary point of view, she cannot refrain from criticizing. As Barrett Browning writes her 'private & individual opinion', she is engaging in an internal dialogue with Mitford even while she writes to her, her own opinion crystallizing in opposition to what she imagines Mitford might 'imagine' or 'estimate'.

In Barrett Browning's next letter on the subject of Austen, she writes: 'she wants (admit it honestly, because *you know* she wants it) she wants a little touch of poetry'.[24] This is a skirmish in which the argument over Austen is coming to stand for something larger: whether or not these are two readers who can agree over what makes great literature. It is worth noting that, in 1847, G. H. Lewes makes the claim that great literature needs verisimilitude, writing that truth to nature is 'the real purpose of literature', glorifying Austen for her mastery in this field and suggesting that 'Fielding and Miss Austen are the greatest novelists in our language'.[25] Here, as in his well-known correspondence with Charlotte Brontë, Lewes's views are aligned with Mitford's, rather than Barrett Browning's, although he was later partially to revise his opinion.

Barrett Browning adopts a variety of strategies in the letter of 7 December to persuade Mitford of her point of view. She suggests that *The Neighbours* is an ideal title for Austen – 'The title is, *The Neighbours* – just a title for Miss Austen you see!' – thus demonstrating her own familiarity with Austen's subject matter. She also recognizes an important aspect of Austen's novels, in which the depiction of neighbourly relationships is, as Sarah Emsley rightly argues, key to appreciating 'Jane Austen's complex understanding of the nature of the theological virtue of charity'.[26] Barrett Browning hence establishes her right to comment on Austen's work. Conciliatorily, she continues, 'and for Miss Austen, you shall praise her as much as you please', but adds, 'she is delightful exquisite *in her degree!*' The sting in the tail of the sentence is neatly calculated: it keeps Austen firmly in her place, both socially and in the realms of literature. Barrett Browning then claims to enjoy Mitford's own work far more than Austen's: 'I w^{dnt} have one of your dear hands "cut off" that you sh^d "write one page like her's with the other", – because, really & earnestly, your Village & Belford Regis are more charming to me than her pages in congregation'. The compliment is charming and disarming, and thus puts her reader off balance before a coercive syntactical structure: 'she wants (admit it honestly because *you know* she wants it) she wants a little touch of poetry'.[27] By implicitly suggesting that Mitford's own writing has the 'touch of poetry' lacking in Austen's, Barrett Browning gives Mitford a strong motive for agreeing with her judgements. For Elizabeth Barrett Browning, great literature must have 'poetry', and so, if she can get Mitford to agree that Austen's writing lacks 'poetry', Barrett Browning assumes that she has won her particular case: Austen would accordingly be a competent but second-rate writer.

It seems from the quotations from Mitford's letter that *her* concern is not only with the question of 'poetry' or lack of it, but also with the question of style or craftsmanship. The desire to 'write one page like her's' – to emulate her style – does away with the rhetoric of 'ideal aspiration', 'Godward tendency' or the 'inner life', concentrating instead on the small and tangible: 'one page', rather than Barrett Browning's 'pages in congregation'. It also focuses on a concrete desire: 'to write one page', while Barrett Browning's condemnation seems abstract and idealized in comparison. Mitford could have made a strong case for the perfection of Austen's craftsmanship, but instead, it appears that she chooses to engage with her friend's criticisms about 'poetry', claiming for Austen the very virtues that Barrett Browning deems her to lack. '"Persuasion" (ah! You are cunning to bring "Persuasion" to me!) is the highest & most touching of her works – and I agree with you gladly that it is perfect in its kind, & with touches of a higher impulse in it than we look generally to receive from her genius', writes Barrett Browning.[28] Again, though, her reservations are clear. *Persuasion* is only 'perfect in its kind', and has better things in it 'than we look generally to receive from her genius'. This is surely damning the book with faint praise: all she has admitted is that it is a better book than the rest of Austen's novels, which she had already relegated to an inferior realm of literature.

Elizabeth Barrett Browning's views of Austen's work as 'perfect in its kind', 'delightful' and 'exquisite' but lacking in 'passion' or 'poetry' find a counterpart in comments by Charlotte Brontë. Brontë recognizes Austen's 'miniature delicacy in the painting', but (famously) misses any sense of passion: 'the Passions are perfectly unknown to her; she rejects even a speaking acquaintance with that stormy Sisterhood'.[29] Austen's own tongue-in-cheek description of her work as a 'little bit (two Inches wide) of Ivory, on which I work with so fine a Brush, as produces little effect after much labour',[30] transmitted to her readers in Henry Austen's 'Biographical Notice', led many of her critics to describe her as a miniaturist, her art perfect within its tiny compass. Related to this idea is the belief that Austen was unable to depict passion. G. H. Lewes, for example, characterizes her works as 'miniatures',[31] and, although he admires the novels, writes of her 'deficiencies in poetry and passion', suggesting that she has 'little or no sympathy with what is picturesque and passionate'.[32] Despite the 'delight which Miss Austen's works have always given us', and his view of her as a perfect artist, he concludes that her 'genius, moving only amid the quiet scenes of every-day life, with no power over the more stormy and energetic activities which find vent even in every-day life, can never give her a high rank among great artists'.[33] Tennyson called her novels 'perfect works on a small scale – beautiful bits of stippling',[34] while Julia Kavanagh writes that 'her range of vision was limited [...] The grand, the heroic, the generous, the devoted, escaped her, or, at least, were beyond her power',[35] but that 'in her own range, and admitting her cold views of life to be true, she is faultless, or almost faultless'.[36] E. S. Dallas suggests that George Eliot is a greater writer than Austen because she 'undertakes to set forth the issues of a more tumultuous life, to work out deeper problems, and to play with torrents where Miss Austen played with rills'.[37] According to the *New Monthly Magazine* of 1852, Austen is 'perfect mistress of all she touches [...] if not with the embellishments of idealism and romance, at least with the fresh strokes of nature'.[38] Elizabeth Barrett Browning's comments on Austen reflect similar views.

Barrett Browning disliked what she felt Austen had come to epitomize – a female writer who did not take her literary self seriously enough. While G. H. Lewes admires the fact that Austen 'made herself known without making herself public', Barrett Browning takes the opposite view.[39] She writes:

> I think, for instance, that you, as your Miss Austen did & as Mrs Radcliffe did, care more for the respect paid to you on mere social grounds, than you care for any acknowledgement of your power as a writer & on literary grounds. I think that you have a sort of satisfaction in saying 'People do not talk literature to me' or 'people like me for myself better than they do for my books'. I think moreover, that you have a tendency to laugh to scorn […] the pain of that wrestling for merited distinction under which so many great hearts have groaned aloud.[40]

Barrett Browning was right about Mitford's tendency to play down her literary talents. Her identification of the trait of false literary modesty with Jane Austen as well as Mary Mitford is, however, the result of the prevailing myth, begun by Henry Austen in the 'Biographical Notice' (and perpetuated in Maria Jane Jewsbury's account of Jane Austen in her 'Literary Women' series of 1831) in which Henry writes of Austen's dislike of the public character of an authoress.[41] Austen's art was rarely represented as being of the kind that demanded 'the pain of that wrestling for merited distinction under which so many great hearts have groaned aloud'; instead, she is presented as an artist blessed by nature or some higher (sometimes supernatural) power. Rather as Milton represented Shakespeare as 'Fancy's child', warbling 'his native Wood-notes wild',[42] the *Edinburgh Review* of July 1839 characterizes Austen as 'one who plays by ear […] led to right conclusions by an intuitive tact'.[43] Julia Kavanagh invests Austen with the 'veneration and awe' due to a 'seer',[44] Virginia Woolf fancifully imagines her literary endeavours blessed by 'one of those fairies who perch upon cradles',[45] and Margaret Oliphant likens her genius to 'witchcraft and magic'.[46] The related version of Austen is as a writer who wrote for amusement – 'an authoress entirely from taste and inclination'[47] – writing with 'ease and naturalness'.[48] Barrett Browning dislikes what she believes to be Austen's facility of composition as much as she does the lack of 'poetry' or depth in her art, seeing the latter as the natural result of the former. She is also scornful of 'Miss Austen's reluctance to be mixed up with "writing people"', commenting, 'Mrs Radcliffe had or appeared to have a like feeling – & so has my own dear friend Miss Mitford! Well! – Or … ill!! Which is the word?'[49] Barrett Browning, author of *Aurora Leigh*, the passionate exploration of the difficulties of the professional female writer, feels undermined and betrayed by a predecessor who seems to her to have done it all too easily.

On 3 March 1843, Elizabeth Barrett Browning writes to tell Mitford of Macaulay's review in the *Edinburgh Review*: 'Did you see [...] in the number before last of the Edinburgh Review, a notice of Ma^{dme} d'Arblay, very admirable in all ways, but chiefly interesting to you for the sake of the high estimate of your Miss Austen, who is called *second to Shakespeare* in the nice delineation of character'.[50] Barrett Browning knows that the idea that Austen is '*second to Shakespeare*', or, as Macaulay actually writes, 'nearest to the manner of the great master',[51] will be ammunition on Mitford's side of their affectionate argument about the depth of Austen's art. Her recommendation of the article to Mitford also signals a willingness to return to their old argument. Five days later, Barrett Browning then writes, on 8 March 1843, of her 'surprise at your considering Miss Edgeworth & Miss Austen mistresses in pathos – when the fault of both those excellent writers appears to me (if indeed that can be a fault which is so closely allied to the peculiarity of their excellencies) a defect in passion altogether, through their habit of considering life & humanity on the cold conventional side'. She complains of Edgeworth's works that 'the depths of the heart & the heights of Heaven have no part or lot in them – and pastoral Nature is as utterly shut out', and that they are not 'poetical & passionate'.[52] She then asks, 'will you answer me one more question ... Is not the "Simple Story" more pathetic than "Persuasion"?'[53] What is lacking in both the earlier writers, according to Barrett Browning, is warmth, pathos and, once again, 'poetry', although her sense that the 'defect in passion' is allied to 'the peculiarity of their excellencies' does suggest a willingness to accept and understand Austen and Edgeworth on what she believes to be their terms rather than her own.

Barrett Browning's full objections to Austen, most of which appear in some form in the previous passages quoted, are expressed clearly in a letter of 1 June 1843, which is worth reproducing at length:

> My dearest friend you mistake a little in your view of the Austen controversy. I thought you w^d know what I meant by denying the beauty. I meant of course, the poet's beauty, the ideal! [...]
>
> Ah – you talk of 'Persuasion'! – & you may well talk of 'Persuasion' – because there is more of the Beautiful in an intense sense, in that work, than in all the rest of Jane Austen's writings. It is in fact an exception, and proves the rule.
>
> My very dear friend, I no more think of denying *her perfection in her sphere*, than I deny the rainyness of this May [...] She is perfect in what she attempts – she is admirable in all that she undertakes: but the excellence lies, I do hold, rather in the execution than the aspiration. It is a narrow, earthly, & essentially unpoetical view of life: It is only half a true view. Her human creatures never look up; and when they look within it is not deeply. We rise from her books, ...

amused, pleased ... charmed, if you like it ... but elevated & purified in soul, we never rise. Now is this not the true statement? Conventional Life is not the Inward Life ... and a writer who is not one-sided, must comprehend *both* in his view of Humanity. Jane Austen is one-sided – and her side is the inferior & darkest side. God, Nature, the Soul ... what does she say, or suggest of these? What proof does she give of consciousness of these? She is, I must repeat my persuasion, essentially unpoetical, ...& does not approach so nearly to Ideal beauty, as Natural picturesqueness! In her works, we do not discern even 'the trees' ... much less, the voice of God stirring them.[54]

These comments expose clearly Barrett Browning's own sense of the duty of the writer and of the reader, and they gesture suggestively towards the constraints she feels when writing about Austen. Although the correspondence with Mitford is a relatively safe space (private, intimate, friendly) in which to practise criticism of a female writer, it seems that Barrett Browning still imposes some self-censorship, forcing herself to acknowledge Austen's 'perfection', but repeatedly qualifying it. Despite her apparent concessions to Mitford, and to the popular critical view of Austen's greatness (familiar to Barrett Browning from Macaulay's review, if not from elsewhere), the calculated and bathetic dismissiveness of her analogy between Austen's 'perfection' and 'the rainyness of this May' suggests her unwillingness to attribute 'perfection' to Austen. This is borne out in her characterization of Austen as comprehending only 'the inferior and darkest side' of humanity. Elizabeth Barrett Browning is afraid of the possibility of representing 'truth' without 'passion' or 'poetry'. In her conception of great writing, a reader must rise from the books 'elevated & purified in soul'. Reading must be a spiritual experience. She wants to find 'Ideal beauty', 'God, Nature, the Soul'. Many of Barrett Browning's reservations about Austen stem from her sense that Austen lacks 'aspiration'; she clearly feels that a 'narrow' view of life must be 'essentially unpoetical'. Failure in a great attempt, in Elizabeth Barrett Browning's thought, is obviously preferable to success in a more minor undertaking, and she resents therefore what Henry James was later to call Austen's 'narrow unconscious perfection of form'.[55]

John Henry Newman (1801–1890)

John Henry (later Cardinal) Newman felt a similar lack of spirituality and ambition in Jane Austen's novels, writing to his sister, Jemima Mozley, in January 1837:

> I have been reading Emma. Everything Miss A. writes is clever, but I desiderate something. There is a want of *body* to the story. The action is frittered away in

over-little things. There are some beautiful things in it. Emma herself is the most interesting to me of all her heroines. I feel kind to her whenever I think of her. But Miss A. has no romance, none at all. What vile creatures her parsons are! She has not a dream of the high Catholic *ethos*. That other woman, Fairfax, is a dolt – but I like Emma.[56]

Although Newman's comments may seem puzzling in the light of Jane Austen's very real piety, evidenced not only by her family in her epitaph and the 'Biographical Notice', but also in the prayers she herself wrote, it is in fact explicable on both personal and theological grounds. Newman's dislike of Austen's treatment of the clergy makes perfect sense in the light of his own religious fervour and vocation, as well as his serious engagement with what he saw as the problems in mainstream Anglican theology and worship. At the time of writing this letter, Newman was an Anglican priest, and extremely active in the revolution in religious thought that would come to be called the Oxford (or Tractarian) Movement, a movement which, among other things, wished to reform the Anglican clergy by reforming a perceived secularization of the Church of England. Austen's 'parsons' (Mr Elton, Henry Tilney, Mr Collins, Edward Ferrars, Edmund Bertram, even the minor character Charles Hayter), who are seen in the pursuit of secular, human love, and who all have a strong sense of the importance of worldly goods, are thus almost exact counter-examples to what Newman thought a priest should be. Austen says little about her clergymen's spiritual life, and the closest she comes to an outright statement on the role of the clergy is Edmund Bertram's response to Mary Crawford's contention that 'a clergyman is nothing':

> I cannot call that situation nothing which has the charge of all that is of the first importance to mankind, individually or collectively considered, temporally and eternally, which has the guardianship of religion and morals, and consequently of the manners which result from their influence. No one here can call the *office* nothing. If the man who holds it is so, it is by the neglect of his duty, by foregoing its just importance, and stepping out of his place to appear what he ought not to appear.[57]

Although this is a strong statement of the importance of the clergyman, it is also one which focuses on his societal role, rather than his soul. Edmund does not forget the 'temporal', along with the 'eternal', in his defence of the clergy above. In addition, a number of Austen's clergymen show a preoccupation with economic and financial affairs that is profoundly unspiritual. Edward and Elinor, we should remember, are 'neither of them quite enough in love to think that three hundred and fifty pounds a-year would supply them with the comforts of life'.⁵⁸ (This fact prompted Katherine Mansfield, too, to revulsion – 'My God, say I!', she recorded in her diary after copying out this sentence from *Sense and Sensibility* in 1914).⁵⁹ Mr Elton's determined pursuit of two heiresses – first Emma, then Augusta – reveals him as a fortune hunter, and, while Edmund Bertrum and Henry Tilney are less obviously interested in money, their world-view is nonetheless grounded in a clear understanding of the value of material possessions. Charles Hayter's conversation, from the tiny glimpses we see of him in *Persuasion*, is also strongly preoccupied with his worldly promotion. We can see why Austen's clerics were indeed 'vile creatures' from Newman's perspective. Newman was not, of course, alone in thinking this, although he expresses it more strongly than most – we have already seen Mrs Wroughton's disapproval of Austen's clergymen on the grounds that the times were, by 1815, already too secular for such portrayals to be safe.

Newman's perception of Austen was also no doubt influenced by a personal and theological disagreement with his former friend and mentor, Richard Whately. In his influential review of *Northanger Abbey* and *Persuasion* for the *Quarterly* in 1821, Whately had called Austen 'evidently a Christian writer', and commended her religion for being the more effective because unobtrusive.⁶⁰ During the 1830s, the relationship between Newman and Whately became increasingly strained and difficult, as Whately's religious views became progressively more liberal, and Newman's opinions pulled him in the opposite direction. Whately and Newman quarrelled irretrievably over their differences, with Newman eventually feeling it necessary to tell Whately 'how deeply I deplore the line of ecclesiastical policy adopted under your archiepiscopal sanction' in a letter of 28 October 1834.⁶¹ Newman's views of Austen were thus negatively influenced by Whately's positive opinion of her. Admired by and aligned with liberal, middle-of-the-road Anglicans, Austen was therefore a writer tainted by association for Newman.

Although he had not yet converted to Catholicism in 1837, Newman already believed strongly in the importance of what he calls here 'the high Catholic *ethos*'. James Pereiro argues that the concept of *ethos* was at the heart of the Tractarian Movement, and that it represented a complex theory of religious knowledge, based on the Aristotelian emphasis on the place of practical wisdom in the search for truth.⁶² References to *ethos* abound in Newman's letters, and it clearly held a central place in his structures of thought, best understood as the idea that holiness was a prerequisite for understanding truth. His condemnation of Austen as lacking the high Catholic *ethos* is, in fact, extremely damning, given that Austen's reputation, at this point in time, partly depended on her novels' 'decided tendency to improve the hearts of those that read them', as Thomas Henry Lister wrote in the *Edinburgh Review* in 1830,⁶³ and on their claims to depicting the world more 'truthfully' than other novelists. Coupled with his opinion that she 'has no romance, none at all', Newman is here suggesting that Austen's mind was too earthly and materialistic for her novels to be considered either salubrious or great art. Her verisimilitude, in other words, had nothing to do with 'truth', which, for Newman, came from God. Newman, then, agrees exactly with Barrett Browning's criticisms of Austen's novels as lacking in a tendency to lift the heart towards God, and his comments on her works reflect both his dislike of middle-of-the-road, mainstream Anglicanism, which he saw Austen as epitomizing, and his belief that Jane Austen's realistic depictions of human manners constituted an inferior kind of art.

Newman's use of the word 'clever' to describe Austen's works is also telling. In 1837, it did already carry some of its modern meaning ('intelligent'), but was by no means generally complimentary. Of all the *OED*'s examples of this usage, all have some negative connotations, including those closest in period to Newman's use in his letter to his sister. Charles Lamb opposed 'genius' to 'cleverness', for example, and Charles Kingsley famously suggested that 'good' maids should 'let who will be clever'.[64] Johnson's *Dictionary* of 1755 described 'clever' as 'a low word',[65] and Austen herself had used it in *Emma* to denote ambiguity in her portrayal of her heroine. Although being 'handsome, clever and rich' may appear on first reading to be unambiguously delightful, alert readers of *Emma*'s opening lines are put on their guard by the narrator's assertion that Emma only '*seemed* [my italics] to unite some of the best blessings in existence'.[66] Our suspicions about the true value of cleverness are confirmed when we learn from Mr Knightley that Emma is 'spoiled by being the cleverest of her family',[67] and strengthened when we read Austen's record of Martha Lloyd's opinion of the same work: 'as *clever* (her emphasis) as either of the two others, but did not receive as much pleasure from it as from P. & P. – & MP.'[68] There is, it seems, something suspicious about 'cleverness', that it may compromise the pleasure that a reader takes in a book. Newman is, in fact, using Austen's own trick here, to condemn while seeming to praise, as his later comments about *ethos* and 'romance' make clear. It is hence surprising that he should like clever Emma best of all Austen's heroines, and 'feel kind' towards her, but perhaps this is, in itself, an example of Newman's own attempts to have and demonstrate the right *ethos* – that is, being in the frame of mind to put the Christian virtues of charity and kindness into practice.

The 'Austen Controversy' Continued

Unlike Newman and Barrett Browning, Mary Russell Mitford believed that Austen was both an ambitious and a spiritually satisfying writer. For her, the depiction of life as it is, rather than as it should be, was as difficult and worthwhile as representing what Barrett Browning called the Ideal, and Newman the high *ethos*. What her friend saw as narrowness and lack of aspiration, Mitford saw as fidelity to detail. Mitford's own work, like Austen's, depicted village life with verisimilitude, but also with humour. Her aim, as she wrote in the introduction to the first volume of *Our Village*, was to describe the village and its people 'with the closest and most resolute fidelity' but she also recognized that she might have depicted them with 'a brighter aspect [...] than is usually met with in books'.[69] Mitford goes on, in the first pages of the first *Village* sketch, to place herself in a literary tradition exemplified, for her, by Austen:

> Even in books I like a confined locality, and so do the critics when they talk of the unities. Nothing is so tiresome as to be whirled half over Europe at the chariot wheels of a hero, to go to sleep at Vienna and awaken at Madrid; it produces a real fatigue, a weariness of spirit. On the other hand, nothing is so delightful as to sit down in a country village in one of Miss Austen's delicious novels, quite sure before we leave it to become intimate with every spot and every person it contains.[70]

We are reminded here, of Austen's teasing comment to Anna Lefroy, written after reading Anna's novel in manuscript in 1814: 'Your Aunt C. does not like desultory novels, & is rather fearful yours will be too much so, that there will be too frequent a change from one set of people to another, & that circumstances will be sometimes introduced of apparent consequence, which will lead to nothing [...] I allow much more Latitude than she does.'[71] Mitford, too, wished to avoid 'desultory' novels. Not only is Mitford naming her debt to Austen here, she is (deliberately, it seems) associating Austen with the unities of Classical tragedies, with all of their traditional high-culture connotations, and thus implying that, as a writer who observes the unity of place, Austen deserves the same sort of critical recognition as the classical tragedians. She therefore claims for Austen, and, through Austen, for herself, a classical lineage and tradition.

Austen's early critics had also commented approvingly on Austen's adherence to the classical unities. The *British Critic*'s reviewer, for example, contrasted *Emma* with the majority of other novels to the former's credit: 'In few novels is the unity of place preserved; we know not of one in which the author has sufficient art to give interest to the circle of a small village. The author of *Emma* never goes beyond the boundaries of two private families, but has contrived in a very interesting manner to detail their history and to form out of so slender materials a very pleasing tale.'[72] It may be that Mitford was thinking of such reviews as she wrote the section from *Our Village* quoted above. Later in *Our Village*, in the sketch entitled 'Nutting', Mitford directly references Austen once again, discussing the purity and propriety of her language use, in a footnote that defends her own use of the word 'deedily' by giving it a precedent in the work of 'the most correct of female writers, Miss Austen'.[73] Again, she aligns herself with Austen, simultaneously claiming literary authority for Austen and providing herself with a legitimate literary ancestress. Mitford saw Austen's 'correctness', her apparent adherence to codes of propriety, the geographical and social limitations of her work and her focus on detail and verisimilitude as both pleasing and suitable for a female writer to emulate. For Mitford, Austen was not so much a literary 'mother' as a much-needed friend, a guide as well as a literary inspiration.

Charlotte Brontë, however, as we have seen, found in Austen nothing to admire: 'no glance of a bright, vivid physiognomy, no open country, no fresh air, no blue hills, no bonny beck'.[74] Barrett Browning, too, comments on the lack of 'Nature' in Austen, and, like Brontë, misses a sense of the outdoors in Austen's work: 'we do not discern even "the trees"'. Where Mitford found the geographical limitations of Austen's work to be both classically inspired and reassuring, both Barrett Browning and Brontë seem to feel a sense of claustrophobia when reading Austen. Brontë literalizes and localizes hers by claiming that she would not like to live in Austen's 'elegant but confined houses',[75] while Barrett Browning's equally claustrophobic reaction locates itself less geographically in Austen's want of literary or spiritual 'aspiration'. Yet Barrett Browning herself deploys a rhetoric of anti-aspiration, endeavouring, as we saw earlier ('*in her degree*') to minimize Austen's achievement; to keep her '*in her sphere*'. Once again, Elizabeth Barrett Browning adopts the discourse of the social world to describe the literary – like 'her degree', 'her sphere' refers dismissively both to Austen's place in the 'Conventional world' and in the realm of literature. Barrett Browning articulates both a snobbishness towards Austen's 'correct pictures of middle life', the 'class' of which is '*low*',[76] and the reverse snobbery of suggesting that she is 'too obviously a *lady*'.[77]

The complicated question of what it means to be a lady underpins not only Barrett Browning's comments, but also Charlotte Brontë's dislike of Austen on the grounds that she was 'a complete and most sensible lady, but a very incomplete, and rather insensible (*not senseless*) woman'.[78] This view is echoed in the *Englishwoman's Domestic Magazine* of 1866, in which the reviewer compares Brontë and Austen, writing, 'Charlotte Brontë wrote like an inspired woman, Jane Austen like a cultivated lady',[79] and becomes axiomatic in Virginia Woolf: 'If we say that Jane Austen was a lady and that Charlotte Brontë was not one, we do as much as need be done in the way of definition'.[80] Elizabeth Barrett Browning explicitly dismisses Austen as 'too obviously a *lady*', but she clearly feels some anxiety about doing so. She writes: 'I have put it in the shape of blame – & many might remark the same thing for praise: I mean however, that her *ladyhood* is stronger in her than her humanity'.[81] The term 'lady', by the middle of the nineteenth century, was a vexed one. While it still carried some of its older, feudal, rank-based connotations (originally denoting a woman to whom obedience or feudal homage is due),[82] thus embodying within it a discourse of class, it had also come to denote a variety of characteristics, both social and inward, chief of which were self-possession under the most trying circumstances, refinement and cultivation of manners, propriety of demeanour and careful self-censorship.[83] What makes the term so slippery is that it is possible to be born a lady (using the term to denote rank) but to behave in an unladylike manner (using the term to signify behaviour), and *vice versa*. In Elizabeth Barrett Browning's rejection of Austen as 'too obviously a *lady*', we see the beginning of its pejorative use, an early version of the Women's Movement's rejection of the term as out-dated and limiting. Despite the fact that Austen was described by her own niece in 1869 as 'not so *refined* as she ought to have been from her *talent*',[84] by 1866, in the wider world, she had come to symbolize what it was to be 'a cultivated lady'.

Barrett Browning was right to think that 'many might remark' on Austen's 'ladyhood' as praiseworthy. We have already seen Arthur Hallam's endorsement of her novels on the grounds that 'none but a woman & a lady could possess that tact of minute observation, & that delicacy of sarcasm', and Lady Gordon and Mrs Pole's approval on similar grounds.[85] The anonymous reviewer of the *Englishwoman's Domestic Magazine* similarly approvingly describes Austen as 'a singularly gifted woman, of refined, and, as would have been said in her day, "elegant" mind'.[86] Richard Simpson commends both her language and subject matter: 'she is neat, epigrammatic, and incisive, but always a lady', whose 'patience, perseverance, modest study, and a willingness to keep her compositions for the test of time' make her 'an example for the aspiring artist'.[87] Barrett Browning's rejection of Austen's '*ladyhood*' in favour of 'humanity' indicates a strong repudiation of conventional or modest femininity in favour of the greater duty of the professional female writer to depict those aspects of life incompatible with modesty. Such an attitude is of a piece with her disapproval of those writers who undervalue their literary talents in favour of their social place. It is perhaps no wonder that Elizabeth Barrett Browning found Austen's ladylike indirections of style to be irritating rather than pleasurably challenging.

The exchange between Mary Russell Mitford and Elizabeth Barrett Browning clearly demonstrates the ways in which they came to a sense of themselves as readers. Barrett Browning writes, for example, that she has been 'reading quite lately & for your sake' *Persuasion* and *Mansfield Park*, '& really my impressions do grow stronger & stronger in their old places'.[88] Through Mitford's opposition, imagined or otherwise, Barrett Browning strengthens her own opinions, concluding:

> surely, surely I am not a niggard in my praise of Jane Austen! To call her a great writer & learned in the secrets, heights & depths of our nature, or a poet in anywise, is all that I refuse to call her – and indeed I have not breath & articulation for such an opinion: & it astonishes me that you sh^d be so exorbitant my dearest Miss Mitford, in your claim for her![89]

It is precisely the 'exorbitance' of Mitford's claims that have allowed Barrett Browning's 'impressions' to grow 'stronger & stronger', and that have allowed her to articulate her view of what constitutes a 'great writer'. In Barrett Browning's rejection of Austen's claims to greatness, she demonstrates her own aspirations as a writer, ruefully recognizing that she 'may be suspected of a prejudice involved in my own faults, against such writers as Jane Austen'.[90] Barrett Browning stuck tenaciously to her opinion of Austen, writing in 1855 to John Ruskin that her argument with Mitford had not caused her to admire Austen's works:

> She [Mitford] never taught *me* anything but a very limited admiration of Miss Austen, whose people struck me as wanting souls, even more than is necessary for men and women of the world. The novels are perfect as far as they go – that's certain. Only they don't go far, I think. It may be my fault.[91]

Although this extract reiterates some of the points she made to Mitford (lack of soul, focus on the conventional life, the novels' perfection in their sphere and Austen's limitation of aspiration), there is a note of hesitancy ('I think'), even apology ('it may be my fault'). She here dismisses the effects of her correspondence with Mitford, but it seems that Barrett Browning's confidence in her opinion has been paradoxically both shaken and strengthened by Mitford's opposition. Over the course of their epistolary argument, Barrett Browning is forced to justify her position, which confirms her belief in her convictions, but Mitford's steadfast opposition also forces her to recognize the possibility that her opinions may stem from 'a prejudice involved in my own faults', and thus prompts a recognition of the features of her own writing, and what matters to her. Barrett Browning couches her critical stance on Austen in terms of 'fault', suggesting that she feels both social and literary pressure to admire Austen in terms more extravagant than her own 'very limited admiration'. The modesty, delicacy, domesticity and ladyhood of the prevailing representations of Austen made her, as Simpson put it, 'an example for the aspiring [female] artist'. W. M. Thackeray's daughter, Anne Ritchie, another working writer, certainly felt the pressure to be like Jane Austen, calling Austen's uncomplaining working method 'an oblique reproach upon me', as we see in the next chapter.[92] While Elizabeth Barrett Browning resisted these pressures, her exasperated negotiations with Austen's name bear tribute to their uncomfortable presence.

Charlotte Brontë, like Elizabeth Barrett Browning, was not prepared to admit to more than 'a very limited admiration' of Austen, although she, too, dutifully pays lip-service to the idea of Austen's greatness. Brontë writes to Lewes, 'I will, when I can (I do not know when that will be, as I have no access to a circulating library), diligently peruse all Miss Austen's works, as you recommend'.[93] Brontë's choice of the adverb 'diligently' neatly signals to Lewes that she considers reading Austen's novels to be a chore rather than a pleasure, while her relegation of Austen to the status of a circulating-library novelist is also cleverly calculated to put Austen down. Although she tells Lewes, 'I *think* too I will endeavour to follow the counsel which shines out of Miss Austen's "mild eyes"; to finish more, and be more subdued', she is uncertain of the wisdom of such a course.[94] For Brontë, unlike for Mary Mitford, writing 'like Miss Austen' does not seem a natural course to take, and her later comments about Austen suggest that she swiftly repented considering it. Like Mitford, though, Brontë still considers Austen an important model of a kind, and is delighted to report a triumph over her. She writes to W. S. Williams in 1853:

> I had a letter the other day announcing that a lady of some note who had always determined that whenever she married, her elect should be the counterpart of Mr Knightley in Miss Austen's 'Emma' – had now changed her mind and vowed that she would either find the duplicate of Professor Emanuel or remain forever single!!![95]

Brontë's three exclamation marks point to her pleasure in having beaten Jane Austen at her own game as well as her amusement over the lady's sentiment. For Charlotte Brontë, Austen quickly comes to stand for the 'more subdued' type of novel that she cannot or will not write, rather as, for John Henry Newman, Austen had come to stand for a kind of low-church Anglicanism that he found antithetical to his mind and spirit. Like Elizabeth Barrett Browning and John Henry Newman, Brontë might well be 'suspected' of 'a prejudice involved in my own faults'. For Barrett Browning and Charlotte Brontë, defining themselves through their difference to

Austen is one way of rejecting amateurism for professionalism, conventional life for unconventionality, self-control for freedom of expression, practicality for spirituality, Reason for Imagination. The version of 'Jane Austen' that Barrett Browning and Brontë knew could not be a literary 'mother' to them, not least because they saw her through the distorting lens of her biographical and literary reputation. Austen's own novels do raise uncomfortable questions about the role of intelligent women in a man's world, an issue of burning interest to both Barrett Browning and Brontë. But it seems that the efforts of ingenuity demanded by Austen's stylistic sublimations and subtle ironic plot subversions served to obscure these questions for Brontë and Barrett Browning. As resistant readers, they refuse the texts' invitations to particular kinds of reading, and decline to take up Austen's playful stylistic challenges.

Chapter 8

AUSTEN'S READERS III: FRIENDSHIP AND CRITICISM

A later generation of readers and writers, at a greater chronological distance from Austen herself, were influenced in their turn by the biographical portrait presented to them in James Edward Austen-Leigh's 1870 *Memoir*. It sparked off a new wave of critical interest in Jane Austen, but it also perpetuated a view of Austen that stressed her domesticity and played down her literary commitment. One anecdote in particular – that of Austen's practice of hiding her work under a sheet of blotting paper if surprised in the process of composition – caught the attention of a number of readers. Austen-Leigh writes:

> Most of the work must have been done in the general sitting-room, subject to all kinds of casual interruptions. She was careful that her occupation should not be suspected by servants, or visitors, or any persons beyond her own family party. She wrote upon small sheets of paper which could easily be put away, or covered with a piece of blotting paper. There was, between the front door and the offices, a swing door which creaked when it was opened; but she objected to having this little inconvenience remedied, because it gave her notice when anyone was coming.[1]

The anecdote presents Austen as a writer for whom privacy was all-important, but also as one for whom writing had to give way to 'casual interruptions', and hence who could not give it her whole attention. Austen-Leigh's readers responded in a variety of ways to this representation of his aunt.

Anne Thackeray Ritchie (1837–1919) and Harriet Martineau (1802–1876)

Anne Thackeray Ritchie, who had evidently been reading the *Memoir* in preparation for reviewing it for the *Cornhill Magazine*, jotted down her thoughts on Austen in a memorandum of 1871:

> She never grizzled over her state, nor allowed her conscious superiority or intellig [*sic*] to claim distinction in her home. Tho an artist, she had no artistic

temperament [.] An oblique reproach upon me. Brought up in a kind of atmosphere wherein convention in the things that matter was omnipotent.[2]

Ritchie's view of Austen's portrayed contentment with her lot as 'an oblique reproach upon me' pays tribute to the influence of this particular vein of writing about Austen, which presented her as a contented and domestic woman first and a great artist second. Ritchie evidently feels that her own process of composition does not live up to Austen's methods. Unlike Elizabeth Barrett Browning, but like Mary Mitford, Ritchie approves of 'convention in the things that matter', and sees Austen as a role model for herself as an artist. Ritchie's review, which perpetuates and reinforces the *Memoir*'s picture of Jane Austen, encourages Austen's readers to imagine her as the 'unknown friend who has charmed us so long – charmed away dull hours, created neighbours and companions for us in lonely places'.[3] Her characters are 'familiar old friends', and 'like living people out of our own acquaintance' (perhaps Ritchie was influenced in this by seeing illustrations of Austen's characters depicted in clothing like that worn by living people of her own acquaintance).[4] She writes, 'we gladly welcome one more glimpse of an old friend come back with a last greeting. All those who love her name and her work, will prize this addition, small as it is, to their acquaintance with her'.[5] To give an even clearer idea of the 'unknown friend', she suggests, 'Anne Elliot must have been Jane Austen herself', and, that being so, 'it is impossible not to love her'.[6] Her emphasis on 'friendship', 'greeting' and 'acquaintance', represents, in an altered form, the same kind of desire for personal connection with Austen's writing that we have already seen in Mary Mitford's, Sarah Burney's and Lord Macaulay's writing. Mitford was thrilled to discover a geographical connection with Austen (calling her 'my countrywoman') and was delighted when she became acquainted with her relatives, but since there is no actual social connection with Austen for Ritchie and her own readers, Ritchie's rhetoric of friendship must become more metaphorical. She is persuading her readers to think, as she claims to think herself, of Austen as a trusted friend, whose chronological or historical distance from them is irrelevant in the light of her ability to assuage their loneliness. Ritchie's review is designed to persuade her readers of the validity and truth of such a friendship.

By the time she wrote *A Book of Sibyls* in 1883, her vision of Austen had become even more sentimentalized. She admires Austen's habit of 'writing in secret, putting away her work when visitors come in, unconscious, modest, hidden at home in heart, as she was in her sweet and womanly life, with the wisdom of the serpent indeed and the harmlessness of a dove'.[7] To Ritchie, this picture is charming and inspiring. Austen's 'sweet and womanly' qualities of modesty and self-abnegation are to be admired. Harriet Martineau, on the other hand, deplores the conventions that created the conditions under which Austen was forced to write:

> When I was young, it was not thought proper for young ladies to study very conspicuously; [...] Jane Austen herself, the Queen of novelists, the immortal creator of Anne Elliott, Mr. Knightley, and a score or two more of unrivalled intimate friends of the whole public, was compelled by the feelings of her family to cover up her manuscripts with a large piece of muslin work, kept on the table for the purpose, whenever any genteel people came in.[8]

Unlike Ritchie, who sees in Austen's secretive working methods something to admire and envy, Martineau's tone is one of outrage and deliberate astonishment, as if she can hardly believe that the 'Queen of novelists' should have been 'compelled' to any form of concealment by her family. Martineau's substitution of 'a large piece of muslin work' for the blotting paper of Austen-Leigh's version is an interesting subconscious slip, which voices her indignation that needlework should be valued above writing, and conflates Austen-Leigh's anecdote about concealment with his praise of her sewing ('her needlework both plain and ornamental was excellent, and might almost have put a sewing machine to shame. She was considered especially great in satin stitch').[9] This emphasis on needlework recurs oddly frequently in writing about Austen, suggesting itself, for example, as a metaphor to Henry James, who effaces the workings of her conscious mind into the busy working of her fingers:

> The key to Jane Austen's fortune with posterity has been in part the extraordinary grace of her facility, in fact of her unconsciousness: as if, at the most, for difficulty, for embarrassment, she sometimes, over her work basket, her tapestry flowers, in the spare, cool drawing-room of other days, fell a-musing, lapsed too metaphorically, as one may say, into wool-gathering, and her dropped stitches, of these pardonable, of these precious moments, were afterwards picked up as little touches of human truth, little glimpses of steady vision, little master-strokes of imagination.[10]

James's strained analogy suggests how deeply Austen-Leigh's conflation of Austen's literary and domestic skills ('the same hand which painted so exquisitely with the pen could work as delicately with the needle'[11]) had sunk into the cultural consciousness by the time James was writing in 1905. His Ciceronian repetition of 'little' also pays tribute to the persistent characterization of Austen as miniaturist. The reactions of Anne Thackeray Ritchie and Harriet Martineau show two kinds of response to these ideological constructions of Austen as a needlewoman, a miniaturist, and a Victorian 'angel in the house'[12].

In both cases Austen generates sympathy, but in neither is that sympathy uncomplicated by personal and professional aspirations.

Margaret Oliphant (1828–1897)

Margaret Oliphant was a professional literary critic and prolific writer of novels, who, like Mary Mitford, depended on her literary endeavours to support a household. As an anonymous reviewer for *Blackwood's Edinburgh Magazine*, she had a professional space within which to discuss issues related to gender and writing without necessarily disclosing her own sex, and her relationship to Austen is different from that of Austen's earlier successors, involving a greater degree of chronological distance and a corresponding lessening of the pressure to be 'like Miss Austen'.[13] Nonetheless, Oliphant's negotiations with Austen continue to demonstrate the extent to which Austen's style and her reputation did place demands on the female writer. Joanne Wilkes suggests that Oliphant felt 'frustration at Austen's being held up as some sort of model for women writers', and quotes a letter from Oliphant to John Blackwood in which she expressed 'pure frustration at the way in which that respectable woman's name is shoved down all our throats on any occasion'.[14] Oliphant's words bear tribute to the ubiquity of comparisons between Austen and her successors throughout the nineteenth century. In her *Blackwood*'s article, Oliphant resists and appropriates Austen strategically, deploying her variously as both example and warning.

Like Martineau, Oliphant notices Austen-Leigh's portrayal of the Austen family's ambivalent attitude towards Austen's literary fame, and she, too, relates this to needlework: 'the family were half ashamed to have it known that she was not just a young lady like the others, doing her embroidery'.[15] In her *Autobiography*, she compares the Austens' attitude to that of her own family as she contrasts Austen's working practices with her own:

> Up to this date, 1888, I have never been shut up in a separate room, or hedged off with any observances. My study, all the study I have attained to, is the little second drawing-room of my house, with a wide opening into the other drawing-room where all the (feminine) life of the house goes on; and I don't think I have ever had two hours undisturbed (except at night, when everybody is in bed) during my whole literary life. Miss Austen, I believe, wrote in the same way, and very much for the same reason; but at her period the natural flow of life took another form. The family were half ashamed to have it known that she was not just a young lady like the others, doing her embroidery. Mine were quite pleased to magnify me, and to be proud of my work, but always with a hidden sense that it was an admirable joke, and no idea that any special facilities or retirement was necessary.[16]

Oliphant's comparison is suggestive because it unconsciously stresses many preconceptions about Austen as a feminine, domestic writer, her life circumscribed by convention and duty, and her genius similarly circumscribed by circumstance: turned in upon the '(feminine) life of the house' rather than outwards towards great events. It is also of interest because of its tone of mild resentment ('I don't think I have ever had two hours undisturbed [...] during my whole literary life', for example). Oliphant seems to take some comfort from the similarity of Austen's position, in contrast to the disquiet she feels in comparing herself to George Eliot: 'How I have been handicapped in life! Should I have done better if I had been kept, like her, in a mental greenhouse and taken care of?'[17] For Oliphant, unlike for the many readers who took the *Memoir's* portrayal at face value, Austen's contentment cannot be taken for granted. Oliphant resents the fact that, in her family, writing was 'subordinate to everything, to be pushed aside for any little necessity', and she attributes the same feeling of resentment to Jane Austen in her review of the *Memoir* for *Blackwood's Edinburgh Magazine* of March 1870.[18]

Oliphant's article is an insightful piece of criticism of Austen. It also tells us much about Margaret Oliphant herself. In the review, in which Oliphant compares Jane Austen to Mary Russell Mitford, there is an edge of condescension towards Austen, who is 'fenced from the outer world by troops of friends', and has 'no inducement to come down from her pedestal and go out into the bitter arena where the strong triumph and the needy struggle, except that prick of genius which is like the rising of the sap in the trees'.[19] It is, as in Elizabeth Barrett Browning's case, the contempt of the professional for the amateur (albeit for different personal reasons), and Oliphant's sympathy is engaged, not by Austen, who is loved and protected – 'delightful to the eye and dear to the heart of all the Austens, and all the Leighs, and all Steventon'[20] – but by Mitford, who, 'as she writes, has a sore heart, and does not know how the bills are to be paid, and is weary beyond description of drudging at her pen all day long for daily bread'.[21] Oliphant suggests that, were Austen to depict Mary Mitford's home-life, she 'would set it before you in three sentences, so that you would no longer see any beauty in the scene [...] for our poor part, we would rather have Miss Mitford's sweet flowery picture [...] and all the painful humanity underneath'.[22] Mary Mitford longed to write like Austen, but, by Margaret Oliphant, at least in this review, she herself is considered a more appealing model of a female writer, both as a hard-working literary professional, and as a warm and kindly woman.

Oliphant makes it clear that she considers Austen-Leigh's portrait of his aunt as a pleasant likeness – 'nothing can be more amusing and attractive than the glimpses; very brief and slight as they are, of this girl [...] How pleasant is the picture!'[23] – but as a fiction, and one that does not begin to do justice to the keenness, ruthlessness and subtlety of Austen's mind:

> Mr Austen-Leigh, without meaning it, throws out of his dim little lantern a passing gleam of light upon the fine vein of feminine cynicism which pervades his aunt's mind. It is something altogether different from the rude and brutal male quality that bears the same name. It is the soft and silent disbelief of a spectator who has to look at a great many things without showing any outward discomposure, and who has learned to give up any moral classification of social sins, and to place them instead on the level of absurdities.[24]

In characterizing this cynical 'position of mind' as 'essentially feminine', Oliphant subverts and undercuts the version of femininity so approvingly endorsed by Austen-Leigh.[25] Austen is still presented as the 'sweet woman' of the *Memoir* portrait,[26] but the sweetness is suddenly made threatening; gentleness and propriety become cloaks for a sharp and judgemental intelligence: 'She has but the faculty of seeing her brother clearly all round as if he were a statue, identifying all his absurdities, quietly jeering at him, smiling with her eyes without committing the indecorum of laughter'.[27] Decorum of demeanour, Oliphant suggests, is no guarantee of decorous thought, choosing the harsh and uncompromising term 'jeering' to describe Austen's habitual way of seeing others. This is a writer of whom one should be somewhat afraid. Oliphant's view of Austen's habit of observation as frightening is reminiscent of Mary Mitford's description of Austen as 'a poker of whom every one is afraid', and her comment that 'this silent observation from such an observer is rather formidable'.[28] It also shows up Oliphant's ambivalence towards Austen.

Throughout Oliphant's review, the inability to effect meaningful change in life or people is the basis of Austen's 'feminine cynicism': social powerlessness the impetus of her art. Austen's self-possession is seen as acquired under compulsion, rather than being 'natural' to her; her art is 'learned', not innate. Oliphant's vision of Austen brings to vivid life the constraints under which an art such as Austen's came into existence, describing 'a sense that *nothing is to be done but to look on*, to say perhaps now and then a softening word, to make the best of it practically and theoretically, to smile and hold up one's hands and wonder why human creatures should be such fools' (my italics), as 'the foundations upon which the feminine cynicism which we attribute to Miss Austen is built'.[29] Oliphant identifies in Austen a 'fine stinging yet soft voiced contempt', an 'exquisite sense of the ridiculous',[30] and a 'certain soft despair of any one human creature ever doing any good to another'.[31] The result is 'pictures which are at once so refined and so trenchant, so softly feminine and polite, and so remorselessly true'.[32] Oliphant's insistence on 'softness' suggests a nervousness about her insights. Both feminine and remorseless, polite and true, Austen is no longer the warm and loving 'dear aunt Jane' of the *Memoir*; instead, she is a different type of woman, clear-sighted, delicate, subtle, sophisticated, and deadly. Austen is lacking in human sympathy: 'humankind stands low in her estimation', seeing 'the world as a thing apart from herself and demanding no excess of sympathy'.[33] Her character depiction is 'cruel in its perfection', even 'rather diabolical', her vision 'unflinching', and, rather than sympathizing with human folly, she subjects it to 'consistent remorseless ridicule'.[34] Oliphant cannot wholeheartedly admire Austen's writing: 'we acknowledge its truth, and yet we rebel against this pitiless perfection of art',[35] preferring Mitford's books because, although they are 'more superficial' and thus lower 'art' than Austen's, they are still 'truer to all those deep instinctive unities which art may sometimes ignore, but which nature never ignores'.[36] In this curious turn of phrase, Oliphant appears to be elevating sympathy above artistic achievement, finding Austen deficient where Mitford, 'warm in a kindly sympathy over all the world', flourishes.[37]

In depicting Austen's 'feminine cynicism', Oliphant has to tread carefully, aware that, for most of her readers, a cynical and critical cast of mind is not 'feminine'. This had been the case for many years before Oliphant wrote her review; the *Edinburgh Monthly Review* of 1820, for example, remarks that 'sneering scepticism [...] in man is offensive – in woman, monstrous and revolting'.[38] Henry Austen demonstrates a similar awareness, in his insistence on Austen's 'candour':

> Though the frailties, foibles, and follies of others could not escape her immediate detection, yet even on their vices did she never trust herself to comment with unkindness. [...] Faultless herself, as nearly as human nature can be, she always sought, in the faults of others, something to excuse, to forgive or forget.[39]

Hence Oliphant's repeated qualifications, her frequently reiterated emphasis on 'softness' and 'sweetness', and her careful differentiation of 'feminine' cynicism from 'the rude and brutal male quality that bears the same name'. Austen is threatening in Oliphant's account because she is subversive; her stinging contempt has the potential to reveal painful, usually hidden, truths about gender relations, even though it is concealed under a decorous exterior. Unlike Elizabeth Barrett Browning or Charlotte Brontë, Oliphant here recognizes the subversive potential of Austen's novels, but she shies away from the full implications of her insights, instead concealing them under a rhetoric of 'softness' and 'politeness', emphasizing that Austen's power is, above all, 'feminine'. In addition, she suggests that Austen's character, 'one full of subtle power, keenness, finesse, and self-restraint', is of 'a type not at all unusual among women of high cultivation, especially in the retirement of the country, where such qualities are likely enough to be unappreciated or misunderstood'.[40] She thus uses her analysis of Austen's character to make a more general point about the under-appreciation of 'cultivated' women, continuing a theme begun in 1866 in a private letter to Blackwood: 'it is the sad fate of gifted women in general never to be appreciated'.[41] Austen is therefore used as an example in an implicit argument about the undervaluing of the female intellect, made to stand for under-appreciated gifted women everywhere.[42]

By the time Margaret Oliphant wrote her *Literary History of England* of 1882, however, her threatening and subversive version of Austen had disappeared. Instead of developing or even reiterating her analysis of 1870, she chooses to paraphrase Austen-Leigh's *Memoir* uncritically, portraying Austen as 'pretty, sprightly, well taken care of – a model English girl, simple, and saucy, and fair', and describing her as writing 'out of native instinct, preferring that way of amusing herself to fine needlework, telling stories, as Burns rhymed, "for fun," with no ulterior views'.[43] Any sense of Austen as a serious artist, and a complicated character, whose conditions of work gave rise to a profoundly cynical world view and a disassociation from humanity, has vanished, leaving only an 'ineffable' genius, who 'belongs to humanity in all periods' and whose art can only be explained in terms of the supernatural: 'witchcraft and magic'.[44] There could hardly be a more complete reversal of position, difficult to explain in the light of the rest of Oliphant's writings on Austen, either private or public. It is, of course, possible that she had simply changed her mind about Austen in the course of twelve years. Practical considerations may also have intruded; Oliphant does write, in reference to the *Literary History*, in a letter of 1 February 1882: 'imagine me floundering among Godwin's set, all the grimy citizens of the end of the century and all the novel-writers! This is the real labour of the book',[45] and it is possible that, in her endeavours to get the 'real labour' done, she simply relied on the *Memoir* portrait of Austen to save her time and effort. In the same letter to Craik, she betrays a weariness with reading – 'how much easier to spin a novel than to read and read – so much that there is very little interest in reading!' which gives some credence to the idea that her heart was not totally in the research for the *Literary History*.[46]

Such considerations aside, the *Literary History* is (however modestly) an attempt at canon-shaping, and it seems that Oliphant preferred a ladylike, domestic, uncomplicated version of Austen, a portrait rather like Oliphant's vision of Mary Mitford in the *Blackwood*'s article, in fact, to represent the female writer in this book. 'Kindly sympathy' almost certainly sold better than 'stinging contempt'. It is also, of course, the case that the anonymity of the *Blackwood*'s review gave her greater freedom than a book to which she put her own name, which may have allowed her to air more controversial sentiments about Austen in the review than she could in the *Literary History*. In 1876, Leslie Stephen noted that Austen's 'was the very type of that kind of humour which charms one large class of amiable persons; and Austenolatry is perhaps the most intolerant and dogmatic of literary creeds.'[47] While the Janeite movement was not yet fully-fledged in the 1880s, Stephen's comment suggests that Oliphant's decision to perpetuate Austen-Leigh's depiction of Austen, rather than her own *Blackwood*'s version was a wise one. Austen's reputation as a modest and domestic female writer had a great deal invested in it by 1882. It also had large number of influential defenders among the Janeite *literati*. The 'dogmatism' of these supporters is summed up well in an anecdote in Austen-Leigh's *Memoir*: 'One of the ablest men of my acquaintance said, in that kind of jest which has much earnest in it, that he had established it in his own mind, as a new test of ability, whether people *could* or *could not* appreciate Miss Austen's merits'.[48] The able man in question was R. H. Cheney, son of a Shropshire estate-owner, who had met Austen-Leigh at Winchester, after which both men went up to Oxford.[49] Harman points out that 'the whole passage, with its insistence on "*we* and *they*", was the strongest possible foundation for a literary cult emerging around Austen that addressed the club mentality rather than the subject's actual achievements'.[50] The 'Cheney test', which was picked up by many of the reviews of the *Memoir*, articulated what was already implicit in some nineteenth-century responses to Austen: the sense that her devotees were members of a select club who alone understood what great art was. From 1870 onwards, Austen was on the way to becoming a cult figure, and the Janeites to becoming a cult. In 1900, W. D. Howells first described 'the readers of Jane Austen' as a 'cult', suggesting that, to her adorers, 'she is a passion and a creed, if not quite a religion'.[51] Influential British Janeite professors and teachers, such as A. C. Bradley and George Saintsbury, and novelists, biographers and poets, such as E. M. Forster, Austin Dobson and Rudyard Kipling, all disseminated their view of the 'surpassing excellence' of Jane Austen to the reading public, and the Janeite phenomenon (discussed in greater detail in Chapter 9), took on a strength and force of its own.[52]

Virginia Woolf (1882–1941)

Virginia Woolf, daughter of Leslie Stephen, and frequent reader of Jane Austen's works, was both aware of the Janeite phenomenon, and unwilling to be swayed by it. The *Times Literary Supplement* of 19 July 1917 carried an article on Jane Austen by Virginia Woolf. The article first appeared on 8 May 1913, and was reprinted by popular request to celebrate Austen's centenary in 1917. In it, Woolf writes:

> The time has come, surely, when there is no need to bring witnesses to prove Jane Austen's fame. Arrange the great English novelists as one will, it does not seem possible to bring them out in any order where she is not first, or second, or third, whoever her companions may be.[53]

According to Woolf, by this point, Austen's literary reputation is assured. There is no longer any need to rehash the arguments of the previous century in order to 'prove her fame'. Woolf goes on to offer an explanation for the slow but steady growth of Austen's reputation, writing, 'it has been steady because there is probably no novelist of the nineteenth century who requires us to make so little excuse for her, and it has been slow because she has limitations of a kind particularly likely to cramp a writer's popularity'.[54] Woolf describes the 'limitations' as follows:

> We doubt whether one of her novels was ever a long toil and stumble to any reader with a splendid view at the end. She was never a revelation to the young, a stern comrade, a brilliant and extravagantly admired friend, a writer whose sentences sang in one's brain and were half absorbed into one's blood.[55]

Woolf's assumptions about reading Austen are, as shown in previous chapters, wrong. To Mary Mitford and to Sarah Harriet Burney, Austen was, as demonstrated above, both a 'brilliant and extravagantly admired friend' and 'a writer whose sentences sang in one's brain and were half absorbed into one's blood'. She is a 'friend' too, to W. D. Howells, Katherine Mansfield, Anne Thackeray Ritchie, Arthur Hallam and Lord Macaulay. Austen was 'absorbed' into the 'blood' of the Darwin and Wedgwood families in a very particular way, as we will see in the next chapter. In her focus on Austen's 'limitations', Woolf is articulating many of the prejudices about Austen seen in the previous chapter, and, creating, in a different form, a version of Austen as an artist 'limited' by her 'sphere'. In order to do this, she must ignore the possibility of the kinds of alternative interactions with Austen described in Chapter 6.

Virginia Woolf writes frequently about Jane Austen, intelligently and insightfully. She credits her with creating the perfect English sentence, with being the greatest of all female writers, with having perfect mastery over her domain, with creating characters who 'have a million facets'.[56] In *The Voyage Out* (1915), she even depicts the kind of intense emotional engagement with Austen that she denies in the *TLS* article – Clarissa Dalloway exclaims: 'I really couldn't exist without the Brontës! Don't you love them? Still, on the whole, I'd rather live without them than without Jane Austen'.[57] Woolf recognizes Austen as 'a mistress of much deeper emotion than appears upon the surface',[58] and as 'a great writer'.[59] She admires Austen, believes her to be a remarkable writer, quotes her in one of her own novels, sees her writing as a model for that of other women, but she is all the same displeased when she is likened to her.

In 1919, Katherine Mansfield reviewed Virginia Woolf's *Night and Day*, writing in private to Middleton Murry that she objected to the novel – 'my private opinion is that it is a lie in the soul' – on the grounds that 'the war never has been, that is what its message is'. She continues, 'I feel in the *profoundest* sense that nothing can ever be the same that as artists we are traitors if we feel otherwise: we have to take it into account and find new expressions [,] new moulds for our new thoughts & feelings'. She then goes on to say, 'what *has* been – stands – but Jane Austen could not write Northanger Abbey now – or if she did I'd have none of her'.[60] Both Mansfield's antipathy to *Night and Day* and the ambivalent association with Jane Austen came out in the review, in which Mansfield explicitly compares *Night and Day* with 'the novels of Miss Austen', suggesting that Austen's novels had a greater 'feeling for life' than Woolf's, and that *Night and Day*, 'a novel in the tradition of the English novel', made her feel 'old and chill'.[61] She thus evokes Austen in order to point out both where Woolf succeeds (in an echo of Barrett Browning's faint praise of Austen, *Night and Day*'s style is 'exquisite') and where Woolf falls short, calling the novel 'unaware of what has been happening' (i.e. the First World War). Woolf records in her diary: 'K. M. wrote a review which irritated me – I thought I saw spite in it. A decorous elderly dullard she describes me; Jane Austen up to date'.[62] A week later, Woolf is still annoyed: 'I had rather write in my own way of "four Passionate Snails" [a reference to her short story, 'Kew Gardens' (1919), also reviewed by Katherine Mansfield for the *Athenaeum*] than be, as K. M. maintains, Jane Austen over again'.[63] For Woolf, as for Barrett Browning, comparison with Austen is irritating, at least in part because she perceptively recognizes that Mansfield's comparison diminishes her by refusing to recognize either her originality or her social relevance. It is apt that Woolf's rejection of Austen here should echo so closely Austen's own defence of *her* type of writing to James Stanier Clarke: 'I must keep to my own style & go on in my own Way; And though I may never succeed again in that, I am convinced that I should totally fail in any other', since it is indicative of both writers' similarly protective sense of the value of their respective styles.[64]

Woolf's prickly response to the Austen comparison should be seen in the context of her difficult relationship with Mansfield, characterized by professional rivalry and personal ambivalence. She objects as much to the use to which Mansfield puts Austen ('a decorous elderly dullard') as to the actual comparison with her. The fact remains, though, that Virginia Woolf did not want to write 'like Miss Austen', believing in the value of her own voice, her own style of novel. Undervaluing the depth of Austen's literary commitment, and the allusiveness of her writing, and overestimating the 'divine' nature of her talent, she also believed that the 'divine spontaneity' of the women's writing of the past should be superseded by a new type of female-authored novel:

> In future, granted time and books and a little space in the house for herself, literature will become for women, as for men, an art to be studied. Women's gift will be trained and strengthened. The novel will cease to be the dumping-ground for the personal emotions. It will become, more than at present, a work of art like any other; and its resources and limitations will be explored.[65]

Woolf's rejection of Austen is thus inextricably linked to her vision of a future where a female writer's sex no longer impedes her professional ability, and where the novel, no longer the preserve of untaught women, can be taken seriously as a genre. For Woolf, who makes the famous argument that a woman needs five hundred pounds a year and a room of her own to write fiction, Austen is an uncomfortable counter-example, a great writer with neither an independent income nor a room of her own. She explains Austen's writing as an anomaly, but it nonetheless jars her argument. Unlike Margaret Oliphant, who could take comfort from the similarity of her working conditions to Austen's, Woolf rejects such working conditions on behalf of womankind. Woolf's public and private discussions of Austen make it clear that, even one hundred years after Austen's death, she remained an implicit standard against which the female writer was measured and often found wanting.

Austen was not, of course, only read by professional female writers. By the time Virginia Woolf was writing, she had increasingly become an interesting object of study for professional literary men, including Virginia Woolf's own father. An article of March 1870 in the *St. Paul's Magazine* claims:

> Jane Austen's works, – though not devoured by young ladies of our period with the same greediness as the new stories just come from Mudie's, – are still taken down by 'the girls' from the maternal shelf, when there is nothing else to be had, and are read, – by them, – with tranquil interest. But they are pondered over with most attention and most appreciation by men of thought and literary education.[66]

Here, Austen's novels are appropriated as the preserve of 'men of thought and literary education', supposed too good for 'the girls' of the reading public, who read them with no more than 'tranquil interest'. In this account, Austen has become, by reputation, not only a safe author (to be found on 'the maternal shelf'), but a good one, her merit assured by the fact that she is read by 'men of thought and literary education'. The reviewer is, as we have seen in the strongly engaged responses from women discussed above, wrong to imagine that Austen is treated with 'most attention and most appreciation' by the male sex in the period of which he is writing, but his assumption that 'literary education' was necessary to appreciate Austen's works reveals the extent to which her novels were differentiated from other female-authored works of her period. It also reflects the gender bias about the 'reading public' that we have seen many times before. Many of Austen's female readers may have been less publicly visible and less vocal than her male admirers but their 'attention' and 'appreciation' were no less real.[67] Nonetheless, the writer for the *St. Paul's Magazine* makes an important point when he suggests that, by 1870, Austen was on the way to becoming a canonical writer, deemed worthy of study by men of the literary establishment. To some extent, this was nothing new – Whately, Scott, Macaulay, and Lewes had all 'pondered over' Austen's novels with 'attention and appreciation', and in doing so had each helped to shape and establish her reputation. By 1948, of course, Austen was securely established in F. R. Leavis's 'great tradition', but as Brian Southam points out, the 1870s formed something of a watershed in Austen appreciation and criticism, as Austen-Leigh's *Memoir* sparked off a new wave of 'widespread interest' in the author and her works, and the Janeite movement began to grow.[68] Southam's introduction to the second volume of the *Critical Heritage* gives an excellent summary of Austen's critical fortunes in the period 1870 to 1945, Claire Harman details the growth of her reputation in this period, and Claudia Johnson discusses the role of prominent Janeites at this time. We will therefore not rehearse that tale here. Instead, we will consider the more private responses of some 'men of thought and literary education' through a brief discussion of some letters and diaries.

Alfred, Lord Tennyson (1809–1892)

The Tennyson household, according to Emily Tennyson's journal, was one in which reading aloud together was both a daily habit, and a shared pleasure. Tennyson very frequently read both his own compositions and a large variety of other books aloud with his wife. Both Tennyson and Emily often read to the children, and Jane Austen's novels formed a part of the wide variety of reading matter that they enjoyed.[69] Tennyson read Jane Austen in an 1853 reprint of Bentley's Standard Novels edition, and he knew and loved her works before the resurgence of interest prompted by Austen-Leigh's *Memoir*. He explicitly planned a trip to the Cobb at Lyme Regis in the company of F. T. Palgrave and William Allingham in 1867, because he had 'wanted to see the Cobb there ever since [he] first read *Persuasion*'.[70] Once they had seen the steps 'from which Louisa Musgrove fell', Allingham read aloud to Tennyson 'out of *Persuasion*, the passage where Louisa Musgrave hurts her ankle'. During the walk that followed, they sat down on a bank to 'talk of Morris, Ned Jones, Swinburne, etc., Whitechapel Rock.' They then 'return[ed] by winding paths to the town', discussing 'Miss Austen, Scott, novel-writing.'[71] The trip and the location naturally prompted conversation about Jane Austen, though it is impossible to know what was said on this occasion.

Tennyson's comments elsewhere, however, show him to have also been familiar with at least some of the critical debates surrounding her reputation in the 1870s. Hallam Tennyson records that his father 'read and re-read' Austen's novels, and discussed them on more than one occasion, along with those of Thackeray and Scott. Hallam tells us that, in the 1890s, for instance:

> He would always talk of Thackeray's novels, *Esmond, Pendennis*, and *The Newcomes* as being 'delicious: they are so mature. But now the days are so full of false sentiment that, as Thackeray said, one cannot draw a man as he should be.' He would read and re-read them as well as Walter Scott's and Miss Austen's novels. His comments on Walter Scott and Miss Austen were: 'Scott is the most chivalrous literary figure of this century, and the author with the widest range since Shakespeare. I think *Old Mortality* is his greatest novel. The realism and life-likeness of Miss Austen's Dramatis Personae come nearest to those of Shakespeare. Shakespeare however is a sun to which Jane Austen, tho' a bright and true little world, is but an asteroid.'[72]

In this snippet of Tennyson's conversation, we see once again a response to Austen that characterizes her as a miniaturist: it is a 'little' world that she depicts. Making reference to Macaulay's famous comparison of Austen and Shakespeare, Tennyson clarifies the difference between the two writers as one of scale, suggesting, rather as Elizabeth Barrett Browning did, that Austen's was a 'narrow sphere of life', but that within the constraints of her imaginary world, 'she pictured human character as truthfully as Shakespeare.'[73]

Samuel Langhorne Clemens ('Mark Twain') (1835–1910)

In contrast to Tennyson, Mark Twain was a reader who loathed Jane Austen's work. Rather than seeing her characters as 'living friends', he considered them as enemies, writing: '[s]he makes me detest all her people, without reserve'.[74] Of Austen herself, he notoriously wrote in 1898:

> I haven't any right to criticize books and I don't often do it except when I hate them. I often want to criticize Jane Austen, but her books madden me so that I can't conceal my frenzy from the reader; and therefore I have to stop every time I begin. Every time I read *Pride and Prejudice* I want to dig her up and hit her over the skull with her own shin-bone.[75]

Though many readers did (and do) dislike Austen's novels on fairly straightforward grounds, the violent antipathy expressed in this letter suggests a deeper motivation than simple aversion to the works. Emily Auerbach posits the suggestion that Twain was in fact 'a closet Janeite, a fake who read and appreciated far more of Jane Austen than he admitted', and that his dislike of Austen was a pose because 'he could no longer reconcile his virile desire to disparage Austen with the fact that he actually "got" her'.[76] In part, Twain's need to present himself in this way is explicable in terms of his conscious self-presentation as an American adventurer. Like Charlotte Brontë and Elizabeth Barrett Browning, Twain saw Austen's novels as representing a kind of writing that was antithetical to his own, but unlike the female writers, Twain did not feel the need to soften his criticism, or couch his discomfort in terms of faint praise. Instead, he rejects Austen's works outright. Austen's focus on the domestic and the matrimonial is a long way from Twain's masculine adventure novels, and the Home Counties Englishness of her settings from the rugged America depicted in such works as *Tom Sawyer* (1876) and *Huckleberry Finn* (1884). American novelists of Twain's generation were still in the process of defining what the great American novel should be, and part of this attempt was a rejection of English culture and English values.[77] Jane Austen herself celebrated Englishness, as when she describes the view of Abbey Mill Farm as 'a sweet view – sweet to the eye and the mind. English verdure, English culture, English comfort, seen under a sun bright, without being oppressive', and waxes lyrical about 'its appendages of prosperity and beauty, its rich pastures, spreading flocks, orchard in blossom, and light column of smoke ascending'.[78] Austen was also frequently represented as the epitome of Englishness in critical writing, such as Oliphant's description of her as 'a model English girl', or enlisted in the service of patriotism, as when Kipling described her as 'England's Jane'.[79] It is therefore easy to understand Twain's dislike and rejection of the novelist and all she stood for within this context. Forty years earlier, another American, Ralph Waldo Emerson, had criticized Austen's novels on the grounds that they were not only narrow, but too English:

> I am at a loss to understand why people hold Miss Austen's novels at so high a rate, which seem to me vulgar in tone, sterile in artistic invention, imprisoned in the wretched conventions of English society, without genius, wit or knowledge of the world. Never was life so pinched and narrow [...] 'Tis 'the nympholepsy of a fond despair', say, rather, of an English boarding-house. Suicide is more respectable.[80]

Emerson's sensation that Austen's novels reflect the 'imprisonment' of conventional English society is, to some extent analogous to Barrett Browning's and Charlotte Brontë's claustrophobia on reading the works. All three writers oppose themselves to convention, and find her work too limited for genius. There is an important difference, however, in that Emerson focuses specifically on the national context of Austen's novels, conflating Englishness with being 'narrow', 'wretched', 'pinched' and 'conventional'. Where Brontë and Barrett Browning take the English settings of the novels for granted, there is an issue of national identity at stake for Emerson. Emerson's association of Austen with English conventions is important in this account, because both stand for a national literature that must be rejected by readers if Emerson's own kind of writing (American transcendentalism) is to survive and flourish. As in the case of Newman, Emerson's philosophical and literary beliefs were antithetical to what he saw in Austen's writing. Transcendentalism, with its emphasis on spirituality and intuition, and its rejection of the doctrines of established religion, stands opposed to Austen's more bleakly materialistic world view. And, as in the correspondence between Barrett Browning and Mitford, what is at stake here is the question of the future of literature, and in this case the future direction of a relatively new national literature. Both gender and national identity are thus at issue in these responses to Austen's works.

Twain was writing and publishing his own novels during the period that saw the rise of the near-hysterical adoration of Jane Austen represented by Janeite cults and cultures, and his responses to Austen's novels should also be seen in this context, as an attempt to counterbalance some of the more excessive praise heaped upon her. To his friend Howells, an arch-Janeite, Twain wrote in January of 1908:

> I have to write a line, lazy as I am, to say how your Poe article delighted me; and to say that I am in agreement with substantially all you say about his literature. To me his prose is unreadable – like Jane Austin's [*sic*]. No, there is a difference.

I could read his prose on salary, but not Jane's. Jane is entirely impossible. It seems a great pity that they allowed her to die a natural death.[81]

The calculated unkindness of the last line of this letter no doubt owes something to Twain's enjoyment of teasing Howells. Like Barrett Browning and Mitford, Twain and Howells enjoyed their own much smaller – though long-running – argument over Austen, with Howells jokingly writing to Twain in 1903, when the latter was ill in bed, 'Now you're sick, I've a great mind to have it out with you about Jane Austen. If you say much more I'll come out and read "Pride and Prejudice" to you'.[82] However, Twain had taken up his position in the anti-Austen camp well before this correspondence with Howells. In his 1897 travelogue, *Following the Equator*, Twain noted that the ship's library had no Jane Austen novels, and quipped that '[j]ust that omission alone would make a fairly good library out of a library that hadn't a book in it'.[83] His was clearly a deep-seated and long-lived aversion. Twain was, like Austen herself, a resistant, oppositional and critical reader with a strong sense of his own authorial voice and identity. This authorial identity – which proved to be effective when deployed as a marketing strategy to sell his books – depended on a model of American masculinity which could have nothing to do with the kind of English domestic femininity that Austen had come to represent by the end of the nineteenth century. Nor could Twain risk being associated with the perceived effeminacy of the Janeites who were her ardent 'adorers' and defenders.[84]

Austen's successors thus responded not only to the invitations of her prose style, but also to her reputation. Such responses are an integral part of discussions of Jane Austen and generate creative energies of their own. Interactions with texts are personal, political, and gendered, and emotions are raised as much by assumptions about the author as by the novels themselves. The same might be said of any author, and perhaps more particularly of those who attain celebrity in their own lifetimes, but Jane Austen's name enjoys a peculiar resonance, her reputation an unusual degree of power. As Arnold Bennett observed in July 1927, 'the reputation of Jane Austen is surrounded by cohorts of defenders who are ready to do murder for their sacred cause. They are nearly all fanatics'.[85] The following chapter considers some of those that Bennett characterized as 'fanatics', as well as some whose more temperate responses to Austen constitute a different kind of devotion.

Chapter 9

AUSTEN'S READERS IV: SOCIABILITY AND DEVOTION

It is clear that, from their earliest incarnations, Austen's novels were read as family entertainment. Jane Austen's collection of opinions of *Mansfield Park* and *Emma* contains a number of comments which demonstrate that reading the books was a family activity. Austen records, for example, the views on *Mansfield Park* of 'the families at Deane' and 'the Kintbury family'.[1] These were communal opinions, arrived at after discussion. Austen's aunt and uncle, Mr and Mrs Leigh Perrot, similarly provided a joint opinion of *Emma*, as did Mrs Craven and her daughter, Austen's brother James and his wife, and 'the family at Upton Gray'.[2] As we have seen, the 'morality' and 'good sense' of Austen's work is commended in a number of these early responses, emphasizing the novels' suitability as books for families to read together. It is also noticeable how often the opinions of both *Mansfield Park* and *Emma* collected by Jane Austen focus on scenes of sociability and family life in those novels. Mrs Cage felt, on reading *Emma*, for example, that she was 'at Highbury all day', and could not 'help feeling I have just got into a new set of acquaintance'.[3] Admiration of *Mansfield Park*'s 'Portsmouth scene' (in which, of course, Austen depicts the boisterous family life and sibling rivalries of the Price family) was recorded not only by the male readers already discussed in Chapter 5, but also by her niece, Anna Austen, sister-in-law Mrs James Austen, and friend Alethea Bigg, who found 'the Price family at Portsmouth' to be 'delightful in their way'.[4]

As her reputation became ever more established over the course of the nineteenth century, Jane Austen was gradually absorbed into a canonical tradition, and promoted in series designed to appeal to those seeking respectable family entertainment. She was frequently recommended as a 'healthy' and 'moral' writer to both young women and working-class men, often in contrast to other writers of fiction, and her novels were promoted over others. George Gissing advised his sister, Margaret in June of 1880, for example: 'Don't read *too* many novels, but try to know all the best. You should get hold of Jane Austen's novels; they are very healthy.'[5] A particular anecdote in Elizabeth Wordsworth's autobiography, *Glimpses of the Past*, describes one way in which Austen could be enjoyed by intelligent men and women together. Wordsworth, the future Head of the first women's college in Oxford, Lady Margaret Hall, records a visit to Dr Whewell, Master of Trinity College, Cambridge in 1866, in which she describes sitting 'for some time capping Miss Austen, Emma breaking her boot lace, Frank Churchill going to have his hair cut'. She records their ensuing conversation: 'I think he asked me, "What was the name of Emma's governess?" to which I rejoined, "Can you tell me Mr. Knightley's Christian name?"'[6] (The answers are, of course, 'Miss Taylor' and 'George' respectively). The point of the game was, presumably, not only to illustrate one's own knowledge of the texts (as in the schoolboy game of capping Latin quotations), but to do so *together*, gaining pleasure in challenging a fellow devotee by thinking of ever more recondite questions and answers. Georgina Battiscombe's *Charlotte Mary Yonge: The Story of an Uneventful Life* (1943) confirms that Elizabeth Wordsworth played the game with more than one person, describing a visit from Wordsworth to Charlotte Yonge in 1872, during which Yonge could apparently 'correct Miss Wordsworth as to the colour of Fanny Price's eyes' while 'capping Miss Austen *con amore*'.[7] The phrase *con amore* (with love) epitomizes the point of the activity. 'Capping Miss Austen' is an act of devotion to the writer, but it also creates a bond of friendship (however temporary or transitory) between the players of the game. 'Capping Miss Austen' was not, however, limited to the rarefied atmosphere of novelist's houses and the parlours of Masters' Lodges. The relationship between Austen's novels, sociability and reading communities forms the focus of this chapter.

Austen's works were enjoyed by Charles Darwin's wife, Emma (*née* Wedgwood), who was 'especially devoted to Jane Austen's novels and almost knew them by heart'.[8] According to her daughter, 'in an examination paper set on them [the novels], she answered the question: "What is Mr Woodhouse's Christian name?" without an instant's thought. His name [Henry], it must be explained is only known by inference, as it is never actually given'.[9] Literary parlour games, 'examination papers' about Jane Austen like the one answered by Emma Darwin, appear in journals read by both men and women. There is one in the 1903 *Good Words* annual, which contains questions such as: 'What degree of expectation might fairly be raised in a young lady's breast by (i) "a partiality", (ii) a "promising inclination" (iii) "attentions too marked to be mistaken" (iv) "objectionable particularity"?' and 'Mention any little habits, peculiarities, or points of etiquette, in which the age of Miss Austen differed from our own'.[10] This suggests that discussing Jane Austen's novels was an activity that took place not only in a gentleman's library or study, but also in the feminine space of the household: the parlour. Although the tone is light, and the parlour games may seem at first to demand no critical engagement with Austen's work, they actually encourage close and careful reading of the novels. In the first cited question in particular, sensitivity to the valence of words is crucial, as is knowledge and understanding of contextual relevance. The question may be explicitly about love, but it implicitly demands critical interpretation. The second question demands careful engagement with cultural and social history. These questions encourage in particular affectionate familiarity with the writer, emphasising shared knowledge and shared enjoyment: family participation in getting to know an author.

The Darwin Family (1812–1952)

In *Mansfield Park*, Jane Austen writes, 'children of the same family, the same blood, with the same first associations and habits, have some means of enjoyment in their power, which no subsequent connections can supply'.[11] 'Associations and habits' can, of course, be literary, as they were for the Austen family, and it is noticeable that Austen's novels and characters are often deployed in family jokes and family allusions. Henrietta Litchfield records the Darwin family joke of the 1820s that 'Susan Darwin and Jessie Wedgwood, [...] both great flirts in an innocent way, received the nicknames of "Kitty and Lydia" in allusion to Kitty and Lydia in *Pride and Prejudice*'.[12] Litchfield's mother, Emma Darwin, amuses her sister Elizabeth Wedgwood with an apt allusion to *Emma*: 'Thank you for your letter which came to-day. I forgot to mention the basket. All the poultry was quite fresh and Fanny says the turkey was excellent, and Maer tongues are quite as superior as Hartfield pork'.[13] Emma's marriage to Charles Darwin is described by the close friend of the family Georgina Tollet in a letter as 'very like a marriage of Miss Austen's'. Tollet adds, 'can I say more!': it is self-evident that nothing more needs to be said about the suitability of the match; her reader will understand that 'a marriage of Miss Austen's' is the pinnacle of romantic achievement.[14] The Darwins frequently read Austen's novels together as a family, and it is clear that the jokes resounded down through subsequent generations.

Gwen Raverat, Emma Darwin's granddaughter, writes in her memoir *Period Piece* (1952):

> Every time I re-read *Emma* I see more clearly that we must be somehow related to the Knightleys of Donwell Abbey; both dear Mr. Knightley and Mr. John Knightley seem so familiar and cousinly. Surely no one, who had not Darwin or Wedgwood blood in their veins, could be as cross as Mr. John Knightley was, when he had to turn out to dine at the Weston's [*sic*]. 'The folly of not allowing people to be comfortable at home! And the folly of people's not staying comfortably

at home when they can!' – it might be Uncle Frank himself speaking. But it is obvious, too, that there is some strain of the Woodhouses of Hartfield in us, of Mr. Woodhouse in particular. There was a kind of sympathetic gloating in the Darwin voices, when they said, for instance, to one of us children: 'And have you got a *bad* sore throat, my poor cat?' which filled me with horror and shame. It was exactly the voice in which Mr. Woodhouse must have spoken of 'Poor Miss Taylor'. But it had one good effect: it quite cured us of *enjoying* ill health. I denied having a sore throat at all if I possibly could.[15]

Raverat takes the idea of being a 'friend' of the author a step further even than Anne Thackeray Ritchie, playfully imagining her own family as 'related' to two of Austen's fictional ones, and finding Austen's characters 'so familiar and cousinly'. The expected hierarchy of the comparison is inverted: the Darwins and Wedgwoods are not descended from the Knightleys as chronology would suggest; instead, Raverat claims that John Knightley must have had 'Darwin or Wedgwood blood' in his veins. The chronology is reversed once more when Raverat suggests that 'there is some strain of the Woodhouses of Hartfield in us', and the effect is to mingle Darwin, Wedgwood, Knightley and Woodhouse genes so thoroughly that the text of *Emma* is inscribed with Raverat's family history. Although it is told in a tone of childlike simplicity, these are not the thoughts of a child – Raverat is not writing of a childhood encounter with *Emma*, but of 'every time I re-read *Emma*'. It is a sophisticated interaction with a much-loved author, making use of Raverat's own playful ingenuity. Raverat's account self-consciously touches on her family's long-running interest in Jane Austen. It subsumes Austen into the family, making her a part of the Darwin-Wedgwood clan. It is perhaps no surprise that the grand-daughter of Charles Darwin should be particularly interested in the evolution of familial traits, but it is affectionate familiarity with Austen's characters as if they were family members that allows Raverat to write in such a way, appropriating Austen's genealogies for her own purposes, injecting her own family's blood into Austen's characters, and making loving fun of her relatives as Austen does of her characters.

The Macaulay Family (1820–1860)

In Thomas Babington Macaulay's family, also, references to Austen functioned as loving shorthand, and an appreciation for Austen's novels was transmitted down through the generations. As we have seen, Macaulay himself was an extraordinary reader, with a photographic memory and an almost total recall of everything he had read. Macaulay's letters to his sisters,

Hannah, Margaret, Selina and Frances, also reveal a deep and intimate *familial* knowledge of the novels. It is evident from the letters to his sisters that they too shared their brother's taste for Austen, and that he urged them to pass this love on to the next generation. Writing to Frances Macaulay about his niece Alice's education, for example, he hoped 'that you let the dear child have plenty of Miss Austen. All her lessons will not do her half so much good'.[16] He wished also that he could talk to Frances about Jane Austen himself: 'I should very much like to see you and Aunty and Alice at Broadstairs, and to have a walk on the sands, and a talk about Mr. Elton and Miss Crawford. But I fear, I fear that it cannot be.'[17]

The letters abound in casual and familiar allusions, Such small details as Mrs Norris's determination to have a spare bedroom, John Thorpe's disapproval of novels, Sir Walter Elliot's recommendation of Gowland's lotion, Mrs Elton's pride in her barouche-landau, Mrs Bennet's dislike of the 'artful' Lucas family, the content of Maria and Julia Bertram's education, and Harriet Smith's favourite cow all make an appearance in the correspondence, scattered over a period of about thirty years. Most often, these references are used to add humour to a description, or as shorthand to describe an acquaintance, and the result is that Austen's characters become part of the Macaulay siblings' private world. Putting his photographic memory to use, Macaulay teasingly asks his sisters to identify obscure quotations. To Hannah Macaulay, in 1833, he writes, for example: 'Henry is quite like a hero of an "old romance and glories in his chains". Where is that? I will bet you three kisses and a pint of whiskey to be drunk on Loch Katrine that you do not guess'.[18] The answer is, of course, to be found in *Mansfield Park*. More than twenty-five years later, the siblings are still playing the same game; he writes to Frances Macaulay in 1859: 'By the bye, why does not George write either to me or to his sister? "I am sorry to say it: but that young man is not the thing." Where is that?'.[19] Readers in the know will immediately recognize Mr Woodhouse's description of Frank Churchill.

Macaulay used the medium of a repeated reference to *Pride and Prejudice*'s Sir William Lucas to signal his amused disapproval of the pomposity of particular acquaintances. In June 1832, he wrote to Hannah and Margaret: 'He [Mr Edwin Pearson] condescended to quiz me through his glass, and then to extend his hand and congratulate me on my appointment [to the House of Commons]. "Such instances of elegant breeding," as Sir William Lucas says, "are not uncommon at the Court"'.[20] A year later, he repeated the joke, writing to Margaret, 'On Monday the House does not sit on account of the Queen's Birthday. But Lord Goderich has asked me to dinner – such instances of elegant breeding not being uncommon, as Sir William Lucas well observed, about the court; and I must go in all my official finery.'[21] Writing to

Hannah, in June of 1831, Macaulay describes a conversation with a friend about doctors:

> I hear good accounts of Jephson's success. Sir G Philips told me that he was a sad quack. "Why", said I, "I am no believer in any people who pretend to be much better physicians than others of equal experience and opportunities." "No", said Sir George. "My friend Prout is indeed a prodigy. But I do not believe in Jephson." I said nothing. But I thought my friend's hatred of quacks rather partial. He and Selina would hold a dialogue together resembling that of Mr. Woodhouse and Mrs. J. Knightley about their doctors.[22]

The result of these allusions is to emphasize and strengthen the bond of understanding between the siblings; Hannah and Margaret, Macaulay knows, will immediately recognize and appreciate the humour of the imagined dialogue between his friend Philips and their sister Selina.

Like Mary Mitford, Macaulay clearly recognized Jane Austen's claims on the city of Bath, and caught something of the spirit of her writing when he described it:

> I have been at Bath. I have seen all the spots made classical by Miss Austen, – the pump-room and the identical bench whereon Miss Thorpe and Miss Morland discussed the merits of novels, – the nasty buildings wherein Mrs. Smith lodged, – the street where Captain Wentworth made his proposals to Anne. The assembly room, I own, I did not see. But I climbed the hill whereon the Revd Henry Tilney M A, Miss Tilney, and Catherine held their conversation; – and I did not agree, I must say, with their opinion that the city of Bath might with advantage have been struck out of the landscape.[23]

Macaulay's familiarity with *Northanger Abbey* stands him in good stead in Bath; every landmark is reminiscent of an event or character in the novel, and the very landscape reminds him of Austen's satire on the picturesque. In refusing to 'agree' with 'their opinion that the city of Bath might with advantage have been struck out of the landscape', Macaulay is, of course, responding to Austen's irony, taking up one of her challenges to be an 'ingenious' reader. In the scene to which he refers in *Northanger Abbey*, the company are assembled on Beechen Cliff, above Bath. Austen discusses the 'advantages of natural folly in a beautiful girl', suggesting that 'a good-looking girl, with an affectionate heart and a very ignorant mind, cannot fail of attracting a clever young man, unless circumstances are particularly untoward.' Catherine Morland then 'confesse[s] and lament[s] her want of knowledge' and declares 'that she would give any thing in the world to be able to draw'. A 'lecture on the picturesque' immediately follows, given by Henry Tilney.[24] This 'lecture' is a masterly pastiche of writing on the picturesque, rendered with characteristic ellipses and lightness of touch: 'He talked of fore-grounds, distances, and second distances – side-screens and perspectives – lights and shades...'.[25] Catherine responds to it by beginning 'to see beauty in every thing admired by him' and 'voluntarily reject[ing] the whole city of Bath, as unworthy to make part of a landscape'.[26] Austen has prepared the reader for this response by poking gentle fun both at Catherine's earnest desire to think exactly as Henry Tilney does, and Henry's attempts to impress a pretty girl with his knowledge of the fashionable subject of the day. We – like Macaulay – see that their judgements on the picturesque are thus coloured by their motives, and so can recognize the extravagance of Catherine's 'rejection' of 'the whole city of Bath' for what it is – a naive endeavour to impress Henry with the rapidity of her progress as a scholar of the picturesque. Macaulay's response is thus apt: he rejects the 'natural folly' of Catherine's judgement and so signals his understanding of the author's irony in a way that includes his sisters in his warm admiration of the work.

Discussing the attitude of his friends the Hyde brothers to their sister, Macaulay writes: 'They seem to love the very ground that she treads on; and she is undoubtedly a charming woman, pretty, clever, lively, polite, and very attentive to me! She seemed to be on a very easy, friendly, footing with her husband, but to keep him in strict order. "She called him Tom. How delightful"'.[27] It is not only the pertinence of the quotation that is noteworthy here, but also the fact that Macaulay draws attention to the close and loving relationship between the brothers and their sister – and mediates this through a reference to Jane Austen. When Margaret married, in August 1832, Macaulay was devastated. William Thomas suggests, in fact, that Macaulay 'came close to emotional collapse' when his sisters married.[28] On the occasion of Margaret's marriage, Macaulay wrote to Hannah and Margaret:

> I had a heavy day of it on Saturday, and not a very light one yesterday. But to day I am in tolerable spirits again. I do not think that I ever felt any event so sharply as this separation, though accompanied with many pleasing circumstances; not that I am at all of the mind of Mr. Woodhouse, or in the least disposed to talk about "poor Margaret." It has always been my wish to see my dearest girls honourably and happily married. But still it is impossible not to feel keenly the pain of parting from one whom I have loved so dearly, and of resigning to new claims that place which I had gained for myself in her affection.[29]

In this context, it is tempting to speculate that Macaulay's reference to Austen is not just a generous attempt to make light of his own pain and thus lighten the mood and tone of the letter. It is also a reminder to Margaret of the familial closeness – the joking intimacy that is possible between siblings – that she was giving up in order to begin her new life.

Macaulay noted in his diary that 'there are in the world no compositions which approach nearer to perfection' than Austen's novels,[30] and he wrote to Selina in 1855, having just finished re-reading all six novels, that it would be impossible to find a better novel than *Persuasion*: 'She was an excellent writer from the very first. But her manner became better and better, till, just before her death, she produced Persuasion, beyond which it seems impossible to go.'[31] Macaulay's references to Jane Austen throughout the correspondence with his sisters reflect the extent of his own admiration of the author, but also the delight the family took in sharing their reading. Allusions to Gowland's lotion and Welsh cows, benches and barouche-landaus became a kind of private language for the Macaulay siblings, a language in which, like the young Austens, they could remind themselves of their affection for one another through reference to a shared history of reading.

The XII Club (1895–1950)

In 1895, in a quiet suburb of Reading, Berkshire, six Quaker couples decided to form a literary society, the purpose of which would be to read and discuss together works of literature, to give papers on literary subjects, and, occasionally, to enjoy excursions to places of local interest. The membership would always be twelve, in principle six couples, but in practice the club also admitted suitable unmarried literary enthusiasts. These members would be Quakers, or those who held similar views to the Society of Friends. The membership was largely drawn from the local professional and gentry classes, and each meeting took place in the home of a different pair of members (or member if unmarried). The society agreed to buy books for the year's meetings, which would then be dispersed among the members of the club at the end of the year. The founding members decided to keep strict minutes of every meeting (the club was to meet approximately once a month), and this practice has been maintained from the club's inception until the present day (2012).

The minute books record that the club's meetings always followed the same format. Firstly, the minutes of the previous meeting were read aloud, and either approved or emended. The date of the next meeting was agreed, followed by the subject to be discussed at that meeting. A committee to prepare the next subject was formed and any other business (such as the selection of the next year's books, or an auction of the books owned by the club, the organization of an excursion, the election of new members, and so on) was discussed. Then came the bulk of the meeting, made up of readings and discussion of literature, usually bisected by supper (during the war years 1914–18 and 1939–45, supper was replaced by lemonade and biscuits). Occasionally, music was introduced, often in the form of songs which were settings of poems by a well-known writer such as Robert Burns, and, on a number of occasions, the society enjoyed a play-reading, in which the members of the society took different roles. From the beginning, the XII Club, as it was named, flourished, and it has changed remarkably little, in terms both of the character of its membership and its activities, in over one hundred years.[32] The club's membership appears to have been both long-standing and long-lived, and there is a remarkably slow turnover of members, which may account for its stability.

The society's records reflect the wide range of literature read in the one hundred and sixteen years of its existence, and the different tastes of succeeding generations of members. Sometimes the meetings seem to have included a variety of writers and even genres. At one meeting in September 1895, for example, the club discussed Annie Besant's *An Autobiography*, Frederic Harrison's *The Meaning of History* and Andrew Martin Fairbairn's *The Place of Christ in Modern Theology*. More commonly, the meetings were clearly themed around a particular writer or topic. On 6 October 1896, the club had a Wordsworth evening, with readings from his poetry by a number of the ladies of the club, and 'a short paper on Wordsworth and Poetic diction', read by the Secretary, Alfred Rawlings.[33] On 6 October 1898, there was a 'programme of selections from and papers on Kingsley', including a paper on Charles Kingsley as a religious leader.[34] In July 1896, 'a part reading from the Midsummer Night Dream was then given, nearly all the members present taking part', which was followed by readings from *Macbeth*.[35] Evenings dedicated to the *Rubáiyát of Omar Khayyám*, Robert Browning's poetry, Lewis Carroll, 'Rudyard Kipling and his books',[36] a performance of *The Tempest* and, on a separate occasion 'readings and songs from Shakespeare'[37], were all enjoyed in the 1890s.

Throughout its existence, the club seems to have tried to balance meetings dealing with the important social issues and literature of the day with study of authors from the more distant past. The 1900s, for example, saw a meeting on the modern writer H. G. Wells; a session on 'the soul of a people' (this included readings from Harold Fielding Hall's *The Soul of a People*, Edwin Arnold's *Light of Asia* and the *Dhammapada*), and an evening's discussion of Benjamin Rowntree's *Poverty: a Study of Town Life*. The older poets were represented by evenings on Chaucer and Edmund Spenser, and the Classics by one dedicated to Marcus Aurelius. The Romantic poets were represented by evenings consecrated to, variously, 'Burns and his books', P. B. Shelley, and Keats. From this period, Charles Lamb was also awarded a whole evening's study. Overall, though, the 1900s were dominated by the high Victorians, with separate evenings devoted to 'Tennyson and his books', Walter Savage Landor,

Carlyle, Thackeray, Robert Louis Stevenson, George Meredith, William Morris, Matthew Arnold, and Ruskin. The session on Ruskin clearly provoked heated controversy; Alfred Rawling's paper on Ruskin's *Modern Painters* 'met with strong dissent' from the assembled company.[38] Light relief was provided by an evening of 'readings from Punch', and transatlantic writers were represented by an evening on Ralph Waldo Emerson, and one on 'selections from American authors', although this ended up only comprising a reading from John Greenleaf Whittier's *The Meeting*. The only women writers chosen by the society for an evening's study during this decade were George Eliot and Jane Austen, and the only non-Anglophone writer was Tolstoy.

The decade 1910 to 1920 suggests a membership with more eclectic interests. The programme contained more evenings on topics, rather than single authors, such as 'English Ballads', 'parodies', 'Vers de Societé', 'Christian Science', 'Recent Irish Literature', 'Three modern poets' (these were Alfred Noyes, Henry Newbolt and Rupert Brooke), 'William Barnes and west country songs', 'Bain's Indian Stories', 'Child Study', 'the Nature of Poetry', 'Psychical Phenomena', 'The Comic', 'Mountains', and a selection of literature dealing with the Faustus legend. Evenings devoted to single authors were still popular – the club chose a variety of authors, once again maintaining a reasonable balance between modern writers and more canonical ones, though the latter were distinctly more numerous. Evenings were dedicated to Thomas Hardy, Oliver Wendell Holmes, J. M. Barrie, Goldwin Smith, W. W. Jacobs, W. Pett Ridge, John Galsworthy, Bret Harte, Lewis Carroll, George Bernard Shaw, Robert Browning, Alfred Russel Wallace, Edmund Gosse, Joseph Conrad, Gilbert Murray and George Gissing, among others. There was a more international flavour to the society's reading: Ibsen, Dante, Henri Bergson, Anatole France, Balzac, Rabindranath Tagore, Cervantes, Mark Twain and Dostoievsky all made an appearance in this decade. Women writers were limited to a session on the Brontë sisters. Play readings were less numerous than earlier, perhaps reflecting a waning of thespian talent in the club, but included John Drinkwater's *Abraham Lincoln*. The club also returned to a number of authors that they had discussed in the previous decades, namely Chaucer, Shakespeare, Shelley, Tolstoy, Thackeray, Meredith, Wordsworth, Morris, H. G. Wells, Stevenson, and Keats.

Between 1920 and 1930, play readings revived in popularity, with readings of Shakespeare's *A Winter's Tale*, *Two Noble Kinsmen*, and *The Tempest*, and Gilbert Murray's translation of *The Agamemnon*. Although the minute book records a suggestion that the society was in the doldrums and should be dissolved, it seems that the members were keen to continue with the meetings. Again, they chose a certain number of authors that the society had already discussed: Tolstoy, Shakespeare, Browning, Anatole France, Galsworthy, and Thomas Hardy, but they also considered a number of new ones, such as Ben Jonson, William Henry Hudson, Fanny Burney, Thomas Love Peacock, John Bunyan, Maurice Hewlett, Samuel Johnson, Laurence Housman, John Masefield, Quiller Couch, Sabine Baring Gould, Yeats, Trollope, 'Mark Rutherford' [William Hale White], Lord Byron, William de Morgan, Walt Whitman, Herman Melville, Hugh Walpole, William Blake, Voltaire, Plato, Charles Reade, de Quincey, Pepys and Victor Hugo. Once again, the society held an evening on 'Ballads' (these sessions seem to have provided a good opportunity for some of the members of the society to sing), and there were evenings dedicated to 'Humour', 'Joan of Arc' 'Letters and letter writing', 'modern poets', 'Gardens' and 'Berkshire' (which included a history of the county, performances of Berkshire folksongs and readings from Berkshire authors). The only women writers considered for a whole evening were George Sand and Elizabeth Gaskell, though Austen made a brief appearance in the session on 'Humour' (see below).

In the 1930 and 40s, the society revisited 'Berkshire in literature' and John Masefield, Housman, Galsworthy, William Morris, Austen and Shelley once again. They discussed Molière, Goethe, the Sitwells, Walter Scott, George William Russell and William Fryer Harvey for the first time, and had evenings devoted to readings from Nobel prizewinning authors, 'Medieval Social Life' (which somehow became Renaissance Social Life in the preparation), cricket in literature, 'the Jew in literature', 'London', 'Witches', and Irish literature, among many other authors and topics. The society's Quaker roots and interests no doubt dictated their choice of reading to some extent, and certainly influenced some of the recorded discussions. There is also a strong local flavour to much of the material chosen. Members' individual interests must also have played an important part both in the choice of reading matter and the approaches to it. But it is evident from the existing minutes that the members of the society were strongly motivated by a desire to read works of literature that were 'important' in some way – politically, morally or aesthetically – and it is possible to extrapolate a number of significant facts from the available data, analysed across four decades. There is a heavy bias towards male writers. American literature and Irish literature are clearly considered to be separate categories. Scottish literature hardly makes a showing. There are also some surprising omissions – Dickens hardly appears in the society's discussions, for example, and Scott is not discussed until the 1930s. The presence of Austen on a number of occasions is therefore significant, since the members' decision to discuss Austen goes against the trend for male writers and suggests that she was considered by the members to be more important (or at least more appealing) than Dickens or Scott, as early as 1901.

Within this broader understanding of the XII Club's habits and interests, we will now consider the society's various interactions with Jane Austen in detail. On 7 June 1901, the XII Club had a Jane Austen evening, and listened to 'A paper [...] on Jane Austen' read by Mrs Lilian Goadby, 'followed by readings from her novels by Mrs Ridges, C. E. Stansfield, S. A. Reynolds & a duologue by Mrs Edminson & Mr Goadby'.[39] Regrettably, the content of the readings and the duologue is not recorded in the minute book. Twenty-eight years later, on 3 May 1929, the society, by then with some new members, revisited Jane Austen in a session dedicated to 'Humour', when Mrs Mary Robson read the scene from *Pride and Prejudice* where Mr Collins proposes.[40] The purpose of the evening was 'to enjoy the following selections chosen to represent English Humour in literature down the Ages', and Austen appeared in company with Chaucer, Shakespeare, Dickens, Charles Lamb, Lewis Carroll, Jerome K. Jerome and Hilaire Belloc.[41] It was not until April 1937 that the club (by then with an almost entirely new membership) dedicated another evening specifically to Jane Austen. This had been a few months in the planning; the minutes of the meeting of 15 September 1936 recorded 'a general desire that before long we might read "Green Pastures"', and – in telling phraseology – 'spend an evening with Jane Austen'.[42] In the April meeting, Victor Alexander, the secretary of the club, read 'a paper on Jane Austen, half biographical sketch & half an appreciation of her style'. The conflation of biography and appreciation of style was perhaps learned from his reading of nineteenth-century articles on Jane Austen, such as those discussed earlier. The knowledgeable Francis Pollard 'quoted from Lucy Harrison's Literary Papers some telling and illuminating remarks, particularly about Fanny Price in Mansfield Park', and readings followed. These were 'from Northanger Abbey by Celia Burrows[;] from Persuasion by Rosamund Wallis[;] from Sense and Sensibility by Francis & Mary Pollard[;] from Love and Friendship by Elizabeth Alexander[;] from Pride and Prejudice by Victor Alexander'.[43] The inclusion of *Love and Freindship* is particularly interesting, since Austen's juvenilia was, at this period, generally considered to be unrepresentative of her writing, and to be unworthy of her. The XII Club's choice of *Love and Freindship* in preference to the much better-known *Emma* or *Mansfield Park* thus suggests that the club's members had a high degree of knowledge of Austen's works, that they were prepared to listen to even the more eclectic parts of her *oeuvre*, and that they were a body of people who wished to make up their own minds about the writer, rather than being swayed by the criticism of others.

The XII Club had not yet had enough of Jane Austen. On 21 February 1945, in the last days of the Second World War, one or more of the members of the club (their identity unrecorded) requested that the secretary add Jane Austen to the list of proposed subjects for discussion that year. It was not until September of 1947, however, that this member (or these members) got their way. At a meeting on 29 September 1947, with Muriel W. Stevens in the chair, the society enjoyed a play reading of Helen Jerome's stage adaptation of *Pride and Prejudice*. Although the membership of the club had changed substantially since the first Jane Austen evening of 1901, one person who had been at that first evening was still an active member of the club: Sylvanus Reynolds. Reynolds, by then aged eighty-four, took a minor role in the play-reading. Francis Pollard (whose 'telling and illuminating remarks' about Fanny Price had enlivened the 1937 evening) read the parts of Mr Wickham and Mr Collins, while his wife took the roles of Lady Lucas and Lady Catherine de Bourgh. The remainder of the roles were played by newer members of the society. Like the young Austens, acting out plays in the Steventon Rectory, the XII Club found play-reading to be agreeable entertainment; unlike the Crawfords and Bertrams of *Mansfield Park*, the members do not seem to have suffered from the practice.

It seems clear that the members of the XII Club considered Austen's works to be both intellectually stimulating and enjoyable. While the minute books do not note individual opinions of her works, they do record that the Austen evenings were lively. As in the Master's Lodge, where Elizabeth Wordsworth and Dr Whewell sat 'capping Miss Austen' in 1866, in the meetings of the XII Club, Austen's works are deployed in the service of sociable activity. This is, of course, of a piece with the role played by books in Austen's own novels. We are reminded of Catherine Morland and Isabella Thorpe, cementing the bonds of friendship as they shut themselves up to read Gothic horror tales together; of Emma and Harriet attempting to read together before the books are put aside in favour of chat and gossip; of Anne Elliot and Captain Benwick, learning to like each other on the promenade at Lyme Regis through a discussion of the poetry of Scott and Byron; of Marianne Dashwood and Willoughby falling in love over Shakespeare, and of Edmund Bertram turning over Fanny's books in the East Room as he comes to her for help and advice. And we are also reminded ironically of Caroline Bingley's transparent attempt to win the affections of Mr Darcy by picking up the second volume of his own choice of book in the drawing-room of Netherfield.

All books can function as social enablers, giving otherwise incompatible characters a mutual topic of conversation, helping to bring people together for the purposes of discussion and/or analysis, providing an excuse to further a promising acquaintanceship, sometimes even becoming the medium through which illicit love letters are exchanged. The borrowing, lending and recommendation of books thus has an evident social function, and this is, to some people and in some cases, much more important than what is inside the books' covers. It is no surprise that Austen's novels – first written, as we have seen, to be read in a small and close community, and dealing with the social events of such communities – should be used in the service of creating, maintaining and perpetuating reading communities such as the XII Club. Reading communities of this kind are formed to share literary tastes. Depending on the viewpoint of the observer, they can be perceived as vibrant, stimulating and enjoyable, or as complacent and exclusive, relying as they often do on shared literary experiences, which give rise to jokes and allusions to literature. These, like those in Austen's novels and letters, can only be recognized by those 'in the know'.

'Janeites' (1870–1950)

Rudyard Kipling, himself a lifelong reader of Austen's works, early recognized (and satirized) such communities and shared literary references in his short story, 'The Janeites' (1924), in which the fictional Janeites of the title are military men for whom intimate knowledge of Austen's novels becomes a kind of Freemasonry in the trenches (not coincidentally, the story is set in a Masonic Lodge, wherein the narrator, Humberstall, describes how knowing such passwords as 'Tilniz and trapdoors' reaped numerous benefits during the war).[44] The comedy of the story lies partly in the gap between Humberstall's incomplete understanding of Austen's novels (he was coached in them by a superior officer so was able, parrot-fashion, to repeat important facts and names, but had little proper knowledge of context or meaning, although he has since become, he says, a true Janeite) and the assumed knowledge and understanding of the reader. There is comedy also in the disjunction between the strongly masculine settings of the Masonic Lodge, Officers' Mess, and gun emplacements, and what was perceived as the entirely domestic preoccupations of Austen's novels. For many years it was a critical truism that Jane Austen had no interest in the wider world of politics and war, to the extent that the *Daily Telegraph* could repeat this idea as a fact: 'There is no sound of war in her pages, though she had sailor brothers of distinction, and she lived through the Napoleonic era. All is placid in her Hampshire villages; and the main business of life is to marry off marriageable daughters to eligible young men'.[45] A number of readers shared this belief, as is well demonstrated by Winston Churchill's assessment of *Pride and Prejudice*: 'What calm lives they had, those people! No worries about the French Revolution, or the crashing struggle of the Napoleonic Wars. Only manners controlling natural passion as far as they could, together with cultured explanations of any mischances.[46] As reported by the *Times*, A. B. Walkley suggested in 1922 that Austen's was 'the literature of consolation', a 'refuge' in an age that was 'war-weary and shell-shocked', and 'a house of rest' for those in need of peace.[47] In 'The Janeites', Kipling delights in suggesting the opposite: that Austen's works are more than ever relevant in a wartime society, and employs many of the same strategies as Austen herself, such as irony, misdirection, inviting the reader to exercise 'ingenuity', and undercutting and subverting the characters' certainties. It is probable that Kipling knew that wounded soldiers were advised to read Jane Austen – as Christopher Kent records, H. F. Brett-Smith, acting as an advisor on reading matter for the wounded, selected Jane Austen for the most severely shell-shocked.[48] In the course both of research for his book on the Irish Guards, and in his work to set up the memorial to the Unknown Soldier, Kipling interviewed a number of soldiers, and read their diaries and other letters. It seems likely, therefore, that he knew of this advice, and that he was implicitly referring to it in 'The Janeites', when we hear that Humberstall is 'liable to a sort o' quiet fits' which 'came on after the dump blew up at Eatables' and that he reads 'all her six books now for pleasure', believing that 'there's no one to touch Jane when you're in a tight place'.[49]

The story is also, at least in part, an in-joke directed at Janeites of his own acquaintance, and very possibly at those within his family, including himself. Although Kipling had not always been a wholehearted admirer of Austen – Lisa Lewis identifies a 'mildly disparaging' reference to Jane Austen in an early comic poem, 'The Mare's Nest' (1885)[50] – he gained appreciation of her writing later in life. Lewis suggests that at least four of Kipling's mature stories – 'Marklake Witches', 'The Janeites', 'Mary Postgate' and 'The Gardener' – contain 'echoes of Jane Austen', claiming that Kipling learned both style and the indirect method – where a writer simultaneously hides and reveals truths from the reader – from Austen.[51] The Kipling family read Jane Austen together in the dark days of the First World War, when their soldier son, Jack, went missing, and Mrs Kipling recorded the comfort and 'great delight' that the novels brought them in her diary of January 1917.[52] Kipling finished 'The Janeites' after a trip to Bath in 1923. According to Kipling's biographer, Andrew Lycett, the immediate motivation for the story was a discussion with the critic (and Janeite) George Saintsbury, 'about the sense of fellowship felt by people who shared a powerful joint experience – whether fighting in war, or membership of a Mason's Lodge, or even familiarity with the works of an author such as Austen.'[53] Kipling's story brings the three kinds of 'powerful joint experience' together. Presumably Kipling's trip to Bath also brought Austen to mind. Like so many others, he felt Austen's particular claims on that city, having re-read her novels while staying there in March of 1915, and writing to a friend at that point that 'the more I read the more I admire and respect and do reverence' her.[54] The idea of 'Janeites' was also particularly topical in the 1920s following the resurgence of interest in Austen's works prompted by the publication of *Volume the Second* of the Juvenilia in 1922, and Chapman's edition of *Sanditon* in 1925. As Claudia Johnson points out, manifestations of both love and hatred of Jane Austen appeared in the 1920s. H. W. Garrod's

1928 'Jane Austen: A Depreciation', a speech presented at the Royal Society of Literature, depicted her as a 'humdrum' writer, who appealed to sexless, or de-sexed men. Johnson suggests that 'Garrod's mysoygnist "Depreciation" is aimed just as much at male Janeites in the audience as at Austen herself', and that the thrust of Garrod's argument is that admiration of Jane Austen reveals the effeminacy of her admirers.[55] Kipling's story thus intervenes in a debate not only about Jane Austen, but also about the masculinity of her readers. Given the long tradition of conflating the novel genre with a feminized reading public, it is perhaps not surprising that male Janeites should have been perceived as effeminate, though, as Johnson suggests, the flamboyant campness of prominent Janeites such as Lord David Cecil may also have contributed to this perception.[56]

While Kipling's version of the Janeite is, of course, both exaggerated and ironized, the Janeites of the 1920s were a real phenomenon. Made up mainly of elite, male readers, who were members of the *literati*, Janeites were prepared to flaunt their devotion to Jane Austen and to attempt to influence popular opinion in her favour. In 1922, the *Times* reported the death of Austen's great-niece, Mary Austen-Leigh, the author of *Personal Aspects of Jane Austen* (1920), under the headline 'A Link with Jane Austen'. In this brief article, the *Times*' correspondent reports one of Mary Austen-Leigh's remarks:

> There are four different categories of people with regard to Jane Austen; there are those who are quite indifferent; next, the people who like her because other people do; then, those who genuinely like and appreciate her; and, lastly, those of us to whom she is a cult.[57]

Those to whom Austen was a 'cult' were numerous. Writing in the *Evening Standard* in July 1927, Arnold Bennett complained of the 'antics' of 'passionate Janeites', calling them 'fanatics', suggesting humorously that they were 'ready to do murder for their sacred cause', and accusing them of a lack of proportion in seeming to believe that 'Jane and Shakespeare are the only two authors who rightly count'.[58] In 1924, E. M. Forster similarly satirized the idolatry of the Janeite when he described himself as 'a Jane Austenite, and therefore slightly imbecile about Jane Austen.' Forster continues:

> My fatuous expression, and airs of personal immunity – how ill they sit on the face of, say, a Stevensonian! But Jane Austen is so different. She is my favourite author! I read and re-read, the mouth open and the mind closed. Shut up in measureless content, I greet her by the name of most kind hostess, while criticism slumbers. The Jane Austenite possesses little of the brightness he ascribes so freely to his idol. Like all regular churchgoers, he scarcely notices what is being said.[59]

In this suggestive passage, Forster pretends to a vacuity that is in fact very far from the truth, following this introductory declamation with some rigorous textual exegesis. Forster's admiration of Jane Austen is real, but the Janeite pose is here designed to differentiate 'criticism' from the kind of mindless hagiography that such writers as Forster, Bennett and, elsewhere, Henry James, found hard to stomach. Forster and Bennett no doubt had in mind not only biographical accounts such as those written by Austen's own family and the critical writings of what Johnson calls 'an insider's society of scholar-gentlemen at play' –Saintsbury, Lord David Cecil and others[60]– but also the many more material manifestations of Austen's popularity with the general public.

From the 1880s onwards, various appeals for funds for subscriptions for memorials to Jane Austen (in Winchester, Bath and Chawton) and the preservation, repair or upkeep of buildings relating to the author appeared frequently in the letters pages of the *Times*, usually followed only a little later by a notice of the unveiling of the memorial or the improvement of the building.[61] Many of the links with Jane Austen were, at best, faint, but it is evident that those seeking for subscribers believed that even the smallest link with Austen made preservation of the artefact or building worthwhile. The strong support of the public for Austen memorials of all kinds in the last decade of the nineteenth century and the first decades of the twentieth onwards suggests that Janeites were not only prepared to love their favourite author, but to provide financial proof of their devotion. Memorials included the Jane Austen memorial window in Winchester Cathedral, paid for by contributions from the public and unveiled in 1900, a tablet outside her house in College Street in Winchester, a tablet outside No. 4 Sydney Place and a memorial in the Pump Room in Bath (unveiled in 1899 and 1912 respectively), a tablet outside Chawton Cottage to mark Austen's centenary in 1917, and a bronze mural tablet in Steventon Church, unveiled in 1936. The formation of the Jane Austen Society in 1940 by Miss Dorothy Darnell was a significant moment for Janeites in Britain. The Society was formed 'with the object of getting possession of the house formerly known as Chawton Cottage' to become the Jane Austen House Museum, and 'set itself to raise at least £5000', no mean sum in a country ravaged by war and then suffering under austerity measures.[62] Nonetheless, the Society raised the necessary funds, and the Museum was opened in 1947, the same year that the XII Club performed Jerome's stage adaptation of *Pride and Prejudice*. In forming the Society, its founder members gave Janeites a common purpose and aim, and the Society's programme of events became (and remains) an opportunity for Janeites to meet each other in order, as the Society puts it, 'to foster the appreciation and study of the life, work and times of Jane Austen and the Austen family'.[63]

Numerous books and newspaper articles catered for the public's seemingly insatiable appetite for even the most trivial details about Austen's life and fed the Janeites' pleasure in ever more arcane textual quibbles, throughout the 1920s and 30s. Noticeably, correspondence about very specialized biographical, historical or textual issues relating to Austen did not always take place in dedicated literary journals such as *Notes and Queries*, or even in the *Times Literary Supplement*; instead it often appeared in the letters pages of the *Times* itself, thus suggesting a large general readership in addition to Austen's critical following.[64] Advertisers too cashed in on Austen's popularity – two property advertisements claiming 'a link with Jane Austen' appeared in the *Times* in the first half of 1928 (the link in both cases is fairly spurious).[65] In 1920, the *Times* reported that 'the amusing parlour-game of Jane Austen topography is always being played somewhere'[66] – and a book that encouraged literary pilgrimages, Constance and Edith Hill's *Jane Austen: Her homes and her friends* (1902), enjoyed renewed popularity in the 1920s, going into a new edition in 1923.

The interest in all things Austen in this period is well illustrated in Caroline Ticknor's *Glimpses of Authors* (1924), a collection of anecdotes about predominantly American authors, although there are also chapters on Dickens, Anne Thackeray Ritchie, Du Maurier and Coleridge in addition to Austen. In the chapter entitled 'Jane Austen's Grand-Niece' (the 'grand-niece' in question is Mary Austen-Leigh, though she is not named), the author records a visit to the Austen-Leigh household during which she was shown 'Aunt Jane's desk', 'her last unfinished manuscript', a collection of 'delightful letters [...] all to the very last penned with the same beauty and neatness', 'an elaborately embroidered muslin scarf', a 'tiny "huswife"' and 'a carefully folded paper on which were written a couple of graceful verses touching upon the tiny gift', 'a sketch made from life by her sister', 'her ring', presentation copies of Austen's novels, and lastly, 'a soft brown curl, silken and beautiful'.[67] The impression throughout the description of these items is that of a worshipper at a shrine, strengthened by Ticknor's characterization of the ownership of the items as a 'sacred trust'.[68] Following this line of thought, Ticknor commends the 'beautiful memorial window' in Winchester Cathedral, but writes, 'better than any view of a cathedral window, or fitting epitaph, is a brief glimpse of that which brings the fortunate beholder near to Jane Austen through her intimate belongings'.[69] Ticknor clearly believed that a readership existed for this 'collection of enchanting memories', rejoicing in being able to pass on her own experience of gazing upon the Austen-Leighs' carefully guarded relics to her readers.[70]

It is impossible to deny that there is an element of whimsy in much Janeite writing such as Ticknor's, as there is in Hugh Thomson's illustrations of the novels. Kipling's poem, 'Jane's Marriage', which immediately follows

'The Janeites' in the collection *Debits and Credits* (1926), and imagines Austen's arrival in Paradise, is another (and particularly egregious) piece of whimsy. The premise of the poem is that 'Jane' arrives in Paradise and is welcomed by a number of other great writers – Scott, Fielding, Smollett, Cervantes and Shakespeare. Offered 'Anything in heaven's gift / That she might command', 'Jane' chooses 'Love'. Seraphim and Cherubim ask the question, 'Who loved Jane?', and 'a Hampshire gentleman' in limbo hears the question ringing through Heaven. He happens to be reading a book called *Persuasion* which 'told the plain / Story of the love between / Him and Jane' and so he answers the question with 'I did – and do!' and immediately enters into Paradise. The gentleman is likened to Captain Wentworth and the reader is left to draw the inference that the 'Hampshire gentleman' of the poem was the model for that fictional character.[71] The poem itself is trifling, and was presumably designed as the sort of occasional poem written as a *jeu d'esprit* of the kind that Austen herself sometimes penned. It is noticeable that Kipling is using Austen's own strategy of discussing characters (in this case 'the late Captain Wentworth R. N.') as if they were real people.

Some readers entered into the spirit of the poem, writing to Kipling to identify some 'factual' inconsistencies. Ellen M. Barnes, for example, wrote in December of 1931, asking whether the 'Sir Walter' who meets Jane Austen in Paradise was Sir Walter Scott or Sir Walter Raleigh. She pointed out that Scott's death occurred after Austen's, and hence Sir Walter could not have reached Paradise before her. Kipling chose to defend the anachronism to Miss Barnes (although he later revised the poem):

> In reply to your note of the 24th re the late Miss J. Austen Mr K. desires me to say that he has no precise knowledge of the exact date after her death when that Lady "went to Paradise" but, from the evidence of the next line, it would appear that there may have been an interval during which Justice occupied itself with the consideration of her claims to proceed thither. Mr Kipling does not know the length of that interval nor for what cause it was imposed but he conceives that it would have given time for the late Sir W. Scott to have preceded her. It is to be noted also that the late Captain Wentworth R.N. was set to wait in 'a private Limbo' his Paradise obviously being conditional on Miss Austen's view of him.[72]

In December of 1932, he was still defending the anachronism, this time to a different correspondent, S. A. Courtauld:

> As to the late Miss Austin [*sic*] (Have you looked at the Oxford press edition of her letters?) the explanation is simple. No date in time is given for her entry

into Paradise, *or* Sir Walter's. There is a period of preparation and squaring of accounts. Sir Walter, when he wasn't with Marjorie, spent that time trying to give Hogg some idea of his hoggishness, and listening to all the world's best ballads from the mouths of their makers. This took time. No one knows how Jane occupied herself. She was on the Ladies' side of Limbo. At the fit hour, she made her entry, just as she was used to make it at the little dances which she loved, and was, as I have described, met with some circumstance. But if people *will* go by almanacks and dates and things – what can you expect?[73]

There is something particularly telling about these pieces of correspondence, which demonstrate Kipling's and his correspondents' willingness to enter into a humorous discussion of even the most whimsical trivialities if 'Jane' is the subject. The poem and letters provide evidence, not only of Kipling's intimate knowledge of Austen, but also of his assumption that his correspondents would share this knowledge. The assumption of shared knowledge about, as well as shared devotion to, the author, is at the heart of a large number of Janeite interactions, as Kipling's short story unerringly pinpoints. Though they did not always meet in the parlours of Masters' Lodges, many Janeites spent time 'capping Miss Austen', either in letters to the newspapers or each other, or at face to face meetings, either at Jane Austen Society events or private gatherings. Austen's novels therefore helped to create both imagined communities of 'unknown friends' who communicated by letter, and real communities of readers who came together to discuss the novels.

CONCLUSION

Many of the interactions with Jane Austen described in these final chapters do not appear, at first glance, to take up the challenging invitations of her style. Readers who find in Austen 'morality', 'health' and 'consolation' are, it could be argued, resisting her challenges to ideology and ignoring the disruptive energies of her novels. Or it could be argued that these readers are in fact interpreting Austen more accurately, that whatever the energies of the prose style, the eventual result of the novels is a confirmation or affirmation of domestic sociability, peaceful country life and happy marriages. Readers who value and trust in Austen's happy endings are, of course, many. Winston Churchill was not the only person to find Austen's novels to be consolatory in war time – an anonymous Mass Observation respondent similarly 'could read nothing but Jane Austen's *Emma* when war broke out',[1] and Anna Neagle, who starred in a war-time stage production of *Emma*, called it 'perfect escapist entertainment'.[2] A whole novel, Karen Joy Fowler's *The Jane Austen Book Club* (2004), takes as its premise the idea that regularly reading Jane Austen is the way to find a happy marriage, ending with the words:

> We'd let Austen into our lives, and now we were all either married or dating. Could O'Brian have done this? How? When we needed to cook aboard ship, play a musical instrument, travel to Spain dressed like a bear, Patrick O'Brian would be our man. Till then, we'd just wait. In three or four years it would be time to read Austen again.[3]

There is no doubt that for some readers, reading Austen's novels is simply a form of pleasurable escapism, particularly suitable for times of melancholy or illness. Churchill was cured of influenza, he felt, by a combination of Jane Austen and antibiotics.[4] William Morris, sent to the countryside for a rest cure in 1895 wrote to Georgiana Burne Jones: 'I brought my University book down with me but deserted it yesterday afternoon for Jane Austen's "Pride and Prejudice," which I have just finished. I am getting better here, but was better on Sunday for the matter of that'.[5] And, with a disjunction between ailment and cure that reminds us comically of Mrs Jennings' belief in the curative value of constantia wine and olives for a broken heart in *Sense and Sensibility*, Sir Henry Holland recorded Austen's salutary effects on Lord Holland's gout: 'I have the picture still before me of Lord Holland lying on his bed, when attacked with gout, his admirable sister, Miss Fox, beside him reading aloud, as she always did on these occasions, some one of Miss Austen's novels, of which he was never wearied.'[6]

In many cases, it is the apparent stability and certainties of the world that Austen depicts, rather than its problematic epistemologies, which appeal to her readers. And for many readers, the response to the elliptical challenges of Austen's style manifests itself in acts of imaginative engagement, not with the works, but with the character of the author, showing itself as a desire to know more about Austen herself. The interest in Austen memorabilia is one facet of this particular kind of engagement with Jane Austen, as is the popularity of literary pilgrimage to places associated with her. In *Pride and Prejudice*, Lizzie finds the pursuit of knowledge irresistible: 'it was impossible not to long to know' the cause of the *froideur* between Mr Darcy and Mr Wickham.[7] For many of Austen's readers, the pursuit of knowledge does not lead them to desire to fill in the gaps in the pre-history of *Pride and Prejudice*, but the tantalizing gaps in their knowledge of Austen's own history. For a number of these readers (as for Anne Thackeray Ritchie), Austen is an oxymoronic 'unknown friend', and in reading the novels, as a writer for the *Retrospective Review* put it in 1823, 'we see and know herself'.[8] A feeling of closeness with the author is what these readers seek and find in Austen's novels. Many are also drawn to the feeling of being part of an exclusive community of readers who get the jokes, understand the allusions, and align themselves on the side of the good or witty characters, against the villains and fools of the novels.

This sense of community is at the heart of the pleasure that many readers take in Austen's novels, and it is directly related to Austen's own habits of writing and reading within a close and homogenous community of readers with a shared frame of reference, as we saw in Chapter 1. For readers such as the Macaulays, the Darwins, the Kiplings, and many others, Austen's novels came to function as Richardson, Cowper, Shakespeare and Crabbe had for the young Austens – they provided a shared source of humour and allusion and a ready stock of character types by which to measure their own acquaintance.

For some readers, such as D. H. Lawrence, Austen's writing – and the kind of communities it encourages – represents a particularly unpleasant narrowness. Lawrence notoriously described Austen as an 'old maid', who epitomized 'the sharp knowing in apartness' contrasted to the 'knowing in togetherness' that he ascribed to Defoe and Fielding, calling her 'English in the bad, mean, snobbish sense of the word, just as Fielding is English in the good generous sense'.⁹ There is, of course, both a gender and a class dimension to Lawrence's criticism, which implicitly suggests both that Austen's spinsterhood was limiting and that those who read (or at least, those who enjoy reading) Jane Austen are complicit in the 'snobbishness' of her writing.¹⁰ Kipling's 'The Janeites' simultaneously reflects a similar assumption (the 'Janeites' are initially all male members of the officer class) and questions it, since the working-class Humberstall does eventually become a true Janeite, thus suggesting that, in fact, love of Jane Austen's novels transcends class and dissolves class barriers.

There is little evidence in the historical record that this was, in fact the case, since the records of working-class readers of Jane Austen are so scarce, and very rarely depict sociable readings of Austen's works. In Philip Inman's autobiography, *No Going Back* (1952), he describes reading Austen's novels as a young labourer:

> The world of which she wrote, in which elegant gentlemen of fortune courted gentle, punctiliously correct ladies in refined drawing rooms, was a remote fairy-tale country to me. Some day, I thought, perhaps I would get to know a world in which voices were always soft and modulated and in which lively and witty conversation was more important than 'brass'.¹¹

Austen's world is figured as completely different from his own, and as such, it was one that he desired to know. Inman's account suggests a solitary encounter with Austen's novels, and an aspiration to encounter 'lively and witty conversation' which suggests he might have enjoyed some Janeite reading communities and activities. For Inman, however, exposure to such conversations came later, and was focused not on the reading of Jane Austen, but on Labour politics. In contrast to Inman's thwarted wish to enter Jane Austen's world, however, reading Austen's novels made Mark Twain feel 'like a bar-keeper entering the Kingdom of Heaven', watching good Presbyterians filing 'self-complacently along'.¹² These suggestive phrases point to the sense of exclusion felt by some readers that is the inevitable flipside of the kind of writing that both demands insider knowledge and creates communities based on it. Many such readers (and their numbers are large) reject the novels and their author entirely, considering her fictional world to be either too far from their own experience or too 'complacent', to use a term employed by both Twain and Henry James, to be interesting. And, of course, there are plenty of readers who are simply unmoved or untouched by Austen's novels. Some find them trivial or uninteresting; others find them overly focused on the middle classes and regional England, still others cannot accept the conventions of a romance plot. For such readers, the challenges of her style go either unremarked or ignored, and they find no pleasure in participating in the 'games of ingenuity' offered by Austen's writing.

Some readers, such as Elizabeth Barrett Browning, engage intensely with the works, but resist their charms. In such responses, we can see the kind of 'rational opposition' that Austen clearly admired, and practised in her own reading and writing. Barrett Browning and Charlotte Brontë, working against stereotypes of the proper lady, reacted strongly against Austen partly because her reputation – as a female writer who was contented, gentle, domestic, ladylike and intuitive – made her complicit with the kinds of patriarchal structures that their protagonists struggle against, and with the kinds of constraints on writing women that nineteenth-century female authors continued to feel. Other successors, on the other hand, such as Margaret Oliphant and Anne Thackeray Ritchie, saw Austen as a role model, socially and stylistically, taking comfort from the fact that they could conceptualize her as a 'friend' to be admired and emulated. Some writers, such as Kipling, Macaulay and Mitford, engaged so intensely with Austen that they appropriate and then reflect some of her strategies in their own writing, sometimes seriously, sometimes ironically, as Austen did with the writing of her own admired predecessors.

Part of the legacy of Austen's reputation must be to make us recognize the complexities of 'thinking back through our mothers if we are women'. If we try to 'think back through' Jane Austen (or indeed, through any writer with a long reception history), we find, as Elizabeth Barrett Browning unconsciously did, that myths, semi-truths, and historically contingent or convenient attitudes towards the writer impinge on our strictly literary judgements. When we 'think back through our mothers', then, we are also thinking back through other people's perceptions, our opinions haunted by those of past readers. In Austen's case, some of the most pervasive and influential half-truths about her are also about the relationship between gender and writing. They therefore press most strongly on Austen's female readers, in particular her female successors, whose responses to Jane Austen – whether resistant, complicit, or appropriative – demonstrate particularly high levels of energy and engagement.

Those taking part in discussions about Austen are, consciously or unconsciously, rehearsing debates already implicit (or, occasionally, explicit) in the novels, and often enact in their conversations with and about Austen the concerns over reading, writing and femininity that her works address. In readers' manoeuvres with Austen's name in such debates, we can see the extraordinarily far-reaching consequence of the combination of her stylistic choices and her biographers' mythologizing abilities. Austen's very style demands 'hard reading', which promotes discussion and debate. As explored in Chapters 1 to 3, its conciseness and allusiveness enable multiple responses. Both resistant and compliant readings are called for in the novels, thematically and stylistically, and the responses to Austen considered here provide evidence of the ways in which opposition and compliance can manifest themselves. Austen's historical readers interact with her novels in ways that a hypothetical reader, however literary, does not, bringing to the texts their own emotions, priorities and prejudices. In 1870, Margaret Oliphant suggested that the 'dim lantern' of Austen-Leigh's *Memoir* shed a 'passing gleam of light' on his aunt's work. This book has turned the spotlight on Jane Austen's readers, arguing that a close look at the responses of Austen's historical readers illuminates the novels rather differently from more traditional approaches, encouraging us to recognize not only the qualities of the original works, but the sometimes unexpected energies that they generate in their readers.

NOTES

Part One: Introduction

1 Deirdre Le Faye (ed.), *Jane Austen's Letters* (Oxford: Oxford University Press, 1995), 306. Hereafter *Letters*.
2 Mary Russell Mitford, *Recollections of a Literary Life; or, Books, Places and People*, 3 vols (London: Richard Bentley, 1852), ii, 197.
3 My focus is on Austen's British readers. The term 'readers' throughout should therefore be taken to mean 'British readers' unless otherwise specified. Those interested in Austen's reception outside Britain should consult Anthony Mandal and Brian Southam (eds), *The Reception of Jane Austen in Europe* (London: Continuum, 2007) and two special issues of *Persuasions Online*: 'Global Jane Austen', 28.2 (Spring 2008) http://www.jasna.org/persuasions/on-line/vol28no2/index.html (accessed 23 November 2011); and 'New Directions in Austen Studies', 30.2 (Spring 2010) http://www.jasna.org/persuasions/on-line/vol30no2/index.html (accessed 23 November 2011).
4 Claire Harman, *Jane's Fame: How Jane Austen Conquered the World* (Edinburgh: Canongate, 2009), 7.
5 Lionel Trilling, '*Emma* and the Legend of Jane Austen', in *Beyond Culture* (Oxford: Oxford University Press, 1980; first published 1965), 28.
6 Claudia Johnson, 'The Divine Miss Jane: Jane Austen, Janeites, and the Discipline of Novel Studies', *boundary 2*, 23.3 (Autumn 1996): 146.
7 Ibid., 150.
8 Ibid., 163.
9 Claudia Johnson, 'Austen cults and cultures', in *The Cambridge Companion to Jane Austen*, ed. Edward Copeland and Juliet McMaster (Cambridge: Cambridge University Press, 1997), 224.
10 Deidre Lynch (ed.), *Janeites: Austen's Disciples and Devotees* (Princeton and Oxford: Princeton University Press, 2000), 6.
11 Bharat Tandon, *Jane Austen and the Morality of Conversation* (London: Anthem Press, 2003), 36.
12 Thanks are due to Hilary Adams, Tom and Elizabeth Heydeman, Shirley Gould-Smith, and William St Clair for permission to quote from their manuscript materials.
13 Trilling, *Beyond Culture*, 29–30.
14 Ibid., 30.
15 Ibid., 29.
16 Jacques Derrida, *On the Name*, ed. Thomas Du Toit, trans. David Wood, John P. Leavey Jr. and Ian McLeod (Stanford: Stanford University Press, 1995), 12–13.
17 Willy Maley, 'Spectres of Engels', in *Ghosts: Deconstruction, Psychoanalysis, History*, ed. Peter Buse and Andrew Stott (Houndsmills and London: Macmillan, 1999), 24.

18 Emily Auerbach's *Searching for Jane Austen* (Madison: University of Wisconsin Press, 2004) contains an excellent illustrated account of the actual images of Jane Austen that readers could have encountered at different historical periods. See Auerbach, 18–35.
19 Virginia Woolf, 'Jane Austen', in *The Common Reader: First Series* (1925), ed. Andrew McNeillie (London: Hogarth Press, 1984), 138.
20 Jacques Lacan, 'Desire and the Interpretation of Desire in *Hamlet*', *Yale French Studies*, 55/56 (1977): 39.
21 Jocelyn Harris, 'Jane Austen and the Burden of the (Male) Past: The Case Reexamined', in *Jane Austen and Discourses of Feminism*, ed. Devoney Looser (Houndsmills and London: Macmillan, 1995), 88.
22 Woolf, *Common Reader*, 136.
23 *Letters*, 203.
24 Quoted in Deirdre Le Faye, *Jane Austen: A Family Record*, 2nd edn (Cambridge: Cambridge University Press, 2004), 206. Hereafter *Family Record*. By 'working', Marianne means needlework.
25 Quoted in ibid., 202.
26 Those interested in twentieth-century and contemporary responses to Jane Austen's works, in particular the ways in which film and television imaginatively respond to her novels, should consult John Wiltshire, *Recreating Jane Austen* (Cambridge: Cambridge University Press, 2001); Suzanne R. Pucci and James Thompson (eds), *Jane Austen and Co: Remaking the Past in Contemporary Culture* (Albany: State University of New York, 2002); Andrew Wright, 'Jane Austen Adapted', *Nineteenth-Century Fiction* 30.3 (December 1975: 421–53; Sue Parrill, *Jane Austen on Film and Television: A Critical Study of the Adaptations* (Jefferson, NC: McParland, 2002); Linda Troost and Sayre Greenfield (eds), *Jane Austen in Hollywood* (Lexington: University Press of Kentucky, 1998); and Gina and Andrew Macdonald (eds), *Jane Austen on Screen* (Cambridge: Cambridge University Press, 2003).
27 Judith Fetterley, *The Resisting Reader: A Feminist Approach to American Fiction* (Bloomington and London: Indiana University Press), 1978.
28 Acknowledgements are due to Brian Southam's invaluable *Critical Heritage* volumes (London: Routledge, 1968–87), David Gilson's *A Bibliography of Jane Austen* (Winchester and New Castle, DE: Oak Knoll Press, 1997), and the British Fiction Database, 1800–1829 (http://www.british-fiction.cf.ac.uk/, accessed 23 November 2011) all of which provide a number of helpful references to Austen's readers. Thanks are due too to my colleagues and fellow researchers on the *Reading Experience Database* project, who alerted me to a number of fruitful avenues of research.
29 *Letters*, 234.
30 Ibid., 283.
31 'Plan of a Novel, according to hints from various quarters', in Jane Austen, *Later Manuscripts*, ed. Janet Todd and Linda Bree (Cambridge: Cambridge University Press, 2008), 226–9. Hereafter *Later Manuscripts*.
32 *Letters*, 234.
33 Ibid., 26.
34 [Walter Scott], review of *Emma*, *Quarterly Review*, 14 (1816): 188.
35 Jane Austen, *Sense and Sensibility*, ed. Edward Copeland (Cambridge: Cambridge University Press, 2006), 286. Hereafter *Sense and Sensibility*.
36 'Opinions of *Emma*', in *Later Manuscripts*, 237.
37 Jane Austen, *Emma*, ed. Richard Cronin and Dorothy Macmillan (Cambridge: Cambridge University Press, 2005), 362.

38 Jane Austen, *Persuasion*, ed. Janet Todd and Antje Blank (Cambridge: Cambridge University Press, 2006), 105. Hereafter *Persuasion*.
39 Lady Jane Davy to Sarah Posonby, 14 May 1813, in Eva Mary Bell, *The Hamwood papers of the Ladies of Llangollen and Caroline Hamilton* (London: Macmillan, 1930), 350–1.
40 Mary Russell Mitford to Sir William Elford, 20 December 1814, in *The Life of Mary Russell Mitford: Related in a Selection from her Letters to her Friends*, ed. A. G. L'Estrange, 3 vols (London: Richard Bentley, 1870), i, 300.
41 John Wiltshire, *Jane Austen and the Body: 'The Picture of Health'* (Cambridge: Cambridge University Press, 1992), passim.
42 *Later Manuscripts*, 189.
43 Ibid., 192.
44 Virginia Woolf, *A Room of One's Own* (1929), ed. Michèle Barrett (London: Penguin, 1993), 61.
45 Margaret Oliphant's unsigned article, 'Miss Austen and Miss Mitford' (1870), is discussed in detail in Chapter 8.
46 Mary Poovey, *The Proper Lady and the Woman Writer: Ideology as Style in the Works of Mary Wollstonecraft, Mary Shelley and Jane Austen* (Chicago and London: University of Chicago Press, 1984), 172–246.
47 D. A. Miller, *Jane Austen, or, The Secret of Style* (Princeton: Princeton University Press, 2003), passim.
48 Janet Todd (ed.), *The Cambridge Introduction to Jane Austen* (Cambridge: Cambridge University Press, 2006), 47–48, 72–74, 127–31.
49 D. W. Harding, 'Regulated Hatred: An aspect of the work of Jane Austen', *Scrutiny*, 7 (1940): 346–62.
50 Two excellent examples are Robyn Warhol's 'The Look, the Body, and the Heroine of *Persuasion*: A Feminist Narratological View of Jane Austen', and Christine Roulston's 'Discourse, Gender, and Gossip: Some Reflections on Bakhtin and *Emma*', both in Kathy Mezei (ed.), *Ambiguous Discourse: Feminist Narratology & British Women Writers* (Chapel Hill and London: University of North Carolina Press, 1996), 21–39, 40–65.
51 *Persuasion*, 261.
52 Such criticism takes its cue from Dale Spender, *Mothers of the Novel: 100 Good Women Writers Before Jane Austen* (London: Pandora, 1986), and includes Anne K. Mellor, *Romanticism and Gender* (New York and London: Routledge, 1993), Catherine Gallagher, *Nobody's Story: The Vanishing Acts of Women Writers in the Marketplace, 1670–1820* (Berkeley and Los Angeles: University of California Press, 1994), Margaret J. M. Ezell, *Writing Women's Literary History* (Baltimore and London: The Johns Hopkins University Press, 1993) and Mary Hammond, *Reading, Publishing and the Formation of Literary Taste in England, 1880–1914* (Aldershot: Ashgate, 2006).
53 Henry Austen, 'Biographical Notice of the Author', in *Persuasion*, ed. John Davie (Oxford and New York: Oxford University Press, 1990), 4. Hereafter 'Biographical Notice'.
54 Q. D. Leavis, 'A Critical Theory of Jane Austen's Writings', *Scrutiny*, 10.1 (1942): 61–87.
55 *Letters*, 182.
56 Ibid., 201.
57 Quoted in James Edward Austen-Leigh, *A Memoir of Jane Austen by her Nephew* (London: Folio Society, 1989; first published 1870), 140. Hereafter *Memoir*.
58 *Letters*, 306.
59 Ibid., 306.

60 Ibid., 252.
61 Ibid., 287.
62 I take the term 'hard reading' from Coleridge, as explained in Chapter 1, to describe a particular kind of engaged, sensitive and critical reading. It is used it as both compound noun – 'hard reading' as well as adjective – 'hard-reading'.

Chapter 1: Jane Austen's Reading in Context

1 Copies of a large number of the books mentioned in Austen's letters and novels can still be found in the Knight Collection, held at Chawton House Library, some of them bearing the signatures of Austen's close family, including Henry Austen, Edward Knight, Elizabeth Austen, and Marianne Knight. The Godmersham Library Catalogue of 1818 records the books held in the collection at that time, including details of the edition (place and date of publication), and where it was located in the room at Godmersham. Careful research in the Knight collection suggests that it still contains some of the actual copies of books read by Austen, including Mary Brunton's *Self-Control* (2nd edn, Edinburgh, 1811), Frances Burney's *The Wanderer* (London, 1814), Gay's *Fables* (London, 1746), Barretti's *Italian Library* (London, 1757), Blair's *Sermons* (London, 1801), Gisborne's *An Enquiry into the Duties of the Female Sex* (London, 1797), Hannah More's *Cœlebs in Search of a Wife* (9th edn, London, 1809), Hester Chapone's *Letters on the Improvement of the Mind* (London, 1773), Madame de Genlis's *Adèle et Théodore* (various editions), Vicesimus Knox's *Elegant Extracts* (London, 1801), Walter Scott's *Marmion* (6th edn, Edinburgh 1810), Maria Edgeworth's *Patronage* (London, 1814), Voltaire's *History of the King of Sweden* (London, 1732) and about twenty others. It seems very probable that Austen based her account of Sir Walter Elliot's additions to the Elliot family entry in the *Baronetage* on some similar entries by the name of 'Bridges' in the 1804 edition of the *Baronetage*, belonging to Godmersham Park. These entries seem to relate to the births of the children of her brother, Edward Knight.
2 Little is known about the Chawton Book Society. Its existence is extrapolated from references to the circulation of books within a small circle of acquaintances and friends in and around Chawton, and Austen's comment in a letter of 1813 to Cassandra that 'The Miss Sibleys want to establish a Book Society in their side of the Country, like ours. What can be a stronger proof of that superiority in ours over the Steventon & Manydown Society, which I have always foreseen & felt? – no emulation of this kind was ever inspired by their proceedings; no such wish of the Miss Sibleys was ever heard, in the course of the many years of that Society's existence...' Deirdre Le Faye (ed.) *Jane Austen's Letters* (Oxford: Oxford University Press, 1995), 199. Hereafter *Letters*.
3 For a full account of those books known to have belonged to Jane Austen, see David Gilson, *A Bibliography of Jane Austen* (Winchester and New Castle, DE: Oak Knoll Press, 1997), 429–46.
4 Jane Austen, *Northanger Abbey*, ed. Barbara M. Benedict and Deirdre Le Faye (Cambridge: Cambridge University Press, 2006), 110. Hereafter *Northanger Abbey*.
5 For discussion of the Goldsmith annotations, see Jane Austen, *Juvenilia*, ed. Peter Sabor (Cambridge: Cambridge University Press, 2006), 316–18. Hereafter *Juvenilia*. For a discussion of the Knox annotations, see Deirdre Le Faye, 'New Marginalia in Jane Austen's Books', *Book Collector*, 49 (2000): 222–6. The annotations to both Goldsmith and Knox are reproduced in *Juvenilia*, 318–55.

6 Isobel Grundy, 'Jane Austen and literary traditions', in *The Cambridge Companion to Jane Austen*, ed. Edward Copeland and Juliet McMaster (Cambridge: Cambridge University Press, 1997), 190.
7 See Deirdre Le Faye, *Jane Austen: A Family Record*, 2nd edn (Cambridge: Cambridge University Press, 2004), 57. Hereafter *Family Record*.
8 Paula Byrne, *Jane Austen and the Theatre* (Hambledon and London: Continuum, 2002; repr. 2007), 28.
9 Caroline Austen, *My Aunt Jane Austen: A Memoir* (London: Spottiswood, Ballantyne and Co., 1952), 10.
10 Patricia Howell Michaelson, 'Reading *Pride and Prejudice*', *Eighteenth-Century Fiction*, 3.1 (October 1990): 65.
11 *Letters*, 201.
12 'We admire your Charades excessively, but as yet have guessed only the 1st. The others seem very difficult. There is so much beauty in the Versification however, that the finding them out is but a secondary pleasure' (*Letters*, 202).
13 'Uncle Henry writes very superior sermons. – You [James Edward] and I must try to get hold of one or two, & put them into our Novels; - it would be a fine help to a volume; & we could make our Heroine read it aloud of a Sunday Evening, just as well as Isabella Wardour in the Antiquary, is made to read the History of the Hartz Demon in the ruins of St Ruth – tho' I believe [*sic*], on reflection, Lovell is the Reader' (*Letters*, 232).
14 Although there is still some uncertainty about the authorship of the 'Sophia Sentiment' letter, Austen scholars generally concur that it is by Jane Austen. See *Juvenilia*, Appendix D, 356–61.
15 The *Grandison* manuscript is held at Chawton House Library. Attribution of authorship is uncertain. It is possible, as Brian Southam suggested in his transcription of the manuscript (Oxford: Clarendon, 1980), that Austen wrote the play herself (scholars agree without exception that it is her handwriting). Austen family tradition, however, claimed that the playlet was dictated to Austen by her niece, Anna Austen. Vigorous critical debate still surrounds the manuscript, but it seems most probable that it was a collaboration between the young Anna Austen and her aunt, and that Jane and Anna worked together on the manuscript.
16 *Letters*, 44.
17 *Juvenilia*, 142.
18 Ibid.
19 Ibid., 176.
20 Ibid., 96.
21 See *Juvenilia*, Introduction, xxxvi for further examples.
22 *Family Record*, 96.
23 *Letters*, 121.
24 Ibid., 43.
25 Ibid., 47.
26 Ibid., 199. The book to which Austen refers is James and Horace Smith's *Rejected Addresses: Or the new Theatrum Poetarum* (1812).
27 This appeared in the first edition of *Persuasion* and *Northanger Abbey*, published together posthumously in four volumes by John Murray in December 1817 (though 1818 appears on the title pages).
28 Henry does not specify which of Gilpin's works on the picturesque Austen knew, but if she was 'enamoured', it seems probable that she had read at least the major works; that

is, the *Essay on Prints* (1768), the *Observations on the River Wye* (1782) and the *Three Essays on the Picturesque* (1792), and may well also have known some of Gilpin's other works, such as the *Observations* on the Lake District, the Highlands of Scotland and Wales.

29 Henry Austen, 'Biographical Notice of the Author', in *Persuasion*, ed. John Davie (Oxford and New York: Oxford University Press, 1990), 5. What Henry means by the 'best essays and novels in the English language' is open to interpretation, but other evidence suggests that these categories would certainly have included the *Rambler*, *Idler* and *Spectator* essays; the works of Dr Johnson, and the novels of Goldsmith, Sterne, Richardson, Burney, Scott and Edgeworth. In 1818, the Godmersham Library contained a large number of volumes of essays, including the *Rambler*, the *Idler*, the *Spectator* and the *Tatler* as well as copies of those novels named above.

30 Like most gentlemen's libraries of the period, the Godmersham Library also had a very large number of histories, including Smollett's *History of England* (London, 1757), Catherine Macaulay's *History of England* (London, 1763), Hume's *History of England* (London, 1762), Bossuet's *Universal History* (London, 1749), Goldsmith's *History of England* (London, 1762), Hooke's *Roman History* (London, 1738), Orme's *History of Indostan* (London, 1763), Gifford's *History of Spain* (London, 1793), a number of local and regional histories, and many others.

31 James Edward Austen-Leigh, *A Memoir of Jane Austen by her Nephew* (London: Folio Society, 1989; first published 1870), 79.

32 Ibid., 80.

33 See page 31 of this volume for discussion of representative conduct-book reading lists.

34 Jane Austen, *Later Manuscripts*, ed. Janet Todd and Linda Bree (Cambridge: Cambridge University Press, 2008), 183.

35 Jane Austen, *Mansfield Park*, ed. John Wiltshire (Cambridge: Cambridge University Press, 2005), 25. Hereafter *Mansfield Park*.

36 Quoted in *Family Record*, 239.

37 Margaret Anne Doody, 'Jane Austen's Reading', in *The Jane Austen Handbook*, ed. J. David Grey, Walton Litz and B.C. Southam (London: Athlone, 1986), 356.

38 For a fuller account of the texts Austen is known to have read, see Gillian Dow and Katie Halsey, *Jane Austen's Reading: The Chawton Years* (University of Southampton and Chawton House Library, 2009). I am grateful for permission to reproduce the argument rehearsed in that pamphlet here. See also Jane Stabler, 'Literary Influences' in *Jane Austen in Context*, ed. Janet Todd (Cambridge: Cambridge University Press, 2005), 41–50; Jacqueline Pearson, *Women's Reading in Britain, 1750–1835* (Cambridge: Cambridge University Press, 1999), 122–52, and Grundy, 189–210.

39 See, for example, Jocelyn Harris, *Jane Austen's Art of Memory* (Cambridge: Cambridge University Press, 1989); Marilyn Butler, *Jane Austen and the War of Ideas* (Oxford: Clarendon Press, 1975); Kenneth Moler, *Jane Austen's Art of Allusion* (Lincoln, NE: University of Nebraska Press); Frank W. Bradbrook, *Jane Austen and her Predecessors* (Cambridge: Cambridge University Press, 1966); Henrietta Ten Harmsel, *Jane Austen: A Study in Fictional Conventions* (The Hague: Mouton, 1964); Peter L. DeRose, *Jane Austen and Samuel Johnson* (Washington: University of Washington Press, 1980); Warren Roberts, *Jane Austen and the French Revolution* (London: Athlone Press, 1995; first published 1979) and Frank Bradbrook, 'Jane Austen and Choderlos de Laclos', *Notes and Queries*, 199 (1954): 75.

40 Grundy, 192–202.

41 Doody, 355.
42 Harris, *Jane Austen's Art of Memory*, x.
43 Olivia Murphy, 'From Pammydiddle to *Persuasion*: Jane Austen Rewriting Eighteenth-Century Literature', *Eighteenth-Century Life*, 32.2 (Spring 2008): 38.
44 Jocelyn Harris, *A Revolution almost beyond Expression: Jane Austen's* Persuasion (Newark, DE: University of Delaware Press, 2007), 18.
45 Mary Waldron, *Jane Austen and the Fiction of her Time* (Cambridge: Cambridge University Press, 1999), 3.
46 See Harold Bloom, *The Anxiety of Influence: A Theory of Poetry* (New York: Oxford University Press, 1973), passim.
47 Waldron, 17.
48 Sandra Gilbert and Susan Gubar, *The Madwoman in the Attic: The Woman Writer and the Nineteenth-Century Literary Imagination* (New Haven, CT and London: Yale University Press, 1979), 107–83.
49 Harris, *Jane Austen's Art of Memory*, x.
50 Grundy, 190.
51 For previous discussions of Austen's reading of conduct literature, see Grundy, who argues that Austen gave 'the pedagogical tradition (which dealt largely in stereotypes) [...] short shrift' (202), and Ilona Dobosiewicz, *Female Relationships in Jane Austen's Novels: A Critique of the Female Ideal Propagated in 18th Century Conduct Literature* (Opole: Uniwersytet Opolski, 1997), which argues that Austen's work constitutes a sustained attack on the ideology perpetuated in conduct books (passim). See also Pearson, 122–52. In fact, Austen read conduct literature with care and attention, and did not dismiss it out of hand. She writes to Cassandra, for example, that 'I am glad you recommended "Gisborne", for having begun, I am pleased with it, and I had quite determined not to read it' (*Letters*, 112). 'Gisborne' is Thomas Gisborne (1758–1846), whose *An Enquiry into the Duties of the Female Sex* (1797) was one of the standard conduct books of the 1790s, and popular well into the nineteenth century. Austen also gave a copy of Ann Murry's *Mentoria, or the Young Ladies' Instructor* (1778) to her niece, Anna Austen. The motive behind Austen's gift is uncertain, but it certainly suggests that she was not, as Grundy, Pearson and Dobosiewicz suggest, single-mindedly opposed to the genre, but instead considered individual books on their different merits.
52 Erasmus Darwin, *A Plan for the Conduct of Female Education in Boarding Schools* (Derby: J. Johnson, 1797), 103.
53 Hannah More, *Strictures on the Modern System of Female Education* (1799), 2 vols (New York and London: Garland Publishing, 1974), i, 165–8.
54 Mary Wollstonecraft, *Thoughts on the Education of Daughters* (1787) (Oxford and New York: Woodstock Books, 1994), 58.
55 R. L. Edgeworth and Maria Edgeworth, *Practical Education* (1798), 3 vols, ed. Jonathan Wordsworth (New York: Woodstock Books, 1996), iii, 6.
56 John Gregory, *A Father's Legacy to his Daughters* (1774) (London: W. Lane, 1795), 21; John Bennett, *Letters to a young lady on a variety of useful and interesting subjects*, 2 vols (Warrington: W. Eyres, 1789), i, 6.
57 Adam and Eve are:
    Not equal, as their sex not equal seemed;
    For contemplation he and valour formed
    For softness she and sweet attractive grace,
    He for God only, she for God in him.

John Milton, *Paradise Lost* (1667), ed. Alastair Fowler (London and New York: Longman, 1968), iv, 296–9.
58 Pearson, 16.
59 Hester Chapone, *Letters on the Improvement of the Mind, Addressed to a Young Lady* (1773), 2 vols (London: J. Walter, 1774), ii, 115.
60 Edgeworth and Edgeworth, iii, 52.
61 Such disapproval already had a long tradition, exemplified most famously in Cervantes' *Don Quixote* (1605–15), and re-gendered to disapprove of feminine addiction to romances in the eighteenth and early nineteenth centuries in such works as Charlotte Lennox's *Female Quixote* (1752) and E. S. Barrett's *The Heroine* (1813). Austen's *Northanger Abbey* famously substitutes the Gothic novel for the chivalric romance.
62 Chapone, ii, 144.
63 Bennett, *Letters to a Young Lady*, ii, 71.
64 The Marquis Caraccioli, *Advice From a Lady of Quality to her Children; in the last stage of a lingering illness*, trans. S. Glasse, 4th edn (Gloucester: R. Raikes, 1786), 163.
65 Edgeworth and Edgeworth, ii, 51–2.
66 More, *Strictures*, i, 168, 166 and 160.
67 Bennett, *Strictures on Female Education; chiefly as it relates to the culture of the heart, in four essays* (London: T. Cadell, 1788), 78–9.
68 Jane West, *Letters to a Young Lady* (1806) 3 vols, in *Female Education in the Age of Enlightenment*, 6 vols (London: Pickering and Chatto, 1996), v, 452–3.
69 Ibid., 453–4.
70 More, *Strictures*, i, 195.
71 Thomas Gisborne, *An Enquiry into the Duties of the Female Sex* (London: T. Cadell, 1798), 225.
72 Chapone, ii, 144.
73 More, *Strictures*, i, 187–8.
74 Mary Wollstonecraft, *A Vindication of the Rights of Woman* (1792) (London: Everyman, 1992), 43 and 55.
75 S. T. Coleridge, 'On the Constitution of the Church and State', in *The Collected Works of Samuel Taylor Coleridge*, ed. John Colmer, 16 vols (London: Routledge and Kegan Paul, 1976), x, 134.
76 I am using the term here as verb, rather than noun, although the writers of conduct books also recommend the 'dry tough reading' that we might now designate 'hard reading'.
77 More, *Strictures*, i, 165.
78 Gisborne, 226.
79 Bennett, *Letters to a Young Lady*, i, 44.
80 Gisborne, 228–9.
81 More, *Strictures*, i, 164.
82 Nancy Armstrong, *Desire and Domestic Fiction: A Political History of the Novel* (Oxford and New York: Oxford University Press, 1987), 75.
83 Philip Skelton to Samuel Richardson, 10 June 1749, quoted in Tom Keymer, *Richardson's Clarissa and the Eighteenth-Century Reader* (Cambridge: Cambridge University Press, 1992), xviii.
84 Armstrong, *Desire and Domestic Fiction*, 63.
85 For an excellent account of how Austen's juvenile works respond to conservative ideas about gender roles, see John C. Leffel, '"Everything is Going to Sixes and Sevens": Governing the Female Body (Politic) in Jane Austen's Catharine, Or the Bower (1792)', *Studies in the Novel*, 43.2 (Summer 2011): 131–51.
86 Dobosiewicz, passim.

Chapter 2: Jane Austen's Negotiations with Reading

1. Jane Austen, *Juvenilia*, ed. Peter Sabor (Cambridge: Cambridge University Press, 2006), 248. Hereafter *Juvenilia*.
2. Jane Austen, *Emma*, ed. Richard Cronin and Dorothy Macmillan (Cambridge: Cambridge University Press, 2005), 73.
3. Hannah More, *Strictures on the Modern System of Female Education* (1799), 2 vols (New York and London: Garland Publishing, 1974), i, 60.
4. Jane Austen, *Pride and Prejudice*, ed. Pat Rogers (Cambridge: Cambridge University Press, 2006), 43. Hereafter *Pride and Prejudice*.
5. Thomas Gisborne, *An Enquiry into the Duties of the Female Sex* (London: T. Cadell, 1798), 224.
6. Jane Austen, *Persuasion*, ed. Janet Todd and Antje Blank (Cambridge: Cambridge University Press, 2006), 108–9. Hereafter *Persuasion*.
7. *Pride and Prejudice*, 62.
8. Deirdre Le Faye (ed.) *Jane Austen's Letters* (Oxford: Oxford University Press, 1995), 312. Hereafter *Letters*.
9. Walter Scott, *Marmion* (1808) (London: Alexander Murray, [1869]), vi, 38.
10. *Letters*, 202.
11. Ibid., 131.
12. Ibid., 202.
13. It is worth remembering that Austen wrote verse as well as prose.
14. *Letters*, 59.
15. Margaret Anne Doody, 'Jane Austen's Reading', in *The Jane Austen Handbook*, ed. J. David Grey, Walton Litz and B.C. Southam (London: Athlone, 1986), 351.
16. See Jane Austen, *The History of England, by a Partial, Prejudiced & Ignorant Historian*, ed. Deirdre Le Faye (London: The British Library, 1993). This edition contains Cassandra Austen's delightful illustrations.
17. *Letters*, 59.
18. *Pride and Prejudice*, 76–7.
19. Ibid., 77.
20. See Paul Kaufman, 'The Community Library: A Chapter in English Social History', *Transactions of the American Philosophical Society*, n.s. 57 (1967): 3–67 and 'In Defence of Fair Readers', *Review of English Literature*, 8 (1967): 68–76; Jan Fergus, 'Eighteenth-Century Readers in Provincial England: The Customers of Samuel Clay's Circulating Library and Bookshop in Warwick, 1770–72', *Papers of the Bibliographical Society of America*, 78 (1984): 155–213, and Edward Jacobs, 'Anonymous Signatures: Circulating Libraries, Conventionality, and the Production of Gothic Romances', *ELH*, 62.3 (1995): 603–29 for further discussion of circulating libraries in Austen's period.
21. *Letters*, 26.
22. *Juvenilia*, 249.
23. Jane Austen, *Northanger Abbey*, ed. Barbara M. Benedict and Deirdre Le Faye (Cambridge: Cambridge University Press, 2006), 108. Hereafter *Northanger Abbey*.
24. Ibid., 30.
25. James Fordyce, *Sermons for Young Women* (1765), 2 vols (London: A. Millar & T. Cadell, 1766), i, 279–80.
26. *Northanger Abbey*, 31.

27 Horace, *Ars Poetica*, 343: 'Ome tulit punctum qui miscuit utile dulci, / lectorem delectando pariterque monendo', translated as 'The man who combines pleasure with usefulness wins every suffrage, delighting the reader and also giving him advice' in Horace, *The Art of Poetry*, trans D. A. Russell, in *Classical Literary Criticism*, ed. D. A. Russell and Michael Winterbottom (Oxford and New York: Oxford University Press, 1972; repr. 1998), 107.
28 *Northanger Abbey*, 7.
29 Ibid., 109.
30 Ibid., 241.
31 Ibid., 205.
32 Ibid., 206.
33 Ibid., 232–3.
34 Jane Austen, *Later Manuscripts*, ed. Janet Todd and Linda Bree (Cambridge: Cambridge University Press, 2008), 169. Hereafter *Later Manuscripts*.
35 Ibid., 183.
36 Ibid., 167.
37 Ibid., 169.
38 Ibid., 183.
39 R. L. Edgeworth and Maria Edgeworth, *Practical Education* (1798), 3 vols, ed. Jonathan Wordsworth (New York: Woodstock Books, 1996), ii., 51.
40 *Later Manuscripts*, 184.
41 Ibid., 183.
42 More, *Strictures*, i., 161.
43 *Later Manuscripts*, 181–2.
44 Ibid., 169, 176, 177 and 183.
45 *Persuasion*, 108.
46 Edward Copeland notes that Austen 'originally wrote "Seccar's explanation of the Catechism", alluding to *Lectures on the Catechism of the Church of England* (1769) by Archbishop Thomas Secker.' Copeland suggests that, when Jane Austen revised the fragment in the early 1800s, the use of Secker's work would have seemed dated. Copeland points out that Austen's choice of More's *Cœlebs* to replace Secker's *Catechism* represents her own dislike of that work, as demonstrated by extracts in the letters. *Juvenilia*, 501n114.
47 More, *Strictures*, i, 6–10.
48 *Juvenilia*, 287.
49 Ibid., 287.
50 Ibid., 287–8.
51 Gisborne, 224.
52 Jane Austen, *Mansfield Park*, ed. John Wiltshire (Cambridge: Cambridge University Press, 2005), 25. Hereafter *Mansfield Park*.
53 *Pride and Prejudice*, 67.
54 Villars tells Evelina, 'nothing is so delicate as the reputation of a woman: it is, at once, the most beautiful and most brittle of all human things'. Frances Burney, *Evelina; or, a Young Lady's Entrance into the World* (1798), ed. Susan Kubica Howard (Ontario: Broadview Press, 2000), 279.
55 *Pride and Prejudice*, 319.
56 Nancy Armstrong, *Desire and Domestic Fiction: A Political History of the Novel* (Oxford and New York: Oxford University Press, 1987), 60.
57 *Northanger Abbey*, 252–3.

58 *Persuasion*, 270.
59 *Northanger Abbey*, 250.
60 Ibid., 249.
61 Gisborne, 224.
62 Hester Chapone, *Letters on the Improvement of the Mind, Addressed to a Young Lady* (1773), 2 vols (London: J. Walter, 1774), i, 9.
63 *Northanger Abbey*, 71.
64 Ibid., 261.
65 *Mansfield Park*, 74.
66 Gisborne, 39.
67 *Mansfield Park*, 3.
68 Ibid., 53.
69 Ibid., 44.
70 Ibid., 45.
71 Ibid., 14.
72 Ibid., 326, 320.
73 Ibid., 320
74 Claudia L. Johnson, *Jane Austen: Women, Politics and the Novel* (Chicago: University of Chicago Press, 1988), 94–120.
75 *Mansfield Park*, 360.
76 Ibid., 363.
77 Ibid., 370.
78 Ibid., 362, 366, 367 and 369.
79 Ibid., 365.
80 Ibid., 364–9.
81 Ibid., 367–8.
82 Ibid., 367.
83 Ibid., 367.
84 Ibid., 369.
85 Ibid., 368–9.
86 Ibid., 366–7.
87 Ibid., 368.
88 Ibid., 380.
89 Ibid., 381.
90 Ibid., 381.
91 Ibid., 425.
92 Ibid., 384.
93 Ibid., 395.
94 Ibid., 402; original emphasis.
95 Ibid., 404.
96 Ibid., 410.
97 Ibid., 540.
98 Ibid., 545–6.
99 Ibid., 533.
100 Henry James, *Notes on Novelists* (1914); repr. in Brian Southam, *Jane Austen: The Critical Heritage*, 2 vols (London: Routledge, 1968–87), ii, 231.
101 *Mansfield Park*, 544.
102 'Opinions of *Mansfield Park*', in *Later Manuscripts*, 230–4.

103 E. M. Forster to Donald Windham, 30 July 1959, in *E. M. Forster's Letters to Donald Windham* (Verona: Sandy Campbell, 1975), 25.
104 See, for example, Brian Wilkie, 'Structural Layering in Jane Austen's Problem Novels', in *Nineteenth-Century Literature*, 46, (1991–92): 517–44 (esp. 530).

Chapter 3: Jane Austen's Games of Ingenuity

1 Mary Poovey, *The Proper Lady and the Woman Writer: Ideology as Style in the Works of Mary Wollstonecraft, Mary Shelley and Jane Austen* (Chicago and London: University of Chicago Press, 1984), 182.
2 Ibid., 182.
3 Hannah More, *Strictures on the Modern System of Female Education* (1799), 2 vols (New York and London: Garland Publishing, 1974), i, 170–2.
4 Unsigned notice of *Emma*, *Gentleman's Magazine*, 86 (1816): 248.
5 [Richard Whately], review of *Northanger Abbey* and *Persuasion*, *Quarterly Review*, 34 (1821): 352.
6 Frances Burney, *Evelina; or, a Young Lady's Entrance into the World* (1798), ed. Susan Kubica Howard (Ontario: Broadview Press, 2000), 95.
7 Maria Edgeworth, 'Advertisement', to *Belinda* (1801), ed. Kathryn J. Kirkpatrick (Oxford: Oxford University Press, 1994), 4.
8 Jane Austen, *Northanger Abbey*, ed. Barbara M. Benedict and Deirdre Le Faye (Cambridge: Cambridge University Press, 2006), 30. Hereafter *Northanger Abbey*.
9 Ibid., 30.
10 Poovey, 242.
11 Ibid., 183.
12 Mary Lascelles, *Jane Austen and her Art* (Oxford: Oxford University Press, 1939; repr. 1974), 43.
13 M .M. Bakhtin, *Problems of Doestoevsky's Poetics* (1963), trans. C. Emerson (Minneapolis: University of Minnesota Press, 1984), 181–269.
14 The first type, 'unidirectional double-voiced discourse', includes 'stylization, narrator's narration and unobjectified discourse of a character who carries out (in part) the author's intentions', and 'tends towards a fusion of voices'– i.e. it is discourse in which both consciousnesses in the utterances have the same goal. The second type includes parody, parodic narration, 'discourse of a character who is parodically represented' and 'any transmission of someone else's words with a shift in accent'. The third type is 'the active type', also described as 'reflected discourse of another', which consists of 'hidden internal polemic, polemically coloured autobiography and confession, any discourse with a sideways glance at someone else's work, a rejoinder of dialogue and hidden dialogue', in which 'diverse forms of interrelationship with another's discourse are possible [...] as well as various degrees of deforming influence exerted by one discourse on the other' (Bakhtin, 199).
15 Ibid., 197.
16 Ibid., 197.
17 Ibid., 227.
18 Ibid., 199.
19 Jane Austen, *Mansfield Park*, ed. John Wiltshire (Cambridge: Cambridge University Press, 2005), 533, 544. Hereafter *Mansfield Park*.
20 *Northanger Abbey*, 30, 253.

21 Jane Austen, *Persuasion*, ed. Janet Todd and Antje Blank (Cambridge: Cambridge University Press, 2006), 270. Hereafter *Persuasion*.
22 Jane Austen, *Pride and Prejudice*, ed. Pat Rogers (Cambridge: Cambridge University Press, 2006), 3. Hereafter *Pride and Prejudice*.
23 Jane Austen, *Emma*, ed. Richard Cronin and Dorothy Macmillan (Cambridge: Cambridge University Press, 2005), 177. Hereafter *Emma*.
24 Jane Austen, *Later Manuscripts*, ed. Janet Todd and Linda Bree (Cambridge: Cambridge University Press, 2008), 77. Hereafter *Later Manuscripts*.
25 Jane Austen, *Sense and Sensibility*, ed. Edward Copeland (Cambridge: Cambridge University Press, 2006), 429.
26 *Northanger Abbey*, 5.
27 *Later Manuscripts*, 172–3.
28 Ibid., 146.
29 Ibid., 148–9.
30 The shifting meaning of the word 'enthusiast' may obscure Austen's point; in 1817 it still carried overtones of excessive or misplaced visionary or quasi-religious fervour (*OED* n. 2b & 3). Austen is thus suggesting that Sanditon is Mr Parker's idol, rather than being simply a financial speculation.
31 *Emma*, 197.
32 *Persuasion*, 148–9.
33 Ibid., 150.
34 *Mansfield Park*, 151.
35 For a full and excellent discussion of Austen's punctuation, including editorial interventions, see Kathryn Sutherland's *Jane Austen's Textual Lives* (Oxford: Oxford University Press, 2005).
36 An earlier version of this section appeared as 'The Blush of Modesty or the Blush of Shame? Reading Jane Austen's Blushes', *Forum for Modern Languages Studies*, 42 (2006): 226–38.
37 Henry Austen, 'Biographical Notice of the Author', in *Persuasion*, ed. John Davie (Oxford and New York: Oxford University Press, 1990), 3. Hereafter 'Biographical Notice'.
38 John Donne, *The Second Anniversarie of the Progres of the Soule* (London: A. Mathewes for Tho. Dewes, 1621), ll. 242–5.
39 Ruth Bernard Yeazell, *Fictions of Modesty: Women and Courtship in the English Novel* (Chicago and London: University of Chicago Press, 1991), 67.
40 Wollstonecraft, 'Preface', *The Female Reader* (1789), ed. Moira Ferguson (Delmar, NY: Scholars' Facsimiles & Reprints, 1979), xiii–xiv.
41 Yeazell, 67.
42 John Cleland, *Fanny Hill; or, Memoirs of a Woman of Pleasure* (1748–49), ed. Peter Wagner (Harmondsworth: Penguin, 1985), 27.
43 John Gregory, *A Father's Legacy to his Daughters* (1774) (London: W. Lane, 1795), 38.
44 Anon., 'On Shamefacedness', *New Lady's Magazine*, 1 (1786): 27.
45 Burney, *Evelina*, 180.
46 Laurence Sterne, *The Life and Opinions of Tristram Shandy, Gentleman* (1759–66), ed. Tim Parnell (London: Everyman, 2000), 524.
47 Jonathan Swift, *Cadenus and Vanessa: A Poem* (London: J. Roberts, 1726).
48 Samuel Richardson, *Pamela; or, Virtue Rewarded* (1740), ed. Margaret A. Doody (London: Penguin, 1985), 332.
49 Ibid., 84.

50 Ibid., 85.
51 *Persuasion*, 234.
52 Burney, *Evelina*, 181.
53 *Northanger Abbey*, 148.
54 *Mansfield Park*, 365.
55 Burney, *Evelina*, 460.
56 Mary Hays, *The Memoirs of Emma Courtney* (1796), ed. Eleanor Ty (Oxford: Oxford University Press, 2000), 118.
57 *Emma*, 63.
58 Jane Austen, *Juvenilia*, ed. Peter Sabor (Cambridge: Cambridge University Press, 2006), 274.
59 Ibid., 291.
60 *Mansfield Park*, 268.
61 Ibid., 30, 102.
62 Ibid., 172, 263.
63 Ibid., 290.
64 *Persuasion*, 27.
65 Ibid., 28.
66 *Emma*, 441.
67 Ibid., 237.
68 Ibid., 262.
69 Ibid., 262.
70 Ibid., 240.
71 Ibid., 322.
72 Ibid., 377.
73 Ibid., 378.
74 Ibid., 372, 380.
75 Ibid., 457.
76 Ibid., 148.
77 Ibid., 185.
78 Ibid., 308.
79 Ibid., 355.
80 Ibid., 367, 407.
81 Ibid., 419.
82 Ibid., 435, 520.
83 Ibid., 463.
84 Ibid., 486.
85 *Pride and Prejudice*, 81.
86 Mary Ann O' Farrell, *Telling Complexions: The Nineteenth-Century English Novel and the Blush* (Durham, NC and London: Duke University Press, 1997), 18.
87 *Emma*, 310.
88 *Persuasion*, 195.
89 Katherine Mansfield, *Novels and Novelists* (London: Constable & Co, 1930), 304.
90 More, *Strictures*, ii, 2.
91 Ibid., ii, 65.
92 More, *Cœlebs in Search of a Wife* (1808), ed. Mary Waldron (Bristol: Thoemmes Press, 1995), 218.
93 Ibid., 218.

94 Deirdre Le Faye (ed.) *Jane Austen's Letters* (Oxford: Oxford University Press, 1995), 306. Hereafter *Letters*.
95 Henry Fielding, *The History of Tom Jones, a Foundling* (1749) (Ware: Wordsworth Classics, 1992), 171.
96 For the term 'spectral texts', I am indebted to Kate Griffiths in 'Scribbling Ghosts: The Spectral Texts and Textual Spectres of Émile Zola', in *Possessions: Essays in French Literature, Cinema and Theory*, ed. Julia Horn and Lynsey Russell-Watts (Oxford: Peter Lang, 2003), 51–65.
97 An earlier version of this section first appeared as 'Spectral Texts in *Mansfield Park*' in Jennie Batchelor and Cora Kaplan (eds), *British Women's Writing in the Long Eighteenth Century: Authorship, Politics and History* (Basingstoke: Palgrave Macmillan, 2005), 48–61. Reproduced with permission of Palgrave Macmillan.
98 Notable exceptions include Jonathan Bate's 'Culture and Environment: from Austen to Hardy', *New Literary History*, 30 (1999): 541–60; Jocelyn Harris's analysis of the links between *Sir Charles Grandison* and *Mansfield Park* in *Jane Austen's Art of Memory* Cambridge: Cambridge University Press, 1989; repr. 2003); and Bharat Tandon's discussion of Austen's 'conversations' with literary figures in *Jane Austen and the Morality of Conversation* London: Anthem Press, 2003).
99 Close considerations of the role of *Lovers' Vows* in *Mansfield Park* can be found in Lionel Trilling's essay on *Mansfield Park* in *The Opposing Self* (London: Secker & Warburg, 1955), 206–30; Avrom Fleishman's *A Reading of* Mansfield Park (Minneapolis: University of Minnesota Press, 1967); A. Walton Litz's *Jane Austen: A Study of her Artistic Development* (New York: Oxford University Press, 1967); Douglas Bush's *Jane Austen* (London: Macmillan, 1975) and Marilyn Butler's *Jane Austen and the War of Ideas* (Oxford: Clarendon Press, 1975). See also Poovey, *The Proper Lady and the Woman Writer*, and Claudia L. Johnson, *Women, Politics and the Novel* (Chicago: University of Chicago Press, 1988), passim.
100 Such diverse texts as Home's *Douglas* (1757), Johnson's *Rasselas* (1759) and Macartney's *Journal of the Embassy to China* (1807) are also significant, although they lie outside the scope of this discussion.
101 After its first performance in 1756, *Douglas* enjoyed a reputation as a play to rival, or even outclass, any of Shakespeare's. David Hume wrote that it was 'one of the most interesting and pathetic pieces, that was ever exhibited on any theatre', commenting on its 'fire and spirit', 'tenderness and simplicity', and the 'unparalleled command which [the author] appeared to have over every affection of the human breast'. These, he said, were 'incontestible proofs that you possess the true theatric genius of Shakespeare and Otway, refined from the unhappy barbarism of the one and licentiousness of the other'. Hume, *Four Dissertations* (London: A. Millar, 1757), 'Dedication', iv–vi.
102 The original: 'Blest leaf! Whose aromatic gales dispense / To Templars modesty, to Parsons sense', becomes 'Blest Knight! whose dictatorial looks dispense / To Children affluence, to Rushworth sense' (*Mansfield Park*, 189).
103 'Biographical Notice', 5.
104 *Letters of Mary Russell Mitford, second series*, ed. Henry Chorley, 2 vols (London: Richard Bentley & Son, 1872), i, 73. Hereafter Chorley.
105 Anon., review of *Emma*, *The Champion*, 31 March 1816, 103.
106 James Edward Austen-Leigh, *A Memoir of Jane Austen by her Nephew* (London: Folio Society, 1989; first published 1870), 79.

107 *Letters*, 218, 220.
108 Ibid., 243.
109 Isobel Grundy, 'Jane Austen and literary traditions', in *The Cambridge Companion to Jane Austen*, ed. Edward Copeland and Juliet McMaster (Cambridge: Cambridge University Press, 1997), 191.
110 George Crabbe, Preface to *Tales* (1812) (London: J. Hatchard, 1813). Austen mentions reading Crabbe's prefaces in a letter of 21 October 1813 (*Letters*, 243).
111 *Mansfield Park*, 161.
112 The commentary on Margaret Oliphant's article 'Miss Austen and Miss Mitford' in Chapter 8 of this book discusses the issue of 'feminine cynicism' in greater detail.
113 *Mansfield Park*, 326.
114 Crabbe, 'The Confidant' (Tale XVI) in *Tales*, 285–6.
115 Ibid., 286.
116 *Mansfield Park*, 79.
117 William Cowper, *The Task* (1785), in *The Task and Selected Other Poems*, ed. James Sambrook (London and New York: Longman, 1994), i, 749. Hereafter *Task*.
118 *Task*, i, 755–9.
119 *Mansfield Park*, 80, 244.
120 *Task*, i, 685–6.
121 *Mansfield Park*, 312.
122 *Task*, i, 389–91.
123 *Task*, i, 102; *Mansfield Park*, 84.
124 *Task*, i, 475–7.
125 *Mansfield Park*, 190.
126 *Task*, iii, 764–5.
127 Ibid., iii, 755–6. See Alistair M. Duckworth, *The Improvement of the Estate: A Study of Jane Austen's Novels* (Baltimore and London: The Johns Hopkins University Press, 1971), passim, for a discussion of the social, cultural and political resonances of the discourse of improvement in Jane Austen's novels.
128 *Mansfield Park*, 538.
129 *Task*, iii, 75–9.
130 See, for example, *Mansfield Park*, 10, 208, 258.
131 Ibid., 107–9.
132 *Task*, ii, 400–1, and ii, 423–5.
133 *Mansfield Park*, 109, 393–5.
134 *Task*, iii, 108.
135 *Mansfield Park*, 66. The reference is to *Task*, i, 338–9.
136 Ibid., 244.
137 Ibid., 132.
138 *The Correspondence of William Cowper*, ed. Thomas Wright, 4 vols (London: Hodder & Stoughton, 1904), ii, 252.
139 *Task*, iv, 243–53. Austen knew this book of *The Task* particularly well; she quotes a later phrase from the same section ('Myself creating what I saw') in *Emma* (340).
140 *Task*, iv, 260–1.
141 *Mansfield Park*, 390–1.
142 'Domestic happiness, thou only bliss/ Of Paradise that has survived the fall!' *Task*, iii, 41–2.

143 A. Walton Litz proposes that Austen's use of *Lovers' Vows* is primarily political – by rejecting the play, she rejects the author's anti-authoritarian and revolutionary views (A. Walton Litz, *Jane Austen: A Study of her Artistic Development* (New York: Oxford University Press, 1967), passim.). Critics who wish to claim more radical sympathies for Austen suggest that the use of *Lovers' Vows* may be a coded way to express these sympathies, pointing to Fanny's similarities to the sincere young heroine of the play, Amelia. Following Lionel Trilling, some suggest that Austen's choice of play is politically unimportant: what is signified in the rehearsal scenes is a Platonic resistance to impersonation or play-acting of any sort. See, for example, Lionel Trilling, 'Mansfield Park' in *The Opposing Self* (London: Secker and Warburg, 1955), 206–30. However, as Margaret Kirkham, Paula Byrne and Penny Gay have recently made clear in their works on Austen and the theatre, Austen was not opposed to the theatre in principle; indeed, she was an avid theatre-goer and had seen *Lovers' Vows* more than once. Marilyn Butler reminds us that the real problem with the theatricals is that the actors are not acting at all: *Lovers' Vows* is pernicious in *Mansfield Park* because it allows the young Bertrams and Crawfords the freedom to express their real emotions under cover of the rehearsals (Marilyn Butler, *Jane Austen and the War of Ideas* (Oxford: Clarendon Press, 1975; repr. 1987), 232–6).

144 E. M. Butler, '*Mansfield Park* and Kotzebue's *Lovers' Vows*', *MLR*, 28 (1933): 326–37, passim.

145 Dvora Zelicovici, 'The Inefficacy of *Lovers' Vows*', in *ELH*, 50 (1983): 532.

146 Brian Wilkie, 'Structural Layering in Jane Austen's Problem Novels', in *Nineteenth-Century Literature*, 46, (1991–92): 530.

147 *Persuasion*, 255.

148 *Northanger Abbey*, 110.

149 *Persuasion*, 255.

Part Two: Introduction

1 William Galperin, 'The Picturesque, the Real, and the Consumption of Jane Austen', *Wordsworth Circle*, 28.1 (Winter 1997): 23.

2 Mary Poovey, *The Proper Lady and the Woman Writer: Ideology as Style in the Works of Mary Wollstonecraft, Mary Shelley and Jane Austen* (Chicago and London: University of Chicago Press, 1984), 207.

3 Johanna M. Smith, 'The Oppositional Reader and *Pride and Prejudice*', in *A Companion to Jane Austen Studies*, ed. Laura Cooner Lambdin and Robert Thomas Lambdin (Westport, CT: Greenwood Press, 2000), 30.

4 Ruth Perry, 'Clarissa's Daughters; or, The History of Innocence Betrayed. How Women Writers Rewrote Richardson', in *Clarissa and Her Readers: New Essays for the Clarissa Project*, ed. Carol Houlihan Flynn and Edward Copeland (New York: AMS Press, Inc., 1999), 120.

5 Richardson writes: 'But let us suppose the Story to end, as you, Madam, would have it; what of extraordinary would there be in it? After infinite Tryals, Difficulties, Distresses, and even *Disgraces*, (her Delicacy and Situation considered) see her married [...] What is there unusual in all this?' in *Selected Letters of Samuel Richardson*, ed. John Carroll (Oxford: Clarendon Press, 1964), 106.

6 'Opinions of *Mansfield Park*', in Jane Austen, *Later Manuscripts*, ed. Janet Todd and Linda Bree (Cambridge: Cambridge University Press, 2008), 233–4. Hereafter *Later Manuscripts*.
7 'Opinions of *Emma*', in *Later Manuscripts*, 237.
8 Samuel Smiles, *A Publisher and his Friends: Memoir and Correspondence of the late John Murray*, 2 vols (London: John Murray, 1891), i, 282.
9 [Thomas Henry Lister], review of *Women as they are*, *Edinburgh Review*, 53 (July 1830): 448–51, quoted in Brian Southam, *Jane Austen: The Critical Heritage*, 2 vols (London: Routledge, 1968–87), i, 114.
10 Lady Bradshaigh's marginal notes in *Clarissa*, quoted in Janice Broder, 'Lady Bradshaigh Reads and Writes *Clarissa*: The Marginal Notes in Her First Edition', in Flynn and Copeland, *Clarissa and Her Readers*, 109.
11 Jerry C. Beasley, '*Clarissa* and Early Female Fiction', in ibid., 90.
12 Samuel Henry Romilly, *Romilly – Edgeworth letters, 1813–1818* (London: John Murray, 1936), 143; quoted in David Gilson, *A Bibliography of Jane Austen* (Winchester and New Castle, DE: Oak Knoll Press, 1997), 71.
13 Quoted in Marilyn Butler, *Maria Edgeworth: A literary biography* (Oxford: Clarendon Press, 1972), 445.
14 The most influential study of literary influence remains Harold Bloom's *The Anxiety of Influence* (New York: Oxford University Press, 1973); other important accounts include Gilbert and Gubar's response to Bloom in *The Madwoman in the Attic* (New Haven, CT and London: Yale University Press, 1979), Christopher Ricks's *Allusion to the Poets* (Oxford: Oxford University Press, 2002), Jocelyn Harris's *Jane Austen's Art of Memory*, and Robert Douglas-Fairhurst's *Victorian Afterlives: The Shaping of Influence in Nineteenth-Century Literature* (Oxford: Oxford University Press, 2002).
15 William Sharp, *The Life and Letters of Joseph Severn* (London: Sampson Low, Marston, 1892), 85. Severn quotes John Keats's deathbed words.
16 For other discussions of individual readers within their social, historical and cultural contexts, see, for example, Anthony Grafton and Lisa Jardine, '"Studied for Action": How Gabriel Harvey Read his Livy', *Past and Present*, 129 (1990): 30–78; Arianne Baggerman, 'The Cultural Universe of a Dutch Child: Otto van Eck and his Literature', *Eighteenth-Century Studies*, 31.1 (1997): 129–33; Stephen Colclough, '"R R, A Remarkable Thing or Action": John Dawson as Reader and Annotator', *Variants*, 2.3 (2004): 61–78; James A. Secord, 'Self-Development' in his *Victorian Sensation: The Extraordinary Publication, Reception and Secret Authorship of 'Vestiges of the Natural History of Creation'* (Chicago: University of Chicago Press, 2003), 336–63; John Brewer, 'Reconstructing the Reader: Prescriptions, Texts and Strategies in Anna Larpent's Reading' in James Raven, Helen Small and Naomi Tadmor (eds), *The Practice and Representation of Reading in England* (Cambridge: Cambridge University Press, 1996), 226–45; Ruth Clayton Windscheffel, *Reading Gladstone* (Basingstoke: Palgrave Macmillan, 2008); Thomas Wright, *Oscar's Books* (London: Chatto & Windus, 2008); H. J. Jackson, *Romantic Readers: The Evidence of Marginalia* (New Haven, CT: Yale University Press, 2005) and *Marginalia: Readers Writing in Books* (New Haven, CT: Yale University Press, 2001); Jonathan Rose, *The Intellectual Life of the British Working Classes* (New Haven, CT: Yale University Press, 2001), Felicity Stimpson, '"I have spent my morning reading Greek": The marginalia of Sir George Otto Trevelyan', *Library History*, 23.3 (2007): 239–50; and Jacqueline

Pearson, *Women's Reading in Britain, 1750–1835* (Cambridge: Cambridge University Press, 1999), 122–51.
17 Simon Eliot, 'The Reading Experience Database; or, what are we to do about the history of reading?', *The Reading Experience Database, 1450–1945*. http://www.open.ac.uk/Arts/RED/redback.htm (accessed 1 June 2009).
18 See *Readership Research: Theory and Practice (Proceedings of the First International Symposium, New Orleans, 1981)*, ed. Harry Henry (London: Sigmatext, 1982) for a number of excellent accounts of different methods used in readership research.
19 See William A. Belson, *Studies in Readership* (London: Business Publications, 1962) for a detailed account of interview procedures and inherent problems. For discussions of the methods and strategies employed in the history of reading, see *Reading in History: New Methodologies from the Anglo-American Tradition*, ed. Bonnie Gunzenhauser (London: Pickering & Chatto, 2010), in particular the chapters by Daniel Allington, 'On the Use of Anecdotal Evidence in Reception Study and the History of Reading' (11–28); Rosalind Crone, Katie Halsey and Shafquat Towheed, 'Examining the Evidence of Reading: Three Examples from the Reading Experience Database, 1450–1945' (29–46); and Anouk Lang, 'Explicating Explications: Researching Contemporary Reading' (119–54). See also my 'Reading the Evidence of Reading', *Popular Narrative Media*, 1.2 (2008): 123–37.
20 Ariane Baggerman presents a comprehensive and cohesive account of the interpretative issues involved in using diaries as evidence of reading in 'The Cultural Universe of a Dutch Child', 129–33.
21 Allington, 'On the Use of Anecdotal Evidence in Reception Study and the History of Reading', 11–28. See also Roger Chartier, 'Figures of the "Other": Peasant Reading in the Age of the Enlightenment', in *Cultural History: Between Practices and Representations* (Cambridge: Polity Press, 1988), 151–71. For a discussion of the conventions governing oral histories of reading, see Martin Lyons and Lucy Taksa, *Australian Readers Remember: An Oral History of Reading, 1890–1930* (Melbourne, Oxford, Auckland and New York: Oxford University Press, 1992), 15.
22 Jon Klancher, *The Making of English Reading Audiences, 1790–1832* (Madison: University of Wisconsin Press, 1987), 174.
23 Ibid., 174.
24 William St Clair, *The Reading Nation in the Romantic Period* (Cambridge: Cambridge University Press, 2004), 5–6.
25 Eliot, 'The Reading Experience Database; or, what are we to do about the history of reading?' http://www.open.ac.uk/Arts/RED/redback.htm (accessed 1 June 2009).
26 W. H. Auden, 'Letter to Lord Byron', from *Letters from Iceland* (London: Faber & Faber, 1937; repr. 1965), 18.
27 For a full discussion of the Romantic poets' interest in their afterlives, see Andrew Bennett, *Romantic Poets and the Culture of Posterity* (Cambridge: Cambridge University Press, 1999). See also Douglas-Fairhurst, *Victorian Afterlives*, 9–84.
28 Cassandra Austen to Anna Lefroy, 1 February 1844, quoted in David Gilson, *A Bibliography of Jane Austen* (Winchester and New Castle, DE: Oak Knoll Press, 1997), 483.
29 George Gordon, Lord Byron, 'A Fragment', in *Lord Byron: The Major Works*, ed. Jerome J. McGann (Oxford: Oxford University Press, 1986), 1.
30 Lisa A. F. Lewis, 'Kipling's Jane: Some Echoes of Austen', *English Literature in Transition, 1880–1920*, 29.1 (1986): 81.

31 Donald Reiman, *The Study of Modern Manuscripts: Public, Confidential, and Private* (Baltimore: The Johns Hopkins University Press, 1992). For a discussion of how Austen's manuscripts fit into this categorization, see Michelle Levy, 'Austen's Manuscripts and the Publicity of Print', *ELH*, 77.4 (Winter 2010): 1015–40.
32 Deirdre Le Faye (ed.) *Jane Austen's Letters* (Oxford: Oxford University Press, 1995), 282.
33 Ibid., 306.
34 Anon., review of *Emma*, *The Champion*, 31 March 1818, 102.
35 [Richard Whately], review of *Northanger Abbey* and *Persuasion*, *Quarterly Review*, 24 (January 1821): 358.
36 'Opinions of *Emma*', in *Later Manuscripts*, 238.
37 'Opinions of *Mansfield Park*', in *Later Manuscripts*, 234.
38 'Opinions of *Emma*', in *Later Manuscripts*, 237.
39 Ibid., 238.
40 Ibid., 238.
41 'Opinions of *Mansfield Park*' and 'Opinions of *Emma*', in *Later Manuscripts*, 230–39.
42 Anon., Notice of *Sense and Sensibility*, *British Critic*, 39 (May 1812): 527.
43 Anon., Notice of *Pride and Prejudice*, *British Critic*, 41 (February 1813): 190.
44 'Opinions of *Mansfield Park*', in *Later Manuscripts*, 231, 232.
45 'Opinions of *Emma*', in *Later Manuscripts*, 235, 236.
46 'Opinions of *Mansfield Park*', in *Later Manuscripts*, 234.
47 'Opinions of *Emma*', in *Later Manuscripts*, 238.
48 'Opinions of *Mansfield Park*', in *Later Manuscripts*, 230.
49 [Walter Scott], review of *Emma*, *Quarterly Review*, 14 (March 1816): 200.
50 'Opinions of *Mansfield Park*', in *Later Manuscripts*, 232.
51 Ibid., 233.
52 'Opinions of *Emma*', in *Later Manuscripts*, 237.
53 'Opinions of *Mansfield Park*', in *Later Manuscripts*, 232.
54 Ibid., 233.
55 'Opinions of *Emma*', in *Later Manuscripts*, 238.
56 Anon., review of *Sense and Sensibility*, *Critical Review*, n.s., 4.1 (February 1812): 150.
57 'Opinions of *Mansfield Park*', in *Later Manuscripts*, 230.
58 Ibid., 232, 233.
59 'Opinions of *Emma*', in *Later Manuscripts*, 236, 238.
60 Anon., Notice of *Pride and Prejudice*, *British Critic*, 41 (February 1813): 189.
61 Anon., Notice of *Emma*, *Monthly Review*, 80 (July 1816): 320; Anon., review of *Emma*, *The Champion*, 31 March 1818, 103.
62 Anon., Notice of *Northanger Abbey* and *Persuasion*, *Edinburgh Magazine and Literary Miscellany*, n.s. 2 (May 1818): 454.
63 'Opinions of *Emma*', in *Later Manuscripts*, 238.
64 Ibid., 238.
65 Ibid., 237, 236.
66 ibid., 236 ,237.
67 Opinions of *Mansfield Park*', in *Later Manuscripts*, 230.
68 Ibid., 230, 231.
69 Anon., Review of *Pride and Prejudice*, *New Review; or, Monthly Analysis of General Literature*, 1 April 1813, 3393.
70 Anon., Notice of *Northanger Abbey* and *Persuasion*, *Edinburgh Magazine and Literary Miscellany*, n.s. 2 (May 1818): 454.

71 'Opinions of *Emma*', in *Later Manuscripts*, 235.
72 Ibid., 236.
73 Ibid., 235.
74 'Opinions of *Mansfield Park*', in *Later Manuscripts*, 232.
75 'Opinions of *Emma*', in *Later Manuscripts*, 236.
76 Ibid., 235.
77 'Opinions of *Mansfield Park*', in *Later Manuscripts*, 231.
78 'Opinions of *Emma*', in *Later Manuscripts*, 237.
79 Ibid., 237.
80 'Opinions of *Mansfield Park*', in *Later Manuscripts*, 232.
81 Mary Ann O'Farrell, 'Jane Austen's Friendships', in Deidre Lynch (ed.), *Janeites: Austen's Disciples and Devotees* (Princeton and Oxford: Princeton University Press, 2000), 47.
82 Ibid., 47.

Chapter 4: Austen's Readers: Contexts I

1 Anthony Mandal, *Jane Austen and the Popular Novel: The Determined Author* (Basingstoke: Palgrave Macmillan, 2007), passim.
2 *The Brontës, their Friendships, Lives and Correspondence*, ed. T. J. Wise and J. A. Symington, 4 vols (Oxford: Blackwell, 1932), ii, 178. Hereafter Wise and Symington.
3 Brian Southam, *Jane Austen: The Critical Heritage*, 2 vols (London: Routledge, 1968–87), i, 126n1.
4 Wise and Symington, ii, 179–80.
5 For details of the first, second and third editions of *Pride and Prejudice*, see David Gilson, *A Bibliography of Jane Austen* (Winchester and New Castle, DE: Oak Knoll Press, 1997), 18–43; for the Bentley edition and reprints, see Gilson, *Bibliography*, 222–31; for the Carey and Lea American edition, see Gilson, *Bibliography*, 103–6. For a more extensive account of price and cost in the Victorian period, see Simon Eliot, '"Never Mind the Value, What about the Price?", Or, How Much Did Marmion Cost St. John Rivers?', *Nineteenth-Century Literature*, 56.2 (September 2001): 160–97.
6 *The Letters of Thomas Babington Macaulay*, ed. Thomas Pinney, 6 vols (Cambridge: Cambridge University Press, 1974), ii, 253.
7 Ibid., ii, 290.
8 Kathryn Sutherland, *Jane Austen's Textual Lives* (Oxford: Oxford University Press, 2005), 266–313. See 303–5 in particular for a description of the practices of printers and publishing houses in Austen's period.
9 Simon Eliot, '"Faintly Troubling the Darkness": Casting a Little Light on the History of the Book', inaugural lecture, 9 November 2006, Institute of English Studies, Senate House, University of London and '"Never Mind the Value, What about the Price?"', passim.
10 See, for example, Paul Dobraszczyk, 'Useful Reading? Designing Information for London's Victorian Cab Passengers', *Journal of Design History*, 21.2 (2008): 121–41; Mike Esbester, 'Nineteenth-Century Timetables and the History of Reading', *Book History*, 12 (2009): 156–85 and Adrian Bingham, '"Putting literature out of reach"? Reading Popular Newspapers in Mid-twentieth Century Britain', in *The History of Reading: The British Isles, 1750–1950*, ed. Katie Halsey and W. R. Owens (Basingstoke: Palgrave Macmillan, 2011), 139–54.

11 Ruth Clayton Windscheffel, *Reading Gladstone* (Basingstoke: Palgrave Macmillan, 2008), 44–78.
12 Mark Towsey, '"An Infant Son to Truth Engage": Virtue, Responsibility and Self-Improvement in the Reading of Elizabeth Rose of Kilravock, 1747–1815', *Journal of the Edinburgh Bibliographical Society*, 2 (2007): 69–92.
13 Robert Darnton, 'First Steps Towards a History of Reading', in his *The Kiss of Lamourette: Reflections in Cultural History* (London: Faber & Faber, 1990), 167; Andrew Hobbs, 'The Reading World of a Provincial Town: Preston, Lancashire 1855–1900', in Halsey and Owens, 121–38, and Stephen Colclough, *Consuming Texts: Readers and Reading Communities, 1695–1870* (Basingstoke: Palgrave Macmillan, 2007).
14 Jan Fergus, *Provincial Readers in Eighteenth-Century England* (Oxford: Oxford University Press, 2006).
15 Thomas Wright, *Oscar's Books* (London: Chatto & Windus, 2008), 152–61.
16 All reading experiences described here are collected in *The Reading Experience Database, 1450–1945 (RED)*, (www.open.ac.uk/Arts/reading), and will be identified by their record identification number in that resource. I am grateful to my colleagues past and present at *RED*, Stephen Colclough, Rosalind Crone, Simon Eliot, Mary Hammond, Sarah Johnson, Jenny McAuley, Bob Owens, Shafquat Towheed and Alexis Weedon, and to the many volunteer contributors to the project, for their various roles in the collective gathering and collating of this material.
17 *Reading Experience Database* ID 11442. http://www.open.ac.uk/Arts/reading/recorddetails2.php?id=11442 (accessed 1 June 2010).
18 *Reading Experience Database* ID 11467. http://www.open.ac.uk/Arts/reading/recorddetails2.php?id=11467 (accessed 1 June 2010).
19 *Reading Experience Database* ID 11467. http://www.open.ac.uk/Arts/reading/recorddetails2.php?id=11467 (accessed 1 June 2010).
20 *Reading Experience Database* ID 11844. http://www.open.ac.uk/Arts/reading/recorddetails2.php?id=11844 (accessed 2 July 2010).
21 *Reading Experience Database* ID 3391. http://www.open.ac.uk/Arts/reading/recorddetails2.php?id=3391. (accessed 2 July 2010).
22 *Reading Experience Database* ID 17791. http://www.open.ac.uk/Arts/reading/recorddetails2.php?id=17791. (accessed 2 July 2010). Stevenson's first paid publication was, in fact, in the *Portfolio*.
23 *Reading Experience Database* ID 24851. http://www.open.ac.uk/Arts/reading/recorddetails2.php?id=24851. (accessed 2 July 2010).
24 *Reading Experience Database* ID 23688. http://www.open.ac.uk/Arts/reading/recorddetails2.php?id=23688. (accessed 2 July 2010).
25 *Reading Experience Database* ID 1204.http://www.open.ac.uk/Arts/reading/recorddetails2.php?id=1204. (accessed 2 July 2010).
26 *Reading Experience Database* ID 22546. http://www.open.ac.uk/Arts/reading/recorddetails2.php?id=22546. (accessed 3 July 2010).
27 *Reading Experience Database* ID 22594. http://www.open.ac.uk/Arts/reading/recorddetails2.php?id=22594. (accessed 3 July 2010).
28 George Otto Trevelyan, *The Life and Letters of Lord Macaulay, Volumes I & II* (Oxford: Oxford University Press, 1978), ii, 433
29 Claire Harman, *Jane's Fame: How Jane Austen Conquered the World* (Edinburgh: Canongate, 2009), 121; quoting Mary Augusta Austen-Leigh, *Personal Aspects of Jane Austen* (1920), 2.

30 For an extensive discussion of the role of format and paratextual material in the reading experiences of medieval readers, see Paul Saenger, 'Silent Reading: Its Impact on Late Medieval Script and Society', *Viator*, 13 (1982): 367–414.
31 *Reading Experience Database* ID 25994. http://www.open.ac.uk/Arts/reading/record details2.php?id=25994 (accessed 3 July 2010).
32 *Reading Experience Database* ID 11881. http://www.open.ac.uk/Arts/reading/record details2.php?id=11881 (accessed 3 July 2010).
33 *Reading Experience Database* ID 25222. http://www.open.ac.uk/Arts/reading/record details2.php?id=25222 (accessed 3 July 2010).
34 *Reading Experience Database* ID 3767. http://www.open.ac.uk/Arts/reading/record details2.php?id=3767 (accessed 3 July 2010).
35 *Reading Experience Database* ID 19970. http://www.open.ac.uk/Arts/reading/record details2.php?id=19970 (accessed 3 July 2010).
36 *Reading Experience Database* ID 3661.http://www.open.ac.uk/Arts/reading/record details2.php?id=3661 (accessed 5 July 2010).
37 *Reading Experience Database* ID 19208. http://www.open.ac.uk/Arts/reading/record details2.php?id=19208 (accessed 5 July 2010).
38 *Reading Experience Database* ID 19688. http://www.open.ac.uk/Arts/reading/record details2.php?id=19688 (accessed 5 July 2010).
39 *Reading Experience Database* ID 14890. http://www.open.ac.uk/Arts/reading/record details2.php?id=14890 (accessed 5 July 2010).
40 *Reading Experience Database* ID 11378. http://www.open.ac.uk/Arts/reading/record details2.php?id=11378 (accessed 10 July 2010).
41 *Reading Experience Database* ID 7393. http://www.open.ac.uk/Arts/reading/record details2.php?id=7393 (accessed 10 July 2010).
42 *Reading Experience Database* ID 6624. http://www.open.ac.uk/Arts/reading/record details2.php?id=6624 (accessed 10 July 2010).
43 *Reading Experience Database* ID 6864. http://www.open.ac.uk/Arts/reading/record details2.php?id=6864 (accessed 10 July 2010).
44 Further relevant readers' responses, commending on translations, bindings, editions, costs, illustrations and legibility can be found in the *Reading Experience Database*. See in particular ID numbers 24851, 4309, 10372, 24083, 3670, 6880, 7210, 8594, 7393, 11447, 18344.
45 David Gilson's invaluable *Bibliography of Jane Austen* provides bibliographical information about all known editions and impressions of Austen's work from 1811 to 1976. I have relied heavily on this work, and on his 'Later publishing history, with illustrations', in *Jane Austen in Context*, ed. Janet Todd (Cambridge: Cambridge University Press, 2005), 121–59. Where possible, I have inspected extant copies of works by Jane Austen and her contemporaries, and I am indebted to John Spiers, William Urquhart, and William St Clair for allowing me to examine their substantial private collections of rare books of different types. I am also grateful to the rare books and special collections librarians and archivists of the Houghton Library, Chawton House Library, the Bodleian Library, the British Library, Cambridge University Library, the National Art Library, the Women's Library, Dr Williams's Library, Innerpeffray Library, the National Library of Scotland and Senate House Library.
46 'From Few to Expensive to Many and Cheap: The British Book Market 1800–1890' in *A Companion to the History of the Book*, ed. Simon Eliot and Jonathan Rose (Oxford: Blackwell, 2007), 291.
47 Samuel Smiles, *A Publisher and his Friends: Memoir and Correspondence of the late John Murray*, 2 vols (London: John Murray, 1891), i, 288.

48 Malcolm Elwin, *Lord Byron's Wife* (London: Macdonald, 1962), 159.
49 *The Letters of Sarah Harriet Burney*, ed. Lorna J. Clark (Athens, GA and London: University of Georgia Press, 1997), 176.
50 Harold William Thompson, *A Scottish Man of Feeling: Some account of Henry Mackenzie, Esq. of Edinbugh and of the golden age of Burns and Scott* (London: Oxford University Press, 1831), 354.
51 John Cam Hobhouse, Lord Broughton, *Recollections of a Long Life*, 6 vols (London: John Murray, 1907), i, 167.
52 For a full account of the far-reaching influence of Henry Austen's 'Biographical Notice' on Austen's readers, see my chapter, '"Faultless herself, as nearly as human nature can be": The construction of Jane Austen's public image, 1817–1917', in *Women Writers and the Artifacts of Celebrity*, ed. Ann R. Hawkins and Maura Ives (Aldershot: Ashgate, forthcoming).
53 William Smith Ward lists 16 reviews of Austen's novels between 1811 and 1826 of which 8 were of *Emma*; William Smith Ward, *Literary Reviews in British Periodicals, 1798–1820: A Bibliography with a Supplementary List of General (Non-Review) Articles on Literary Subjects* (New York: Garland, 1972). In his bibliography, David Gilson includes a publication not listed in Ward, a review of *Pride and Prejudice* in *The New Review; or Monthly Analysis of General Literature*, 1 (April 1813): 393–6. Ongoing research by Ann R. Hawkins suggests that there were many more reviews of women writers than those listed by Ward or Gilson. According to Hawkins, 'Ward misses between 20% and 70% of the reviews of women in every year' (private correspondence with Ann R. Hawkins, 29 September 2008). Austen may, therefore, have been more widely reviewed, and thus readers might have come across quotations from her work in a far larger number and far wider range of publications than has previously been assumed. I am grateful to Ann Hawkins for alerting me to this fact.
54 Although Mathew Carey's records of publishing *Emma* are no longer extant, I extrapolate from Gilson that the edition must have been small from the fact that 'only three copies have so far come to light' (in comparison to the far larger numbers of copies of the British first edition of *Emma* recorded as having been traced by Gilson). Gilson, *Bibliography*, 100.
55 J. G. Williamson, 'The structure of pay in Britain, 1710–1911', *Research in Economic History*, 7 (1982): 1–54.
56 For accounts of the use of various kinds of libraries by members of the working and middle classes, see Paul Kaufman, *Libraries and their Users: Collected Papers in Library History* (London: The Library Association, 1969); idem, *Reading Vogues at English Cathedral Libraries of the Eighteenth Century* (New York: New York Public Library, 1964); idem, *Borrowings from the Bristol Library 1773–1784: A Unique Record of Reading Vogues* (Charlottesville: Bibliographical Society of Virginia, 1960); Jan Fergus, 'Eighteenth-Century Readers in Provincial England: The Customers of Samuel Clay's Circulating Library and Bookshop in Warwick, 1770-2', *PBSA*, 78 (1984): 155–213; Vivienne S. Dunstan, 'Glimpses into a Town's Reading Habits in Enlightenment Scotland: Analysing the Borrowings of Gray Library, Haddington, 1732–1816', *Journal of Scottish Historical Studies*, 26 (2006): 42–59; Mark Towsey, '"The Talent Hid in a Napkin": Castle Libraries in Eighteenth-Century Scotland' in Halsey and Owens, 15–31; and idem, 'First Steps in Associational Reading: The Foundation and Early Use of the Wigtown Subscription Library, 1790–1815', *PBSA*, 103 (2009): 455–95.
57 Gilson, 'Later publishing history, with illustrations', 127.
58 Gilson, *Bibliography*, 230.
59 See letter to Richard Bentley, 2 April 1827: 'I want at the usual trade allowance (if that be proper in an Author's case) a complete set of the Standard Novels up to this time, if

you will have the goodness to direct them to be sent to me – and also the numbers to follow, as they come out.' *The Letters of Charles Dickens*, ed. Madeline House and Graham Storey, 12 vols (Oxford: Clarendon, 1965), i, 250.
60 *The Letters of Thomas Babington Macaulay*, ii, 253, 290.
61 Eliot, '"Never mind the value"', 167.
62 A representative illustration, from *Sense and Sensibility*, is reproduced in Gilson, 'Later publishing history, with illustrations', 126.
63 Ibid.
64 See Mary Hammond, 'Sensation and Sensibility: W. H. Smith and the Railway Bookstall' in her *Reading, Publishing and the Formation of Literary Taste*, 51–83, for analysis of the role of railway bookstalls in forming Victorian readers' tastes.
65 See John Spiers, ed., *The Culture of the Publisher's Series*, 2 vols (Basingstoke: Palgrave Macmillan, 2011).
66 Gilson, 'Later publishing history, with illustrations', 139.
67 [Richard Simpson], review of James Edward Austen-Leigh, *A Memoir of Jane Austen*, *North British Review*, 52 (April 1870): 129.
68 'M. A. W.' [Mrs Humphry Ward], 'Style and Miss Austen', *Macmillan's Magazine*, 51 (1885): 91.
69 *Henry James' Letters 1875–83*, ed. Leon Edel (London: Macmillan, 1978), 422.
70 [Leslie Stephen], 'Humour', *Cornhill Magazine*, 33 (1876): 324.
71 Harman, 160.
72 Gilson, *Bibliography*, 267.
73 Henry James, 'The Lesson of Balzac', in *The House of Fiction: Essays on the Novel*, ed. Leon Edel (London: Hart-Davis, 1957), 62.
74 [R. H. Hutton], 'Miss Austen's Posthumous Pieces', *Spectator*, 22 July 1871, 891.
75 Virginia Woolf, 'Jane Austen' in *The Common Reader*, ed. Andrew McNeillie, 2 vols (London: Vintage, 2003; first published 1925), i, 137.
76 Ibid., i, 138.
77 For a comprehensive survey of Austen criticism from 1811 to 1940, see Southam, *Critical Heritage*, i, 1–33 and ii, 1–158. See also Ian Littlewood (ed.), *Critical Assessments*, 4 vols (Sussex: Helm Information, 1998); Annika Bautz, *The Reception of Jane Austen and Walter Scott: A Comparative Longitudinal Study* (London: Continuum, 2007); Mary Waldron, 'Critical responses, early', Nicola Trott, 'Critical responses, 1830–1970', and Rajeswari Sunder Rajan, 'Critical responses, recent', all in Todd (ed.), *Jane Austen in Context*, 83–110. For a discussion of the 'Janeite' tradition, see the works already discussed by Deidre Lynch and Claudia Johnson, For analysis of Austen's translation into television and film, see John Wilshire, *Recreating Jane Austen* (Cambridge: Cambridge University Press, 2001) and Gina Macdonald and Andrew F. Macdonald (eds), *Jane Austen on Screen* (Cambridge: Cambridge University Press, 2003), in particular 44–66.
78 [T. B. Macaulay], 'The Diary and Letters of Mme D'Arblay', *Edinburgh Review*, 76 (1842–43): 561.
79 Scott's praise of Austen in his 1816 review was also often extracted for advertising purposes. See examples using quotations from Scott and Macaulay in advertisements for Bentley's edition in the *Times*'s 'Column of New Books and New Editions' of Monday 27 November 1871, Wednesday 1 July 1874, Wednesday 28 July 1875, Saturday 16 October 1875.
80 Lady Charlotte Schreiber, *Extracts from her Journal 1853–1891*, ed. the Earl of Bessborough (London: John Murray, 1952), 134.

Chapter 5: Austen's Readers: Contexts II

1. See David Vincent, *The Rise of Mass Literacy: Reading and Writing in Modern Europe* (Cambridge: Polity, 2000) for discussion of the implications of greater literacy in Britain in Austen's period. See Rob Banham, 'The Industrialization of the Book, 1800–1970', in *A Companion to the History of the Book*, ed. Simon Eliot and Jonathan Rose (Oxford: Blackwell, 2007), 273–90, for a description of the inventions and industrial processes which made possible the greater availability of cheap print, and Eliot, 'From Few and Expensive to Many and Cheap', 291–302, for information about the price and availability of novels and the marketing and distribution policies of publishers and booksellers of the period.
2. Anon., 'Moral and Political Tendency of the Modern Novels', *Church of England Quarterly Review*, 11 (1842): 287–8.
3. Plato, *Republic*, X, 605b and 605c, in Plato, *Republic*, trans. Paul Shorey, 2 vols, Loeb Classical Library, 276 (Cambridge, MA and London: Harvard University Press, 1935; repr. 1994), ii, 459. For more on Plato's views of imitative art, see *Plato on Poetry*, ed. Penelope Murray (Cambridge: Cambridge University Press, 1996).
4. Plato, *Republic*, X, 597e.
5. T. A. [Thomas Arnold], 'Recent Novel Writing', *Macmillan's Magazine*, 13 (1865–66): 202.
6. Richard Brinsley Sheridan, *The Rivals* (1775), i, 2, in *The Dramatic Works of Richard Brinsley Sheridan*, 2 vols, ed. Cecil Price (Oxford: Clarendon Press, 1973), i, 84.
7. [Walter Scott], review of *Emma*, *Quarterly Review*, 14 (1816): 188.
8. Jane Austen, *Northanger Abbey*, ed. Barbara M. Benedict and Deirdre Le Faye (Cambridge: Cambridge University Press, 2006), 30. Hereafter *Northanger Abbey*.
9. Scott, review of *Emma*, 189, 192.
10. Ibid., 193.
11. Ibid., 200.
12. Unsigned review of *Sense and Sensibility*, *Critical Review*, n.s. 4, i (1812): 149.
13. Unsigned notice of *Pride and Prejudice*, *British Critic*, 16 (1813): 189.
14. Unsigned review of *Northanger Abbey* and *Persuasion*, *British Critic*, n.s. 9 (1818): 294.
15. Anon., 'Sensation Literature', *Ladies' Treasury: An Illustrated Magazine of Entertaining Literature, Education, Fine Art, Domestic Economy, Needlework and Fashion*, n.s. 7.37 (1862): 14.
16. [Richard Whately], review of *Northanger Abbey* and *Persuasion*, *Quarterly Review*, 24 (January 1821): 352.
17. *Northanger Abbey*, 30.
18. See, for example, Sarah Scott's Preface to *The Test of Filial Duty* (1772), in which she writes: 'Though it is almost established into a custom, I shall not begin my Preface by reminding the town that it swarms with novels [...] Nor shall I endeavour to depreciate other performances of this nature, in order to hint that mine is designed as a sort of antidote to the poison conveyed in them; which would be no less unjust than insolent', in *Bluestocking Feminism, Writings of the Bluestocking Circle 1738–1785*, 6 vols (London: Pickering & Chatto, 1999), vi, 5.
19. 'Doubleday' [Alfred Ainger], 'Books and their Uses', *Macmillan's Magazine*, 1 (1859–60): 111.
20. Louisa Emily Dorrée, 'A Girl's Leisure Moments', *Quiver*, 19 (1884): 307.
21. Anon., 'On Fiction as an Educator', *Blackwood's Edinburgh Magazine*, 108 (1870): 449.
22. Anon., 'Recent Novels', *Edinburgh Review or Critical Journal*, 97 (1853): 380.
23. Ibid., 381.

24 Sir Philip Sidney, *Defence of Poesie* (1595) (Menston: Scolar Press Facsimile, 1968), sig. D3 ʳ.
25 Anon., 'Sensation Literature', 14.
26 T. A., 'Recent Novel Writing', 202.
27 Anon., 'Different Classes of Readers', *Leisure Hour: A Family Journal of Instruction and Recreation*, 1 (1852), 15.
28 'Doubleday', 'Books and their Uses', 111.
29 Ibid., 110.
30 T. A., 'Recent Novel Writing', 204.
31 F. T. Palgrave, 'On Readers in 1760 and 1860', *Macmillan's Magazine*, 1 (1859–60): 488.
32 'M. A. W', 'Style and Miss Austen', 84.
33 [Mowbray Morris], 'General Readers; by One of Them', *Macmillan's Magazine*, 53 (1885–86): 453.
34 Ibid., 456.
35 Anon., 'Aunt Anastasia on Modern Novels', *Tinsley's Magazine*, 1 (1867): 308.
36 Ibid., 309.
37 Ibid., 310.
38 Ibid., 312.
39 Ibid., 313.
40 Ibid., 315.
41 Ibid., 316.
42 [William Gifford], unsigned review of works by Felicia Hemans, *Quarterly Review*, 24 (1820–21): 131.
43 Anon., '*Clarissa*', *Tinsley's Magazine*, 3 (1868–69): 311–2.
44 Anon., 'On Fiction as an Educator', 457.
45 Anon., 'Some Thoughts about Novels', *Macmillan's Magazine*, 55 (1886–87): 361.
46 Ibid., 361.
47 The *Englishwoman's Domestic Magazine*, for example, refreshingly adopts an indignant attitude, explicitly rejecting the image of women perpetuated elsewhere and adopted by 'men': 'When, therefore, we compare the acquirements of Lady Jane Grey with those of an accomplished young woman of our own time, we have no hesitation in awarding the superiority to the latter, and men are mistaken in thinking that the great-great-grandmothers of their great-great-grandmothers were superior to their sisters and wives'. Anon., 'Learned Ladies Three Hundred Years Ago', *Englishwoman's Domestic Magazine*, 5.7 (November 1856): 207.
48 'Opinions of *Mansfield Park*', in Jane Austen, *Later Manuscripts*, ed. Janet Todd and Linda Bree (Cambridge: Cambridge University Press, 2008), 233. Hereafter *Later Manuscripts*.
49 William Gilmore Simms, *Beauchampe; or, The Kentucky Tragedy: A Tale of Passion*, 2 vols (Philadelphia: Lea and Blanchard, 1842), i, 241.
50 Anon., 'Literary Notices', *Ladies' Treasury*, 4 (1860): 254.
51 Opinions of *Mansfield Park*', in *Later Manuscripts*, 234.
52 Deirdre Le Faye (ed.), *Jane Austen's Letters* (Oxford: Oxford University Press, 1995), 26.
53 *The Letters of Mary Russell Mitford*, ed. R. Brimley Johnson (London: John Lane The Bodley Head Ltd, 1925), 175.
54 *The Letters of Thomas Moore*, ed. Wilfred S. Dowden (Oxford: Clarendon Press, 1964), 396.
55 *Felicia Hemans, Selected Poems, Letters, Reception Materials*, ed. Susan J. Wolfson (Princeton and Oxford: Princeton University Press, 2000), 476.

56 *Extracts of the Journals and Correspondence of Miss Berry from the Year 1783 to 1852*, ed. Lady Theresa Lewis, 3 vols (London: Longmans, Green, & Co., 1865), i, 11.
57 Ibid., ii, 112.
58 Ibid., ii, 313.
59 *Memoir and Correspondence of Susan Ferrier*, ed. John A. Doyle (London: John Murray, 1898), 125.
60 Ibid., 128.
61 *The Journals of Mary Shelley 1814–1844*, ed. Paula R. Feldman and Diana Scott-Kilvert (Baltimore and London: The Johns Hopkins University Press, 1987; repr. 1995), 460.
62 *Women of Letters: Selected Letters of Elizabeth Barrett Browning and Mary Russell Mitford*, ed. Meredith B. Raymond and Mary Rose Sullivan (Boston: Twayne Publishers, 1987), 156.
63 *The Letters of William and Dorothy Wordsworth: The Middle Years*, ed. Ernest de Selincourt, 2 vols (Oxford: Clarendon Press, 1937), ii, 464. She refers to Thomas Avory's *Life of John Buncle* (1756–66).
64 Ibid., ii, 491.
65 Ibid., ii, 497.
66 *The Journals of Claire Clairmont*, ed. Marion Kingston Stocking (Cambridge, MA: Harvard University Press, 1968), 31, 40.
67 See, for example, John Brewer's discussion of Anna Larpent's reading, in 'Reconstructing the reader: prescriptions, texts and strategies in Anna Larpent's reading', in James Raven, Helen Small and Naomi Tadmor (eds), *The Practice and Representation of Reading in England* (Cambridge: Cambridge University Press, 1996), 226–45.
68 *The Barretts at Hope End: The Early Diary of Elizabeth Barrett Browning*, ed. Elizabeth Berridge (London: John Murray, 1974), 170.
69 Ibid., 86.
70 Ibid., 256
71 Ibid., 228.
72 Ibid., 258.
73 For a full discussion of the books that became fashionable during the nineteenth century, see William St Clair, *The Reading Nation in the Romantic Period* (Cambridge: Cambridge University Press, 2004), esp. 413–32.
74 Unsigned review of *Sense and Sensibility*, *Critical Review*, n.s. 4, i (1812): 150.
75 *The Letters of Mary Wollstonecraft Shelley*, ed. Betty T. Bennett, 3 vols (Baltimore and London: The Johns Hopkins University Press, 1980–88), ii, 207.
76 Ibid., ii, 222.
77 Ibid., ii, 63.
78 *Harriet Martineau's Letters to Fanny Wedgwood*, ed. Elisabeth Sanders Arbuckle (Stanford: Stanford University Press, 1983), 24.
79 *Letters of Mary Russell Mitford, second series*, ed. Henry Chorley, 2 vols (London: Richard Bentley & Son, 1872), i, 265, 79.
80 Mary Russell Mitford, 'MS Diary', written in *The Literary Pocket-Book* (London: C. J. Ollier, 1819). British Library C.60.b.7.
81 Of the 3,428 recorded experiences of reading fiction in the *Reading Experience Database* for the period 1800–1900, 1,767 are men and 1,664 are women. While this may partly reflect a gender imbalance towards male readers in the database as a whole, owing to the greater survival of sources written by men, the figures for fiction reading are

nonetheless a helpful correlative to Victorian assumptions that the primary market for fiction in the period was female.
82 *The Croker Papers. The Correspondence and Diaries of the Late Right Honourable John Wilson Croker, LL.D., F. R. S., Secretary to the Admiralty from 1809 to 1830*, ed. Louis J. Jennings, 3 vols (London: John Murray, 1884), iii, 306.
83 Ibid., iii, 8 and 13.
84 *Byron's Letters and Journals*, ed. Leslie A. Marchand, 12 vols (London: John Murray, 1973–1994), vii, 45.
85 *The Diary of a Canny Man 1818–1828: Adam Mackie Farmer, Merchant, and Innkeeper in Fyvie*, ed. David Stevenson (Aberdeen: Aberdeen University Press, 1991), 33.
86 Ibid., 33.
87 James Glass Bertram, *Some Memories of Books, Authors and Events* (Westminster: Constable & Co., 1893), 26.
88 Peter Berresford Ellis, *H. Rider Haggard. A Voice from the Infinite* (London: Routledge and Kegan Paul, 1978), 24.
89 *The Selected Letters of Leslie Stephen*, ed. John Bicknell, 2 vols (Basingstoke: Macmillan, 1996), i, 54.
90 *Croker Papers*, iii, 306.
91 George Moore, *Confessions of a Young Man* (1886); quoted in Philip Waller, *Writers, Readers, and Reputations: Literary Life in Britain 1870–1918* (Oxford: Oxford University Press, 2006), 666.
92 Joseph Stamper, *So Long Ago* (London: Hutchinson, 1960), 42.
93 Georgina Battiscombe, *Charlotte Mary Yonge: The Story of an Uneventful Life* (London: Constable & Co., 1943), 87.
94 Janet Penrose Trevelyan, *The Life of Mrs Humphry Ward* (London, Constable & Co., 1923), 44.
95 Inman's response to Austen is recorded in his *No Going Back* (London: Williams and Norgate, 1952), 35–47.
96 'Opinions of *Mansfield Park*', in Jane Austen, *Later Manuscripts*, ed. Janet Todd and Linda Bree (Cambridge: Cambridge University Press, 2008), 230–4.
97 Ibid.
98 Quoted in Jonathan Rose, *The Intellectual Life of the British Working Classes* (New Haven, CT: Yale University Press, 2001), 31.
99 Thomas Burt, *Thomas Burt, M. P., D. C. L., Pitman & Privy Councillor: An autobiography* (London: Unwin, 1924), 116.
100 For a representative contemporary discussion that asserts the dangers of cheap popular fiction in the shape of 'penny bloods', see Hugh Chisholm, 'How to Counteract the "Penny Dreadful"', *Fortnightly Review*, 58 (November 1895), 771. See Anna Vaninskaya, 'Learning to Read Trash: Late-Victorian Schools and the Penny Dreadful', in Halsey and Owens, 67–83, for a comparison of cultural commentators' pronouncements on the reading of 'penny bloods' and actual historical reading practices.
101 Thomas Okey, *A Basketful of Memories: An autobiographical sketch* (London: J. M. Dent, 1930), 20.
102 Ibid., 20.
103 Hans Robert Jauss, 'Literary History as a Challenge to Literary Theory', trans. Elizabeth Benzinger, *New Literary History*, 2.1, *A Symposium on Literary History* (Autumn 1970): 12.

Chapter 6: Austen's Readers I: Affection and Appropriation

1 Kathryn Sutherland, *Jane Austen's Textual Lives* (Oxford: Oxford University Press, 2005), 55–117.
2 Henry Austen, 'Biographical Notice of the Author', in *Persuasion*, ed. John Davie (Oxford and New York: Oxford University Press, 1990), 1. Hereafter 'Biographical Notice'.
3 Ibid., 4.
4 Ibid., 5.
5 Jane Austen, *Mansfield Park*, ed. John Wiltshire (Cambridge: Cambridge University Press, 2005), 71. Hereafter *Mansfield Park*.
6 'Biographical Notice', 5.
7 Ibid., 4.
8 Marginal notes on last page of National Art Library copy of Jane Austen's *Northanger Abbey*, class mark Dyce 8vo 597.
9 Nineteenth-century critical accounts that make extensive use of the 'Biographical Notice' (before the publication of Austen-Leigh's *Memoir*) include the *British Critic*'s review of *Northanger Abbey* and *Persuasion* (March 1818), cited Chapter 5, n14; the *Retrospective Review*'s review of the *Life and Adventures of Peter Wilkins* (1823), repr. in Brian Southam, *Jane Austen: The Critical Heritage*, 2 vols (London: Routledge, 1968–87), i, 107–14; Maria Jane Jewsbury's 'Literary Women: No. 2', *Athenaeum*, 27 August 1831, 553–4, and the unsigned articles on 'Miss Austen', *Englishwoman's Domestic Magazine*, July and August 1866, repr. in Brian Southam, *Jane Austen: The Critical Heritage*, 2 vols (London: Routledge, 1968–87), i, 200–14.
10 Virginia Woolf, *A Room of One's Own* (1929), ed. Michèle Barrett (London: Penguin, 1993), 69.
11 Oliphant refers to the founding of Girton College, Cambridge, in 1869.
12 *Autobiography and Letters of Mrs Margaret Oliphant*, ed. Mrs. Harry Coghill (Leicester: Leicester University Press, 1974), 221.
13 *Letters of Mary Russell Mitford, second series*, ed. Henry Chorley, 2 vols (London: Richard Bentley & Son, 1872), i, 129.
14 Catherine Hutton to John Murray, 14 November 1838, National Library of Scotland, John Murray Archive, MS Acc. 12604/124.
15 Quoted in Marjorie Astin, *Mary Russell Mitford – Her Circle and her Books* (London: Noel Douglas, 1930), 48.
16 For a fuller account of Mitford's habitually oppositional reading practices, see my '"Tell me of some booklings": Mary Russell Mitford's Literary Networks', *Women's Writing*, 18.1 (2011): 121–36.
17 Mary Russell Mitford, *Recollections of a Literary Life; or, Books, Places and People*, 3 vols (London: Richard Bentley, 1852), ii, 235.
18 *The Compact Edition of the Dictionary of National Biography*, 2 vols (Oxford: Oxford University Press, 1975), i, 1387.
19 Mitford, *Literary Life*, i, 1–2.
20 Ibid., i, dedicatory letter to H. F. Chorley.
21 Ibid., i, 202.
22 Ibid., i, vii.
23 Anne does not, in fact, take refuge in a shoe shop, but in a confectioner's: Molland's [at 2 Milsom St]. There is, however, a discussion about the relative thickness of Mrs Clay's and Anne's boots in the passage to which Mitford is referring, which may explain the slight misrecollection.
24 Mitford, *Literary Life*, ii, 197.

25 Elizabeth Wordsworth, *Glimpses of the Past* (London and Oxford: A.R. Mowbray and Co., 1912), 61.
26 *Tennyson: Interviews and Recollections*, ed. Norman Page (London and Basingstoke: Macmillan, 1983), 57.
27 Hallam Tennyson, *Alfred, Lord Tennyson: A Memoir*, 2 vols (London: Macmillan and Co, 1897), ii, 47.
28 *Tennyson: Interviews and Recollections*, 101; *Alfred, Lord Tennyson: A Memoir*, ii, 371.
29 Mitford, *Literary Life*, i, vii.
30 *Letters of Anne Thackeray Ritchie*, ed. Hester Ritchie (London: John Murray, 1924), 114.
31 Mitford, *Literary Life*, ii, 97.
32 *Mansfield Park*, 390–91.
33 *The Letters of Elizabeth Barrett Browning to Mary Russell Mitford, 1836–1854*, ed. Meredith B. Raymond and Mary Rose Sullivan, 3 vols (Waco, TX: Armstrong Browning Library of Baylor University, The Browning Institute, Wedgestone Press and Wellesley College, 1983), ii, 109. Hereafter Raymond and Sullivan. Barrett Browning quotes a letter of Mitford's (now lost) back to her.
34 James Edward Austen-Leigh, *A Memoir of Jane Austen by her Nephew* (London: Folio Society, 1989; first published 1870), 129. Hereafter *Memoir*.
35 *The Letters of Mary Russell Mitford*, ed. R. Brimley Johnson (London: John Lane The Bodley Head Ltd, 1925), 127. Hereafter Brimley Johnson.
36 Ibid., 127–28. Mitford refers to the controversial lawsuit over the Knight entail. For a full account, see Deirdre Le Faye, *Jane Austen: A Family Record*, 2nd edn (Cambridge: Cambridge University Press, 2004), 216–17.
37 Ibid., 127.
38 Ibid., 146.
39 Raymond and Sullivan, ii, 161 and ii, 183.
40 Brimley Johnson, 229.
41 [Richard Whately], review of *Northanger Abbey* and *Persuasion*, *Quarterly Review*, 24 (January 1821): 367.
42 Mitford, *Literary Life*, i, 241.
43 *The Letters of Sarah Harriet Burney*, ed. Lorna J. Clark (Athens, GA and London: University of Georgia Press, 1997), 176.
44 Ibid., 199.
45 Ibid., 201.
46 Ibid., 201.
47 Ibid., 420.
48 Ibid., 469.
49 *The Letters of Arthur Henry Hallam*, ed. Jack Kolb (Columbus: Ohio State University Press, 1981), 717. The quotation is from Tennyson's 'Marion'.
50 Ibid., 717.
51 Ibid., 734.
52 Alfred, Lord Tennyson, *In Memoriam A.H.H.*, vi, in *Poems of Tennyson*, introduced by Herbert Warren (London: Oxford University Press, 1921), 320.
53 Henry James, 'The Lesson of Balzac', in *The House of Fiction: Essays on the Novel*, ed. Leon Edel (London: Hart-Davis, 1957), 62.
54 *The Letters of Thomas Babington Macaulay*, ed. Thomas Pinney, 6 vols (Cambridge: Cambridge University Press, 1974), ii, 72.
55 *The Letters of Arthur Henry Hallam*, 734.

56 'Opinions of *Mansfield Park*', in Jane Austen, *Later Manuscripts*, ed. Janet Todd and Linda Bree (Cambridge: Cambridge University Press, 2008), 232. Hereafter *Later Manuscripts*.
57 'Opinions of *Emma*', in *Later Manuscripts*, 235 and 235–6.
58 George Otto Trevelyan, *The Life and Letters of Lord Macaulay, Volumes I & II* (Oxford: Oxford University Press, 1978), ii, 388.
59 Ibid., i, 222 and ii, 226.
60 Ibid., i, 329.
61 Ibid., ii, 388.
62 Ibid., ii, 389.
63 'Proposed Monument to Jane Austen', Letters to the Editor, *Times*, 3 January 1885.
64 *Memoir*, 79.
65 *Letters of Thomas Babington Macaulay*, ii, 344.
66 Ibid., ii, 245.
67 Ibid., ii, 280 and ii, 249.
68 Ibid., ii, 243 and ii, 142.
69 *Life and Letters of Lord Macaulay*, ii, 401.
70 See *Marginal Notes by Lord Macaulay*, ed. G. O. Trevelyan (London: Longmans, Green, & Co., 1907).
71 *Life and Letters of Lord Macaulay*, ii, 388.
72 Ibid., ii, 388.

Chapter 7: Austen's Readers II: Opposition and Resistance

1 *The Letters of Elizabeth Barrett Browning to Mary Russell Mitford, 1836–1854*, ed. Meredith B. Raymond and Mary Rose Sullivan, 3 vols (Waco, TX: Armstrong Browning Library of Baylor University, The Browning Institute, Wedgestone Press and Wellesley College, 1983), ii, 238. Hereafter Raymond and Sullivan.
2 Ibid., ii, 99.
3 *The Brontës, their Friendships, Lives and Correspondence*, ed. T. J. Wise and J. A. Symington, 4 vols (Oxford: Blackwell, 1932), ii, 180–81. Hereafter Wise and Symington.
4 P. B. Shelley, *A Defence of Poetry*, in *Shelley's Poetry and Prose*, ed. Donald H. Reiman and Sharon B. Powers (New York and London: Norton, 1977), 482.
5 Ibid., 484.
6 Ibid., 483.
7 Ibid., 480.
8 Ibid., 482.
9 Mary Russell Mitford, *Recollections of a Literary Life; or, Books, Places and People*, 3 vols (London: Richard Bentley, 1852), i, 242.
10 *Letters of Mary Russell Mitford, second series*, ed. Henry Chorley, 2 vols (London: Richard Bentley & Son, 1872), ii, 129.
11 Ibid., ii, 129.
12 Margaret Forster suggests that Elizabeth Barrett Browning's familiarity with her female predecessors and contemporaries can be attributed both to Mary Barrett's approval of female writers whom she encouraged her daughter to read, and to her daughter's desire to rebel against her perception of the frustration of her mother's confined life. Margaret Forster, *Elizabeth Barrett Browning: A Biography* (London: Chatto & Windus, 1988), 18–29.

13 Elizabeth Barrett Browning, *Aurora Leigh* (1856), ii, 232–36, in *Aurora Leigh and Other Poems*, ed. Cora Kaplan (London: The Women's Press Ltd, 1978; repr. 2001).
14 Raymond and Sullivan, ii, 99.
15 Deirdre Le Faye (ed.), *Jane Austen's Letters* (Oxford: Oxford University Press, 1995), 308. Hereafter *Letters*.
16 Ibid., 309.
17 Ibid., 212.
18 James Edward Austen-Leigh, *A Memoir of Jane Austen by her Nephew* (London: Folio Society, 1989; first published 1870), 79.
19 *Daily Telegraph*, 19 July 1917. Quoted in Claire Harman, *Jane's Fame: How Jane Austen Conquered the World* (Edinburgh: Canongate, 2009), 188.
20 'A. I. T.' [Anne Thackeray Ritchie], 'Jane Austen', *Cornhill Magazine*, 24 (1871): 158.
21 Raymond and Sullivan, iii, 118.
22 Ibid., ii, 99.
23 Ibid.
24 Ibid., ii, 99 and ii, 109.
25 [G. H. Lewes], 'Recent Novels: French and English', *Fraser's Magazine*, 36 (1847): 687.
26 Sarah Emsley, 'Laughing at our Neighbours: Jane Austen and the Problem of Charity', *Persuasions Online*, 26.1 (Winter 2005), http://www.jasna.org/persuasions/on-line/vol26no1/emsley.htm (accessed 5 August 2011).
27 Raymond and Sullivan, ii, 109.
28 Ibid., 110.
29 Wise and Symington, iii, 99.
30 *Letters*, 323.
31 [G. H. Lewes], 'The Novels of Jane Austen', *Blackwood's Edinburgh Magazine*, 86 (1859): 99.
32 Ibid., 106.
33 Ibid., 112–13.
34 *Tennyson: Interviews and Recollections*, ed. Norman Page (London and Basingstoke: Macmillan, 1983), 101.
35 Julia Kavanagh, *English Women of Letters: Biographical Sketches*, 2 vols (London: Hurst and Blackett, 1863), ii, 190.
36 Ibid., ii, 235.
37 [E. S. Dallas], review of *Felix Holt, the Radical*, *Times*, 26 June 1866, 6.
38 Anon., 'Female Novelists', *New Monthly Magazine*, 95 (May 1852): 18.
39 Lewes, 'The Novels of Jane Austen', 100.
40 Raymond and Sullivan, ii, 161.
41 For an account of the afterlife of Jewsbury's Austen article, see Joanne Wilkes, *Women Reviewing Women in Nineteenth-Century Britain: The Critical Reception of Jane Austen, Charlotte Brontë and George Eliot* (Farnham: Ashgate, 2010), 31–36.
42 John Milton, 'L'Allegro', ll. 133–34, in *Complete English Poems*, ed. Gordon Campbell (London: Everyman, 1994).
43 Unsigned review of Harriet Martineau's *Deerbrook*, *Edinburgh Review*, 69 (1839): 496.
44 Kavanagh, ii, 190.
45 Virginia Woolf, 'Jane Austen', in *Collected Essays*, 4 vols (London: Hogarth Press, 1966–67), i, 146.
46 Margaret Oliphant, *The Literary History of England in the End of the Eighteenth and Beginning of the Nineteenth Century*, 3 vols (London: Macmillan & Co., 1882), iii, 206.

47 Henry Austen, 'Biographical Notice of the Author', in *Persuasion*, ed. John Davie (Oxford and New York: Oxford University Press, 1990), 4.
48 [G. H. Lewes], 'A Word about *Tom Jones*', *Blackwood's Edinburgh Magazine*, 87 (1860): 335.
49 Raymond and Sullivan, ii, 167.
50 Ibid., ii, 183.
51 [T. B. Macaulay], 'The Diary and Letters of Mme D'Arblay', *Edinburgh Review*, 76 (1842–43): 561.
52 Raymond and Sullivan, ii, 185.
53 Ibid., ii, 186.
54 Ibid., ii, 238.
55 *Henry James' Letters 1875–83*, ed. Leon Edel (London: Macmillan, 1978), 422–3.
56 *The Letters and Diaries of John Henry Newman*, ed. Thomas Gornall et al., 32 vols (Oxford: Clarendon Press, 1961–2008), vi, 16.
57 Jane Austen, *Mansfield Park*, ed. John Wiltshire (Cambridge: Cambridge University Press, 2005), 107–8.
58 Jane Austen, *Sense and Sensibility*, ed. Edward Copeland (Cambridge: Cambridge University Press, 2006), 418.
59 *The Journal of Katherine Mansfield*, ed. J. Middleton Murry (Hamburg, Paris, Bologna: The Albatross, 1935), 23.
60 [Richard Whately], review of *Northanger Abbey* and *Persuasion*, *Quarterly Review*, 24 (January 1821): 359.
61 *Life and Correspondence of Richard Whately, D. D.*, ed. Elizabeth Jane Whately, 2 vols (London: Longmans, Green & Co., 1866), i, 235.
62 James Pereiro, *Ethos and the Oxford Movement: At the Heart of Tractarianism* (Oxford: Oxford University Press, 2008), passim.
63 [Thomas Henry Lister], review of *Women as they are*, *Edinburgh Review*, 53 (July 1830): 448–51, quoted in Brian Southam, *Jane Austen: The Critical Heritage*, 2 vols (London: Routledge, 1968–87), i, 113.
64 See *OED*, 'clever', adj. 3a and b.
65 Samuel Johnson, *Dictionary of the English Language* (London: Richard Bentley, 1755), 'clever', 4. Also available at http://johnsonsdictionaryonline.com/?page_id=7070&i=389 (accessed 19 January 2012).
66 Jane Austen, *Emma*, ed. Richard Cronin and Dorothy Macmillan (Cambridge: Cambridge University Press, 2005), 3.
67 Ibid., 37.
68 'Opinions of *Emma*', in Jane Austen, *Later Manuscripts*, ed. Janet Todd and Linda Bree (Cambridge: Cambridge University Press, 2008), 236. Hereafter *Later Manuscripts*.
69 Mary Russell Mitford, *Our Village: Sketches of Rural Character and Scenery* (London: G. & W. B. Whittaker, 1824), v.
70 Ibid., 1–2.
71 Deirdre Le Faye (ed.) *Jane Austen's Letters* (Oxford: Oxford University Press, 1995), 269.
72 Anon., Notice of *Emma*, *British Critic*, n.s. (6 July 1816): 96.
73 Mitford, *Our Village*, 244n.
74 Wise and Symington, ii, 179.
75 Ibid., ii, 179–180.
76 Raymond and Sullivan, ii, 262. In this letter Elizabeth Barrett Browning is reporting the words of her acquaintance F. G. Kenyon as 'words as nearly as possible as I should select them to express my own opinions'.

77 Ibid., ii, 260.
78 Wise and Symington, iii,99.
79 Anon., 'Miss Austen', *Englishwomen's Domestic Magazine*, 3rd series, 11 (July 1866): 238.
80 Virginia Woolf, 'Outlines: Mary Russell Mitford', in *Collected Essays*, iv, 105.
81 Raymond and Sullivan, ii, 260.
82 *OED*, 'lady', n. 1, 2a and 4a.
83 *OED*, 'lady', n. 5.
84 Deirdre Le Faye, *Jane Austen: A Family Record*, 2nd edn (Cambridge: Cambridge University Press, 2004), 279.
85 *The Letters of Arthur Henry Hallam*, 717; 'Opinions of *Mansfield Park*', in *Later Manuscripts*, 234.
86 'Miss Austen', *Englishwomen's Domestic Magazine*, 238.
87 [Richard Simpson], 'Jane Austen', *North British Review*, n.s. 13 (1870): 152.
88 Raymond and Sullivan, ii, 260.
89 Ibid., ii, 260.
90 Ibid., ii, 262.
91 *The Letters of Elizabeth Barrett Browning*, 2 vols, ed. Frederic G. Kenyon (London: Smith, Elder, & Co., 1897), ii, 217.
92 Anne Thackeray Ritchie, memorandum, spring or summer 1871, in *Anne Thackeray Ritchie: Journals and Letters*, ed. Abigail Burnham Bloom and John Maynard, with notes and biographical commentary by Lillian F. Shankman (Athens, OH: Ohio State University Press, 1994), 177.
93 Wise and Symington, ii, 181.
94 Ibid., ii, 179.
95 Ibid., iii, 99.

Chapter 8: Austen's Readers III: Friendship and Criticism

1 James Edward Austen-Leigh, *A Memoir of Jane Austen by her Nephew* (London: Folio Society, 1989; first published 1870), 91. Hereafter *Memoir*.
2 Ritchie, memorandum, spring or summer 1871, in *Anne Thackeray Ritchie: Journals and Letters*, ed. Abigail Burnham Bloom and John Maynard, with notes and biographical commentary by Lillian F. Shankman (Athens, OH: Ohio State University Press, 1994), 177–8.
3 'A. I. T.' [Anne Thackeray Ritchie], 'Jane Austen', *Cornhill Magazine*, 24 (1871): 159.
4 Ibid., 164.
5 Ibid., 159.
6 Ibid., 166.
7 Anne Thackeray Ritchie, *A Book of Sibyls* (London: Smith, Elder, & Co., 1883), 199–200.
8 Harriet Martineau, *Autobiography, with Memorials by Maria Weston Chapman*, 3 vols (London: Smith, Elder & Co., 1877), i, 100.
9 *Memoir*, 87.
10 Henry James, 'The Lesson of Balzac', in *The House of Fiction: Essays on the Novel*, ed. Leon Edel (London: Hart-Davis, 1957), 63.
11 *Memoir*, 88.
12 Coventry Patmore, *The Angel in the House* (Boston: Ticknor & Fields, 1856).
13 Recent studies that discuss Oliphant's self-positioning and her reviewing voice include Joanne Wilkes, *Women Reviewing Women in Nineteenth-Century Britain: The Critical Reception of Jane Austen, Charlotte Brontë and George Eliot* (Farnham: Ashgate, 2010), 113–24; Ann

Heilmann, 'Mrs Grundy's Rebellion: Margaret Oliphant Between Orthodoxy and the New Woman', *Women's Writing*, 6.2 (1999): 215–37; and Joanne Shattock, 'Work for Women: Margaret Oliphant's journalism', in Laurel Brake, Bill Bell and David Finkelstein (eds), *Nineteenth-Century Media and the Construction of Identities* (Basingstoke: Palgrave Macmillan, 2000), 165–77.
14 Wilkes, 128.
15 Margaret Oliphant, *The Autobiography*, ed. Elisabeth Jay (Oxford and New York: Oxford University Press, 1990), 30.
16 Ibid., 30.
17 Ibid., 15.
18 Ibid., 30.
19 [Margaret Oliphant], 'Miss Austen and Miss Mitford', *Blackwood's Edinburgh Magazine*, 108 (1870): 291.
20 Ibid., 291.
21 Ibid., 297.
22 Ibid., 297.
23 Ibid., 291.
24 Ibid., 294.
25 Ibid., 294.
26 Ibid., 291.
27 Ibid., 295.
28 *The Letters of Mary Russell Mitford*, ed. R. Brimley Johnson (London: John Lane The Bodley Head Ltd, 1925), 127.
29 Oliphant, 'Miss Austen and Miss Mitford', 295.
30 Ibid., 294.
31 Ibid., 295.
32 Ibid., 296.
33 Ibid., 295.
34 Ibid., 300.
35 Ibid., 301.
36 Ibid., 297.
37 Ibid., 296.
38 Quoted in *Felicia Hemans, Selected Poems, Letters, Reception Materials*, ed. Susan J. Wolfson (Princeton and Oxford: Princeton University Press, 2000), 531.
39 Henry Austen, 'Biographical Notice of the Author', in *Persuasion*, ed. John Davie (Oxford and New York: Oxford University Press, 1990), 4.
40 Oliphant, 'Miss Austen and Miss Mitford', 294.
41 *Autobiography and Letters of Mrs Margaret Oliphant*, ed. Mrs. Harry Coghill (Leicester: Leicester University Press, 1974), 210.
42 Joanne Wilkes discusses Oliphant's 'recurrent concern with the lack of respect with which women, including women writers, are often treated, compared with men', in *Women Reviewing Women*, 115.
43 Margaret Oliphant, *The Literary History of England in the End of the Eighteenth and Beginning of the Nineteenth Century*, 3 vols (London: Macmillan & Co., 1882), iii, 222.
44 Ibid., iii, 205, 206.
45 *Autobiography and Letters of Mrs Margaret Oliphant*, 303.
46 Ibid., 304.
47 [Leslie Stephen], 'Humour', *Cornhill Magazine*, 33 (1876): 324.
48 *Memoir*, 121.

49 Deirdre Le Faye, '*The Memoir of Jane Austen* and the Cheney Brothers', *Notes and Queries*, 56.3 (September 2009): 375.
50 Claire Harman, *Jane's Fame: How Jane Austen Conquered the World* (Edinburgh: Canongate, 2009), 158.
51 W. D. Howells, *Heroines of Fiction* (1901). Quoted in Brian Southam, *Jane Austen: The Critical Heritage*, 2 vols (London: Routledge, 1968–87), ii, 227.
52 A. C. Bradley, 'Jane Austen', *Essays and Studies* (1911). Quoted in *Critical Heritage*, ii, 234.
53 Virginia Woolf, 'Jane Austen', *Times Literary Supplement*, 19 July 1917.
54 Ibid.
55 Ibid.
56 Virginia Woolf, '*Jane Eyre* and *Wuthering Heights*', in *Collected Essays*, 4 vols (London: Hogarth Press, 1966–67), i, 186.
57 Virginia Woolf, *The Voyage Out*, ed. C. Ruth Miller and Lawrence Miller (Oxford: Blackwell, 1995; first published 1915), 51.
58 Virginia Woolf, 'Jane Austen', *Collected Essays*, i, 148.
59 Virginia Woolf, 'Jane Austen at Sixty', *New Republic* (New York), 37 (30 January 1924): 261.
60 *Katherine Mansfield: Selected Letters*, ed. Vincent O'Sullivan (Oxford and New York: Oxford University Press, 1990), 147.
61 Katherine Mansfield, 'A Ship Comes into the Harbour', *Athenaeum*, 4650 (13 June 1919), repr. in *Novels and Novelists* (London: Constable & Co, 1930), 108–11.
62 *The Diary of Virginia Woolf*, ed. Anne Olivier Bell, 5 vols (Harmondsworth: Penguin, 1979; first published 1977), i, 314. Woolf quotes the phrase 'Jane Austen up to date' from Mansfield's review.
63 *Diary of Virginia Woolf*, i, 316.
64 Deirdre Le Faye (ed.), *Jane Austen's Letters* (Oxford: Oxford University Press, 1995), 312.
65 Virginia Woolf, 'Women and Fiction', in *Collected Essays*, ii, 148.
66 Anon., 'Jane Austen', *St. Paul's Magazine*, 5 (1870): 643.
67 It is nevertheless worth pointing out that a number of journal articles about Austen in the 1870s and beyond are by women – Margaret Oliphant, Mrs Humphry Ward, Juliet Pollock and Anne Thackeray Ritchie among them.
68 *Critical Heritage*, ii, 7.
69 *The Farringford Journal of Emily Tennyson, 1853–1864*, ed. Richard J. Hutchings and Brian Hinton (Newport: Isle of Wight Country Press, 1986).
70 Ibid., 57.
71 *Tennyson: Interviews and Recollections*, ed. Norman Page (London and Basingstoke: Macmillan, 1983), 58–9.
72 Hallam Tennyson, *Alfred, Lord Tennyson: A Memoir*, 2 vols (London: Macmillan and Co, 1897), ii, 371–72.
73 *Tennyson: Interviews and Recollections*, 101.
74 Mark Twain, undated fragment, 'Jane Austen', DV201, Mark Twain Papers, University of California, Berkeley.
75 Mark Twain, letter to Joseph Twichell, 13 September 1898, quoted in *Critical Heritage*, ii, 232.
76 Emily Auerbach, *Searching for Jane Austen* (Madison: University of Wisconsin Press, 2004), 299, 301.
77 Since the eighteenth century, American writers had been seeking to write a new kind of American literature that differed from British models: 'Ideas about new kinds of literature were part of the optimistic progression to nationhood because it seemed that

this was one of the most potent areas in which to express *difference* from Britain.' Bill Ashcroft, Gareth Griffiths and Helen Tiffin, *The Empire Writes Back: Theory and practice in post-colonial literatures* (London: Routledge, 1989), 16.
78 Jane Austen, *Emma*, ed. Richard Cronin and Dorothy Macmillan (Cambridge: Cambridge University Press, 2005), 391.
79 Oliphant, *Literary History of England*, iii, 222; Rudyard Kipling, 'Jane's Marriage', in *Debits and Credits* (London: Macmillan, 1926), 175–6.
80 *Journals of Ralph Waldo Emerson 1856–1863*, ed. E. W. Emerson and W. E. Forbes (Boston: Houghton, 1913), 336–7.
81 *Mark Twain – Howells Letters*, ed. Henry Nash Smith and William M. Gibson, 2 vols (Cambridge, MA: Harvard University Press, 1960), ii, 841.
82 Ibid., ii, 769.
83 Mark Twain, *Following the Equator*, in *The Writings of Mark Twain*, Definitive Edition, 37 vols (New York: Gabriel Wells, 1922–25), xxi, 289.
84 W. D. Howells, *Heroines of Fiction* (1901). Quoted in *Critical Heritage*, ii, 227.
85 Arnold Bennett, 'Books and Persons' column, *Evening Standard*, 21 July 1927.

Chapter 9: Austen's Readers IV: Sociability and Devotion

1 'Opinions of *Mansfield Park*', in Jane Austen, *Later Manuscripts*, ed. Janet Todd and Linda Bree (Cambridge: Cambridge University Press, 2008), 232. Hereafter *Later Manuscripts*.
2 'Opinions of *Emma*', in *Later Manuscripts*, 235–6.
3 Ibid., 238.
4 'Opinions of *Mansfield Park*', in *Later Manuscripts*, 230–32.
5 *The Collected Letters of George Gissing*, ed. Paul F. Mattheisen, Arthur C. Young and Pierre Coustillas, 9 vols (Athens, OH: Ohio University Press, 1994), i, 286.
6 Elizabeth Wordsworth, *Glimpses of the Past*, 61; journal entry for 18 February 1866.
7 Georgina Battiscombe, *Charlotte Mary Yonge: The Story of an Uneventful Life* (London: Constable & Co., 1943), 58.
8 *Emma Darwin: A Century of Family Letters 1792–1896*, ed. Henrietta Litchfield, 2 vols (London: John Murray, 1915), ii, 275.
9 Ibid.
10 Anon., 'Literary Examination Paper No 7: Miss Austen's Novels: *Pride and Prejudice, Emma, Mansfield Park*', *Good Words*, 44 (1903): 526.
11 Jane Austen, *Mansfield Park*, ed. John Wiltshire (Cambridge: Cambridge University Press, 2005), 273. Hereafter *Mansfield Park*.
12 *Emma Darwin: A Century of Family Letters*, i, 141.
13 Ibid., ii, 39.
14 Ibid., ii, 11.
15 Gwen Raverat, *Period Piece: A Cambridge childhood* (London: Faber & Faber, 1987; first published 1952), 122.
16 *The Letters of Thomas Babington Macaulay*, ed. Thomas Pinney, 6 vols (Cambridge: Cambridge University Press, 1974), v, 465.
17 Ibid., iv, 351.
18 Ibid., ii, 262. The reference is to *Mansfield Park*, 416.
19 Ibid., vi, 227. The reference is to *Emma*, and is a slight misquotation. Mr Woodhouse actually says, 'That young man (speaking lower) is very thoughtless. Do not tell his

father, but that young man is not quite the thing. He has been opening the doors very often this evening, and keeping them open very inconsiderately. He does not think of the draught. I do not mean to set you against him, but indeed he is not quite the thing!' Jane Austen, *Emma*, ed. Richard Cronin and Dorothy Macmillan (Cambridge: Cambridge University Press, 2005), 268. Hereafter *Emma*.

20 Ibid., ii, 142.
21 Ibid., ii, 230.
22 Ibid., ii, 39.
23 Ibid., ii, 130–31.
24 Jane Austen, *Northanger Abbey*, ed. Barbara M. Benedict and Deirdre Le Faye (Cambridge: Cambridge University Press, 2006), 112.
25 Ibid., 113.
26 Ibid.
27 *Letters of Thomas Babington Macaulay*, ii, 157. The reference is to *Emma*, 293: 'He called her "Augusta". How delightful!'
28 *The Journals of Thomas Babington Macaulay*, ed. William Thomas, 5 vols (London: Pickering & Chatto, 2008), i, xii.
29 *Letters of Thomas Babington Macaulay*, ii, 185.
30 George Otto Trevelyan, *The Life and Letters of Lord Macaulay, Volumes I & II* (Oxford: Oxford University Press, 1978), ii, 226.
31 *Letters of Thomas Babington Macaulay*, v, 451.
32 I am indebted to Tom and Elizabeth Heydeman for their kindness and hospitality in allowing me access to the XII Club minute books and, for sharing with me their wealth of knowledge of the history of the club.
33 Secretary of the XII Club, MS 'XII Club Minute Book', 5 vols, i, 12. Private collection.
34 Ibid., i, 29.
35 Ibid., i, 11.
36 Ibid., i, 35.
37 Ibid., i, 40.
38 Ibid., i, 48.
39 Ibid., i, 60.
40 Ibid., ii, 189–90.
41 Ibid., ii, 189–90.
42 Ibid., iii, 176–7.
43 Ibid., iii, 186.
44 Rudyard Kipling, 'The Janeites', in *Debits and Credits* (London: Macmillan, 1926), 155.
45 *Daily Telegraph*, 19 July 1917. Quoted in Claire Harman, *Jane's Fame: How Jane Austen Conquered the World* (Edinburgh: Canongate, 2009), 190.
46 Winston Churchill, *The Second World War Volume V: Closing the Ring*, ed. John Kegan (New York: Houghton Mifflin, 1985; first published 1951), 377.
47 'Mr. Walkley's Sketch', *Times*, 1 April 1922.
48 Christopher Kent, 'Learning History with, and from, Jane Austen,' in *Jane Austen's Beginnings: The Juvenilia and Lady Susan*, ed. J. David Grey (Ann Arbor and London: UMI Research Press, 1989), 59.
49 'The Janeites', 173.
50 Lisa A. F. Lewis, 'Kipling's Jane: Some Echoes of Emma', *English Literature in Transition, 1880–1920*, 29.1 (1986): 76.
51 Ibid., 80–1.

52 Charles Carrington, *Rudyard Kipling: His Life and Work* (London: Macmillan, 1955). Carrie Kipling's diaries were destroyed by the trustees of her daughter's will in 1976. The quotation is therefore taken from Carrington's notes on Mrs Kipling's diaries.
53 Andrew Lycett, *Rudyard Kipling* (London: Weidenfeld & Nicolson, 1999), 513–14.
54 *The Letters of Rudyard Kipling*, ed. Thomas Pinney, 6 vols (London: Macmillan, 1990), iv, 296.
55 Claudia Johnson, 'The Divine Miss Jane: Jane Austen, Janeites, and the Discipline of Novel Studies', *boundary 2*, 23.3 (Autumn 1996): 149.
56 Ibid.
57 'A Link with Jane Austen', *Times*, 13 May 1922.
58 Arnold Bennett, 'Books and Persons', *Evening Standard*, 21 July 1927.
59 E. M. Forster, *Abinger Harvest*, quoted in Brian Southam, *Jane Austen: The Critical Heritage*, 2 vols (London: Routledge, 1968–87), ii, 279.
60 Claudia Johnson, 'The Divine Miss Jane', 150.
61 See, for example, 'Letters to the Editor', *Times*, 21 February 1898; 'Letters to the Editor', *Times*, 30 December 1925; 'Jane Austen's House: Condition of the Building', *Times*, 1 January 1926; 'Jane Austen's Old School', *Times*, 1 May 1926; 'Jane Austen's Village Home', *Times*, 31 August 1926.
62 'Jane Austen's Home', Letters to the Editor, *Times*, 7 December 1946.
63 'Aims of the Society', The Jane Austen Society Website, http://www.janeaustensoci.freeuk.com (accessed 1 December 2010).
64 See, for example, the letters on the Christian names preferred by Jane Austen (from R. Gillbard), 'Jane Austen and Richard', *Times*, 1 June 1934 and (from David Rhydderch), 'Jane Austen's "Marriage": Names of Characters', *Times*, 4 September 1936; on her opinion of the Prince Regent: 'George IV and Jane Austen' (from C.A. Whitton), *Times*, 6 May 1935 and (from H. M. Walter), 'Jane Austen and the Prince Regent', *Times*, 21 April 1926; on the changing meaning of Austen's words: (from F. S. Boas and A. K. Cook) 'Words and their Meanings', *Times*, 30 December 1921, and on the specific details of the Longbourn entail (from G. R. Y. Radcliffe), 'Jane Austen's Law: Tenants for life', *Times*, 2 April, 1929.
65 See 'The Estate Market. Usk and Test. A Link with Jane Austen', *Times*, 30 May 1928 and 'The Estate Market. Shotton Hall For Sale', *Times*, 8 February 1928.
66 A. B. W. [A. B. Walkley], 'Jane Austen: The Topographical Game', *Times*, 21 April 1920.
67 Caroline Ticknor, *Glimpses of Authors* (London: T. Werner Laurie Ltd, 1924), 305–8. A number of these items are now in the Jane Austen House Museum, Chawton, and the sketch of Jane Austen by Cassandra is in the National Portrait Gallery, London.
68 Ibid., 309.
69 Ibid., 309.
70 Ibid., 308.
71 Kipling, 'Jane's Marriage', in *Debits and Credits*, 175–6.
72 *Letters of Rudyard Kipling*, vi, 67.
73 Ibid., 150.

Conclusion

1 Mass Observation Survey File Report 1332, July 1942, *Books and the Public*, http://www.massobservation.amdigital.co.uk (accessed 29 December 2010).
2 Anna Neagle, *Anna Neagle says 'There's always tomorrow': An autobiography* (London: W. H. Allan, 1974), 146.

3 Karen Joy Fowler, *The Jane Austen Book Club* (London: Penguin, 2005; first published 2004), 249.
4 Winston Churchill, *The Second World War Volume V: Closing the Ring*, ed. John Kegan (New York: Houghton Mifflin, 1985; first published 1951), 377.
5 *The Collected Letters of William Morris*, ed. Norman Kelvin (Princeton: Princeton University Press, 1996), 341.
6 Quoted in James Edward Austen-Leigh, *A Memoir of Jane Austen by her Nephew* (London: Folio Society, 1989; first published 1870), 131.
7 Jane Austen, *Pride and Prejudice*, ed. Pat Rogers (Cambridge: Cambridge University Press, 2006), 81.
8 Anon., Review of *The Life and Adventures of Peter Wilkins*, *Retrospective Review*, 7 (1823): 133.
9 D. H. Lawrence, *Sex, Literature, and Censorship* (New York: Viking, 1959), 109.
10 An interesting perspective on Lawrence's relationship with Austen is provided by Faye Hammill in her analysis of Stella Gibbons' novel *Cold Comfort Farm*, in which she suggests that Gibbons deliberately satirizes Lawrence's view of Austen. See Faye Hammill, 'Cold Comfort Farm, D. H. Lawrence, and English Literary Culture Between the Wars', *Modern Fiction Studies*, 47.4 (Winter 2001): 831–54.
11 Philip Inman, *No Going Back* (London: Williams and Norgate, 1952), 35–47.
12 Mark Twain, undated fragment, 'Jane Austen', DV201, Mark Twain Papers, University of California, Berkeley.

BIBLIOGRAPHY

Source Materials

Anon., *The Whole Duty of Woman; or, A Complete System of Female Morality* (London: J. Wallis, 1794).

_____, *The New Female Instructor; or, Young Woman's Guide to Domestic Happiness* (London: Thomas Kelly, 1817).

_____, *The New Whole Duty of Man, Containing the Faith as Well as Practice of A Christian: Made Easy for the Practice of the Present Age* (London: W. Bent, 1841).

Aikin, J., *Letters From a Father to his Son on Various Topics, Related to Literature and the Conduct of Life. Written in the Years 1792 & 1793*, 3rd edn (London: J. Johnson, 1796).

Aikin, J. and L. Barbauld, *Evenings at Home; or, The Juvenile Budget*, 4 vols (London: T. Johnson, 1794).

Argyle, Archibald, *Instructions to a Son, Containing Rules of Conduct in Publick and Private Life, Written 1660 During his Confinement* (Glasgow: R. Foulis and Edinburgh: Hamilton & Balfour, 1743).

Arbuthnot, Harriet, *The Journal of Mrs. Arbuthnot, 1820–1832*, ed. Francis Bamford and the Duke of Wellington (London: Macmillan & Co., Ltd, 1950).

Austen, Jane, *Sense and Sensibility* (1811), ed. Edward Copeland (Cambridge: Cambridge University Press, 2006).

_____, *Pride and Prejudice* (1813), ed. Pat Rogers (Cambridge: Cambridge University Press, 2006).

_____, *Mansfield Park* (1814), ed. John Wiltshire (Cambridge: Cambridge University Press, 2005).

_____, *Emma* (1816), ed. Richard Cronin and Dorothy Macmillan (Cambridge: Cambridge University Press, 2005).

_____, *Northanger Abbey* (1818), ed. Barbara M. Benedict and Deirdre Le Faye (Cambridge: Cambridge University Press, 2006).

_____, *Persuasion* (1818), ed. Janet Todd and Antje Blank (Cambridge: Cambridge University Press, 2006).

_____, *Juvenilia*, ed. Peter Sabor (Cambridge: Cambridge University Press, 2006).

_____, *Later Manuscripts*, ed. Janet Todd and Linda Bree (Cambridge: Cambridge University Press, 2008).

_____, *The History of England, by a Partial, Prejudiced & Ignorant Historian*, ed. Deirdre Le Faye (London: British Library, 1993).

_____, *Jane Austen's Letters*, ed. Deirdre Le Faye (Oxford: Oxford University Press, 1995).

Austen, Henry, 'Biographical Notice of the Author', in *Persuasion*, ed. John Davie (Oxford and New York: Oxford University Press, 1990).

Auden, W. H., 'Letter to Lord Byron', in *Letters from Iceland* (London: Faber & Faber, 1937; repr. 1965).

Ashcroft, Bill, Gareth Griffiths and Helen Tiffin, *The Empire Writes Back: Theory and practice in post-colonial literatures* (London: Routledge, 1989).

Barker, Juliet, *The Brontës: A Life in Letters* (Harmondsworth: Penguin, 1997).

Barrett, Eaton Stannard, *The Heroine; or, Adventures of a Fair Romance Reader*, 3 vols (London: Henry Colburn, 1813).

Bell, Anne Olivier (ed.), *The Diary of Virginia Woolf*, 5 vols (Harmondsworth: Penguin, 1979; first published 1977).

Bell, Eva Mary, *The Hamwood papers of the Ladies of Llangollen and Caroline Hamilton* (London: Macmillan, 1930).

Bennett, John, *Strictures on Female Education; Chiefly as it Relates to the Culture of the Heart, in Four Essays* (1787) (London: T. Cadell, 1788).

———, *Letters to a young lady on a variety of useful and interesting subjects*, 2 vols (Warrington: W. Eyres, 1789).

Bennett, Betty T. (ed.), *The Letters of Mary Wollstonecraft Shelley*, 3 vols (Baltimore and London: The Johns Hopkins University Press, 1980–88).

Bell, Vanessa, *Selected Letters of Vanessa Bell*, ed. Regina Marler (London: Bloomsbury, 1993).

Berquin, Arnaud, *The Children's Friend*, trans. Lucas Williams, 6 vols (London: J. Stockdale et al., 1793).

———, *L'Ami de l'Adolescence* (Paris: n.p., 1786).

Berridge, Elizabeth (ed.), *The Barretts at Hope End: The Early Diary of Elizabeth Barrett Browning* (London: John Murray, 1974).

Berry, Mary, *Extracts of the Journals and Correspondence of Miss Berry from the Year 1783 to 1852*, ed. Lady Theresa Lewis, 3 vols (London: Longmans, Green, & Co., 1865).

Bertram, James Glass, *Some Memories of Books, Authors and Events* (Westminster: Constable & Co., 1893).

Bessborough, Earl of, *The Diary of Lady Charlotte Guest* (London: John Murray, 1950).

Bicknell, John (ed.), *The Selected Letters of Leslie Stephen*, 2 vols (Basingstoke: Macmillan, 1996).

Brimley Johnson, R. (ed.), *The Letters of Mary Russell Mitford* (London: John Lane The Bodley Head Ltd, 1925).

Broughton, John Cam Hobhouse, Lord, *Recollections of a Long Life*, 6 vols (London: John Murray, 1907).

Browning, Elizabeth Barrett, *Aurora Leigh* (1856), in *Aurora Leigh and Other Poems*, ed. Cora Kaplan (London: The Women's Press Ltd, 1978; repr. 2001).

Burney, Frances, *Cecilia, or Memoirs of an Heiress* (1782), ed. Margaret Anne Doody and Peter Sabor (Oxford: Oxford University Press, 1999).

———, *Camilla; or, a Picture of Youth* (1796), ed. Edward A. Bloom and Lillian D. Bloom (Oxford: Oxford University Press, 1995).

———, *Evelina; or, a Young Lady's Entrance into the World* (1798), ed. Susan Kubica Howard (Ontario: Broadview Press, 2000).

———, *The Diary and Letters of Madame D'Arblay*, ed. W. C. Ward, 3 vols (London: Frederick Warne & Co, n.d.).

Burnham Bloom, Abigail and John Maynard (eds), *Anne Thackeray Ritchie, Journals and Letters* (Athens, OH: Ohio State University Press, 1994).

Burt, Thomas, *Thomas Burt, M. P., D. C. L., Pitman & Privy Councillor: An autobiography* (London: Unwin, 1924).

Byron, George Gordon, Lord, 'A Fragment', in *Lord Byron: The Major Works*, ed. Jerome J. McGann (Oxford: Oxford University Press, 1986).
Caraccioli, Marquis, *Advice From a Lady of Quality to her Children; in the Last Stage of a Lingering Illness*, 4th edn, trans. S. Glasse (Gloucester: R. Raikes, 1786).
Carey, Frances Jane, *Journal of a Tour in France in the Years 1816 and 1817* (London: Taylor and Hessey, 1823).
Caroll, John, (ed.), *Selected Letters of Samuel Richardson* (Oxford: Clarendon Press, 1964).
Cervantes, Miguel, *Don Quixote* (1605–15) (Ware: Wordsworth Classics, 1993).
Chapone, Hester, *Letters on the Improvement of the Mind, Addressed to a Young Lady* (1773), 2 vols (London: J. Walter, 1774).
_____, *A Letter to a New-Married Lady* (London: E. & C. Dilly and J. Walter, 1777).
Chapple, J. A. V. and Arthur Pollard (eds), *The Letters of Mrs Gaskell* (Manchester: Mandolin, 1997).
Chesterfield, Earl of, *Advice to his Son, on Men and Manners* (1774), 7th edn (London: W. J. and J. Richardson, 1799).
_____, *Characters of Eminent Personages of his own Time, Written by the Late Earl of Chesterfield* (London: William Fleckney, 1777).
Chorley, Henry (ed.), *Letters of Mary Russell Mitford Second Series*, 2 vols (London: Richard Bentley & Son, 1872).
Churchill, Winston, *The Second World War Volume V: Closing the Ring*, ed. John Kegan (New York: Houghton Mifflin, 1985; first published 1951).
Clark, Lorna (ed.), *The Letters of Sarah Harriet Burney* (Athens, GA and London: University of Georgia Press, 1997).
Cleland, John, *Fanny Hill; or, Memoirs of a Woman of Pleasure* (1748–49), ed. Peter Wagner (Harmondsworth: Penguin, 1985).
Clinton, Catherine (ed.), *Fanny Kemble's Journals* (Cambridge, MA: Harvard University Press, 2000).
Coleridge, S. T., 'On the Constitution of the Church and State', ed. John Colmer, in *The Collected Works of Samuel Taylor Coleridge*, 16 vols (London: Routledge & Kegan Paul, 1976), x.
Cowper, William, *The Task* (1785), in *The Task and Selected Other Poems*, ed. James Sambrook (London & New York: Longman, 1994).
_____, *Poems 1782* (Ilkley & London: The Scolar Press, 1973).
Crabbe, George, *Tales* (1812), 2nd edn (London: J. Hatchard, 1813).
Darwin, Erasmus, *Zoonomia* (1794–96), ed. Thom Verhase and Paul R. Bindler, 2 vols (New York: A.M.S. Press, Inc., 1974).
_____, *A Plan for the Conduct of Female Education in Boarding Schools* (Derby: J. Johnson, 1797).
de Selincourt, Ernest (ed.), *The Letters of William and Dorothy Wordsworth: The Middle Years*, 2 vols (Oxford: Clarendon Press, 1937).
Dibdin, T. F., *Bibliomania: or Book-madness; a Bibliographical Romance* (London: J. M'Creery, 1811).
Dickinson, Emily, *The Complete Poems*, ed. Thomas H. Johnson (London and Boston: Faber & Faber, 1970).
Donne, John, *The Second Anniversarie of the Progres of the Soule* (London: A. Mathewes for Tho. Dewes, 1621).
Dowden, Wilfred S. (ed.), *The Letters of Thomas Moore* (Oxford: Clarendon Press, 1964).
Doyle, John A. (ed.), *Memoir and Correspondence of Susan Ferrier 1782–1854* (London: John Murray, 1898).

Edel, Leon (ed.), *Henry James' Letters 1875–83* (London: Macmillan, 1978).
Edgeworth, Maria, *Letters for Literary Ladies* (London: J. Johnson, 1795).
_____, *Belinda* (1801), ed. Kathryn J. Kirkpatrick (Oxford: Oxford University Press, 1994).
_____, *The Novels and Selected Works of Maria Edgeworth*, general editor Marilyn Butler, 11 vols (London: Pickering & Chatto, 1999–2003).
Edgeworth, Maria and R. L. Edgeworth, *Practical Education* (1798), ed. Jonathan Wordsworth, 3 vols (New York: Woodstock Books, 1996).
Emerson, E. W. and W. E. Forbes (eds), *Journals of Ralph Waldo Emerson 1856–1863* (Boston: Houghton, 1913).
Feldman, Paula R. and Diana Scott-Kilvert, *The Journals of Mary Shelley 1814–1844* (Baltimore and London: The Johns Hopkins University Press, 1987; repr. 1995).
Ferrier, Susan, *Marriage* (1818), ed. Herbert Foltinek (Oxford: Oxford University Press, 2001).
Fielding, Henry, *The History of Tom Jones, a Foundling* (1749) (Ware: Wordsworth Classics, 1992).
Fordyce, James, *Sermons for Young Women* (1765), 2 vols (London: A. Millar & T. Cadell, 1766).
Forster, E. M., *E. M. Forster's Letters to Donald Windham* (Verona: Sandy Campbell, 1975).
Fowler, Karen Joy, *The Jane Austen Book Club* (London: Penguin, 2005; first published 2004).
Gisborne, Thomas, *An Enquiry into the Duties of the Female Sex* (1797) (London: T. Cadell, 1798).
_____, *An Enquiry into the Duties of Men in the Higher and Middle Classes of Society in Great Britain* (London: n.p., 1794).
_____, *The Principles of Moral Philosophy Investigated, and Briefly Applied to the Constitution of Civil Society* (London: B. White & Son, 1789).
_____, *Walks in a Forest* (London: n.p., 1794).
_____, *Poems, Sacred and Moral* (London: n.p., 1798).
Godwin, William, *Things As They Are; or, The Adventures of Caleb Williams* (1794), ed. David McCracken (Oxford: Oxford University Press, 1982).
Gornall, Thomas, Ian Ker, Gerard Tracey, Francis McGrath, and Charles Dessain (eds), *The Letters and Diaries of John Henry Newman*, 32 vols (Oxford: Clarendon Press, 1961–2008).
Gregory, John, *A Father's Legacy to his Daughters* (1774) (London: W. Lane, 1795).
Halifax, Earl, *The Lady's New-Year's-Gift: or Advice to a Daughter* (1680), 10th edn (Dublin: A. Rhames, 1724).
Harris, Margaret and Judith Johnston (eds), *The Journals of George Eliot* (Cambridge: Cambridge University Press, 1998).
Hale, Sarah Josepha, *Biography of Distinguished Women; or, Woman's Record, from the Creation to A. D. 1869* (New York: Harper & Bros, 1876; first published 1851).
Hawkins, Ann. R. and Maura Ives (eds), *Women Writers and the Artifacts of Celebrity* (Aldershot: Ashgate, 2012).
Hays, Mary, *The Memoirs of Emma Courtney* (1796), ed. Eleanor Ty (Oxford: Oxford University Press, 2000).
Heydon, Peter N. and Philip Kelley (eds), *Elizabeth Barrett Browning's Letters to Mrs. David Ogilvy 1849–1861, with Recollections by Mrs. Ogilvy* (London: John Murray, 1974).
Home, John, *Douglas: A Tragedy* (London: A. Millar, 1757).
House, Madeline and Graham Storey (eds), *The Letters of Charles Dickens*, 12 vols (Oxford: Clarendon, 1965).

Hume, David, *Four Dissertations* (London: A. Millar, 1757).
Hunter, Robert, *Advice from a Father to his Son Just Entered into The Army and About to Go Abroad into Action. In Seven Letters* (London: J. Johnson, 1776).
Hutchings, Richard J., and Brian Hinton (eds), *The Farringford Journal of Emily Tennyson, 1853–1864* (Newport: Isle of Wight Country Press, 1986).
Hutton, Catherine, *Letter to John Murray*, 14 November 1838, National Library of Scotland, John Murray Archive, MS Acc. 12604/124.
Inchbald, Elizabeth, *Lovers' Vows*, adapted from the German of August von Kotzebue (1798) (Oxford and New York: Woodstock Books, 1990).
Inman, Philip, *No Going Back* (London: Williams and Norgate, 1952).
Jameson, Anna, *Letters & Friendships 1812–1860*, ed. Mrs Steuart Erskine (London: T. Fisher Unwin, Ltd, 1915).
Jennings, Louis J., *The Croker Papers. The Correspondence and Diaries of the Late Right Honourable John Wilson Croker, LL.D., F.R.S., Secretary to the Admiralty from 1809 to 1830*, 3 vols (London: John Murray, 1884).
Johnson, Samuel, *Dictionary of the English Language* (London: Richard Bentley, 1755).
_____, *The History of Rasselas Prince of Abissinia* (1759), ed. J. P. Hardy (Oxford: Oxford University Press, 1988).
Kavanagh, Julia, *English Women of Letters: Biographical Sketches*, 2 vols (London: Hurst and Blackett, 1863).
Kingston Stocking, Marion (ed.), *The Journals of Claire Clairmont* (Cambridge, MA: Harvard University Press, 1968).
Kipling, Rudyard, *Debits and Credits* (London: Macmillan, 1926).
Kenyon, Frederick G. (ed.), *The Letters of Elizabeth Barrett Browning*, 2 vols (London: Smith, Elder, & Co., 1897).
Kelvin, Norman (ed.), *The Collected Letters of William Morris* (Princeton: Princeton University Press, 1996).
Kolb, Jack (ed.), *The Letters of Arthur Henry Hallam* (Columbus: Ohio State University Press, 1981).
Lawrence, D .H., *Sex, Literature, and Censorship* (New York: Viking, 1959).
Lennox, Charlotte, *The Female Quixote* (1752), ed. Margaret Dalziel (Oxford: Oxford University Press, 1989).
L'Estrange, A. G. (ed.), *The Friendships of Mary Russell Mitford as Recorded in Letters from her Literary Correspondents*, 2 vols (London: Hurst and Blackett, 1870).
_____ (ed.), *The Life of Mary Russell Mitford: Related in a Selection from her Letters to her Friends*, 3 vols (London: Richard Bentley, 1870).
Leveson Gower, F., *Letters of Harriet, Countess Granville 1810–1845*, 2 vols (London: Longmans, Green, & Co., 1894).
Lewis, Matthew, *The Monk* (1796), ed. Howard Andersen (Oxford: Oxford University Press, 1989).
Litchfield, Henrietta (ed.), *Emma Darwin: A Century of Family Letters 1792–1896*, 2 vols (London: John Murray, 1915).
Macartney, George, *An Embassy to China: Lord Macartney's Journal*, ed. Lancelot Cranmer-Byng (London: Longmans, Green & Co., 1962).
Marchand, Leslie A. (ed.), *Byron's Letters and Journals*, 12 vols (London: John Murray, 1973–1994).
Martineau, Harriet, *Autobiography, with Memorials by Maria Weston Chapman*, 3 vols (London: Smith, Elder & Co., 1877).

Mattheisen, Paul F., Arthur C. Young and Pierre Coustillas (eds), *The Collected Letters of George Gissing*, 9 vols (Athens, OH: Ohio University Press, 1994).

Mayne, Ethel C., *The Life and Letters of Anne Isabella, Lady Noel Byron* (London: Dawsons of Pall Mall, 1969).

Milton, John, *Paradise Lost* (1667), ed. Alastair Fowler (London and New York: Longman, 1968).

———, *Complete English Poems*, ed. Gordon Campbell (London: Everyman, 1994).

Middleton Murry, J. (ed.), *Journal of Katherine Mansfield* (Hamburg, Paris and Bologna: The Albatross, 1935).

Mitford, Mary Russell, *Recollections of a Literary Life; or, Books, Places and People*, 3 vols (London: Richard Bentley, 1852).

———, manuscript diary, written in and over *The Literary Pocket-Book, 1819*, ed. Leigh Hunt (London: C. J. Ollier, 1819) [British Library C.60.b.7].

———, *Our Village: Sketches of Rural Character and Scenery* (London: G. & W. B. Whittaker, 1824).

More, Hannah, *Strictures on the Modern System of Female Education* (1799), 2 vols (New York and London: Garland Publishing, 1974).

———, *Cœlebs in Search of a Wife* (1808), ed. Mary Waldron (Bristol: Thoemmes Press, 1995).

Murry, Ann, *Mentoria: or the Young Ladies' Instructor, in Familiar Conversations on Moral and Entertaining Subjects Calculated to Improve Young Minds, in the Essential as Well as Ornamental Part of Female Education* (Dublin: Price, Sheppard [...] & Watson, 1779).

Neagle, Anna, *Anna Neagle says 'There's always tomorrow': An autobiography* (London: W. H. Allan, 1974).

Page, Norman (ed.), *Tennyson: Interviews and Recollections* (London and Basingstoke: Macmillan, 1983).

Patmore, Coventry, *The Angel in the House* (1854) (Boston: Ticknor & Fields, 1856).

Okey, Thomas, *A Basketful of Memories: An autobiographical sketch* (London: J. M. Dent, 1930).

Oliphant, Margaret, *The Autobiography*, ed. Elisabeth Jay (Oxford and New York: Oxford University Press, 1990).

———, *Autobiography and Letters*, ed. Mrs Harry Coghill with an introduction by Q. D. Leavis (Leicester: Leicester University Press, 1974).

———, *The Literary History of England in the End of the Eighteenth and Beginning of the Nineteenth Century*, 3 vols (London: Macmillan & Co., 1882).

O'Sullivan, Vincent (ed.), *Katherine Mansfield: Selected Letters* (Oxford and New York: Oxford University Press, 1990).

Plato, *Republic*, trans. Paul Shorey, Loeb Classical Library, 276, 2 vols (Cambridge, MA and London: Harvard University Press, 1935; repr. 1994).

Raverat, Gwen, *Period Piece: A Cambridge Childhood* (1952) (London: Faber & Faber, 1987).

Raymond, Meredith B. and Mary Rose Sullivan (eds), *The Letters of Elizabeth Barrett Browning to Mary Russell Mitford, 1836–1854*, 3 vols (Waco, TX: Armstrong Browning Library of Baylor University, The Browning Institute, Wedgestone Press and Wellesley College, 1983).

———, *Women of Letters: Selected Letters of Elizabeth Barrett Browning and Mary Russell Mitford* (Boston: Twayne Publishers, 1987).

Richardson, Samuel, *Pamela; or, Virtue Rewarded* (1740), ed. Margaret Anne Doody (London: Penguin, 1985).

———, *Clarissa; or, The History of a Young Lady* (1747–48), ed. Angus Ross (Harmondsworth: Viking, 1985).

———, *Sir Charles Grandison* (1753–54), ed. Jocelyn Harris (Oxford: Oxford University Press, 1986).
Ritchie, Anne Thackeray, *A Book of Sibyls* (London: Smith, Elder, & Co., 1883).
Ritchie, Hester (ed.), *Letters of Anne Thackeray Ritchie* (London: John Murray, 1924).
Roland, Marie-Jeanne, *Memoires de Madame Roland* (1793), ed. C. L. Perroud, 2 vols (Paris: Librairie Plon, 1905).
Sanders Arbuckle, Elisabeth, *Harriet Martineau's Letters to Fanny Wedgwood* (Stanford, CA: Stanford University Press, 1983).
Schreiber, Lady Charlotte, *Extracts from her Journal 1853–1891*, ed. the Earl of Bessborough (London: John Murray, 1952).
Secretary of the XII Club, MS 'XII Club Minute Book', 5 vols. Private collection.
Scott, Sarah, *The Test of Filial Duty* (1772), in *Bluestocking Feminism: Writings of the Bluestocking Circle 1738–1785*, ed. Gary Kelly, 6 vols (London: Pickering & Chatto, 1999), vi.
Scott, Walter, *Marmion: A Tale of Flodden Field* (1808) (London: Alexander Murray, [?1869]).
Sidney, Sir Philip, *Defence of Poesie* (1595) (Menston: Scolar Press Facsimile, 1968).
Sharp, William (ed.), *The Life and Letters of Joseph Severn* (London: Sampson Low, Marston, 1892).
Shelley, P. B., *Shelley's Poetry and Prose*, ed. Donald H. Reiman and Sharon B. Powers (New York and London: Norton, 1977).
Sheridan, Richard Brinsley, *The Dramatic Works of Richard Brinsley Sheridan*, ed. Cecil Price, 2 vols (Oxford: Clarendon Press, 1973).
Simms, William Gilmore, *Beauchampe; or, The Kentucky Tragedy: A Tale of Passion*, 2 vols (Philadelphia: Lea & Blanchard, 1842).
Smiles, Samuel, *A Publisher and his Friends: Memoir and Correspondence of the late John Murray*, 2 vols (London: John Murray, 1891).
Smith, Henry Nash and William M. Gibson (eds), *Mark Twain – Howells Letters*, 2 vols (Cambridge MA: Harvard University Press, 1960).
Smollett, Tobias, *The Expedition of Humphry Clinker* (1771), ed. Angus Ross (Harmondsworth: Penguin, 1967).
Stamper, Joseph, *So Long Ago* (London: Hutchinson, 1960).
Sterne, Laurence, *A Sentimental Journey Through France and Italy* (1768) (Harmondsworth: Penguin, 1986).
———, *The Life and Opinions of Tristram Shandy, Gentleman* (1759–66), ed. Tim Parnell (London: Everyman, 2000).
Stevenson, David (ed.), *The Diary of a Canny Man 1818–1828: Adam Mackie Farmer, Merchant, and Innkeeper in Fyvie* (Aberdeen: Aberdeen University Press, 1991).
Swift, Jonathan, *Cadenus and Vanessa: A Poem* (London: J. Roberts, 1726).
Tait, J. G. (ed.), *Journal of Sir Walter Scott* (Edinburgh and London: Oliver & Boyd, 1939; repr. 1950).
Tennyson, Alfred, Lord, *Poems of Tennyson*, introduced by Herbert Warren (London: Oxford University Press, 1921).
Tennyson, Hallam, *Alfred Lord Tennyson: A Memoir by his Son*, 2 vols (London: Macmillan and Co., 1897).
Thomas, William (ed.), *Journals of Thomas Babington Macaulay*, 5 vols (London: Pickering & Chatto, 2008).
Trevelyan, George Otto, *The Life and Letters of Lord Macaulay, Volumes I & II* (Oxford: Oxford University Press, 1978).

_____ (ed.), *Marginal Notes by Lord Macaulay* (London: Longmans, Green, & Co, 1907).
Trevelyan, Janet Penrose, *The Life of Mrs. Humphry Ward by her Daughter* (London: Constable & Co., 1923).
Twain, Mark, 'Jane Austen', DV201, Mark Twain Papers, University of California, Berkeley.
_____, *Following the Equator*, in *The Writings of Mark Twain*, Definitive Edition, 37 vols, New York: Gabriel Wells, 1922–25), xxi.
Wakefield, Priscilla, *Mental Improvement* (1794–97), ed. Ann B. Shteir (East Lansing: Colleagues Press, 1995).
West, Jane, *Letters to a Young Lady* (1818), in *Female Education in the Age of Enlightenment*, 6 vols (London: William Pickering, 1996), iv–vi.
Whately, Elizabeth J. (ed.), *Life and Correspondence of Richard Whately, D. D.*, 2 vols (London: Longmans, Green, & Co., 1866).
Wise, T. J. and J. A. Symington (eds), *The Brontës: Their Lives, Friendships and Correspondence*, 4 vols (Oxford: Blackwell, 1932).
Wollstonecraft, Mary, *Thoughts on the Education of Daughters* (1787) (Oxford and New York: Woodstock Books, 1994).
_____, *A Vindication of the Rights of Woman* (1792) (London: Everyman, 1992).
_____, *Female Reader* (1789), ed. Moira Ferguson (Delmar, NY: Scholars' Facsimiles & Reprints, 1979).
Wolfson, Susan J. (ed.), *Felicia Hemans: Selected Poems, Letters, Reception Materials* (Princeton and Oxford: Princeton University Press, 2000).
Woolf, Virginia, *The Voyage Out* (1915), ed. C. Ruth Miller and Lawrence Miller (Oxford: Blackwell, 1995).
_____, *Kew Gardens* (London: Hogarth Press, 1919).
Wordsworth, Dorothy, *The Grasmere and Alfoxden Journals*, ed. Pamela Woof (Oxford: Oxford University Press, 2002).
Wordsworth, Elizabeth, *Glimpses of the Past* (London and Oxford: A. R. Mowbray & Co., 1912).
Wright, Thomas (ed.), *The Correspondence of William Cowper*, 4 vols (London: Hodder & Stoughton, 1904).

Works of Criticism

A. B. W. [A. B. Walkley], 'Jane Austen: The Topographical Game', *Times*, 21 April 1920.
Altick, Richard D., *The English Common Reader: A Social History of the Mass Reading Public 1800–1900* (Chicago: University of Chicago Press, 1957).
'An Editor', 'Candour in English Fiction', *Macmillan's Magazine*, 61 (1889–90): 314–20.
Anon., 'On Shamefacedness', *New Lady's Magazine*, 1 (1786): 27.
_____, unsigned review of *Sense and Sensibility*, *Critical Review*, n.s. 4.1 (1812): 149–57.
_____, unsigned review of *Sense and Sensibility*, *British Critic*, 39 (1812): 527.
_____, unsigned notice of *Pride and Prejudice*, *British Critic*, 16 (1813): 189–90.
_____, unsigned review of *Pride and Prejudice*, *Critical Review*, 4th series, 3 (1813): 318–24.
_____, unsigned review of *Pride and Prejudice*, *New Review; or, Monthly Analysis of General Literature*, 1 (April 1813): 393–96; repr. in *Nineteenth Century Fiction*, 29 (1974–75): 336–38.
_____, unsigned review of *Emma*, *The Champion*, 31 March 1816, 102–3; repr. in *Nineteenth Century Fiction*, 26 (1971–72): 469–74.

———, unsigned review of *Emma*, *The Augustan Review*, 2 (May 1816): 484–86; repr. in *Nineteenth Century Fiction*, 26 (1971–72): 474–76.
———, unsigned notice of *Emma*, *Literary Panorama*, n.s. 6 (1816): 418.
———, unsigned notice of *Emma*, *Monthly Review*, 80 (July 1816): 320.
———, unsigned notice of *Emma*, *British Critic*, n.s. 6 (July 1816): 96–98.
———, review of *Emma*, *British Lady's Magazine, and Monthly Miscellany*, 4 (September 1816): 180–81.
———, unsigned notice of *Emma*, *Gentleman's Magazine*, 86 (1816): 248–49.
———, unsigned review of *Northanger Abbey* and *Persuasion*, *British Critic*, n.s. 9 (1818): 293–301.
———, unsigned review of Felicia Hemans' *Tales and Historic Scenes* (1819), *Monthly Review*, 2nd series, 90 (December 1819): 408–12.
———, unsigned review of Felicia Hemans' *The Siege of Valencia* (1832), *British Critic*, n.s. 20 (1823): 50–61.
———, review of Harriet Martineau's *Deerbrook*, *Edinburgh Review*, 69 (1839): 494–502.
———, 'Moral and Political Tendency of the Modern Novels', *Church of England Quarterly Review*, 11 (1842): 286–310.
———, 'Easy Spelling and Hard Reading', in *Household Words*, 1 (30 March – 21 September 1850): 561–62.
———, 'Recent Novels', *Edinburgh Review or Critical Journal*, 97 (1853): 380–90.
———, 'Social Employment of Women', *Ladies' Treasury: An Illustrated Magazine of Entertaining Literature, Education, Fine Art, Domestic Economy, Needlework and Fashion*, 1 (1858): 21–31.
———, 'Madame D'Arblay', *Ladies' Treasury*, 1 (1858): 113–15.
———, 'Conduct and Carriage', *Ladies' Treasury*, 1 (1858): 270–72.
———, 'New Books', *Ladies' Treasury*, 1 (1858): 54.
———, 'Learned Ladies Three Hundred Years Ago', *Englishwoman's Domestic Magazine*, 5.7 (November 1856): 203–7.
———, 'Women: Their Duties, Privileges, and Social Position', *What-Not or Ladies' Handy-Book* (1859): 85–86, 111–12, 127–28, 153–54.
———, 'Literary Notices', *Ladies' Treasury*, 4 (1860): 254, 322–23.
———, 'Sensation Literature', *Ladies' Treasury*, n.s. 7.37 (1862): 14–20.
———, 'Aunt Anastasia on Modern Novels', *Tinsley's Magazine*, 1 (1867): 308–16.
———, 'The Reviewer of the Period', *Tinsley's Magazine*, 2 (1868): 617–22.
———, '*Clarissa*', *Tinsley's Magazine*, 3 (1868–69): 311–20.
———, 'Dr. Trusler's Maxims', *Tinsley's Magazine*, 4 (1869): 118–28.
———, 'Modern Views about Women', *Tinsley's Magazine*, 5 (1869–70): 660–64.
———, 'The Uses of Fiction', *Tinsley's Magazine*, 6 (1870): 180–85.
———, 'Jane Austen', *St. Paul's Magazine*, 5 (1870): 631–43.
———, 'On the Forms of Publishing Fiction', *Tinsley's Magazine*, 10 (1872): 411–14.
———, 'Genius and Liberty', *Household Words*, 2 (1850–51): 19–22.
———, 'Free Public Libraries', *Household Words*, 3 (1851): 80–82.
———, 'Mrs. Shelley', *The Ladies' Companion and Monthly Magazine*, 3 (1851): 62–3.
———, 'Sentimental Journalism', *Household Words*, 4 (1851–52): 550–52.
———, 'Female Novelists', *New Monthly Magazine*, 95 (May, 1852): 17–23.
———, 'Different Classes of Readers', *Leisure Hour: A Family Journal of Instruction and Recreation*, 1 (1852): 15.
———, 'Miss Austen', *Englishwomen's Domestic Magazine*, 3rd series, 11 (July 1866): 237–40.

―――, 'On Fiction as an Educator', *Blackwood's Edinburgh Magazine*, 108 (October, 1870): 449–59.

―――, review of Austen-Leigh's *A Memoir of Jane Austen*, and *The Life of Mary Russell Mitford, Authoress of 'Our Village' etc: related in a selection from her letters to her friends*, ed. A. G. L'Estrange, *Quarterly Review*, 128 (1870): 196–218.

―――, 'Harriet Martineau', *Macmillan's Magazine*, 36 (1877): 47–60.

―――, 'Recent Fiction in England and France', *Macmillan's Magazine*, 50 (1884): 250–60.

―――, 'The Office of Literature', *Macmillan's Magazine*, 53 (1885–86): 361–63.

―――, 'Some Thoughts About Novels', *Macmillan's Magazine*, 55 (1886–87): 358–65.

―――, composite review of *The Head of a Family, Agatha's Husband, Villette*, & *Clare Abbey*, *Edinburgh Review or Critical Journal*, 97 (1853): 380–90.

―――, 'Thackeray's Works', *Edinburgh Review*, 99 (1854): 196–243.

―――, review of Harriet Beecher Stowe's *Uncle Tom's Cabin, or Life Among the Lowly*, *Edinburgh Review*, 101 (1855): 294–321.

―――, review of George Eliot's *Middlemarch*, *Edinburgh Review*, 136 (1872): 246–63.

―――, review of *The Life and Adventures of Peter Wilkins*, *Retrospective Review*, 7 (1823): 120–83.

―――, 'Memoir and Letters of Sara Coleridge, edited by her daughter', *Edinburgh Review or Critical Journal*, 139 (1874): 44–68.

―――, 'Letters and reminiscences from Last Century', *Good Words*, 43 (1902): 694–700, 771–7, 859–65.

―――, 'Literary Examination Paper No 7: Miss Austen's Novels: *Pride and Prejudice, Emma, Mansfield Park*', *Good Words*, 44 (1903): 526–27.

Archep, William, 'Criticism as An Inductive Science', *Macmillan's Magazine*, 54 (1886): 45–54.

Armstrong, Nancy, *Desire and Domestic Fiction: A Political History of the Novel* (New York and Oxford: Oxford University Press, 1987).

Armstrong, Nancy and Leonard Tennenhouse, *The Ideology of Conduct: Essays on Literature and the History of Sexuality* (New York and London: Methuen, 1987).

Arnold, Matthew, 'On the Modern Element in Literature', *Macmillan's Magazine*, 19 (1868–69): 304–14.

Astin, Marjorie, *Mary Russell Mitford – Her Circle and her Books* (London: Noel Douglas, 1930).

Austen, Caroline, *My Aunt Jane Austen: A Memoir* (London: Spottiswood, Ballantyne and Co., 1952).

―――, *Reminiscences of Jane Austen's niece Caroline Austen*, ed. Deirdre Le Faye (Chawton: Jane Austen Society, 1986; revised edn 2004).

Austen, Henry, 'Biographical Notice of the Author', in *Persuasion*, ed. John Davie (Oxford and New York: Oxford University Press, 1990).

Austen-Leigh, James Edward, *A Memoir of Jane Austen by her Nephew* (1870), ed. Fay Weldon (London: Folio Society, 1989).

Austen-Leigh, Mary Augusta, *Personal Aspects of Jane Austen* (London: John Murray, 1920).

Auerbach, Emily, *Searching for Jane Austen* (Madison: University of Wisconsin Press, 2004).

Baggerman, Arianne, 'The Cultural Universe of a Dutch Child: Otto van Eck and his Literature', *Eighteenth-Century Studies*, 31.1 (1997): 129–33.

Bakhtin, Mikhail, *Problems of Doestoevsky's Poetics* (1963), trans. Caryl Emerson (Minneapolis: University of Minnesota Press, 1984).

_____, *The Dialogic Imagination*, ed. Michael Holquist, trans. Caryl Emerson and Michael Holquist (Austin and London: University of Texas Press, 1981).
_____, *Speech Genres and Other Late Essays*, ed. Caryl Emerson and Michael Holquist, trans. Vern W. McGee (Austin: University of Texas Press, 1986).
Barker, Gerard A., *Grandison's Heirs: The Paragon's Progress in the Late Eighteenth-Century Novel* (London and Toronto: Associated University Presses, 1985).
Barthes, Roland, *Mythologies* (1956), selected and trans. Annette Lavers (London: Jonathan Cape, 1972).
_____, *S / Z* (1970), trans. Richard Miller (London: Jonathan Cape, 1975).
_____, *The Pleasure of the Text* (1973), trans. Richard Miller (New York: Hill and Wang, 1975).
_____, *Image-Music-Text* (1977), selected and trans. Stephen Heath (London: Flamingo, 1984).
Bate, Jonathan, 'Culture and Environment: From Austen to Hardy', *New Literary History*, 30 (1999): 541–60.
Bautz, Annika, *The Reception of Jane Austen and Walter Scott: A Comparative Longitudinal Study* (London: Continuum, 2007).
Battiscombe, Georgina, *Charlotte Mary Yonge: The Story of an Uneventful Life* (London: Constable & Co., 1943).
Bradbrook, Frank W., *Jane Austen and her Predecessors* (Cambridge: Cambridge University Press, 1966)
_____, 'Jane Austen and Choderlos de Laclos', *Notes and Queries*, 199 (1954): 75.
Belsey, Catharine and Jane Moore, *The Feminist Reader: Essays in Gender and the Politics of Literary Criticism* (Houndsmills: Macmillan, 1989; repr.1997).
Belson, William A., *Studies in Readership* (London: Business Publications, 1962).
Bennett, Andrew, *Romantic Poets and the Culture of Posterity* (Cambridge: Cambridge University Press, 1999).
Bennett, Arnold, 'Books and Persons' column, *Evening Standard*, 21 July 1927.
Bloom, Harold, *The Anxiety of Influence: A Theory of Poetry* (New York: Oxford University Press, 1973).
Brodey, Inger Sigrun and Susan Allen Ford (eds), 'Global Austen', special issue of *Persusaions Online*, 28.2 (Spring 2008).
Buse, Peter and Andrew Stott (eds), *Ghosts: Deconstruction, Psychoanalysis, History* (Houndsmills and London: Macmillan, 1999).
Bush, Douglas, *Jane Austen* (London: Macmillan, 1975).
Butler, Marilyn, *Jane Austen and the War of Ideas* (Oxford: Clarendon Press, 1975; repr. 1987).
_____, *Maria Edgeworth: A literary biography* (Oxford: Clarendon Press, 1972).
Butler, E. M., '*Mansfield Park* and Kotzebue's *Lovers' Vows*', *MLR*, 28 (1933): 326–37.
Byrne, Paula, *Jane Austen and the Theatre* (Hambledon and London: Continuum, 2002, repr. 2007).
Carrington, Charles, *Rudyard Kipling: His Life and Work* (London: Macmillan, 1955).
de Certeau, Michel, *The Practice of Everyday Life*, trans. Steven F. Rendall (Berkeley, Los Angeles and London: University of California Press, 1984).
Chisholm, Hugh, 'How to Counteract the "Penny Dreadful"', *Fortnightly Review*, 58 (November 1895): 765–75.
Colclough, Stephen, '"R R, A Remarkable Thing or Action": John Dawson as Reader and Annotator', *Variants* 2.3 (2004): 61–78.

_____, *Consuming Texts: Readers and Reading Communities, 1695–1870* (Basingstoke: Palgrave Macmillan, 2007).

Colley, Linda, *Britons: Forging the Nation 1707–1837* (New Haven, CT and London: Yale University Press, 1992).

Collins, Irene, *Jane Austen, The Parson's Daughter* (London and Rio Grande: Hambledon Press, 1998).

Comstock, Cathy, *Disruption and Delight in the Nineteenth-Century Novel* (Ann Arbor and London: UMI Research Press, 1988).

Copeland, Edward and Juliet McMaster (eds), *The Cambridge Companion to Jane Austen* (Cambridge: Cambridge University Press, 1997).

Cripps, Matthew, 'Editors and Contributors', *Good Words*, 42 (1901): 620–22.

[Dallas, E. S.], review of *Felix Holt, the Radical*, *Times*, 26 June 1866.

Darnton, Robert, *The Kiss of Lamourette: Reflections in cultural history* (London: Faber & Faber, 1990).

David, Deirdre, *Intellectual Women and Victorian Patriarchy* (Ithaca, NY and New York: Cornell University Press, 1987).

DeRose, Peter L., *Jane Austen and Samuel Johnson* (Washington: University of Washington Press, 1980).

Derrida, Jacques, *Specters Of Marx: The State of the Debt, the Work of Mourning, and the New International*, trans. Peggy Kamuf (London and New York: Routledge, 1994).

_____, *On the Name*, ed. Thomas Du Toit, trans. David Wood, John P. Leavey, Jr. and Ian McLeod (Stanford: Stanford University Press, 1995).

Dobraszczyk, Paul, 'Useful Reading? Designing Information for London's Victorian Cab Passengers', *Journal of Design History*, 21.2 (2008): 121–41.

Dobosiewicz, Ilona, *Female Relationships in Jane Austen's Novels: A Critique of the Female Ideal Propagated in 18th Century Conduct Literature* (Opole: Uniwersytet Opolski, 1997).

Doody, Margaret Anne, 'Jane Austen's Reading', in *The Jane Austen Handbook*, ed. J. David Grey, Walton Litz and B. C. Southam (London: Athlone, 1986), 347–62.

'Doubleday' [Alfred Ainger], 'Books and Their Uses', *Macmillan's Magazine*, 1 (1859–60): 110–13.

Douglas-Fairhurst, Robert, *Victorian Afterlives: The Shaping of Influence in Nineteenth-Century Literature* (Oxford: Oxford University Press, 2002).

Dorée, Louisa Emily, 'A Girl's Leisure Moments', *Quiver*, 19 (1884): 307–8.

Dow, Gillian and Katie Halsey, *Jane Austen's Reading: The Chawton Years* (University of Southampton and Chawton House Library, 2009).

Dow, Gillian and Susan Allen Ford (eds), 'New Directions in Austen Studies', special issue of *Persuasions Online*, 30.2 (Spring 2010).

Duckworth, Alistair M., *The Improvement of the Estate: A Study of Jane Austen's Novels* (Baltimore and London: The Johns Hopkins University Press, 1971).

Dunstan, Vivienne S., 'Glimpses into a Town's Reading Habits in Enlightenment Scotland: Analysing the Borrowings of Gray Library, Haddington, 1732–1816', *Journal of Scottish Historical Studies*, 26 (2006): 42–59.

Eco, Umberto, *The Role of the Reader: Explorations in the Semiotics of Texts* (London: Hutchinson, 1979; repr. 1981).

Eliot, Simon, 'The Reading Experience Database; or, what are we to do about the history of reading?', *The Reading Experience Database, 1450–1945*. http://www.open.ac.uk/Arts/RED/redback.htm (accessed 1 June 2009).

_____, '"Faintly Troubling the Darkness": Casting a Little Light on the History of the Book', inaugural lecture, 9 November, 2006, Institute of English Studies, Senate House, University of London.

———, '"Never Mind the Value, What about the Price?": Or, How Much Did Marmion Cost St John Rivers?' *Nineteenth Century Literature*, 56.2 (September 2001): 160–97.
Eliot, Simon and Jonathan Rose (eds), *A Companion to the History of the Book* (Oxford: Blackwell, 2007).
Ellis, Peter Berresford, *H. Rider Haggard. A Voice from the Infinite* (London: Routledge and Kegan Paul, 1978).
Elwin, Malcolm, *Lord Byron's Wife* (London: Macdonald, 1962), 159.
Emsley, Sarah, 'Laughing at our Neighbours: Jane Austen and the Problem of Charity', *Persuasions Online*, 26.1 (Winter 2005), http://www.jasna.org/persuasions/on-line/vol26no1/emsley.htm (accessed 5 August 2011).
Esbester, Mike, 'Nineteenth-Century Timetables and the History of Reading', *Book History*, 12 (2009): 156–85.
Ezell, Margaret J. M., *Writing Women's Literary History* (Baltimore and London: The Johns Hopkins University Press, 1993).
Farrar, Rev. F. W., 'Learning to Read', *Macmillan's Magazine*, 21 (1869–70): 445–48.
Felman, Shoshana, *What Does a Woman Want? Reading and Sexual Difference* (Baltimore and London: The Johns Hopkins University Press, 1993).
Fendler, Susanne (ed.), *Feminist Contributions to the Literary Canon: Setting Standards of Taste* (Lewiston, Queenston, Lampeter: The Edwin Mellen Press, 1997).
Fergus, Jan, 'Eighteenth-Century Readers in Provincial England: The Customers of Samuel Clay's Circulating Library and Bookshop in Warwick, 1770–72', *Papers of the Bibliographical Society of America*, 78 (1984): 155–213.
———, *Provincial Readers in Eighteenth-Century England* (Oxford: Oxford University Press, 2006).
Fetterley, Judith, *The Resisting Reader: A Feminist Approach to American Fiction* (Bloomington and London: Indiana University Press, 1978).
Fish, Stanley, *Surprised by Sin: the Reader in 'Paradise Lost'* (Berkeley: University of California Press, 1971; first published in 1967).
———, *Is there a Text in this Class?: The Authority of Interpretive Communities* (Cambridge, MA: Harvard University Press, 1980).
Fischer, Steven Roger, *A History of Reading* (London: Reaktion Books Ltd, 2003).
Fleishman, Avrom, *A Reading of* Mansfield Park (Minneapolis: University of Minnesota Press, 1967).
Flint, Kate, *The Woman Reader 1837–1914* (Oxford: Clarendon Press, 1993; repr. 1995).
Flynn, Carol Houlihan and Edward Copeland (eds), *Clarissa and her Readers: New Essays for the Clarissa Project* (New York: AMS Press, Inc., 1999).
Flynn, Elizabeth A., and Patrocinio P. Schweickart (eds), *Gender and Reading: Essays on Readers, Texts, and Contexts* (Baltimore and London: The Johns Hopkins University Press, 1986).
Forster, Margaret, *Elizabeth Barrett Browning: A Biography* (London: Chatto & Windus, 1988).
'F. M.', 'Popular Literature', *The Englishwoman's Magazine and Christian Mother's Miscellany*, n.s. 7 (1852): 25–27.
Fraser, Hilary and R. S. White (eds), *Constructing Gender: Feminism and Literary Studies* (Nedlands, Western Australia: University of Western Australia Press, 1994).
Gallagher, Catherine, *Nobody's Story: The Vanishing Acts of Women Writers in the Marketplace, 1670–1820* (Berkeley and Los Angeles: University of California Press, 1994).
Galperin, William, 'The Picturesque, the Real, and the Consumption of Jane Austen', *Wordsworth Circle*, 28.1 (Winter 1997): 19–27.
Gay, Penny, *Jane Austen and the Theatre* (Cambridge: Cambridge University Press, 2002).

Chartier, Roger, *Cultural History: Between Practices and Representations* (Cambridge: Polity Press, 1988), 151–71.
Gerhart, Mary, *Genre Choices, Gender Questions* (Norman and London: University of Oklahoma Press, 1992).
[Gifford, William], unsigned review of works by Felicia Hemans, *Quarterly Review*, 24 (1820–21): 130–39.
Gilbert, Sandra M. and Susan Gubar, *The Madwoman in the Attic: The Woman Writer and the Nineteenth-Century Literary Imagination* (New Haven, CT and London: Yale University Press, 1979).
Gilmore, Leigh, *Autobiographics: A Feminist Theory of Women's Self-Representation* (Ithaca, NY and London: Cornell University Press, 1994).
Gilson, David, *A Bibliography of Jane Austen*, with introduction and corrections by the author (Winchester and New Castle, DE: St. Paul's Bibliographies, 1997).
Gittings, Robert and Jo Manton, *Claire Clairmont and the Shelleys 1798–1879* (Oxford and New York: Oxford University Press, 1992).
Glover, David and Cora Kaplan, *Genders* (London and New York: Routledge, 2000).
Gonda, Caroline, *Reading Daughters' Fictions 1709–1834: Novels and Society from Manley to Edgeworth* (Cambridge: Cambridge University Press, 1996).
Grafton, Anthony and Lisa Jardine, '"Studied for Action": How Gabriel Harvey Read his Livy', *Past and Present*, 129 (1990): 30–78.
Grier, Sydney C., 'A God-daughter of Warren Hastings', *Temple-Bar*, 131 (1905): 562–71.
Gunzenhauser, Bonnie (ed.), *Reading in History: New Methodologies from the Anglo-American Tradition* (London: Pickering & Chatto, 2010).
Halsey, Katie, 'Reading the Evidence of Reading', *Popular Narrative Media*, 1.2 (2008): 123–37.
_____, '"Tell me of some booklings": Mary Russell Mitford's Literary Networks', *Women's Writing*, 18.1 (2011): 121–36.
Halsey, Katie and W. R. Owens (eds), *The History of Reading: The British Isles, 1750–1950* (Basingstoke: Palgrave Macmillan, 2011).
Hammill, Faye, 'Cold Comfort Farm, D. H. Lawrence, and English Literary Culture Between the Wars', *Modern Fiction Studies*, 47.4 (Winter 2001): 831–54.
Hammond, Mary, *Reading, Publishing and the Formation of Literary Taste in England, 1880–1914* (Aldershot: Ashgate, 2006).
Harding, D. W., 'Regulated Hatred: An aspect of the work of Jane Austen', *Scrutiny*, 7 (1940): 346–62.
Harman, Claire, *Jane's Fame: How Jane Austen Conquered the World* (Edinburgh: Canongate, 2009).
Harris, Jocelyn, *Jane Austen's Art of Memory* (Cambridge: Cambridge University Press, 1989; repr. 2003).
_____, *A Revolution almost beyond Expression: Jane Austen's Persuasion* (Newark, DE: University of Delaware Press, 2007)
Hellerstein, Erna Olafson, Leslie Parker Hume and Karen M. Offen (eds), *Victorian Women: A Documentary Account of Women's Lives in Nineteenth-Century England, France, and the United States* (Brighton: Harvester Press, 1981).
Hemlow, Joyce, 'Fanny Burney and the courtesy books', *PMLA*, 65 (1950): 732–61.
Heilmann, Ann, 'Mrs Grundy's Rebellion: Margaret Oliphant Between Orthodoxy and the New Woman', *Women's Writing*, 6.2 (1999): 215–37.
Henry, Harry (ed.), *Readership Research: Theory and Practice (Proceedings of the First International Symposium, New Orleans, 1981)* (London: Sigmatext, 1982).

Higgins, Elizabeth Jean, assisted by Richard A. Long, *Reading the Novel: From Austen to E. M. Forster* (New York: Vantage Press, 1982).
Horn, Julia and Lynsey Russell-Watts (eds), *Possessions: Essays in French Literature, Cinema and Theory* (Oxford: Peter Lang, 2003).
Horwitz, Barbara J., *Jane Austen and the Question of Women's Education* (New York and London: Peter Lang, 1991).
Howe, Florence (ed.), *Tradition and the Talents of Women* (Urbana and Chicago: University of Illinois Press, 1991).
Hunter, J. Paul, *Before Novels: The Cultural Contexts of Eighteenth-Century English Fiction* (New York and London: W. W. Norton & Co., 1990).
Husbands, H. Winifred, '*Mansfield Park* and *Lovers' Vows*: A Reply', in *MLR*, 29 (1934): 176–9.
[Hutton, R. H.], 'Miss Austen's Posthumous Pieces', *Spectator*, 22 July 1871, 891–2.
'Ignoramus', 'Beauty and Print', *Temple-Bar*, 129 (1904): 687–98.
Iser, Wolfgang, *The Implied Reader; Patterns of Communication in Prose Fiction from Bunyan to Beckett* (Baltimore: The Johns Hopkins University Press, 1974).
_____, *The Act of Reading: A Theory of Aesthetic Response* (1976) (London: Routledge and Kegan Paul, 1978; first published in 1976).
_____, *Prospecting: From Reader Response to Literary Anthropology* (Baltimore: The Johns Hopkins University Press, 1989).
Jacobs, Edwards, 'Anonymous Signatures: Circulating Libraries, Conventionality, and the Production of Gothic Romances', *ELH*, 62.3 (1995): 603–29.
Jacobus, Mary, *Reading Woman: Essays in Feminist Criticism* (New York: Columbia University Press, 1986).
Jackson, H. J., *Romantic Readers: The Evidence of Marginalia* (New Haven, CT: Yale University Press, 2005).
_____, *Marginalia: Readers Writing in Books* (New Haven, CT: Yale University Press, 2001).
James, Henry, *The House of Fiction: Essays on the Novel*, ed. Leon Edel (London: Hart-Davis, 1957).
Jauss, Hans Robert 'Literary History as a Challenge to Literary Theory', trans. Elizabeth Benzinger, *New Literary History*, 2.1, *A Symposium on Literary History* (Autumn 1970): 7–37.
Jewsbury, Maria Jane, 'Literary Women: No. 2', *Athenaeum*, 27 August 1831, 553–4.
Johnson, Claudia L., *Jane Austen: Women, Politics and the Novel* (Chicago: University of Chicago Press, 1988).
_____, 'The Divine Miss Jane: Jane Austen, Janeites and the Discipline of Novel Studies', *boundary 2*, 23.3 (Autumn 1996): 143–63.
Jones, Vivien (ed.), *Women and Literature in Britain 1700–1800* (Cambridge: Cambridge University Press, 2000).
Kaplan, Deborah, *Jane Austen among Women* (Baltimore and London: The Johns Hopkins University Press, 1992).
Kaufman, Paul, *Borrowings from the Bristol Library 1773–1784: A Unique Record of Reading Vogues* (Charlottesville: Bibliographical Society of Virginia, 1960).
_____, *Reading Vogues at English Cathedral Libraries of the Eighteenth Century* (New York: New York Public Library, 1964).
_____, 'The Community Library: A Chapter in English Social History', *Transactions of the American Philosophical Society*, n.s. 57 (1967): 3–67.
_____, In Defence of Fair Readers', *Review of English Literature*, 8 (1967): 68–76.

_____, *Libraries and their Users: Collected Papers in Library History* (London: The Library Association, 1969).
Kavanagh, Julia, *English Women of Letters: Biographical Sketches*, 2 vols (London: Hurst and Blackett, 1863).
Kellman, Steven G., *The Self-Begetting Novel* (New York: Columbia University Press, 1980).
Kent, Christopher, 'Learning History with, and from, Jane Austen,' in *Jane Austen's Beginnings: The Juvenilia and Lady Susan*, ed. J. David Grey (Ann Arbor and London: UMI Research Press, 1989), 59.
Keynes, Geoffrey, *Jane Austen: A Bibliography* (London: Nonesuch Press, 1929).
Keymer, Tom, *Richardson's* Clarissa *and the Eighteenth-Century Reader* (Cambridge: Cambridge University Press, 1992).
Kirkham, Margaret, *Jane Austen, Feminism and Fiction* (London and Atlantic Highlands, NJ: The Athlone Press, 1997).
Klancher, Jon, *The Making of English Reading Audiences, 1890–1832* (Madison: University of Wisconsin Press, 1987).
Labbe, Jacqueline, *Romantic Visualities: Landscape, Gender and Romanticism* (Houndsmills: Macmillan, 1998).
Lacan, Jacques, 'Desire and the Interpretation of Desire in *Hamlet*', *Yale French Studies*, 55/56 (1977): 11–52.
Lambdin, Laura Cooner and Robert Thomas Lambdin (eds), *A Companion to Jane Austen Studies* (Westport, CT: Greenwood Press, 2000).
Lascelles, Mary, *Jane Austen and her Art* (Oxford: Oxford University Press, 1939; repr. 1974).
Leavis, F. R., *The Great Tradition: George Eliot, Henry James, Joseph Conrad* (London: Chatto & Windus, 1948).
Leavis, Q. D., 'A Critical Theory of Jane Austen's Writings', *Scrutiny*, 10.1 (1942): 61–87.
Leffel, John C., '"Everything is Going to Sixes and Sevens": Governing the Female Body (Politic) in Jane Austen's Catharine, Or the Bower (1792)', *Studies in the Novel*, 43.2 (Summer 2011): 131–51.
Levy, Michelle, 'Austen's Manuscripts and the Publicity of Print', *ELH*, 77.4 (Winter 2010): 1015–40.
Lewis, Lisa A. F., 'Kipling's Jane: Some Echoes of Austen', *English Literature in Transition, 1880–1920*, 29.1 (1986): 76–82.
Le Faye, Deirdre, *Jane Austen: A Family Record*, 2nd edn (Cambridge: Cambridge University Press, 2004).
_____, 'New Marginalia in Jane Austen's Books', *Book Collector*, 49 (2000), 222–6.
_____, 'The Memoir of Jane Austen and the Cheney Brothers', *Notes and Queries*, 56.3 (September 2009): 374–6.
[Lewes, G. H.], 'Recent Novels: French and English', *Fraser's Magazine*, 36 (1847): 687–95.
_____, 'The Novels of Jane Austen', *Blackwood's Edinburgh Magazine*, 86 (1859): 99–113.
_____, 'A Word about *Tom Jones*', *Blackwood's Edinburgh Magazine*, 87 (1860): 331–41.
[Lister, T. H.], review of *Women as they are*, *Edinburgh Review*, 53 (July 1830): 448–51.
Littlewood, Ian (ed.), *Jane Austen, Critical Assessments*, 4 vols (Sussex: Helm Information, 1998).
Litz, A. Walton, *Jane Austen: A Study of Her Artistic Development* (New York: Oxford University Press, 1967).
Looser, Devoney (ed.), *Jane Austen and Discourses of Feminism* (Houndsmills and London: Macmillan, 1995).

Lootens, Tricia, *Lost Saints: Silence, Gender and Victorian Literary Canonization* (Charlottesville and London: University Press of Virginia, 1996).
Lycett, Andrew, *Rudyard Kipling* (London: Weidenfeld & Nicolson, 1999).
Lynch, Deidre (ed.), *Janeites: Austen's Disciples and Devotees* (Princeton and Oxford: Princeton University Press, 2000).
Lyons, Martin and Lucy Taksa, *Australian Readers Remember: An Oral History of Reading, 1890–1930* (Melbourne, Oxford, Auckland and New York: Oxford University Press, 1992).
[Macaulay, Thomas Babington], 'The Diary and Letters of Mme d'Arblay', *Edinburgh Review*, 76 (1842–43): 523–70.
Macdonald, Gina and Andrew F. Macdonald (eds), *Jane Austen on Screen* (Cambridge: Cambridge University Press, 2003).
MacNabb, Elizabeth, L., *The Fractured Family: The Second Sex and Its Disconnected Daughters* (New York, San Francisco, Paris, etc.: Peter Lang, 1993).
Magnus, Kate, 'Concerning the Difficulty of Reading', *Good Words*, 45 (1905): 369–70.
Mandal, Anthony, *Jane Austen and the Popular Novel: The Determined Author* (Basingstoke: Palgrave Macmillan, 2007).
Mandal, Anthony and Brian Southam (eds), *The Reception of Jane Austen in Europe* (London: Continuum, 2007).
Mansfield, Katherine, *Novels and Novelists* (London: Constable & Co., 1930).
_____, 'A Short Story' (review of Virginia Woolf's *Kew Gardens*), *Athenaeum*, 4673 (21 November 1919), 1227; repr. in *Novels and Novelists*, 36–38.
_____, 'A Ship Comes into the Harbour' (review of Virginia Woolf's *Night and Day*), *Athenaeum*, 4650 (13 June 1919), 159; repr. in *Novels and Novelists*, 107–11.
Marcus, Jane, *Art and Anger: Reading Like a Woman* (Columbus: Ohio State University Press, 1988).
Marshall, David, 'True Acting and the Language of Real Feeling: *Mansfield Park*', *Yale Journal of Criticism*, 3 (1989–90): 87–106.
'M. A. W.' [Mrs Humphry Ward], 'Style and Miss Austen', *Macmillan's Magazine*, 51 (1884–85): 84–91.
McGann, Jerome, *The Romantic Ideology: A Critical Investigation* (Chicago and London: University of Chicago Press, 1983).
Mellor, Anne K., *Romanticism and Gender* (New York and London: Routledge, 1993).
Mezei, Kathy (ed.), *Ambiguous Discourse: Feminist Narratology and British Women Writers* (Chapel Hill and London: University of North Carolina Press, 1996).
Michaelson, Patricia Howell, 'Reading *Pride and Prejudice*', *Eighteenth-Century Fiction*, 3.1 (October 1990): 65–76.
Miller, D. A., *Jane Austen, or, The Secret of Style* (Princeton: Princeton University Press, 2003).
Mills, Sara (ed.), *Gendering the Reader* (New York, London, Singapore, etc.: Harvester Wheatsheaf, 1994).
Mills, Sara and Lynne Pearce, *Feminist Readings/Feminists Reading* (London, New York Munich, etc.: Prentice Hall, 1996).
Milner, Rev. Joseph, 'The Essentials of Christianity Theoretically and Practically Considered', *Englishwoman's Magazine and Christian Mother's Miscellany*, n.s. 5 (1850): 1–14.
Mitchell, Sally, *The Fallen Angel: Chastity, Class and Women's Reading, 1835–1880* (Bowling Green, OH: Bowling Green University Popular Press, 1981).
Moler, Kenneth L., *Jane Austen's Art of Allusion* (Lincoln, NE: University of Nebraska Press, 1968).

Montefiore, Janet, *Arguments of Heart and Mind: Selected Essays 1977–2000* (Manchester and New York: Manchester University Press, 2002).
Murphy, Olivia, 'From Pammydiddle to *Persuasion*: Jane Austen Rewriting Eighteenth-Century Literature', *Eighteenth-Century Life*, 32.2 (Spring 2008): 29–28.
Murray, Douglas, 'Spectatorship in *Mansfield Park*: Looking and Overlooking', *Nineteenth-Century Literature*, 52 (1998–99): 1–27.
Murray, Penelope (ed.), *Plato on Poetry* (Cambridge: Cambridge University Press, 1996).
O'Farrell, Mary Ann, *Telling Complexions: The Nineteenth-Century English Novel and the Blush* (Durham and London: Duke University Press, 1997).
O'Keefe, Deborah, *Good Girl Messages: How Young Women Were Misled by Their Favorite Books* (New York and London: Continuum, 2000).
[Oliphant, Margaret], 'Miss Austen and Miss Mitford', *Blackwood's Edinburgh Magazine*, 107 (1870): 290–313.
Palgrave, F. T., 'On Readers in 1760 and 1860', *Macmillan's Magazine*, 1 (1859–60): 487–9.
Parrill, Sue, *Jane Austen on Film and Television: A Critical Study of the Adaptations* (Jefferson, NC: McParland, 2002).
Pearce, Lynne, *Feminism and the Politics of Reading* (London, New York, Sydney, Auckland: Arnold, 1997).
Pearson, Jacqueline, *Women's Reading in Britain, 1750–1835* (Cambridge: Cambridge University Press, 1999).
Perkins, Pam, 'A Subdued Gaiety: The Comedy of *Mansfield Park*', *Nineteenth-Century Literature*, 48 (1993–94): 1–26.
Pereiro, James, *Ethos and the Oxford Movement: At the Heart of Tractarianism* (Oxford: Oxford University Press, 2008).
Pinion, F. B., *A Jane Austen Companion* (London and Basingstoke: Macmillan, 1973; repr. 1976).
Pinney, Thomas (ed.), *The Letters of Thomas Babington Macaulay*, 6 vols (Cambridge: Cambridge University Press, 1974).
_____, *The Letters of Rudyard Kipling*, 6 vols (London: Macmillan, 1990).
Poovey, Mary, *The Proper Lady and the Woman Writer: Ideology as Style in the Works of Mary Wollstonecraft, Mary Shelley and Jane Austen* (Chicago and London: University of Chicago Press, 1984).
Pollock, Juliet, 'Novels and Their Times', *Macmillan's Magazine*, 27 (1872): 297–303, 358–67.
Pucci, Joseph, *The Full-Knowing Reader: Allusion and the Power of the Reader in the Western Literary Tradition* (New Haven, CT and London: Yale University Press, 1998).
Pucci, Suzanne R., and James Thompson (eds), *Jane Austen and Co: Remaking the Past in Contemporary Culture* (Albany: State University of New York, 2002).
Raven, James, Helen Small and Naomi Tadmor, *The Practice and Representation of Reading in England* (Cambridge: Cambridge University Press, 1996).
Reiman, Donald, *The Study of Modern Manuscripts: Public, Confidential, and Private* (Baltimore: The Johns Hopkins University Press, 1993).
Ricks, Christopher, *Keats and Embarrassment* (Oxford: Oxford University Press, 1974).
_____, *Allusion to the Poets* (Oxford: Oxford University Press, 2002).
Riffaterre, Michael, *Semiotics of Poetry* (London: Methuen, 1978; repr. 1980).
_____, *Fictional Truth* (Baltimore and London: The John Hopkins University Press, 1990).
Ritchie, Anne Thackeray, *A Book of Sibyls* (London: Smith, Elder, & Co. 1883).
_____ (signed A.I.T.), 'Jane Austen', *Cornhill Magazine*, 24 (1871): 158–74.

Roberts, Warren, *Jane Austen and the French Revolution* (London: Athlone Press, 1995; first published 1979).
Robinson, E. Kay, 'Reading Without Tears', *Good Words*, 40 (1899): 235–39.
Robinson, Rev. H. G., 'On the Use of English Classical Literature in the Work of Education', *Macmillan's Magazine*, 2 (1860): 425–34.
Rose, Jonathan, *The Intellectual Life of the British Working Classes* (New Haven, CT: Yale University Press, 2001).
Roth, Barry, *An Annotated Bibliography of Jane Austen Studies 1952–72* (Charlottesville: University Press of Virginia, 1973).
——, *An Annotated Bibliography of Jane Austen Studies 1973–83* (Charlottesville: University Press of Virginia, 1984).
——, *An Annotated Bibliography of Jane Austen Studies 1984–94* (Athens, OH: Ohio University Press, 1996).
Russell, D. A. and Michael Winterbottom (eds), *Classical Literary Criticism* (Oxford and New York: Oxford University Press, 1972; repr. 1998).
Ruston, Sharon (ed.), *The Influence and Anxiety of the British Romantics: Spectres of Romanticism* (Lewiston, Queenston and Lampeter: The Edwin Mellen Press, 1999).
Saintsbury, George, 'Maria Edgeworth', *Macmillan's Magazine*, 72 (1895): 151–70.
Saenger, Paul, 'Silent Reading: Its impact on Late Medieval Script and Society', *Viator*, 13 (1982): 367–414.
Scholes, Robert, *The Crafty Reader* (New Haven, CT and London: Yale University Press, 2001).
Scholz, Anne-Marie, *An Orgy of Propriety; Jane Austen and the Emergence and the Legacy of the Female Author in America 1826–1926* (Trier: WVT, Wissenschaftlicher Verlag, 1999).
[Scott, Walter], review of *Emma*, *Quarterly Review*, 14 (1816): 188–201.
Secord, James, A., 'Self-Development' in *Victorian Sensation: The Extraordinary Publication, Reception and Secret Authorship of 'Vestiges of the Natural History of Creation'* (Chicago: University of Chicago Press, 2003).
Shattock, Joanne, 'Work for Women: Margaret Oliphant's journalism', in Laurel Brake, Bill Bell and David Finkelstein (eds), *Nineteenth-Century Media and the Construction of Identities* (Basingstoke: Palgrave Macmillan, 2000), 165–77.
Shires, Linda M. (ed.), *Rewriting the Victorians: Theory, History, and the Politics of Gender* (New York and London: Routledge, 1992).
Showalter, Elaine, *A Literature of Their Own: British Women Novelists from Brontë to Lessing* (Princeton: Princeton University Press, 1977).
[Simpson, Richard], 'Jane Austen', *North British Review*, n.s. 13 (1870): 129–52.
Smith, LeRoy W., *Jane Austen and the Drama of Woman* (London and Basingstoke: Macmillan, 1983).
Southam, Brian, *Jane Austen's Sir Charles Grandison* (Oxford: Clarendon, 1980).
—— (ed.), *Jane Austen: The Critical Heritage*, 2 vols (London: Routledge, 1968–87).
Spacks, Patricia Meyer, *Desire and Truth: Functions of Plot in Eighteenth-Century English Novels* (Chicago and London: Chicago University Press, 1990).
Spencer, Jane, *The Rise of the Woman Novelist from Aphra Behn to Jane Austen* (Oxford: Basil Blackwell Ltd, 1986).
Spender, Dale, *Mothers of the Novel: 100 Good Women Writers Before Jane Austen* (London: Pandora, 1986).
Spelman, Elizabeth, *The Inessential Woman* (Boston: Beacon Press, 1988).

Spiers, John, (ed.), *The Culture of the Publisher's Series*, 2 vols (Basingstoke: Palgrave Macmillan, 2011).
Spufford, Francis, *The Child that Books Built: A Memoir of Childhood and Reading* (London: Faber & Faber, 2002).
St. Clair, William, *The Reading Nation in the Romantic Period* (Cambridge: Cambridge University Press, 2004).
Stephen, Leslie, *English Literature and Society in the Eighteenth Century* (London: Duckworth & Co., 1904).
[Stephen, Leslie], 'Humour', *Cornhill Magazine*, 33 (1876): 324–5.
Stewart, Garrett, *Dear Reader: The Conscripted Audience in Nineteenth-Century British Fiction* (Baltimore and London: The Johns Hopkins University Press, 1996).
Stimpson, Felicity, '"I have spent my morning reading Greek": The marginalia of Sir George Otto Trevelyan', *Library History*, 23.4 (2007): 239–50.
Sutherland, Kathryn, *Jane Austen's Textual Lives: from Aeschylus to Bollywood* (Oxford: Oxford University Press, 2005).
'T. A.' [Thomas Arnold], 'Recent Novel Writing', *Macmillan's Magazine*, 13 (1865–66): 202–209.
Tandon, Bharat, *Jane Austen and the Morality of Conversation* (London: Anthem Press, 2003).
Templin, Charlotte, *Feminism and the Politics of Literary Reputation: The Example of Erica Jong* (Lawrence, KS: University Press of Kansas, 1995).
Ten Harmsel, Henrietta, *Jane Austen: A Study in Fictional Conventions* (The Hague: Mouton, 1964).
Thomas, Claudia N., *Alexander Pope and His Eighteenth-Century Women Readers* (Carbondale and Edwardsville: Southern Illinois University Press, 1994).
Thompson, Harold William, *A Scottish Man of Feeling: Some account of Henry Mackenzie, Esq. of Edinburgh and of the golden age of Burns and Scott* (London: Oxford University Press, 1831).
Ticknor, Caroline, *Glimpses of Authors* (London: T. Werner Laurie Ltd, 1924).
Todd, Janet (ed.), *The Cambridge Introduction to Jane Austen* (Cambridge: Cambridge University Press, 2006).
_____ (ed.), *Jane Austen in Context*, (Cambridge: Cambridge University Press, 2005).
Towsey, Mark, '"An Infant Son to Truth Engage": Virtue, Responsibility and Self-Improvement in the Reading of Elizabeth Rose of Kilravock, 1747–1815', *Journal of the Edinburgh Bibliographical Society*, 2 (2007): 69–92.
_____, 'First Steps in Associational Reading: The Foundation and Early Use of the Wigtown Subscription Library, 1790–1815', *PBSA*, 103 (2009): 455–95.
Trilling, Lionel, *The Opposing Self: Nine Essays in Criticism* (London: Secker and Warburg, 1955).
_____, *Beyond Culture: Essays on Literature and Learning* (Oxford: Oxford University Press, 1980; first published 1957).
Troost, Linda and Sayre Greenfield (eds), *Jane Austen in Hollywood* (Lexington: University Press of Kentucky, 1998).
Vickery, Amanda, *The Gentleman's Daughter: Women's Lives in Georgian England* (New Haven, CT and London: Yale University Press, 1998).
Vincent, David, *The Rise of Mass Literaacy: Reading and Writing in Modern Europe* (Cambridge: Polity, 2000).
Volosinov, V. N., *Marxism and the Philosophy of Language*, trans. Ladislav Matejka and I. R. Titunick (Cambridge, MA: Harvard University Press, 1986).
Waldron, Mary, *Jane Austen and the Fiction of her Time* (Cambridge: Cambridge University Press, 1999).

Waller, Philip, *Writers, Readers, and Reputations: Literary Life in Britain 1870–1918* (Oxford: Oxford University Press, 2006).
Ward, William Smith, *Literary Reviews in British Periodicals, 1798–1820: A Bibliography with a Supplementary List of General (Non-Review) Articles on Literary Subjects* (New York: Garland, 1972).
Webling, A. F., 'On Browsing in a Library', *Temple-Bar*, 129 (1904): 466–74.
[Whately, Richard], unsigned review of *Northanger Abbey* and *Persuasion*, *Quarterly Review*, 24 (1821): 352–76.
Wheeler, Michael, *The Art of Allusion in Victorian Fiction* (London and Basingstoke: Macmillan, 1979).
Wilkie, Brian, 'Structural Layering in Jane Austen's Problem Novels', in *Nineteenth-Century Literature*, 46 (1991–92): 517–44.
Williamson, J. G., 'The structure of pay in Britain, 1710–1911', *Research in Economic History*, 7 (1982): 1–54.
Wilkes, Joanne, *Women Reviewing Women in Nineteenth-Century Britain: The Critical Reception of Jane Austen, Charlotte Bronë and George Eliot* (Farnham: Ashgate, 2010).
Wiltshire, John, *Jane Austen and the Body: 'The Picture of Health'* (Cambridge: Cambridge University Press, 1992).
_____, *Recreating Jane Austen* (Cambridge: Cambridge University Press, 2001).
Windscheffel, Ruth Clayton, *Reading Gladstone* (Basingstoke: Palgrave Macmillan, 2008).
Woolf, Virginia, *The Common Reader: First Series* (1925), ed. Andrew McNeillie (London: The Hogarth Press, 1984).
_____, *Collected Essays*, 4 vols (London: Hogarth Press, 1966–67).
_____, *A Room of One's Own* (1929), ed. Michèle Barrett (London: Penguin, 1993).
_____, 'Jane Austen', *Times Literary Supplement*, 19 July 1917.
_____, 'Jane Austen at Sixty', *New Republic* (New York), 37 (30 January 1924): 261.
Wright, Andrew, 'Jane Austen Adapted', *Nineteenth-Century Fiction*, 30.3 (December 1975): 421–53.
Wright, Thomas, *Oscar's Books* (London: Chatto & Windus, 2008).
Yeazell, Ruth Bernard, *Fictions of Modesty: Women and Courtship in the English Novel* (Chicago and London: University of Chicago Press, 1991).
Zaczek, Barbara Maria, *Censored Sentiments: Letters and Censorship in Epistolary Novels and Conduct Material* (Newark, DE: University of Delaware Press, 1997).
Zelicovici, Dvora, 'The Inefficacy of *Lovers' Vows*', *English Literary History*, 50 (1983): 531–40.

Electronic Resources

The Reading Experience Database, 1450–1945, https://www.open.ac.uk/Arts/Reading
Mass Observation Online, http://www.massobservation.amdigital.co.uk

INDEX

XII Club 196–201, 205

Adams, Charles (*Jack and Alice*) 38
Addison, Joseph 26, 31, 43
'Address to Tobacco' (Hawkins Browne) 77
Advice From a Lady of Quality (Carracioli) 40
Advice to a Daughter (Halifax) 31
Ainger, Alfred 122, 125
Akenside, Mark 31
Allan, George 113
Allingham, William 184
American transcendentalism 186
Armstrong, Nancy 34, 47
Arnold, Mary 123
Arnold, Thomas 122
Auden, W. H. 94
Auerbach, Emily 4, 185
'Aunt Anastasia' 123–4, 125
'Austen Controversy, the' (Browning/Mitford) 153–61, 164–5, 166–8
Austen family: and communal reading 19–20, 21–22, 33, 41, 59; and literary discussions 19, 20, 21, 23–4, 39, 76; opinions on Austen's writing 20, 55–6, 97, 98–9, 189; *see also under individual names*
Austen, Anna: *see* Lefroy, Anna
Austen, Caroline 19, 20, 26
Austen, Cassandra 7, 17, 20, 22, 23, 30, 39, 78, 95; Austen's letters to 13, 24, 38, 78, 156
Austen, Charles 98
Austen, Frank 97, 99
Austen, Henry 13, 17, 20, 21–2, 23, 56, 65, 77, 177; 'Biographical Notice of the Author' 13, 24, 109, 111, 135–7, 158, 159
Austen, James 18, 19, 20, 23, 97, 132, 189

Austen, Jane: letters of 13, 18, 23–4, 38, 39–40, 76, 78, 136, 156; use of libraries 17, 27; reading habits/preferences 7, 17–19, 23, 24–8, 39, 78 (*see also under individual names*); researching readers' responses to her novels 3, 20, 95, 96, 148–9, 164, 189
Austen, Mrs 17, 20, 99
Austen, Reverend George 17, 19, 20
Austen's novels: Austen family's responses to 20, 55–6, 97, 98, 99, 108–9, 119, 189–90; books/reading in 25–6, 37, 40–1, 42–4, 45, 46–7, 49, 77–9, 85, 119, 126, 201; first editions of 39, 107–8, 136, 145, 153; illustrated editions of 101–2, 110, 111, 112, 113; male readers of 132–3, 183; prose style of 13, 56, 58–9, 83, 85, 89, 156, 187, 209; readers' responses to 94, 95–6, 110, 142, 143, 211; retail prices of 109–11, 112, 113; reviews of 57–8, 94, 120, 144; *see also under individual names/titles*
Austen-Leigh, James Edward 20, 99, 112, 114, 132, 136–7; *Memoir of Jane Austen* 24–5, 112, 114, 135, 139, 143, 149, 171–2, 173, 174, 175–6, 177, 178–9, 183, 213
Austen-Leigh, Mary Augusta 105, 112, 206; *Personal Aspects of Jane Austen* 204
autobiographies 93; *see also under individual titles*
Autobiography (Oliphant) 174

Baillie, Joanna 154
Bakhtin, M. M. 8, 13, 59–60, 61, 91
Balzac 128, 198

Baretti, Joseph 26
Barnes, Ellen M. 207
Barthes, Roland 8
Bates, Miss (*Emma*) 98
Bath 17, 62, 118, 140–1, 142, 194–5, 203, 205
Battiscombe, Georgina 190
Bautz, Annika 4
Belinda (Edgeworth) 58
Bennet, Elizabeth (*Pride and Prejudice*) 12, 13, 37, 38, 47, 52, 74, 89, 101, 102, 112, 210
Bennet, Kitty (*Pride and Prejudice*) 41
Bennet, Lydia (*Pride and Prejudice*) 41, 47
Bennet, Mary (*Pride and Prejudice*) 26, 45, 47, 56
Bennett, Arnold 105, 106, 187, 204
Bennett, John 22, 30, 32, 34, 118
Bentley, Richard 110
Bentley's 'Steventon Edition' 113
Bentley's Standard Novels series 101–2, 105, 110–11, 112, 147, 150, 153, 183
Benwick, Capt. James (*Persuasion*) 37, 45
Berquin, Arnaud 27; *L'Ami de l'Enfance* 21
Berry, Mary 127–8, 134
Bertram, Edmund (*Mansfield Park*) 46–7, 49, 52–3, 54–5, 64–5, 77, 79, 81, 162, 163, 201
Bertram, James Glass 131
Bertram, Julia (*Mansfield Park*) 52, 64, 193
Bertram, Maria (*Mansfield Park*) 50, 52, 64, 76–7, 80, 193
Bertram, Lady Maria (*Mansfield Park*) 50, 52, 78–9, 81, 99–100
Bertram, Sir Thomas (*Mansfield Park*) 50–1, 68–9, 79, 81
Bible, the 24, 31, 33, 103–4, 129
Bingham, Adrian 103
Bingley, Caroline (*Pride and Prejudice*) 25, 37, 201
'Biographical Notice of the Author' (Austen, H.) 13, 24, 109, 111, 135–7, 158, 159
Blackwood's Edinburgh Magazine 117, 120, 125, 174, 175, 179
Blair, Hugh 26, 31
blushing 59, 65–9, 70–4

book bindings 103, 104, 105–6, 108
book illustrations 101–2, 103–4, 110, 111, 112, 172
Book of Common Prayer 24, 27
Book of Sibyls, A (Ritchie) 172
book prices 103, 104, 109, 110–11, 112, 113
books: access to 17, 19, 27, 103, 110, 201 (*see also* libraries); physical qualities of 102–5, 107; *see also* reading
booksellers 92, 93, 111
Boringdon, Lady 109
Brabourne, Lord 112, 114
Braddon, Mary Elizabeth 131
Bradley, A. C. 179
Bramstone, Mrs 90
Bremer, Frederika 155, 156, 157
Brimley Johnson, R. 112, 113
British Critic 97, 119, 144, 165
Brittain, Vera 105
Brontë, Charlotte 101, 153, 158, 166, 169–70, 186, 212
Browning, Elizabeth Barrett 106, 129–30, 139; correspondence with Mary Russell Mitford 14, 96, 143, 144, (*see also* 'Austen Controversy, the' (Browning/Mitford)); criticism of Austen 160–1, 164, 166–9, 181, 186, 212
Brunton, Mary 26; *Discipline* 128; *Self Control* 10, 129
Brydges, Egerton 27
Buffon, Georges-Louis Leclerc, Comte De 33
Bunyan, John 27, 199
Burke, Edmund 130
Burney, Frances 26, 31; *Camilla*: 18, 44, 58; *Cecilia* 58; *Evelina* 19, 47, 58, 65, 66, 68, 69
Burney, Sarah Harriet 26, 109, 145–6, 180
Burns, Robert 26, 197
Burt, Thomas 107, 133
Butler, E. M. 83
Byrne, Paula 19
Byron, Harriet (*Sir Charles Grandison*) 10, 23, 27, 48
Byron, Lord 26, 28, 95, 108, 128, 131

INDEX

Cabinet of Fashion and Romance, The 117
'Cadenus and Vanessa' (Swift) 67
Cage, Fanny 89–90, 97, 98
Camilla (Burney) 18, 44, 58
Campbell, Thomas 26
Carey and Hart, Philadelphia 111
Carey, Lea and Blanchard, Philadelphia 101
Carey, Mathew 109
Carracioli, Louis-Antoine 40
Carroll, Lewis 197, 198, 200
Carter, Thomas 106–7
Catharine; or, The Bower (Austen) 37, 42, 45, 46, 69, 124
Cecil, Lord David 204, 205
Cecilia (Burney) 58
Centlivre, Susanna 26
Certeau, Michel de 8
Champion, The 77–8, 96
Chapman, R. W. 113, 114, 203
Chapone, Hester 22, 29, 39, 51, 58; *Letters on the Improvement of the Mind* 31, 40
characters/characterization (in Austen's novels) 89–1, 97, 98–100, 101, 132, 140, 141, 142, 156, 162, 210; *see also under individual names*
Chartier, Roger 8
Chaucer, Geoffrey 27, 197, 198, 200
Chawton, Hampshire 17, 139, 205
Chawton Book Society 17, 24
Chawton House Library 18, 27
Cheney, R. H. 179
Chorley, Henry F. 140
Church of England Quarterly Review 118
Churchill, Frank (*Emma*) 70, 71, 73, 99, 193
Churchill, Winston 202, 209
circulating libraries 17, 41, 45, 106, 108, 123, 110, 111, 118, 182
Clairmont, Claire 128–9
Clarissa (Richardson) 44, 49, 50, 89, 90, 124
Clarke, H. G. editions 101, 111
Clarke, James Stanier 95, 181
Clarkson, Thomas 26, 105
Cleland, John 66
Clemens, Samuel Langhorne: *see* Twain, Mark
clergy, representations of the (in Austen's novels) 149, 162, 163; *see also under individual names*

Cœlebs in Search of a Wife (More) 28, 35, 45, 65, 75
Colclough, Stephen 103
Coleridge, Samuel Taylor 33, 56, 121, 129, 132, 206
Collins, Mr (*Pride and Prejudice*) 40–1, 43, 56, 58, 200
Colman, George 26
communal reading 20, 21–22, 33, 59, 189, 201–2, 203: and the Austen family 20, 21–22, 33, 41, 59; and discussion 191–3, 196–201; *see also* reading communities; reading groups
compliant readers 8–9, 143, 154, 212
conduct literature 15, 26, 28, 29–35, 37, 39–41, 45, 46–9, 53, 54, 56, 59; and disapproval of novels 31–2, 43–4, 124; reading recommendations of 31, 32, 40, 41, 83, 130; *see also under individual authors*
Contagious Diseases Acts (1864, 1866, 1869) 138
Cooke, Cassandra 27
Cooke, Mary 98, 99
Cooper, Edward 20, 26
Cooper, Jane 21
Copeland, Edward 23
Corelli, Marie 104
Cornhill Magazine 171
Cowley, Hannah 26
Cowper, William 24, 25, 31, 78, 80–3, 84; *The Task* 76, 77, 80–2, 84; 'Tirocinium' 77
Crabbe, George 24, 25, 26, 80, 83, 84, 210; *Tales* (Crabbe) 76, 77, 78–9
Crawford, Henry (*Mansfield Park*) 50, 51, 52, 53, 54, 55, 56, 69, 70, 76, 77, 80–1, 82–3, 143
Crawford, Mary (*Mansfield Park*) 49, 50, 54, 69, 70, 77, 79, 80, 136
Critical Review 98, 130
critics 4, 5, 97–100, 114, 136, 165; Austen family as 20, 97; male 137, 155; *see also under individual names*
Croker, John Wilson 131
Cumberland, Richard 26
Custody Acts (1839, 1873) 137

Dallas, E. S. 158
Darcy, Mr (*Pride and Prejudice*) 12, 25, 37, 73–4, 201
Darnell, Dorothy 205
Darnton, Robert 8, 103
Darwin family 14, 191–2, 210
Darwin, Charles 132, 191
Darwin, Emma 190, 191
Darwin, Erasmus 29
Dashwood, Elinor (*Sense and Sensibility*) 11, 47, 52, 162–3
Dashwood, Marianne (*Sense and Sensibility*) 11–12, 60, 201
Davy, Lady Jane 12
Debits and Credits (Kipling) 207
dedications (in Austen's works) 21–3
Defence of Poetry (Shelley) 153
Defoe, Daniel 26; *Robinson Crusoe* 131
Denham, Sir Edward (*Sanditon*) 26, 44–5, 56
Dent, J. M. 112
Derrida, Jacques 6
diaries 93, 105, 114–15, 129, 130, 140–1, 163, 183
Dickens, Charles 106, 110, 125, 144, 199; *Tale of Two Cities* 131
Dictionary (Johnson) 164
Discipline (Brunton) 128
Divorce Act (1857) 137
Dixon, Mr (*Emma*) 71, 72, 73
Dobosiewicz, Ilona 35
Dobraszczyk, Paul 103
Dobson, Austin 179
'domestic ideology' 6, 29, 30, 31, 34, 56, 57, 59, 83, 169, 172, 173, 175
Doody, Margaret Anne 26–7, 28, 40
Doré, Gustave 103
Dorrée, Louisa Emily 120
Dorset, Catherine Anne Turner 109
'double-voiced discourse' (Bakhtin) 59–60, 61
Dryden, John 31
Duckworth, Alistair 81
Dyce, Rev. Alexander 136–7

Edgeworth, Maria 24, 25, 26, 124, 131, 149, 155, 160; *Belinda* 58; *Popular Tales* 130; *Practical Education* 31, 32; response to *Emma* 91
Edgeworth, R. L. 31, 32

Edinburgh Monthly Review 177
Edinburgh Review, the 117, 120–1, 159, 160, 163–4
education 28, 29, 30, 31, 37–8, 43, 46, 49, 65, 120;
Egerton editions (of Austen's novels) 39, 101, 102, 107, 108, 109–10, 145, 153, 191
Egerton, Thomas 97, 108, 148
Elegant Extracts (Knox) 18
Elford, Sir William 143–4
Eliot, George 154, 158, 175, 198
Eliot, Simon 8, 92, 94, 103, 108, 110
Elliot, Anne (*Persuasion*) 11, 13, 26, 37, 45, 47, 62, 73, 74, 85, 142, 172, 201
Elliot, Elizabeth (*Persuasion*) 62–3
Elliot, Sir Walter (*Persuasion*) 62–3, 68, 193
Elliot, William (*Persuasion*) 63
Elton, Mr (*Emma*) 61, 70, 72, 73, 98, 149, 162, 163, 193
Elton, Mrs (*Emma*) 97, 98, 193
Emerson, Ralph Waldo 14, 186, 198
Emma 13–14, 37, 155–6, 191–2;
early editions 108, 109; and the female blush 69, 70–3, 74; negative responses to 11, 148; use of parody 60, 61–2; readers' opinions of 20, 90, 91, 95, 96–7, 98, 126, 128, 145, 146, 147, 148–9, 162; reviews of 11, 77–8, 90, 96, 97, 108, 119, 126, 165, 189; *see also under individual names*
Emsley, Sarah 157
Engels, Friedrich 6
'Englishness' 185–6, 210–11
Englishwoman's Domestic Magazine 166, 167
Englishwoman's Magazine and Christian Mother's Miscellany, The 117
Enquiry into the Duties of the Female Sex (Gisborne) 28, 33–4, 46
Esbester, Mike 103
escapism 209
Evelina (Burney) 19, 47, 58, 65, 66, 68, 69

Fairfax, Jane (*Emma*) 60, 70, 71–4, 99
families and shared reading experiences 14, 189, 190–6, 203, 210; *see also* communal reading
Fanny Hill (Cleland) 66

INDEX

Father's Legacy to his Daughters, A (Gregory) 31, 66
Felman, Shoshana 8
'female philospher – A Letter, The' (Austen) 22
Female Quixote (Lennox) 21
female readers: *see* women readers
female sexuality 66, 67
female writers 13, 26, 57, 95, 124, 135, 137, 153–5, 158, 169, 182, 198, 199, 212; *see also under individual names*
femininity 30, 167, 176, 187; and conflation with novel reading 28, 120–6, 146, 147, 204; *see also* conduct literature; domesticity
feminist theory 114, 137, 155, 182
Fergus, Jan 103
Ferrars, Edward (*Sense and Sensibility*) 162
Ferrars, Robert (*Sense and Sensibility*) 11
Ferrier, Susan 128
Fetterley, Judith 8
Feuillide, Eliza de 21, 23
fiction 28, 41, 58, 96, 101, 112, 121, 125, 130–2, 133–4, 141, 142; criticisms of 32, 118, 120, 127, 146; and cultural stereotypes 117, 126–8, 130, 132–3, 150; *see also* novel reading; romances; sensation fiction
Fielding, Henry 25, 75, 125, 136, 138, 139, 157, 210; *Tom Jones* 26, 65, 138
film/television adaptations (of Austen's novels) 4–5, 6, 114
'First Impressions' (Austen) 20, 95
First World War 181, 203
Fish, Stanley 8
Flint, Kate 8
Flynn, Elizabeth 8
Following the Equator (Twain) 187
fonts 107; *see also* type sizes
Fordyce, James 26, 30, 31; *Sermons for Young Women* 40–1, 42–3
Forster, E. M. 56, 132, 179, 204–5
Fowler, Karen Joy 209
Free Opinions (Corelli) 104

Galperin, William 89
Garrod, H. W. 203–4
Gaskell, Elizabeth 199
Gay, John 26

Genlis, Madame de 27; *Theatre d'Education* 31
Gentleman's Magazine 57
Gibbon, Edward 139
Gifford, William 90, 124
Gilbert, Sandra 28, 59
Gilpin, William 24
Gilson, David 110, 111, 112
Girton College, Cambridge 138
Gisborne, Thomas 26, 28, 30, 37, 49, 51, 58; *Enquiry into the Duties of the Female Sex* 28, 33–4, 46
Glimpses of Authors (Ticknor) 206
Glimpses of the Past (Wordsworth, E.) 190
Godwin, William 27, 30, 128, 129
Goethe, Johann von 27, 199
Goldsmith, Oliver 24, 25, 31, 139; *History of England* 18, 21, 31, 114; *Vicar of Wakefield* (Goldsmith) 32
Gordon, Lady 90, 167
Gothic novels 43–4, 58, 90, 128
Grafton, Anthony 8
Gregory, John 31, 66
Groombridge and Sons 112
Grundy, Isobel 18–19, 27, 28, 78
Gubar, Susan 28, 59
Guiton, Mrs 90
Gulliver's Travels (Swift) 24

Haggard, H. Rider 131
Halifax, Marquis of 31
Hallam, Arthur Henry 145–7, 167, 180
Hamilton, Elizabeth 26
Hammond, Mary 8
'hard reading' 15, 33–4, 35, 48, 56, 59, 120, 122, 212
Harding, D. W. 13
Harman, Claire 3, 4, 105, 113, 179, 183
Harris, Jocelyn 7, 8, 27, 28
Hawkins Browne, Isaac 77
Hawkins, Laetitia Matilda 26
Hayter, Charles (*Persuasion*) 163
Heartsease (Yonge) 131–2
Hemans, Felicia 126–7, 155
Herries, Isabella 11, 99
Heywood, Charlotte (*Sanditon*) 41, 44, 61
Hill, Constance and Edith 206
History of England (Austen) 40
History of England (Goldsmith) 18, 21, 31

Hobbs, Andrew 103
Holland, Sir Henry 210
Home, John 26
Homer 31, 129
Howells, W. D. 156, 179, 180, 186–7
Howitt, Mary 155
Huckleberry Finn (Twain) 185
Hume, David 18, 24, 25, 31, 139
humour 23, 38, 40–1, 78, 98, 125, 145, 179, 199, 200, 201, 210
Hunter, Rachel 26
Hutton, Catherine 139, 145
Hutton, R. H. 114

Idler (Johnson) 77
illustrations: *see* book illustrations
Inchbald, Elizabeth 26, 155; *Lovers' Vows* (adaptation of) 28, 76, 78, 83–4; *A Simple Story* 28
Inman, Philip 211
intertextuality 7, 10, 27–8, 38–41, 76; *see also* 'spectral texts'
Iser, Wolfgang 8

Jack and Alice (Austen) 38
Jackson, Thomas 103–4
James, Henry 54, 112, 113–14, 161, 173, 205, 211
Jane Austen Book Club, The (Fowler) 209
Jane Austen House Museum 205
Jane Austen Society 205, 208
Jane Austen: Her homes and her friends (Hill) 206
'Jane's Marriage' (Kipling) 206–8
Janeites 4, 5, 113, 148, 179, 183, 185, 186, 202, 203, 204–5, 206, 208
'Janeites, The' (Kipling) 202–3, 204, 211
Jauss, Hans Robert 8, 134
Jewsbury, Geraldine 155
Jewsbury, Maria Jane 159
John Murray (publisher) 17, 102, 108–9, 110, 142, 145, 153
Johnson, Claudia 4, 5, 50, 76, 183, 203, 204, 205
Johnson, Samuel 23, 24, 25, 26, 27, 77, 139, 140; *Dictionary* 164; *Idler* 77
Journal (Macartney) 77

journals: *see* diaries
juvenilia 7, 18, 19, 20–3, 38, 40, 95, 113, 114, 200; publication of 114, 203; *see also under individual titles*

Kaufman, Paul 41
Kavanagh, Julia 158, 159
Keats, John 95, 129, 197
Kent, Christopher 203
Kerr, Lady Robert 97, 98
Kingsley, Charles 131–2, 164, 197
Kipling family 14, 203, 210
Kipling, Rudyard 179, 203, 208, 212; *Debits and Credits* 207; 'Janeites, The' 202–3, 204, 211; 'Mare's Nest, The' 203; 'Jane's Marriage' 206–8
Klancher, Jon 93, 94
Knight Collection (Chawton House Library) 18, 27
Knight, Edward 17, 23, 55, 132
Knight, Fanny 7, 14, 22, 55–6, 99
Knight, Marianne 7, 19
Knightley, John (*Emma*) 71, 191–2
Knightley, Mr (George) (*Emma*) 69, 72–3, 74, 98, 99, 164, 190, 191–2
Knox, Vicesimus 18
Kotzebue, August von 27, 76; *Lovers' Vows* 28, 76, 83–4

L'Ami de l'Enfance (Berquin) 21
L'Estrange, A. G. 139
Laclos, Choderlos de 27
Ladies' Magazine 126
Ladies' Treasury, The 117, 121, 124
Lady Audley's Secret (Braddon) 131
Lady Margaret Hall College, Oxford 138, 190
Lady Susan (Austen) 60, 95, 114
'ladylike' behaviour 6, 14, 83, 84, 166–7, 169, 178, 212; *see also* 'domestic ideology'
Lamb, Charles 164, 197
Lascelles, Mary 59
laughter 7–8, 38; *see also* humour
Lawrence, D. H. 210–11
Leavis, F. R. 183
Leavis, Q. D. 13

Lefroy, Anna 10, 18, 95, 165; responses to Austen's novels 96, 97, 98, 99, 126, 189; 'Sir Charles Grandison' 20
Lefroy, Benjamin 98, 132
Leigh Perrot, Mr and Mrs 99, 136, 137, 189
Leisure Hour, The 121
Lennox, Charlotte 26; *Female Quixote* 21
Lesley Castle (Austen) 38
letter writing 13, 18, 23–4, 38, 39–40, 76, 78, 91, 93, 136, 156
'Letter to Lord Byron' (Auden) 94
Letters on the Improvement of the Mind (Chapone) 31, 40
Lewes, G. H. 101, 114, 155, 157, 158, 159, 169
Lewis, Lisa 95, 203
Lewis, M. G. 26
libraries 17, 41, 45, 93, 106, 108, 110, 123, 111, 118, 182
library borrowing records 93
Life of Mary Russell Mitford (L'Estrange) 139
light reading 32, 120, 126, 128
Lister, Thomas Henry 90, 163–4
Litchfield, Henrietta 191
Literary History of England (Oliphant) 178, 179
literary references 21, 22, 27, 75, 81–2, 151, 202, 210; *see also* 'spectral texts'
'Literary Women' series (Jewsbury) 159
Lloyd, Martha 17, 20, 21, 39–40, 99, 164
Locke, John 27
Loiterer, The (periodical) 20
Love and Freindship [*sic*] (Austen) 38, 200
love (in Austen's novels) 49, 55–7, 61–2, 69, 70–3, 83, 201
Lovers' Vows (Kotzebue) 28, 83–4; Inchbald adaptation of 76, 78, 83
Lucas, Sir William (*Pride and Prejudice*) 193
Lycett, Andrew 203
Lydon, A. F. 112
Lyme Regis 141, 184
Lynch, Deirdre 4
Lytton, Edward Bulwer 131, 132

Macartney, Lord 26, 83; *Journal* 77
Macaulay, Thomas Babington 14, 105, 110, 114, 132, 155, 184; correspondence with family 192–6; responses to Austen's novels 101–2,

147–50, 183, 194–5, 212; reviews 115, 160, 161
Mackenzie, Margaret 109
Mackie, Adam 131
Macmillan publishers 113
Macmillan's Magazine 122, 123, 125
Making of English Reading Audiences (Klancher) 93
male readers 130–2; of Austen's novels 132, 146, 183, 204; *see also under individual names*
Maley, Willy 6
Mandal, Anthony 101
Mansfield Park 14, 49–56, 68–9, 111, 143, 193; Austen family's responses to 20, 55–6; books/reading in 26, 46–7, 77; early editions of 107, 108, 109; literary references in 76–85; narrative voice 64–5, 90; use of parody 60, 64; posthumous editions of 111, 113; readers' responses to 55, 89–90, 95, 96–7, 98–100, 126, 132, 147, 148, 189, 200
Mansfield, Katherine 74, 106, 135, 163, 180, 181–2
manuscript works: *see* juvenilia
'Mare's Nest, The' (Kipling) 203
marginalia 18, 105, 114, 136–7, 150
Marmion (Scott) 38, 39, 131
marriage: conventions of 46, 50–3; plots in Austen's novels 15, 50–6, 80, 90
Married Women's Property Acts (1870, 1882) 137–8
Martin, Robert (*Emma*) 61, 62, 69, 70
Martineau, Harriet 107, 130, 172–3
Marx, Karl 6
Mass Observation project (1942) 104, 209
Memoir of Jane Austen (Austen-Leigh, J. E.) 24–5, 78, 112, 114, 135, 139, 143, 149, 171–2, 173, 174, 178, 179, 183; reviews of 175–6, 177, 178–9, 213
memoirs: *see* autobiographies
memorabilia 210
memorials (to Austen) 149, 205, 206
Mental Improvement (Wakefield) 40
Mezei, Kathy 8
Michaelson, Patricia Howell 19
middle classes 110, 111, 112, 132–3, 211

Milbanke, Annabella 109
Miller, D. A. 13
Millot, Michel 106
Mills, Sara 8
Milton, John 26, 30, 31, 159; *Paradise Lost* 106–7
Minor Works (Chapman ed.) 113, 114
Mitford, Mary Russell 7, 12, 77, 126, 130, 135, 138–45, 153, 172, 175; admiration of Austen 139, 140, 141, 143–5, 153, 157–8, 180, 212; correspondence with Elizabeth Barrett Browning 14, 96, 128, 143, 144 (*see also* 'Austen Controversy, the' (Browning/Mitford)); literary career 135, 139, 154, 159, 176, 177; *Our Village* 165–6; *Recollections of a Literary Life* 139–40, 141–3
modesty 29, 37, 50, 65–6, 70, 75, 95, 109, 137, 138; *see also* blush
Monk, The (Lewis, M. G.) 26
Montagu, Lady Mary Wortley 89
morality 25, 26, 44, 47, 48, 75, 84, 98, 148, 189
More, Hannah 26, 29, 32, 33, 34, 37, 39, 41, 51; *Cœlebs in Search of a Wife* 28, 35, 45, 65, 75; *Strictures on the Modern System of Female Education* 40, 45–6, 57, 75, 83
Morland, Catherine (*Northanger Abbey*) 18, 43–4, 49, 56, 60, 68, 85, 119, 141, 194–5, 201
Morris, Mowbray 123
Morris, William 198, 199, 209
'much-readers' 33, 120, 123
Mudie's Lending Library 106, 123, 182
Munro, George 112
Murphy, Andrew 8
Murphy, Olivia 27, 28
Murray editions (of Austen's novels): *see* John Murray (publisher)
Murray II, John 108
Musgrove, Louisa (*Persuasion*) 26, 141, 142, 184
Mysteries of Udolpho, The (Radcliffe) 129, 141
Mystery, The (Austen) 114

Napoleonic Wars 202
narrative voice 8, 40, 48–9, 54–5, 56, 59, 63, 64–5, 72, 79, 83, 142; and use of parody 60–4; relationship with reader 69, 70, 73, 74, 75, 77, 80, 85, 90
needlework 79, 173, 174, 178
Neighbours, The (Bremer) 155, 156, 157
New Monthly Magazine 158
New Review, the 99
Newman, John Henry 161–2, 163, 169, 186
Newnham College, Cambridge 138
Nicholson, Norman 106
Night and Day (Woolf) 181
No Going Back (Inman) 211
Norris, Mrs (*Mansfield Park*) 49, 50, 78, 90, 98, 99, 132, 193
Northanger Abbey 23, 48, 141–2, 194; books/reading in 26, 42–4, 49, 119, 126, 201; and the defence of the novel 42–3, 56, 126; early editions of 109, 142; posthumous editions of 102, 111, 113; readers' opinions of 98, 194; reviews of 57–8, 119, 120, 163; *see also under individual names*
notebooks: *see* juvenilia
novel reading 11, 24, 32, 41, 44, 57; critics of 57–9, 120, 123–4; and feminization of the reading public 28, 120–6, 146, 147, 204; male readers 130–1; perceived dangers of 11, 31–2, 33, 41, 43–4, 47, 57, 118, 127–8; *see also* fiction
novel, the (genre) 6, 21, 42–4, 58–9, 118–20; Austen's defence of 42–5, 58–9, 120, 126; critics of 57–9, 118; *see also* fiction; novel reading

O'Farrell, Mary Ann 73–4, 100
Okey, Thomas 133–4
Oliphant, Margaret 13, 138, 159, 174, 182, 212; *Autobiography* 174; *Literary History of England* 178, 179; review of *Memoir* 175–6, 177, 178–9, 213
'oppositional' readers 9, 22, 25, 33, 139, 146, 149, 153, 154
Orlando (Woolf) 106

Our Village (Mitford) 165–6
Owenson, Sydney 26
Oxford Movement: *see* Tractarian Movement

Palgrave, F. T. 122–3, 125–6, 141, 184
Pamela (Richardson) 65, 67
Paradise Lost (Milton) 106–7
Parish Register (Crabbe) 78
Parker sisters (*Sanditon*) 12
Parker, Mr (*Sanditon*) 61
parlour games 190–1
parody 7, 10, 21–2, 27, 38, 39–40, 58, 60–4
Pasley, Charles 26
Peacock, Thomas Love 130, 199
Pearce, Lynne 8
Pearson, Jacqueline 28, 30–1
'penny bloods' 133–4; *see also* fiction
Pepys, Samuel 105
Percival, Catherine (Kitty) (*Catharine; or, The Bower*) 45, 46, 69
Percival, Mrs (*Catharine; or, The Bower*) 45, 46, 124
Pereiro, James 163
periodical essays 43, 58, 120
periodicals 28, 41, 94, 109, 117, 120; *see also under individual titles*
Perry, Ruth 89
Personal Aspects of Jane Austen (Austen-Leigh, M.) 204
Persuasion 7, 13, 26, 37–8, 48, 68, 70, 74, 140, 141–2, 184, 207; books/reading in 45, 85; early editions 109, 142; posthumous editions 102, 111, 113; readers' opinions on 158; reviews of 57–8, 119; *see also under individual names*
Philipotteaux, Felix 103
Pickering, Ellen 155
Piozzi, Hester Lynch 23, 26
'Plan of a Novel' (Austen) 10
Plumptre, John Pemberton 56, 98, 132
Poovey, Mary 13, 57, 59
Pope, Alexander 26, 31, 77
Popular Tales (Edgeworth) 130
Portraiture of Quakerism (Clarkson) 105
Practical Education (Edgeworth and Edgeworth) 31, 32

Price, Fanny (*Mansfield Park*) 11, 26, 46, 47, 49–56, 65, 68–9, 70, 77–80, 81–2, 84, 201
Pride and Prejudice 12, 19–20, 38, 58, 73, 193, 201, 210; books/reading in 25, 26, 37, 40–1, 43, 47; early editions 39, 101, 107, 145, 191; influence of conduct books 40–1; posthumous editions 101–2, 112, 113; readers' opinions on 101, 202; reviews of 90, 97, 98, 119; *see also under individual names*
Pritchett, V. S. 104

Quarterly Review, the 11, 58, 97, 108, 117, 119–20, 124, 126
Quarterly, the 90, 163
Quiver, The 117, 120

Radcliffe, Ann 26, 155; *Mysteries of Udolpho, The* 129, 141
railway bookstalls 111
Raverat, Gwen 191–2
Rawling, Alfred 197, 198
reading 92–3, 121–2; as a family activity 189, 190, 191–6, 203; *see also* 'hard reading'; light reading; shared reading experiences
reading aloud 19–20, 33, 183; *see also* communal reading
reading communities 190, 201–2, 208, 210; within families 20, 21–22, 33, 41, 59, 191–3, 203; *see also* reading groups
reading experiences, records of 7, 18–20, 21, 33, 39, 59, 91, 92–4, 96, 102–4, 107, 129, 130–2, 133, 143; difficulties in interpreting 9–10, 18, 92–3; *see also* XII club
reading groups 196–201
Recollections of a Literary Life (Mitford) 139–40, 141–3
Reiman, Donald 95
'resisting readers' 8–9, 10, 89, 115
Richardson, Samuel 10, 25, 26, 27, 31, 37, 57, 89, 138; *Clarissa* 44, 49, 50, 89, 90, 124; *Pamela* 65, 67; *Sir Charles Grandison* 10, 21, 24, 32, 38, 45, 48, 125, 149

ridicule 38, 45, 176, 177; *see also* humour
Ritchie, Anne Thackeray 156, 169, 171–2, 180, 192, 206, 212; *Book of Sibyls, A* 172
Rivals, The (Sheridan) 28, 118
Robertson, William 25, 139
Robinson Crusoe (Defoe) 131
Roche, Regina Maria 26
Rollin, Charles 31
romances 41, 42, 56, 119, 124, 126, 128, 211; perceived dangers of reading 31–2, 58; *see also* novel reading
Romilly, Lady Anne 91
Rose, Jonathan 8
Rousseau, Jean-Jacques 27, 129
Routledge's Railway Library series 111–12
Ruskin, John 105, 106, 168, 198

Said, Edward 4
Saintsbury, George 113, 179, 203, 205
Sand, George 154, 199
Sanditon (Austen) 12, 26, 38, 41, 44, 60–1, 203
Schreiber, Lady Charlotte 114–15
Schweickart, Patrocinio 8
Scott, Sir Walter 25, 28, 38–9, 108, 124, 125, 131, 132, 145, 155, 184, 199, 207: *Marmion* 38, 39, 131; review of *Emma* (*Quarterly Review*) 11, 97, 108, 119, 126; *Waverley* 24, 131, 145
'Seaside Library, The' 112
Second World War 8, 200
Self Control (Brunton) 10, 129
self-regulation (of reading) 33, 33–4, 35, 167
sensation fiction 6, 112, 119, 124, 131
Sense and Sensibility 11, 17, 47, 60, 162–3; early editions of 14, 107; opinions/reviews of 97, 98; posthumous editions of 111, 112, 147; *see also* under individual names
Sentimental Journey, A (Sterne) 76
Sermons for Young Women (Fordyce) 40–1, 42–3
sexuality: *see* female sexuality
Shakespeare, William 24, 25, 26, 31, 107, 115, 129, 150, 197, 198; Austen being compared with 155, 160,
184, 204, 207; featuring in Austen's novels 12, 79, 82–3, 143, 201
shared reading experiences 19, 20, 21–3, 38, 39, 40, 190–1, 203, 208, 210; and humour/jokes 23, 38, 39, 78, 95, 194, 202, 210; within families 14, 19–20, 21–2, 33, 41, 59, 190, 191–6; *see also* communal reading
Sharpe, Anne 89, 98
Shelley, Mary 59, 128, 129, 130
Shelley, P. B. 95, 154, 197, 198; *Defence of Poetry* 153
Sheridan, Richard Brinsley 26; *Rivals, The* 28, 118
Sherlock, Thomas 26
Simple Story, A (Inchbald) 28
Simpson, Richard 112, 167, 169
'Sir Charles Grandison' (Austen, A.) 20
Sir Charles Grandison (Richardson) 10, 21, 24, 32, 38, 45, 48, 125, 149
Smith, Harriet (*Emma*) 37, 61–2, 69, 70–1, 73, 99, 193, 201
Smith, Johanna M. 89
Smollett, Tobias 139, 207
Solo Trumpet: Some memories of Socialist agitation and propaganda (Jackson) 103–4
Somerville Hall, Oxford 138
Southam, Brian 4, 101, 183
Southampton 17, 19
Southey, Robert 106, 132
Spectator, the 42, 43
'spectral texts' 75, 83, 84–5, 143
Spenser, Edmund 27, 197
St Clair, William 93, 94
St. Paul's Magazine 182, 183
Staël, Germaine de 27, 149
Stanley, Camilla (*Catharine; or, The Bower*) 37
Steele, Richard 31, 43
Stephen, Leslie 112, 131, 179, 182
Sterne, Laurence 26, 83, 139; *A Sentimental Journey* 76; *Tristram Shandy* 66–7
Stevenson, Robert Louis 104–5, 198
Steventon, Hampshire 17, 19, 20, 205
Strictures on the Modern System of Female Education (More) 40, 45–6, 57, 75, 83
Susan (Austen) 95; *see also* Northanger Abbey

Sutherland, Kathryn 102, 135
Swift, Jonathan 26; 'Cadenus and Vanessa' 67; *Gulliver's Travels* 24
Sykes, Henrietta 26

Tale of Two Cities (Dickens) 131
Tales (Crabbe) 76, 77, 78–9
Tandon, Bharat 4
Task, The (Cowper) 76, 77, 80–2, 84
Tauchnitz editions (of Austen's novels) 111
teasing 10, 23, 27, 165; *see also* humour
television adaptations: *see* film/television adaptations (of Austen's novels)
Tennyson, Alfred, Lord 132, 141, 146, 147, 148, 183–4, 197
Tennyson, Emily 183
Tennyson, Hallam 184
Thackeray, W. M. 125, 142, 144, 184, 198
Theatre d'Education (Genlis) 31
Thomson, Christopher 133
Thomson, Hugh 113, 133
Thorpe, Isabella (*Northanger Abbey*) 68, 119, 201
Thorpe, John (*Northanger Abbey*) 23, 26, 193
'Three Sisters, The' (Austen) 23
Ticknor, Caroline 206
Tilney, Eleanor (*Northanger Abbey*) 26, 44
Tilney, General (*Northanger Abbey*) 44
Tilney, Henry (*Northanger Abbey*) 26, 42, 48, 49, 68, 163, 195
Times Literary Supplement 179–80, 206
Times, the 202, 204, 205, 206
Tinsley's Magazine 117, 123–4
'Tirocinium' (Cowper) 77
Todd, Janet 13
Tom Jones (Fielding) 26, 65, 138
Tom Sawyer (Twain) 185
Towsey, Mark 103
Tractarian Movement 162, 163
transcendentalism: *see* American transcendentalism
Trevelyan, George Otto 105, 149, 150
Trilling, Lionel 4, 5, 76
Tristram Shandy (Sterne) 66–7
Trollope, Frances 105
Twain, Mark 14, 132, 184–5, 186–7, 198, 211; *Huckleberry Finn* 185; *Following the Equator* 187; *Tom Sawyer* 185

type sizes 103–5, 107–8
Tyrold, Camilla (*Camilla*) 27

Uncle Tom's Cabin (Stowe) 133

Vicar of Wakefield (Goldsmith) 32
Vincent, David 8
Vindication of the Rights of Women (Wollstonecraft) 34, 129
Virgil 31, 150
Volume the First (Austen) 20–1, 23
Volume the Second (Austen) 22, 40, 203
Volume the Third (Austen) 21
Voyage Out, The (Woolf) 180–1

W. H. Smith 111
Wakefield, Priscilla 40
Waldron, Mary 28
Walkley, A. B. 202
war 8, 181, 200, 202, 203
Ward, Maria (*Mansfield Park*): *see* Bertram, Lady Maria (*Mansfield Park*)
Watsons, The (Austen) 114
Waverley (Scott) 24, 131, 145
Wedgwood, Elizabeth 191
Wentworth, Capt. (*Persuasion*) 13, 26, 207
West, Jane 26, 32, 57, 83
Whately, Richard 57, 96, 119–20, 144, 163
What-Not, The 117
Wickham, George (*Pride and Prejudice*) 73–4
Wilde, Oscar 103
Wilkes, Joanne 174
Wilkie, Brian 84
Willoughby, John (*Sense and Sensibility*) 12, 201
Wiltshire, John 4, 12
Winchester Cathedral 205, 206
Windham, Donald 56
Windscheffel, Ruth Clayton 103
Wollstonecraft, Mary 27, 29–30, 33, 59; *Vindication of the Rights of Women* 34, 129
women readers 14–15, 28–9, 30–1, 37, 117, 118–19, 128–9; and Austen's novels 89–91, 96–100, 212; and censorship 32–3, 167; and education 28, 29, 30, 31, 37, 39–40,

65, 120; and novels 21, 31–2, 34, 42–4, 118–19, 120, 124–5; and regulation of reading habits 30, 31, 32–4, 35, 43, 49, 56, 124, 130, 167; and self-improvement 46–7, 49, 125; *see also* conduct literature

women: and the domestic sphere 6, 29, 30, 31, 83 175; and education 28, 29–30, 37; and moral conduct 30, 33–4

women's education 28, 29, 33, 37, 138, 173, 190; and books 30–1, 35, 40, 45, 97, 183

Women's Rights Movement 138, 167

Women's Suffrage 138

Wood, Mrs Henry 131

Woodhouse, Emma (*Emma*) 11, 13–14, 47, 52, 61–2, 70–4, 99, 162, 164, 201

Woolf, Leonard 106

Woolf, Virginia 7, 13, 114, 135, 137, 155, 159, 166, 179–82; and feminist theory 137, 155, 182; *Night and Day* 181; *Orlando* 106; *Voyage Out, The* 180–1

Wordsworth, Dorothy 105, 128

Wordsworth, Elizabeth 140–1; *Glimpses of the Past* 190

Wordsworth, William 26, 28, 132, 197, 198

working classes 110, 112, 117, 132–3, 189, 211

Wright, Thomas 103

Yeazell, Ruth Bernard 65–6

'yellowbacks' 112

Yonge, Charlotte M. 131–2, 190

Zelicovici, Dvora 83–4

www.ingramcontent.com/pod-product-compliance
Lightning Source LLC
Chambersburg PA
CBHW021820300426
44114CB00009BA/254